lonely planet

D0951319

Discover
Maui

Experience the best
of Maui

This edition written and researched by

Amy C Balfour, Paul Stiles

Contents

Plan Your Trip Discover Maui

In Focus

Survival Guide

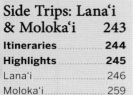

West Maui
'Iao Valley & Central Maui — p57
Side Trips: Lana'i & Moloka'i — p243
The Road to Hana — p205
p31
p93
p151
Lahaina
Kihei & South Maui — p121
p183
p225 — Hana & East Maui
North Shore & Upcountry
Haleakalā National Park

This is Maui

Snorkelers pause for green sea turtles. Zip-liners swoop over jungles. Couples exchange vows on the beach. And early risers watch the sun punch through the clouds from their perch on the edge of a lofty volcano. The most visited of the Neighbor Islands, Maui lures travelers with a revitalizing mix of outdoor adventure and gorgeous scenery.

The beaches alone are reason enough to visit.

Maui's entire western coast is fringed with sun-kissed strands, some backed by resorts, some full of boogie boards and cabana chairs, others as bare as the day they were born. Golden sand, red sand and black sand – take your pick.

Maui boasts world-class conditions for anything that involves a wave.

Yet each of its shores has a different temperament. You can ride monster breaks if you're a pro or learn to surf in gentle waves if you're not. Snorkel beside manta rays. Kayak with dolphins. Stand up paddle in a quiet bay. Or pin a sail to your board and fly with the wind.

Exploring on land is equally awesome.

Lace up your boots and hike the crunchy moonscape surface of the world's largest dormant volcano. Twist along the jungly, cliff-hugging Hana Hwy, soaking up waterfalls and swimming holes. Or take it airborne on an adrenaline-charged swoop down the West Maui Mountains.

Maui's natural charms are enhanced by top-notch restaurants and lodging.

From scrappy food trucks to white-linen dining rooms, Maui's eateries embrace local food and its traditions. Resorts wow guests with impeccable service and oceanside locations, with B&Bs providing more personal alohas. For more adventure – or quietude – a quick leap across the channel delivers you into the arms of Maui's smaller siblings, Lana'i and Moloka'i.

> *You can ride monster breaks or learn to surf in gentle waves*

A surfer rides massive North Shore waves at Jaws (p166)
RON DAHLQUIST/GETTY IMAGES ©

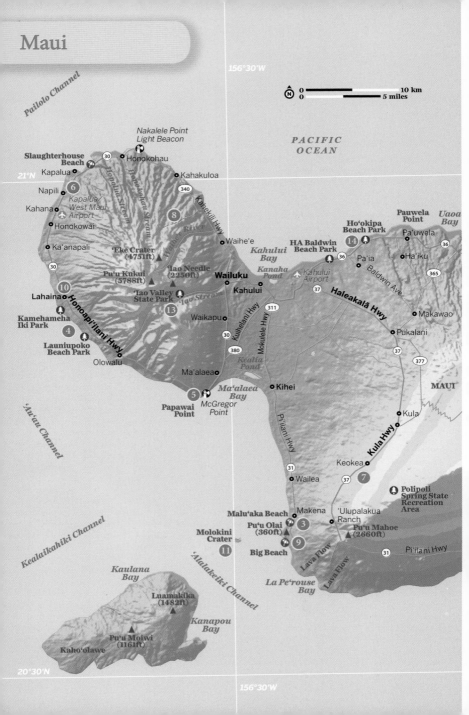

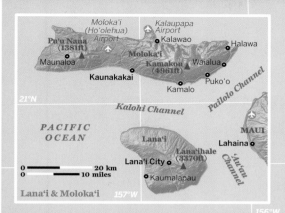

Lana'i & Moloka'i

14
Top Highlights

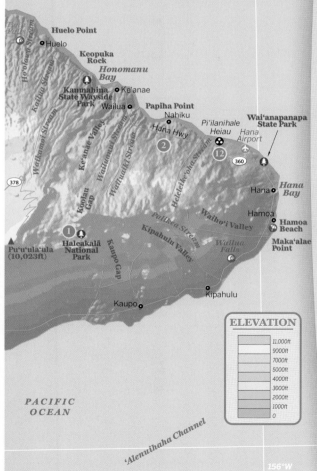

ELEVATION

11,000ft
9000ft
7000ft
5000ft
4000ft
3000ft
2000ft
1000ft
0

14 Maui's Top Highlights

Sunrise at Haleakalā National Park

As you shiver in the inky darkness, bumping elbows with strangers and wishing for your warmer coat, it's easy to grumble, 'What was I thinking?' But then a soft, orange glow pierces the darkness. The crowd leans forward, holding its breath. Cottony clouds appear, stretching to horizon's end, encircling your lofty summit perch (p198). Rich tones of amber and ocher blaze on the crater floor below. Elemental. Communal. Spiritual. And to quote Mark Twain: 'The sublimest spectacle I ever witnessed.'

1

WATERFALL, WILLIAM/GETTY IMAGES ©

2

Road to Hana

Of all the heart-stoppingly dramatic drives in Hawaii, this is the Big Kahuna. A roller-coaster ride, the Hana Hwy (p205) winds down jungly valleys and up towering cliffs, curling around 600 turns along the way. Some 54 one-lane bridges cross nearly as many waterfalls – some of them torrents and others so gentle they beg a dip. But the ride's only half the thrill. Swim in a Zen-like pool, stroll a ginger-scented trail and stop once, or twice, for banana bread.

Snorkeling at Malu'aka Beach

Don your mask and snorkel on the shores of stunning Malu'aka Beach (p144) in Makena and start swimming in the direction of the tour boats. Before you get halfway you'll likely spot a magnificent green sea turtle nibbling algae on the ocean floor. You may see another swimming gracefully through the surf. Welcome to 'Turtle Beach' – where the underwater scenery is nothing short of mesmerizing.

The Best...
Beaches

BIG BEACH (ONELOA)
If one beach embodies the spirit of Maui, it's this aptly named mile-long stretch of sand. (p146)

KA'ANAPALI BEACH
This West Maui resort beach is action central. (p66)

KEAWAKAPU BEACH
There's no finer place for a sunset swim. (p125)

KAPALUA BEACH
A beautiful beach with calm waters year-round. (p79)

PA'ILOA BEACH
Maui's finest black-sand beach. (p221)

HAMOA BEACH
Hawaii author James Michener waxed lyrical over this unspoiled Hana beach. (p229)

The Best...
Hikes

KARL LEHMANN/GETTY IMAGES ©

4 Surfing West Maui

This is Hawaii – of course you're going to catch some waves. The best part is, you don't have to be Laird Hamilton to enjoy the Maui surf. Just stick to Lahaina and West Maui, where the waves are more accessible, and you'll be hanging 10 in no time. Up-and-at-'em surf schools cluster near Kamehameha Iki Park (p40) in Lahaina, ready to launch newbies on easy waves beside the breakwall. Got your surf legs? Head to Launiupoko Beach Park (p60) for a picture-perfect day.

ROBINSON ED/GETTY IMAGES ©

5 Whale-Watching

Humpback whales keep things lively off Maui's west coast each winter, when thousands arrive to court and calve. If you're in Maui at the time, treat yourself to a whale-watching cruise. Whales are also spotted from cliffside lookouts such as Papawai Point (p61), from west-facing beaches and from oceanfront condos. Snorkelers and divers who duck underwater at the right time can even hear them singing: love songs, we presume!

Masters of Hawaiian Slack Key Guitar Concert Series

Feel like part of a family jam session at this intimate concert series (p78) in Napili. Slack key tuning, with its simultaneous bass and melody, virtually defines Hawaiian music. The host, Grammy Award–winning George Kahumoku Jr, interweaves the music with banter on growing up, Hawaiian-style.

Upcountry Drive

The Upcountry (p151) is Maui's garden, bursting to the brim with pastures and bountiful crops. This region supplies Maui's locavore cuisine and is heaven to foodies. Sample cheeses at Surfing Goat Dairy, munch on scones at Ali'i Kula Lavender, sip Maui-grown coffee at Grandma's Coffee House, tour Ocean Vodka's organic farm and distillery, and join a pick-your-own organic lunch tour at O'o Farm. For the finale, raise a toast at Maui's Winery.

Waiheʻe Ridge Trail

Hiking doesn't get much better than the Waiheʻe Ridge Trail (p90), an inviting footpath that climbs the rugged green slopes of the West Maui Mountains. The trail is alternately covered and exposed, winding through a dense grove of guava trees before darting up a grassy ridgeline with bird's-eye views of cloud-topped peaks and overgrown valleys. After 2.5 miles of gentle climbing, the lonely summit is a sweet reward.

8

The Best...
Ocean Adventures

DIVING AT MOLOKINI
The crystal waters of this submerged volcano teem with sea creatures. (p114)

KAYAKING AT MAKENA BAY
A paddle here takes you through waters visited by humpback whales. (p144)

SNORKELING AT MALUʻAKA BEACH
See for yourself why this pretty strand is dubbed 'Turtle Beach'. (p144)

WINDSURFING AT KANAHA BEACH PARK
This windward beach shimmers with sailriders. (p96)

SURFING AT HONOLUA BAY
Like Oʻahu's famed North Shore, Honolua Bay is a surfer's dream. (p79)

STAND UP PADDLE BOARDING IN WAILEA
The latest craze off the Maui coast. (p137)

Big Beach (Oneloa), Makena State Park

If one beach captures the spirit of Maui, this is it: wild, vast and in a completely natural state. But unvisited, no. This is where Mauians come to celebrate Maui the way it used to be. An endless expanse of gleaming sands (p146), no development in sight, unbelievably blue water, a surfer scanning for the next perfect wave. For a sweeping view of the place – and an iconic photograph – climb the rocky outcrop just north. Take a few steps. Turn. And whoa. Paradise.

The Best...
Views

HALEAKALĀ CRATER
Be awed by the volcanic wonderland on the crater floor 3000ft below. (p186)

WAILEA BEACH WALK
Grand coastal views any time plus fabulous whale-watching in winter. (p139)

KALALOA POINT
Gaze across Honomanu Bay and see the cars crawling on the Road to Hana cliffside. (p213)

PU'U KEKA'A (BLACK ROCK)
The view at sunset when the tiki torches are lit is smolderingly romantic. (p66)

SUN YAT-SEN PARK
The panorama from this Upcountry picnic spot is so vast that half of Maui unfolds below. (p179)

LAHAINA
There's a fine view of Lana'i right from Front St. (p34)

Old Lahaina Luau

10

They had us at aloha, but who are we to refuse the cool mai tai and sweet-smelling lei that followed? At Maui's most authentic luau (p53), Hawaiian history, culture and culinary prowess are the focus. Highlights? The unearthing of the *imu*-cooked pig, the dancing of the hula *ka-hiko* and, of course, the savoring of the feast – a spread of hearty salads, fresh fish, and grilled and roasted meats. But it's the sense of shared community that will linger longest in your memory.

Diving Molokini Crater

11

Hawaiian legend says that Molokini (p114) was a beautiful woman turned to stone by a jealous Pele, the goddess of fire and volcanoes. Today Molokini is the stuff of legends in the diving community. The crescent-shaped rock, which sits about 3 miles from the South Maui coast, is the rim of a volcanic crater. The shallow waters cradled within are a hospitable spot for coral and serve as a calling card for more than 250 fish species. For an iconic Hawaiian dive, this is the place.

RYAN SIU/GETTY IMAGES ©

Pi'ilanihale Heiau

Standing in front of Hawaii's largest temple (p219) – five stories high – it's impossible not to feel dwarfed by the scale. The remote setting on a windswept coast adds to the sense of being in a sacred place. Be still. You can almost hear the footsteps of the ancients and see the high priest walking up the terraced stone steps to offer sacrifices to the gods. The surrounding Polynesian gardens – swaying coconut palms, sturdy breadfruit trees – add depth to the vision of how it must have looked centuries ago.

'Iao Valley State Park

Nowhere is Maui's moody beauty better captured than at 'Iao Valley (p111), where the 'Iao Needle shoots straight up from the valley floor. Snuggled into deep folds of rainforested mountains, 'Iao Valley State Park is such a sumptuous sight it's hard to imagine that it was the scene of a violent, inter-island battle in the late 18th century. This melding of breathtaking scenery and tragic history makes it a compelling place of reflection. View towards 'Iao Needle

Ho'okipa & Pa'ia

If you're on the pro windsurfing circuit, meet your buddies at Ho'okipa Beach Park (p154). The rest of us can grab a voyeur's seat on the adjacent hillside and watch the death-defying action. Want the ultimate North Shore experience? Follow Ho'okipa's windsurfing theatrics by immersing yourself in the funky vibe of nearby Pa'ia (p154), Maui's hippest burg. Hang-loose Pa'ia will woo you with artsy shops, cool surfer haunts and the island's hottest cafe scene. You could bump into just about anyone here, from Willie Nelson to the Dalai Lama.

The Best...
Local Cuisine

ALOHA MIXED PLATE
Affordable Hawaiian fare pairs with a million-dollar view at this seaside eatery. (p48)

CAFÉ O'LEI
Order the blackened mahi-mahi with papaya salsa and just see if you can resist coming back the next day. (p133)

DA KITCHEN
Maui's ultimate plate lunch joint dishes up carb-loaded plates with two-scoop rice. (p103)

MAMA'S FISH HOUSE
The menu reveals who caught your fish and where! Now that's local. (p162)

SAM SATO'S
It's all about the noodles at this quintessential local eatery. (p109)

Maui's Top Itineraries

Pailolo Channel

PACIFIC OCEAN

3 **KAPALUA**

4 **KAHEKILI HIGHWAY**

2 **KA'ANAPALI**

5 **WAIHE'E RIDGE TRAIL**

13 **HO'OKIPA BEACH PARK**

PA'IA 12

1 **LAHAINA**

'IAO VALLEY STATE PARK 20

6 **ROAD TO HANA**

'Au'au Channel

14 **MAKAWAO**

MAUI

MAUI OCEAN CENTER 19 **KIHEI** 17

15 **KULA**

HANA 7

HALEAKALĀ NATIONAL PARK (KIPAHULU AREA)

KEAWAKAPU BEACH 21

16 **HALEAKALĀ NATIONAL PARK**

9

8 **WAILUA FALLS**

MALU'AKA BEACH

MAUI'S WINERY 11

22

KIPAHULU 10

MOLOKINI CRATER 18

24 **BIG BEACH** 23 **LA PE'ROUSE BAY**

'Alalakeiki Channel

Kaho'olawe

'Alenuihaha Channel

- ● **Lahaina to Waihe'e Ridge Trail** four days
- ● **The Road to Hana to 'Ulupalakua Ranch** six days
- ● **Pa'ia to Haleakalā National Park** eight days
- ● **Kihei to Big Beach** 10 days

Lahaina to Waihe'e Ridge Trail

4 DAYS

Pioneer Inn (p51), Lahaina

PETER FRENCH/GETTY IMAGES ©

① Lahaina (p31)

Enjoy a stroll around Maui's captivating old whaling town, relax under the USA's largest banyan tree, and then feast your stomach and your eyes at the Old Lahaina Luau.

② Ka'anapali (p65)

The next morning, plunge into Maui with a plunge into the sea at Ka'anapali Beach. Snorkel out to Pu'u Keka'a (Black Rock) to check out Maui's dazzling underwater scenery then pop into the Whalers Village Museum. Enjoy the sunset on a sailboat cruise or from shore at the Hula Grill.

③ Kapalua (p78)

Start day three early at the Gazebo restaurant in Napili for chocolate macnut pancakes. Swimmers should head to Kapalua Bay, bodysurfers to DT Fleming Beach and snorkelers to Honolua Bay. Ka-palua's menu of adventures also includes hiking and zip-lining. Catch the sunset at Merriman's.

④ Kahekili Highway (p86)

Hit the road on your last day with an adventurous drive around the northern tip of Maui. Seek out Nakalele Blowhole, and don't miss Ohai Viewpoint.

⑤ Waihe'e Ridge Trail (p90)

In the afternoon lace up your hiking boots. Lofty mountain views and waterfalls are just starters on this fun ridge trail that goes deep into the West Maui Mountains. Return to Lahaina or spend the night in Pa'ia.

◆ THIS LEG: 50 MILES

The Road to Hana to 'Ulupalakua Ranch

6 DAYS

Views along the road to Hana (p205)

INGMAR WESEMANN/GETTY IMAGES ©

6 Road to Hana (p205)

Hop onto Hwy 36, aka the Hana Hwy. This magical drive is lined with waterfalls and lush scenery. And there's no need to rush – you're spending the night in Hana. So swing down to Ke'anae Peninsula, be humbled by Hawaii's largest temple at Kahanu Garden and stroll along the coast at Wai'anapanapa State Park.

7 Hana (p228)

This wide spot in the road is well worth a poke around. Enjoy Thai food for lunch, a visit to Hana's museum and the marvelous beaches.

8 Wailua Falls (p240)

It's back on the road in the morning. First stop? This roadside cascade, which is a top contender for Maui's most gorgeous waterfall.

9 Haleakalā National Park (p183)

The road continues to 'Ohe'o Gulch (the Kipahulu Area of the park) with its 24 pools, each backed by its own little waterfall. Make time to hike to the 200ft plunge of Makahiku Falls.

10 Kipahulu (p201)

Seek out the grave of aviator Charles Lindbergh before heading off on the Pi'ilani Hwy for a romp through cowboy country.

11 Maui's Winery (p180)

End your trip with a taste of Maui Splash, a refreshing pineapple wine, at the tasting room at 'Ulupalakua Ranch. Spend the night at a B&B in Haiku.

THIS LEG: 108 MILES

Pa'ia to Haleakalā National Park

Pele's Paint Pot (p193), Haleakalā National Park

M SWIET PRODUCTIONS/GETTY IMAGES ©

⑫ Pa'ia (p154)

Mosey around downtown to find just the right breakfast joint then wander the boutiques or hit the beach.

⑬ Ho'okipa Beach Park (p154)

Watch the windsurfers from the lofty overlook at the eastern end of the beach. Splurge for lunch just down the road at the rightfully renowned Mama's Fish House.

⑭ Makawao (p166)

It's *paniolo*-meets-Picasso in downtown Makawao, an artsy cowboy town. Once you're done shopping, enjoy a melt-in-your-mouth cream puff from Komoda Store & Bakery or hit the trails at the Makawao Forest Reserve.

⑮ Kula (p173)

For Upcountry's sweetest green scene, wind over to Ali'i Kula Lavender and munch on lavender scones as you soak up the rainbow-lit coastal views.

⑯ Haleakalā National Park (p184)

The next morning, grab a coat and picnic lunch, and leave early (3am!) to catch the sunrise atop this magnificent volcano. Follow with a hike into the belly of the beast and climb around those cool cinder cones. Spend the night in Kihei.

⬤ THIS LEG: 95 MILES

Kihei to Big Beach

10 DAYS

Walkers on the beach, Kihei (p124)

GOMABA/GETTY IMAGES ©

17 Kihei (p124)

They open the doors early at Kihei Caffe, a good place to fuel up before a morning of snorkeling.

18 Molokini Crater (p114)

Explore the pristine waters of this sunken crater that harbors brilliant fish and coral.

19 Maui Ocean Center (p114)

Right where the Molokini boat docks you'll find an inviting tropical aquarium. Try to identify all those colorful fish you've just seen.

20 'Iao Valley State Park (p111)

In the afternoon drive to this oh-so-pretty park for cool streams, misty mountains and Maui's emerald jewel, the 'Iao Needle.

21 Keawakapu Beach (p125)

The star of Kihei's beaches, this soft-sand beauty is tops for long swims. Enjoy a sunset cocktail at Five Palms.

22 Malu'aka Beach (p144)

Relax on the sand or slip on a snorkel and swim out to the coral gardens to discover why this one's dubbed Turtle Beach: green sea turtles nibble away on the bottom as you swim past.

23 La Pe'rouse Bay (p148)

A stunning volcanic landscape awaits at land's end. Wander past historic structures and ponder the twisted lava flows.

24 Big Beach (p146)

Catch one of the best sunsets Maui has to offer on your way back to Kihei.

THIS LEG: 57 MILES

Get Inspired

Books

o **Middle Son** (2000) Deborah Iida describes 1950s Maui through the eyes of a sugar plantation laborer.

o **Maui** (2000) A stunning photo book from famed Pacific photographer Douglas Peebles.

Films

o **The Devil at 4 O'Clock** (1961) Spencer Tracy and Frank Sinatra hang out at Lahaina's Pioneer Inn.

o **Just Go With It** (2011) Adam Sandler and Jennifer Aniston have misadventures at the Grand Wailea Resort.

o **Hereafter** (2011) Clint Eastwood's film shot scenes on Lahaina's Front St.

Music

o **Maui On My Mind** (2010) Jeff Peterson, with cowboy roots in the Upcountry, took Hawaii's 2010 Hoku Award for Best Slack Key Album.

o **Peace Love Ukulele** (2011) Hot uke whiz Jake Shimabukuro takes ukulele to the next level.

o **Keʻalaokamaile** (2003) One of the finest of many albums from Maui-born singer, chanter and hula teacher Kealiʻi Reichel.

o **Hapa** (1992) Let the Maui duo Hapa woo you with beautiful harmonies, including the classic song 'Haleakalā Ku Hanohano.'

Websites

o **Maui Visitors Bureau** (www.gohawaii.com/maui) Pretty pictures on the official tourist office site.

o **Maui News** (www.mauinews.com) Maui's main daily newspaper includes a list of weekly events called 'Maui Scene.'

o **Maui Web Cams** (www.mauihawaii.org/webcams) Check out the beach scene live.

o **KPOA Radio** (www.kpoa.com) Listen to live streaming of Hawaiian music, Maui style.

Short on time?

This list will give you an instant insight into Maui.

Read *The Wave* (2010), where Susan Casey chronicles Laird Hamilton's big wave riding on Maui.

Watch *Hoʻokele Waʻa: Turning the Canoe* (2010) by Danny Miller showcases Maui's environmental movement.

Listen *Legends of Hawaiian Slack Key Guitar: Live From Maui* (2007) won George Kahumoku Jr a Grammy for slack key guitar album of the year.

Log on Whalesong Project (www.whalesong.net) lets you listen to humpback whales along Maui's shores.

Surfing big waves, Maui
ERIK AEDER/GETTY IMAGES ©

Maui Month by Month

Top Events

🐋 **World Whale Day Celebration** February

🍴 **East Maui Taro Festival** April

⭐ **Maui Film Festival** June

⭐ **Ki Hoʻalu Slack Key Guitar Festival** June

🐋 **Halloween in Lahaina** October

January

⭐ **Hyundai Tournament of Champions**
This season opener for the PGA tour (www.pgatour.com) tees off in Kapalua in early January, when the prior year's champions compete for a multimillion dollar purse.

February

Between December and April, about 12,000 humpback whales return to Hawaii to breed and give birth in the shallow waters. View them up and down the West Maui coast. February is the best month for spotting them.

🐋 **World Whale Day Celebration**
A whale of a bash, this parade and beachside celebration (p128) in Kihei in mid-February honors Maui's favorite winter visitor – the splashy North Pacific humpback whale.

April

🐋 **Banyan Tree Birthday Party**
Celebrate Maui's most renowned tree with a wild birthday party under its sprawling branches, which cover an entire square in Lahaina. The beloved banyan is more than 140 years old. The event is held on the weekend closest to April 24.

 East Maui Taro Festival
Hana, Maui's most Hawaiian town, throws the island's most Hawaiian party (p233) in late April, with everything from hula dancers and a top-notch Hawaiian music festival to a taro pancake breakfast.

Hula dancer, Maui
RON DAHLQUIST/GETTY IMAGES ©

May

Maui Onion Festival

Whalers Village (www.whalersvillage.com) in Ka'anapali hosts this festival honoring Maui's famous pungent bulb. The mighty onion takes center stage in chef demonstrations and onion-eating contests (gasp) on the first weekend of May.

June

Maui Film Festival

In mid-June, movie lovers gather in Wailea (p141), where the golf course is transformed into the 'Celestial Theater' and Hollywood stars show up for added bling.

Kapalua Wine & Food Festival

Hawaii's hottest chefs vie for attention in this culinary extravaganza (p84) of cooking demonstrations and wine tasting in mid-June.

Ki Ho'alu Slack Key Guitar Festival

Slack key guitar music doesn't get any better than this. Held in late June, the event (www.mauiarts.org) brings in all the big-name players from throughout the state. Plan to spend the afternoon and early evening at the Maui Arts & Cultural Center in Kahului.

July

Makawao Rodeo & Paniolo Parade

Roping contests, daredevil bronco-riding events and a colorful parade (p169) showcase Upcountry's *paniolo* (cowboy) past on the weekend closest to Independence Day.

Lana'i Pineapple Festival

Pineapples, the symbol of hospitality, are feted on the island of Lana'i (www.lanaipineapplefestival.com) on the weekend of July 4 with live music, food and fireworks.

October

Maui County Fair

Maui is a garden land, so it's no surprise that its old-fashioned agricultural fair (www.mauifair.com) is a bountiful event with orchids, luscious produce and all sorts of good food. Plus plenty of carnival rides for kids young and old. Held in early October in Kahului.

Halloween in Lahaina

Lahaina hosts Maui's biggest street festival (p45) on Halloween night, attracting about 28,000 revelers with music, dancing and costume contests. Fun for families early, then things get a bit more wild.

November

Hula O Na Keiki

Talented *keiki* (children) are the headliners of this annual hula competition (www.kbhmaui.com) at the Ka'anapali Beach Hotel in mid-November, with arts, crafts and workshops.

December

Holiday Lighting of the Banyan Tree

On the first weekend of December, Lahaina illuminates America's oldest banyan tree with thousands of bright, colorful holiday lights. Even Santa stops by for this one.

Need to Know

Currency
US dollar ($)

Language
English, Hawaiian

Visas
Generally not required for stays of up to 90 days for citizens of Visa Waiver Program countries.

Money
ATMs common. Credit cards widely accepted; often required for car and hotel reservations.

Cell Phones
International travelers need GSM multiband phones. Buy pre-paid SIM cards locally. Coverage can be spotty outside developed areas.

Wi-Fi
Common in most hotels; available in some condo units. Free at most McDonald's and with purchases at many cafes.

Internet Access
Most towns have cafes offering internet for about $3 for 15 minutes. Available at libraries with a $10 non-resident library card.

Tipping
15% for taxi drivers; 15–20% for restaurant waitstaff; $2 per bag at airports and hotels.

When to Go

Tropical climate, wet & dry seasons

Lahaina GO Dec-Apr

Pa'ia GO all year

Hana GO all year

Kihei GO all year

Haleakalā National Park GO all year

High Season
(mid-Dec–mid-Apr)
- Highest accommodation prices
- Coincides with Christmas holidays
- Prices high through whale season

Shoulder
(Jun–Aug)
- Coincides with school vacations
- Book rental car early; fleets may be reduced
- Lots of festivals in June and July

Low Season
(Apr & May, Sep–mid-Dec)
- Between whale season and summer
- Slow between Thanksgiving and Christmas
- Look for online specials and cheap airfares

Advance Planning

- **Three months before** Make flight, hotel and car rental reservations, particularly if arriving during holidays, whale season or a festival weekend (and watch out for golf tournaments!).

- **One month before** Secure reservations for popular activities with limited seating, such as a whale-watching cruise, outrigger canoe tour or the Old Lahaina Luau.

- **One week before** Make fine-dining reservations, particularly during the holidays. It's also a good idea to make reservations for zip-lining, kayaking or a tour of the Road to Hana.

Daily Costs

Budget less than $150

- Hostel dorm: $29–34
- Semi-private hostel room, guesthouse or budget B&B: $69–112
- Groceries, fast food: $6–12
- Walking tour, beach days: free
- Maui Bus one-way fare: $2

Midrange $150–350

- Most B&Bs, hotel room or condo: $100–275
- Local rental car: per day/week from $35/175
- Dinner at midrange restaurant: $20–35
- Museums, snorkeling, hiking: free–$30

Top End over $350

- Beach resort room: from $275
- New rental car: per day/week from $45/233
- Three-course meal at top restaurant: $75–100
- Diving, zip-lining, spa treatment, sunset cruise: from $69

Exchange Rates

Australia	A$1	$0.94
Canada	C$1	$0.91
Europe	€1	$1.39
Japan	Y100	$0.98
New Zealand	NZ$1	$0.86
UK	£1	$1.67

For current exchange rates see www.xe.com

What to Bring

- **Sunscreen & hat** It's the tropics, baby! It's also usually sunny, so be kind to your skin.
- **Snorkel, mask & fins** There's fantastic snorkeling from Makena north to Kapalua.
- **Binoculars** Nice for roadside whale-watching in winter.
- **Warm jacket** It's chilly on top of Haleakalā all day, but downright frigid before sunrise.
- **Hiking boots or shoes with good traction** Jungle-like trails are often slick with rain and mushy fruit.

Arriving in Maui

Kahului International Airport

Private shuttle To Kihei $29–33, Lahaina $48–50

Taxi To Kihei/Lahaina from $30/70

Rental car $35–110 per day; major rental companies have airport rental booths.

Maui Bus The Upcountry Islander and Haiku Islander routes stop at the airport. Transfers are required for West and South Maui. $2 per ride.

Getting Around

- **Rental car** Due to limited public transportation, renting a car is recommended.
- **Maui Bus** Public bus provides daily service to limited destinations within and between cities in Central, West and South Maui and Upcountry; $2 per trip.
- **Resort shuttles** Complimentary; run regularly within most major resort areas.
- **Taxis** Cluster near malls and shopping areas, but don't expect to flag one down on the street. Drop charge $3.50, and then $3 per additional mile.

Accommodations

- **B&Bs & inns** Homes or small lodgings. Owner usually lives on-site. Fruit, pastries and bread are typically served for breakfast.
- **Condominiums** Individually owned units grouped in one complex. Typically include a full kitchen.
- **Hotels** Price is usually based on room size and view, with bigger rooms and full ocean views garnering top rates.
- **Resorts** Sprawling complexes, often luxurious, with restaurants, pools, nightly entertainment and children's programs. Expect to pay a daily resort fee and/or parking fee.

Be Forewarned

- **Rental car break-ins** Maui is notorious for smash-and-grabs. Don't leave valuables in the car.
- **Rental car availability** If you see a good rate online before your trip, book the car. Unexpected shortages and rate spikes are not uncommon.

Lahaina

Maui's most historic town looks like a port of call for Captain Ahab: weathered storefronts, narrow streets, a bustling harbor and chattering parrots. Is this the 21st century, or an 1850s whaling village? In truth, Lahaina offers an inviting mix of of both.

Tucked between the rainbow-draped West Maui Mountains and a tranquil sea, Lahaina has long been a popular convergence point. Ancient Hawaiian royals were the first to gather here, followed by missionaries, whalers and sugar plantation workers. Today it's a base for eco-minded chefs, passionate artists and dedicated surf instructors.

Storefronts that once housed saloons, dance halls and brothels now teem with art galleries, souvenir shops and still plenty of watering holes. And the whalers have been replaced by a new kind of leviathan hunter: photo-snapping whale-watchers searching for a spout. Fortunately, between January and March, they don't have to look very hard.

Lahaina Harbor (p42)

Lahaina Itineraries

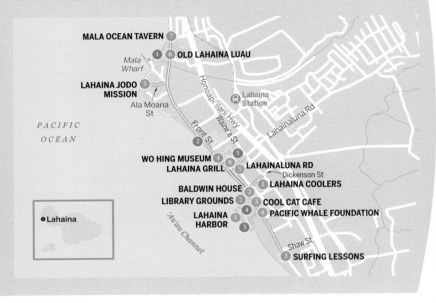

MALA OCEAN TAVERN

Mala Wharf

OLD LAHAINA LUAU

LAHAINA JODO MISSION

Ala Moana St

Honoapi'ilani Hwy

Waine'e St

Lahaina Station

Lahainaluna Rd

PACIFIC OCEAN

Front St

•Lahaina

WO HING MUSEUM
LAHAINA GRILL

LAHAINALUNA RD
Dickenson St

LAHAINA COOLERS

BALDWIN HOUSE
LIBRARY GROUNDS

COOL CAT CAFE

LAHAINA HARBOR

PACIFIC WHALE FOUNDATION

'Au'au Channel

Shaw St

SURFING LESSONS

One Day

1 Lahaina Harbor (p34) Start the day in the heart of Lahaina at the lively harbor where catamarans jostle for attention, the Best Western Pioneer Inn hums with period ambience and the USA's largest banyan tree spreads its branches across Banyan Tree Square.

2 Baldwin House (p35) Step into this simple house for scenes from a medical missionary's life, then walk to Hale Pa'ahao and peer into one of the reconstructed prison cells to read a list of 19th-century criminal offenses committed by hard-partying whalers.

3 Cool Cat Cafe (p49) For a quick but filling lunch, order a juicy burger from award-winning Cool Cat Cafe, a '50s-themed diner near the harbor.

4 Pacific Whale Foundation (p42) Hop aboard a catamaran to see 40-ton humpback whales up close and personal.

5 Lahainaluna Rd (p34) Back on land, a short walk along shop-lined Front St should include a pause at Lahainaluna Rd. It's a prime spot to watch the sun drop behind Lana'i in a blaze of orange and red.

6 Lahaina Grill (p50) A few more steps will drop you at the doorstep of this sparkling restaurant, where fine wine, fresh fish and easy conversation make for a memorable meal. And don't skip the triple berry pie.

➡ **THIS LEG: 1 MILE**

Two Days

1 **Lahaina Coolers** (p49) Start your second day with a hot skillet of *kalua* pork huevos rancheros.

2 **Library Grounds** (p38) After breakfast, follow Dickenson St to Front St and the grounds of the Lahaina Library. Walk to the northwest point, overlooking the ocean. Look down to see the mighty Hauola Stone, a chair-shaped rock used as a birthing stone by ancient Hawaiians and considered to have healing powers.

3 **Surfing Lessons** (p40) To learn the Hawaiian art of wave riding, there's no better place for a lesson than on the gentle waves at the Lahaina Breakwall. Surfing schools can be found along Prison St and at 505 Front St.

4 **Wo Hing Museum** (p37) After your time in the surf, spend the afternoon browsing the shops and galleries on Front St then step inside this ornate museum to glimpse a 1912 Chinese meeting hall. Black-and-white films shot on Maui by Thomas Edison play in the adjacent cookhouse.

5 **Lahaina Jodo Mission** (p38) To escape the crowds, head north to this mission, where a meditative 12ft Buddha honors the centennial of Japanese immigration to Hawaii.

6 **Old Lahaina Luau** (p53) Traditional hula dances trace Hawaii's history, and a hearty buffet celebrates its culinary past. Think *kalua* pig, *laulau,* taro salad and lots, lots more.

7 **Mala Ocean Tavern** (p50) Toast your time in Lahaina at this convivial seaside restaurant and bar with a $12 mega martini. Cheers!

➲ **THIS LEG: 2.3 MILES**

Lahaina Highlights

1 **Best Hawaiian Experience:**
Old Lahaina Luau (p53) Celebrate Hawaiian culture with traditional hula, tropical cocktails and a feast fit for kings.

2 **Best View: Seaside Front St** (p34) Dawdling sailboats and a languid Lana'i are the shimmering backdrop.

3 **Best Activity: Whale-watching cruise** (p42) Odds are good that you'll see a whale in winter. Most companies offer a free second chance if you don't.

4 **Best Green Space: Banyan Tree Square** (p35) Lahaina's landmark banyan is a tree-climber's dream.

5 **Best Fine Dining: Lahaina Grill** (p50) Attentive service, expansive wine list and exquisitely prepared seafood – mahalo (thank you) for the memories.

Banyan Tree Square (p35), Lahaina
PETER FRENCH/GETTY IMAGES ©

Discover Lahaina

History

In ancient times Lahaina – then known as Lele – housed a royal court for high chiefs and was the breadbasket (or, more accurately, the breadfruit basket) of West Maui. After Kamehameha the Great unified the islands, he chose it as his base, and the capital remained here until 1845. Missionaries arrived in the 1820s and within a decade Hawaii's first stone church, missionary school and printing press were in place.

Lahaina became the dominant port for whalers, not only in Hawaii but in the entire Pacific. The whaling years reached their peak in the 1840s, with hundreds of ships pulling into port each year. When the whaling industry fizzled in the 1860s, Lahaina became all but a ghost town. In the 1870s sugarcane came to Lahaina and it remained the backbone of the economy until tourism took over in the 1960s.

◉ Sights

Lahaina's top sights cluster around the harbor, with other sights either on Front St or within a few blocks of it. This makes Lahaina an ideal town to explore on foot. The top free sight? The sunset view from Front St, at its intersection with Lahainaluna Rd.

Old Lahaina Courthouse
Museum

(Map p36; ☏ visitor center 667-9193; www.visitlahaina.com; 648 Wharf St; ◷ 9am-5pm) **FREE** Tucked in the shadows of a banyan tree, Lahaina's 1859 courthouse is a repository of history and art, housing a museum, the town visitor center and two art galleries. Its location beside the bustling harbor is no coincidence. Smuggling was so rampant during the whaling era that officials deemed this the ideal spot for customs operations, the courthouse and the jail – all neatly wrapped into a single building. It also held the governor's office, and in 1898 the US annexation of Hawaii was formally concluded here.

Gifts and a walking tour map are available at the 1st floor visitor center (p55). On the 2nd floor, the **Lahaina Heritage Museum** (Map p36; www.lahainarestoration.org; ◷ 9am-4pm)

Old Lahaina Courthouse
PETER FRENCH/GETTY IMAGES ©

Righteous & Rowdy

Two diametrically opposed groups of New Englanders clashed in Lahaina in the 1820s – missionaries and whalers.

In 1823 William Richards, Lahaina's first missionary, converted Maui's native governor, Hoapili, to Christianity and persuaded him to pass laws against 'drunkenness and debauchery.' However, after months at sea, sailors weren't looking for a prayer service when they pulled into port – to them there was 'no God west of the Horn.' Missionaries and whalers almost came to battle in 1827 when Governor Hoapili arrested a whaler captain for allowing women to board his ship. The crew retaliated by shooting cannonballs at Richards' house. The captain was released, but laws forbidding liaisons between seamen and Hawaiian women remained in force.

It wasn't until Governor Hoapili's death in 1840 that laws prohibiting liquor and prostitution were no longer enforced and whalers began to flock to Lahaina. Among the sailors who roamed Lahaina's streets was Herman Melville, who later penned *Moby Dick*.

FREE, which was completely revamped in 2013, celebrates Lahaina's prominent role in Maui's history. Exhibits spotlight ancient Hawaiian culture, 19th-century whaling, and local plantations and mills. Check out the lemon-shaped sling stones. Made from volcanic rock, they were deadly projectiles used in early Hawaiian warfare.

The basement holds the old jail, used today as a gallery by the Lahaina Arts Society (p53). The cells that once held drunken sailors now display artwork by members of an artists' cooperative. The entrance to the jail is outside, on the north side of the building. Member art is also on display across from the visitor center.

Banyan Tree Square   Park
(Map p36; cnr Front & Hotel Sts) Throngs of citizens gather each year to celebrate the birthday of this leafy landmark which marks the center of Lahaina. This awesome banyan tree sprawls across the entire square and ranks as the largest banyan tree in the US. Planted as a seedling on April 24, 1873, to commemorate the 50th anniversary of missionaries in Lahaina, the tree has become a virtual forest unto itself, with 16 major trunks and scores of horizontal branches reaching across the better part of an acre.

The songs of thousands of mynah birds keep things lively at night. Most weekends artists and craftsmen set up booths beneath the tree's shady canopy.

Fort Ruins   Ruin
(Map p36; cnr Wharf & Canal Sts) A crumbly wall of coral stone blocks stands at attention just south of the courthouse – all that remains of a fort built in 1832 to keep rowdy whalers in line. Each day at dusk a Hawaiian sentinel would beat a drum to alert sailors to return to their ships. Stragglers who didn't make it in time were imprisoned here. At the height of its use the fort had some 47 cannons, most salvaged from foreign ships that had sunk in Lahaina's tricky waters.

When the fort was dismantled in the 1850s, its stone blocks were used to build Hale Pa'ahao, the new prison.

Baldwin House   Museum
(Map p36; www.lahainarestoration.org/baldwin. html; 120 Dickenson St; adult/child $7/free, incl admission to Wo Hing Museum; ☻10am-4pm, candlelit tours 6-8:30pm Fri) Reverend Dwight Baldwin, a missionary doctor, built this house in 1834–35, making it the oldest Western-style building in Lahaina. It served as both his home and

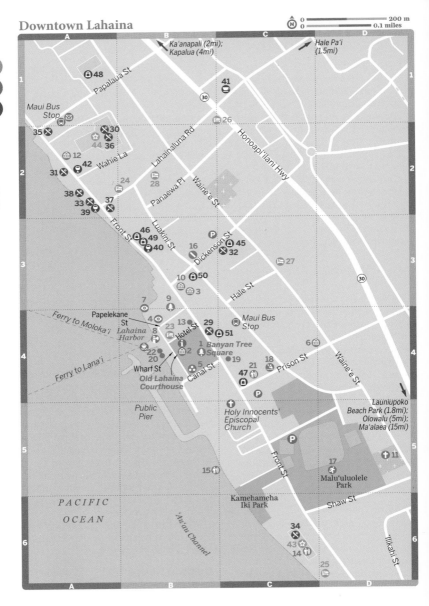

the community's first medical clinic. The coral-and-rock walls are a hefty 24in thick, which keeps the house cool year-round. The exterior walls have been plastered over, but you can get a sense of how they originally appeared next door

at the **Masters' Reading Room** (Map p36), which now houses an art gallery.

It took the Baldwins 161 days to get here from their native Connecticut, sailing around Cape Horn at the southern tip of South America. Dr Baldwin's passport

Downtown Lahaina

and mother Baldwin's sewing box are on display, as well as representative period furniture. A doctor's 'scale of fees' states that $50 was the price for treating a 'very great sickness', while a 'very small sickness' cost $20. It's only a cold, Doc, I swear.

Wo Hing Museum
Museum

(Map p36; www.lahainarestoration.org/wohing. html; 858 Front St; adult/child $7/free, incl admission to Baldwin House; ☉10am-4pm Sat-Thu, 1-8pm Fri) This two-story temple, built in 1912 as a meeting hall for the benevolent society Chee Kung Tong, provided Chinese immigrants with a place to preserve their cultural identity, celebrate festivities and socialize in their native tongue. After WWII, Lahaina's ethnic Chinese population spread far and wide and the temple fell into decline. Now restored and turned into a cultural museum, it houses ceremonial instruments, a teak medicine cabinet c 1900 and a Taoist shrine.

Don't miss the tin-roof cookhouse out back, which holds a tiny theater showing films of Hawaii shot by Thomas Edison in 1898 and 1906, soon after he invented the motion-picture camera. These grainy black-and-white shots capture poignant images of old Hawaii, with *paniolo* (cowboys) herding cattle, cane workers in the fields and everyday street scenes. The wall behind the screen holds a collection

The Best...
Unique Historic Sites

1 Banyan tree (p35)

2 Hauola Stone, behind the Library Grounds

3 Thomas Edison films, Wo Hing Museum (p37)

4 List of punishable offenses, Hale Pa'ahao

5 Sling stones, Lahaina Heritage Museum (p34)

of opium bottles unearthed during an excavation of the grounds.

Hale Pa'ahao — Museum

(Stuck-in-Irons House; Map p36; www.lahaina restoration.org/paahao.html; 187 Prison St; ☺8am-3pm Mon-Fri) FREE As far as prisons go, this coral-stone calaboose doesn't look too intimidating. A remnant of the whaling era, Hale Pa'ahao was built in 1852 and looks much as it did 150 years ago.

One of the tiny cells displays a list of arrests in 1855. The top three offenses were drunkenness (330 arrests), 'furious riding' (89) and lascivious conduct (20). Other transgressions of the day included profanity, aiding deserting sailors and drinking 'awa (kava).

Waine'e (Waiola) Church — Church

(Map p36; 535 Waine'e St) The first stone church in Hawaii, Waine'e Church was built in 1832 then hit with a run of bad luck. In 1858 the belfry collapsed. In 1894 royalists, enraged that the minister supported Hawaii's annexation, torched the church to the ground. A second church, built to replace the original, burned in 1947, and the third blew away in a storm a few years later. The fourth version, now renamed

Waiola Church, has stood its ground since 1953 and still holds Sunday services.

The adjacent **cemetery** holds as much intrigue as the church. Here lie several notables, including Governor Hoapili, who ordered the original church built; Reverend William Richards, Lahaina's first missionary; and Queen Ke'opuolani, wife of Kamehameha the Great and mother of kings Kamehameha II and III.

Library Grounds — Park

(Map p36; 680 Wharf St) A cluster of historic sites – the foundations of Kamehameha I's 'palace,' a birthing stone and a historic lighthouse – surround the Lahaina library. The yard itself was once a royal taro field where Kamehameha II toiled in the mud to instill in his subjects the dignity of labor.

The first Western-style building in Hawaii, the **Brick Palace** (Map p36) was erected by Kamehameha I around 1800 so he could keep watch on arriving ships. Despite the name, this 'palace' was a simple two-story structure built by a pair of ex-convicts from Botany Bay. All that remains is the excavated foundation, which can be found behind the library.

From this foundation, walk to the northern shoreline and look down. There lies the **Hauola Stone** (Map p36), a chair-shaped rock that the ancient Hawaiians believed emitted healing powers to those who sat upon it. It sits just above the water's surface, the middle of three lava stones. In the 14th and 15th centuries royal women sat here while giving birth to the next generation of chiefs and royalty.

About 100ft to the south stands **Lahaina Lighthouse** (Map p36), the site of the first lighthouse in the Pacific. It was commissioned in 1840 to aid whaling ships pulling into the harbor. The current structure dates from 1916.

Lahaina Jodo Mission — Religious

(Map p46; www.lahainajodomission.org; 12 Ala Moana St; ☺sunrise-sunset) FREE A 12ft-high bronze Buddha sits serenely in the courtyard at this Buddhist mission, looking across the Pacific toward its Japanese homeland. Cast in Kyoto, the Buddha is the largest of its kind outside Japan and was installed here in 1968 to celebrate the centennial of Japanese immigration to Hawaii. The grounds also hold a 90ft pagoda and a whopping 3.5-ton temple bell, which is rung 11 times each evening at 8pm. Inside the temple are priceless Buddhist paintings by Haijin Iwasaki.

 Activities

Lahaina is not known for its beaches, which are generally shallow and rocky, though it is a good place to take a surf lesson. For swimming and snorkeling, head up the coast to Ka'anapali.

Considering a sunset cruise? A whale-watching tour? A submarine ride? Wander down to the Lahaina Harbor, located directly behind the Old Lahaina Courthouse, where a lineup of tour operators angle for your business. This is also the departure point for the ferries to Lana'i and Moloka'i.

DIVING & SNORKELING

Dive boats leave from Lahaina Harbor, offering dives suitable for all levels.

Lahaina Divers _Diving_
(Map p36; ☎800-998-3483, 667-7496; www.lahainadivers.com; 143 Dickenson St; 2-tank dives from $129; ☷8am-8pm) Maui's first PADI five-star center offers a full range of dives, from advanced night dives to 'discover scuba' dives for newbies. The latter go to a reef thick with green sea turtles – a great intro to diving.

Maui Dive Shop _Diving, Snorkeling_
(Map p46; ☎800-542-3483, 661-5388; www.mauidiveshop.com; 315 Keawe St; 2-tank dives from $120, snorkeling trip adult/child $139/89; ☷7am-9pm) This full-service operation offers daily scuba and snorkeling trips. Locals recommend the custom-built _Alii Nui_, Maui Dive Shop's 65ft catamaran available for small-group snorkeling excursions. The company has seven shops across Maui; this branch, located in Lahaina Gateway, also rents scuba and snorkel gear.

Snorkel Bob's _Snorkeling_
(Map p46; ☎661-4421; www.snorkelbob.com; 1217 Front St; ☷8am-5pm) If you're driving

1 **WHAT IS THE FOCUS OF THE NEW LAHAINA HERITAGE MUSEUM?**
It's the story of Lahaina's history from pre-contact all the way through present day.

2 **HOW IS LAHAINA DIFFERENT FROM OTHER TOWNS ACROSS MAUI?**
All the eras of Hawaii's history happened here. So pre-contact, before white people came, this is where the chiefs used to come. It was their playground, to relax, and then it became the kingdom's first capital. There was a major missionary infusion here. This was where the whaling ships came to reprovision... After the whaling died down because of the discovery of oil, Lahaina recreated itself as a plantation town. And then it became tourism.

3 **WHY DID LAHAINA PLAY SUCH A PROMINENT ROLE?**
The real reason why that happened is the location. The safe harbor. The abundant streams. It was ideally calm and accessible.

4 **ARE THERE ANY MISCONCEPTIONS ABOUT LAHAINA?**
A big myth is that whaling ships caught whales out here, which is not true. They went up north, to the arctic, to catch whales and then before they would go back to New England they would stop here to reprovision.

5 **WHAT CAN VISITORS SEE IN BALDWIN HOUSE?**
It shows you life in the mid-1800s, when missionaries came over to live here. It's Dr Baldwin's home, and some of his furniture. One thing we've started is the Candlelit Tour on Friday nights. It just changes the whole thing because all of a sudden you feel like you're in that era. All of Front St falls away. It's all dark.

from downtown Lahaina to Ka'anapali to snorkel, stop by Snorkel Bob's for cheap snorkel-set rentals on your way. The store is on Front St north of downtown.

KAYAKING

Maui Kayaks   Kayaking
(Map p36; ☑874-4000; www.mauikayaks.com; 505 Front St; guided tour per person $69-99; ☉shop 8am-4pm, reservations 7am-7pm) This locally owned operation takes guided kayaking and kayaking-snorkel tours along the western coast of Maui. The Lahaina Paddle trip doubles as a whale-watching excursion in season (adult/child $59/49). Kayak rentals are also available (two hours/per day $25/35).

STAND UP PADDLE SURFING

Everybody's trying to stand up paddle surf (SUP) these days, as a quick glance at Maui's western coast quickly confirms. The graceful sport – which requires a longboard, a paddle and some balance – is easy to learn, but Maui's currents can be tricky for newcomers. Beginners should consider a lesson.

Maui Wave Riders   Paddle Boarding
(Map p36; ☑875-4761; www.mauiwaveriders. com; 133 Prison St; 90 min class adult/child from $60/50; ☉7am-3pm, reservations 7am-9pm) Limits class size to six students per instructor. Also offers surfing lessons.

SURFING

If you've never surfed before, Lahaina is a great place to learn, with first-class instructors, gentle waves and ideal conditions for beginners. The section of shoreline known as **Lahaina Breakwall (Map p36)**, north of Kamehameha Iki Park, is a favorite spot for novices. Surfers also take to the waters just offshore from Launiupoko Beach Park.

Several companies in Lahaina offer surfing lessons. Some guarantee you'll be able to ride a wave after a two-hour lesson or the class is free. Rates vary depending upon the number of people in the group and the length of the lesson, but for a two-

Left: Banyan Tree Square (p35);
Below: Buddha statue at Lahaina Jodo Mission (p38)

(LEFT) JOHN ELK/GETTY IMAGES ©; (BELOW) JOHN ELK/GETTY IMAGES ©

hour class expect to pay about $65 in a small group or $150 for private instruction.

Maui Surf Clinics
Surfing

(Map p36; ☏244-7873; www.mauisurfclinics. com; 505 Front St, Suite 224B; ⊙lessons 9am, noon & 2:30pm) The oldest surfing school on the island was started by Nancy Emerson, who was winning international surfing contests by the time she was 14. Now under new ownership, her techniques are still implemented at this welcoming school.

Royal Hawaiian Surf Academy
Surfing

(Map p36; ☏276-7873; www.royalhawaiian surfacademy.com; 117 Prison St; ⊙8am-4pm) In business since 1996, Royal Hawaiian offers group surfing lessons with a maximum of five people per class ($65 per person). Semi-private ($200 for two people) and private lessons ($150 per person) are also available. Stand up paddle board lessons start at $75 per person.

Also rents surfboards ($30 for three hours) and SUP boards ($35 for three hours).

Goofy Foot Surf School
Surfing

(Map p36; ☏244-9283; www.goofyfootsurf school.com; 505 Front St, Suite 123; ⊙6:30am-8pm Mon-Sat, 8am-8pm Sun) This top surf school combines fundamentals with fun. In addition to lessons, it runs day-long surf camps and rents boards to experienced surfers.

CYCLING

West Maui Cycles
Bicycle Rental

(Map p46; ☏661-9005; www.westmauicycles. com; 1087 Limahana Pl; per day $15-60; ⊙9am-5pm Mon-Sat, 10am-4pm Sun) For bike rentals head to West Maui Cycles, which has quality hybrid and mountain bikes, as well as cheaper cruisers fine for kicking around town. Check the website for route maps.

Detour:
Hale Pa'i

A small white cottage on the grounds of Lahainaluna High School, **Hale Pa'i** (Map p62; 667-7040; www.lahainarestoration.org; 980 Lahainaluna Rd; donations appreciated; 10am-4pm Mon-Wed) housed Hawaii's first printing press. Although its primary mission was making the Bible available to Hawaiians, the press also produced, in 1834, Hawaii's first newspaper. Named *Ka Lama Hawaii* (The Torch), it held the distinction of being the first newspaper west of the Rockies. The adjacent school was founded in 1831, and students operated the press.

Typography tools and a replica of the original Rampage Press are on display. The original press was so heavily used that it wore out in the 1850s. There's also an exhibit explaining the history of Hawaii's 12-letter alphabet and a reprint of an amusing 'Temperance Map' ($10), drawn by an early missionary to illustrate the perils of drunkenness. Don't be alarmed if an ear-splitting siren breaks your 1850s reverie; it's not an attack, just the high school's 'bell' for changing classes. Boarding students, about 10% of the student body, have traditionally worked in neighboring fields – so the bell has to be loud.

It's wise to call in advance. Hale Pa'i is staffed by volunteers so hours can be irregular. To get there, follow Lahainaluna Rd 2 miles northeast from Lahaina.

TENNIS

There are public tennis courts at **Lahaina Civic Center** and **Malu'uluolele Park** (Map p36). Both have lights to enable night playing. The Lahaina Civic Center is north of downtown Lahaina. From Honoapi'ilani Hwy, take the first right after passing Leiali'i Pkwy and the Lahaina Post Office.

Tours

Catamarans and other vessels in Lahaina Harbor cater to the tourist trade, and outfitters staff booths along the harbor's edge. Most companies offer discounts or combo deals on their websites. Check with companies about where to meet pre-trip.

During whale season, cocktail cruises often double as whale-watching excursions.

The Lana'i ferry docks behind the Best Western Pioneer Inn. The Moloka'i ferry departs from Slip 3 at Lahaina Harbor.

Pacific Whale Foundation Ecotour
(Map p36; reservations 249-8811, 800-942-5311, store 667-7447; www.pacificwhale.org;

612 Front St; whale-watching adult/child from $25/18; 6am-9pm, snorkel tours from 7am) The well-versed naturalists on this non-profit foundation's cruises are the island's best. The Lana'i Snorkel & Dolphin Watch Cruise and whale-watching excursions leave from Lahaina Harbor. Other trips depart from Ma'alaea Harbor (p114). The whale-watching cruises, which depart several times a day in winter, are immensely popular. In the unlikely event you don't spot whales, your next trip is free.

For the standard whale-watching trips, one child under six is free for every adult. For a small group experience, try the Raft Whalewatch Cruise (adult/child $45/32) on a smooth, anti-slamming raft.

The company also offers half-day volunteering opportunities in Maui through its Volunteering on Vacation (p196) program, which has attracted more than 3900 participants. Visit the website for a program calendar.

Trilogy Excursions Boat Tour
(Map p46; 888-225-6284, 874-5649; www.sailtrilogy.com; 207 Kupuohi St; adult/child from

$39/20; 8:30am-4:30pm Mon-Thu, 8:30am-4pm Fri, noon-3pm Sun) This family-run operation specializes in personable eco-friendly catamaran tours that let you get your feet wet. The 10am trip from Lahaina to Lana'i's Hulopo'e Beach Park & Marine Preserve (adult/child $199/100) includes morning cinnamon rolls and fruit, deli wraps, a van tour of Lana'i City, snorkeling and a barbecue dinner. In winter there's whale-watching along the way and you can spot spinner dolphins year-round.

Scotch Mist II   Cruise

(Map p36; 661-0386; www.scotchmistsailing charters.com; Slip 2, Lahaina Harbor; sunset charter $1200 or per person adult/child $70/35) The *Scotch Mist II* serves champagne, wine, beer and chocolate-covered macadamia nuts on its sunset cruise. The beautiful boat is also a 50ft sailing yacht that's fast and seductive. Book in advance as the boat (which is available for group charters) carries just 18 passengers per sail. Snorkel cruises and whale-watching trips (December to April) are also available.

Lahaina Cruise Company   Cruise

(Map p36; 667-6165; www.mauiprincess.com; 658 Front St, Lahaina Harbor; cocktail cruise adult/child $60/35, dinner cruise adult/child $96/68; 8am-8pm) If you're unsure about your sea legs consider choosing this company for your sunset cruise. Its 70ft-long *Kaulana* is the largest and most stable catamaran in the harbor. The sunset cruise features two complimentary cocktails and appetizers, while the dinner cruise on the 120ft-long *Maui Princess* includes open-air table service and live music. Both vessels depart from the main loading dock behind the Pioneer Inn.

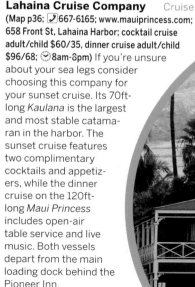

Lahaina Lighthouse (p38)
GREG ELMS/GETTY IMAGES ©

The Best...
Activities for Kids

1 Pacific Whale Foundation cruise

2 Banyan tree (p35)

3 Old Lahaina Luau (p53)

4 Surfing school (p40)

5 Atlantis Submarine

Atlantis Submarine   Boat Tour

(Map p36; 800-381-0237, 661-7827; www.atlantisadventures.com; 658 Wharf St, Best Western Pioneer Inn; adult/child $109/45; tours 9am, 10am, noon, 1pm & 2pm) To see Maui's undersea wonders without getting wet, consider a trip on the *Atlantis*. The price

LAHAINA TOURS

is steep, but this 65-footer is a real sub, and it dives to a depth of 130ft. Sights include coral, tropical fish and the sunken *Carthaginian,* a sailing brig that played a leading role in the 1965 movie *Hawaii*. Check in at the office, which is inside the Pioneer Inn building. The office opens onto Front St.

Reefdancer   Boat Tour
(Map p36; ☎855-249-0087, 667-2133; www.mauiglassbottomboat.com; Slip 6, Lahaina Harbor; adult/child per 1hr $35/19, 90min $45/25; ⏱reservations 7am-10pm, departures 10am-2:15pm) A nice option if you're traveling with young children, this glass-bottomed boat has a submerged lower deck lined with viewing windows. The views aren't as varied as on a submarine, but the underwater scenes are still eye candy and you won't feel claustrophobic.

Sugar Cane Train   Historic Train
(Map p46; ☎661-0080; www.sugarcanetrain.com; 975 Limahana Pl; adult/child $23/16; ⏱Lahaina departures 11:05am, 1pm, 2:30pm & 4pm) The restored century-old steam train that once carried cane from the fields to Lahaina's sugar mill now carries tourists on a 45-minute ride between Lahaina,

Ka'anapali and Pu'uokilli'i, departing from Lahaina Station and running right beside the Honoapi'ilani Hwy. The ride is a bit pokey and there's not really much to see, but younger kids and steam-train buffs will want to hop aboard.

Festivals & Events

Lahaina's top festivals draw huge crowds, with Front St closed to traffic during these events. For updated details on Lahaina festivities, contact the **Lahaina Town Action Committee** (☎event hotline 667-9194; www.visitlahaina.com) or check the events calendar on its website.

Whale & Ocean Arts Festival   Culture
Fete the annual humpback whale migration in mid-March at Banyan Tree Square during this weekend-long celebration with Hawaiian music, hula and games, plus marine-themed art and a few naturalists who share their knowledge about whales.

Banyan Tree Birthday Party   Festival
Lahaina's favorite tree gets a two-day birthday party, complete with a birthday

The Sugar Cane Train

VAUGHN GREG/GETTY IMAGES ©

Halloween, Lahaina Style

By the 1990s Lahaina's modest, kiddie-oriented Halloween parade had exploded into an all-out blast. The event was rechristened 'Mardi Gras of the Pacific,' spiced up with elaborate floats and outrageous costumes, and promoted far and wide. It grew into Maui's biggest bash, attracting upward of 30,000 revelers to the jam-packed Front St for the October 31 celebration. After island families complained that risqué attire and heavy drinking had made the festival unsuitable for children, organizers dropped the Mardi Gras title and ratcheted it down a notch. Consider it a fine-tuning. The event today – dubbed 'Halloween in Lahaina' – has struck a happy medium. In 2013 about 28,000 partygoers came out for a street festival of music, dance and a costume contest. Public drinking and nudity were prohibited, and the event wrapped up by 10:30pm.

cake, music and art, plus piñatas for the *keiki* (children). It's held on the weekend closest to April 24.

King Kamehameha Celebration — Parade
Traditionally dressed Hawaiian riders on horseback, marching bands and floral floats take to Front St to honor Kamehameha the Great on this public holiday in mid-June. An awards ceremony and arts festival follow at Kamehameha Iki Park.

Fourth of July — Public Holiday
Enjoy a concert on the lawn of the public library from 5:30pm then watch fireworks light up the sky over the harbor at 8pm.

Plantation Days — Culture
(www.lahainarestoration.org/plantationdays)
Beneath the Pioneer Mill smokestack, this two-day festival in mid-October spotlights Lahaina's plantation past, with displays about life and work at the former sugar mill (1860–1999). Food booths, live music and Maui-brewed beer add to the fun.

Halloween in Lahaina — Street Carnival
Front St morphs into a costumed street festival on Halloween night. The party is fun for families in the late afternoon, with a *keiki* costume parade, but things get a bit more risqué as the night goes on. Forget parking; it's best to take a bus or taxi to this one.

Holiday Lighting of the Banyan Tree — Christmas
Lahaina lights Hawaii's biggest tree on the first weekend in December with thousands of colorful lights, accompanied by music, carolers, cookie decorating and a craft show. And, of course, Santa shows up for the *keiki*.

Friday Town Party — Street Carnival
(www.mauifridays.com) This outdoor festival features music and food vendors. It's held the second Friday of the month from 5pm to 8pm at Campbell Park, which is across from the Pioneer Inn on Front St.

🛏 Sleeping

Despite the tourists filling its streets, Lahaina is surprisingly sparse on places to stay. West Maui's resort hotels are to the north, where the beaches are better. On the plus side, Lahaina's accommodations tend to be less crowded. Between Lahaina and Ma'alaea Harbor, to the south, are an oceanside campground and a stylish hillside B&B. Prices jump during the height of whale season (January and February).

Lahaina's Last Resort — Hostel $
(Map p36; ☑ 661-6655; www.lahainaslast resort.com; 252 Lahainaluna Rd; dm/r $44/112; Ⓟ ❄ 🛜) Decide what's important to you before booking a bed at this busy hostel at the corner of one of Lahaina's most

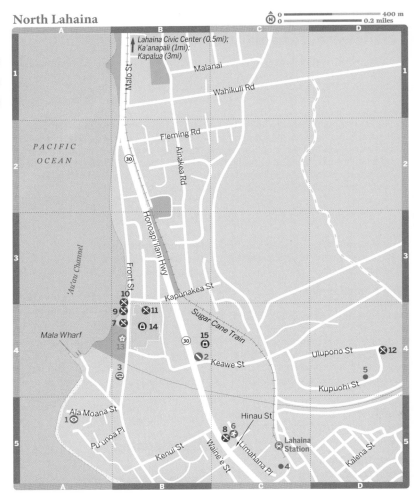

North Lahaina

congested intersections. On the plus side, this hostel, in a small cottage, is just two blocks from Front St. On the flip side, if you're impatient or need lots of space, the small co-ed bathroom and overall tight quarters may be a turnoff.

Rooms have microwaves and mini-refrigerators. The kitchen/common area is outside.

Plantation Inn
B&B **$$**

(Map p36; ☎667-9225, 800-433-6815; www. theplantationinn.com; 174 Lahainaluna Rd; r/ste incl breakfast from $158/248; P❄🛜🏊) Alohas are warm at the 19-room Plantation Inn, a genteel oasis set back from the hustle and bustle of Lahaina's waterfront. Inside the stylish lanai rooms, flat-screen TVs and DVD players blend seamlessly with plantation-era decor. Victorian-style standard rooms come with four-poster beds. The highlight? Complimentary breakfast from Gerard's (p50) served by the pool – we say *mahalo* (thank you) for the savory, piping-hot eggs Florentine.

The property is not on the beach, but guest privileges are provided at its sister property Ka'anapali Beach Hotel (p70).

Best Western Pioneer Inn
Hotel **$$**

(Map p36; ☎800-457-5457, 661-3636; www. bestwestern.com; 658 Wharf St; r $180; P❄@🛜🏊) The historic Pioneer Inn looks a little salty and sea worn on the outside, but step inside for a pleasant surprise. Rooms have undergone a stylish revamp, which includes new flat-screen TVs. The accommodating staff keeps the sailing smooth. Ship figureheads and the saloon's swinging doors give a nod to Lahaina's whaling past.

To avoid the nightly chatter of mynah birds in Banyan Park and the noise from Front St, ask for a courtyard room. All rooms are on the 2nd floor, with no elevators.

Outrigger Aina Nalu
Condo **$$**

(Map p36; ☎800-688-7444, 667-9766; www. outrigger.com; 660 Waine'e St; studio/1br/2br from $149/159/179; P❄🛜🏊) Lush, leafy foliage stretches toward the sun while tropical trees shoot through 2nd-floor breezeways, giving this complex a Kipling-esque ambience. Though not on the beach, it's just one block from the Wharf Cinema Center. Hotel-style guest services are available in the lobby; wi-fi is available in the pool area and the lobby only. Parking is $17.50 per day.

Lahaina Inn
Boutique Hotel **$$**

(Map p36; ☎800-222-5642, 661-0577; www. lahainainn.com; 127 Lahainaluna Rd; r/ste from $135/222; P🛜) Rooms may be small, but they strut their stuff like they belong in the most chic of boutique hotels, with artsy prints, hardwood floors and a touch of greenery. And there's always the balcony if you need more space. The front desk is not staffed overnight. Per day parking is $15 and wi-fi is $10.

Gourmands take note: the 12-room inn is perched above the highly recommended Lahaina Grill (p50).

Lahaina Shores
Condo **$$$**

(Map p36; ☎661-4835, 866-934-9176; www. lahainashores.com; 475 Front St; studio/1br from $225/305; P❄🛜🏊) They'll have you at aloha at Lahaina Shores, where the staff seems genuinely glad to help you. This seven-story property, the only oceanfront condo complex in central Lahaina, operates hotel-style with a front desk and full services. All the units are roomy, and even the studios have a full kitchen and lanai (veranda). Newly remodeled Premier rooms shine with a breezy island style.

The adjacent beach is a good place for beginner surfers, and a small shopping village next door offers dining, entertainment and surf lessons. Parking is $8 and wi-fi is $10 per day.

🍴 Eating

Kalua pork. Spicy ahi *poke* (raw tuna). Juicy burgers. Macnut-crusted fish. Triple berry pie. Need we continue? Lahaina has the finest dining scene on Maui. But remember, fine food draws hungry hordes. Many folks staying in Ka'anapali pour into Lahaina at dinnertime and traffic jams up. Allow extra time.

Need to stock up? **Foodland** (Map p36; ☎661-0975; www.foodland.com; 878 Front St,

Old Lahaina Center; ☺6am-midnight) and **Safeway** (Map p46; ☎667-4392; www.safeway.com; 1221 Honoapi'ilani Hwy, Lahaina Cannery Mall; ☺24hr) supermarkets have everything you need for self-catering, as well as good delis. For discounts, you can use your phone number in place of a customer card in Foodland, and Safeway accepts customer club cards from the mainland.

Choice Health Bar Health Food $

(Map p46; ☎661-7711; www.facebook.com/choice.maui; 1087 Limahana Pl; mains $8-16; ☺8am-4pm Mon-Sat; 🖋) This breezy box of healthy deliciousness whips up addictive organic fare. Dishes are fresh, filling and designed with an artist's touch. The chilly, fruit-stuffed acai bowls, loaded with berries, greens, granola and healthy add-ins, are an invigorating breakfast choice. The Buddha Bowl, one of our favorite lunch dishes on Maui, is a triple-layered nirvana of grains topped by soup and then a salad – trust us, it works. Smoothies, juices and health shots are perfect for on-the-go travelers.

Aloha Mixed Plate Hawaii Regional $

(Map p46; ☎661-3322; www.alohamixedplate.com; 1285 Front St; breakfast $7-12, lunch & dinner $6-17; ☺8am-10pm) This is the Hawaii you came to find: friendly, open-air and beside the beach. The food's first-rate, the prices affordably local. For a thoroughly Hawaiian experience, order the Ali'i Plate, packed with *laulau, kalua* pig, *lomilomi* salmon, poi and *haupia* – and, of course, macaroni salad and rice.

The restaurant now serves breakfast, which stays Hawaiian with dishes like *loco moco* and and *kalua* pig omelets.

Star Noodle Asian $$

(Map p46; ☎667-5400; www.starnoodle.com; 286 Kupuohi St; shared plates $3-30, mains $7-15; ☺10:30am-10pm) Star Noodle has quickly become one of Lahaina's most popular restaurants. Inside this sleek noodle shop, grazers can nibble on an eclectic array of Asian-fusion share plates. Those seeking heartier fare can dive into garlic noodles, *kim chee ramen* and a saimin (local-style noodle soup; Spam included). For heat fiends, ask for the hot sauces, which add to the fun. A central communal table keeps the vibe lively.

Kimo's Hawaii Regional $$

(Map p36; ☎661-4811; www.kimosmaui.com; 845 Front St; most mains lunch $11-17, dinner $23-37; ☺11am-10pm; 👪) This is our favorite oceanside patio on Front St. A locally beloved standby, Hawaiian-style Kimo's keeps everyone happy with reliably good food, a superb water view and a family friendly setting. Try the grilled shrimp beet salad, one of the fresh fish dishes and the towering hula pie. At lunch, if you're seeking lighter fare, order the Caesar salad. Mai tais are served in glass totems.

Kalua pork
LONELY PLANET/GETTY IMAGES ©

Chilly Treats

I scream, you scream, we all scream for...shave ice. And gelato. And yes, even ice cream. Downtown Lahaina whips up delectable versions of all three of these cool refreshments.

Ululani's Hawaiian Shave Ice (Map p36; www.ululanisshaveice.com; 819 Front St; small $4.75; ⊙10:30am-10pm) For over-the-top shave ice, amble up to the counter at Ululani's Hawaiian Shave Ice and take your pick of tropical flavors. A second location has opened at the **Lahaina Marketplace** (Map p36; 790 Front St; ⊙10:30am-9pm).

Ono Gelato Co (Map p36; 🗺495-0203; www.onogelatocompany.com; 815 Front St; small $5; ⊙8am-10pm) At Ono Gelato Company there's always a crowd gazing at the sinful array of silky gelatos, all prepared with Maui cane sugar.

Scoops (Map p36; 🗺661-5632; 888 Front St; scoop $4; ⊙9am-10pm) Serves locally made Lappert's ice cream, but we'll make the choice easy: Kauai Pie, a luscious mix of Kona coffee ice cream, coconut, macadamia nuts and fudge. Cash only.

Cool Cat Cafe   Diner $$

(Map p36; 🗺667-0908; www.coolcatcafe.com; 658 Front St, Wharf Cinema Center; mains $9-26; ⊙10:30am-10:30pm; 👪) It's a hunka-hunka burger love at Cool Cat Cafe, a lively doo-wop diner where most of the burgers, sandwiches and salads are named for 1950s icons, honoring the likes of Marilyn Monroe, Chubby Checker and, of course, Elvis Presley. The 6.5oz burgers, made with 100% Angus beef, consistently rank as Maui's best. The view overlooking Banyan Tree Square isn't bad either.

Honu Seafood & Pizza   Seafood, Pizzeria $$

(Map p46; 🗺667-9390; www.honumaui.com; 1295 Front St; mains lunch $15-32, dinner $15-35; ⊙lunch 11am-3pm, happy hour menu 3-4:30pm, dinner 4:30-9:30pm Mon-Sat, 4:30-9pm Sun) Named for Maui's famous green sea turtles, this stylish venture from restaurateur Mark Ellman is wowing crowds with expansive ocean views and a savory array of wood-fired pizzas, out-of-this-world salads and comfort-food dishes. And we haven't even mentioned the fish (from Hawaii, the Pacific Northwest and the East Coast). Beer connoisseurs can choose from more than 50 brews.

As you dine, scan the water beside the rocky coast – you might just glimpse a green sea turtle.

Lahaina Coolers   American $$

(Map p36; 🗺661-7082; www.lahainacoolers. com; 180 Dickenson St; breakfast $8-15, lunch $10-16, dinner $15-28; ⊙8am-midnight) We like Lahaina Coolers for breakfast, and we remember with affection the homemade hot sauce that kick-starts the delightfully messy huevos rancheros with *kalua* pork. This easygoing spot, just off Front St, has an inviting patio – a nice place to dine on the Evil Jungle Pasta (prepared with spicy peanut sauce), da local pizza with Portuguese sausage, or coconut-crusted fish. The hot sauce is also sold by the bottle.

Thai Chef   Thai $$

(Map p36; 🗺667-2814; www.thaichefrestaurant maui.com; 878 Front St, Old Lahaina Center; mains $11-18; ⊙11am-2pm Mon-Fri, 5-9pm Mon-Sat) Hidden in the back of an aging shopping center, this place looks like a dive from the outside, but the food's incredible. Start with the fragrant ginger coconut soup and the fresh summer rolls and then move on to savory curries that explode with flavor. It's BYOB so pick up a bottle from the nearby Foodland.

The Best...
Spots to Watch the Sunset

1 Front St, south of Lahainaluna Rd (p34)

2 Rooftop Bar at Fleetwood's

3 Old Lahaina Luau (p53)

4 Kimo's (p48)

5 Mala Ocean Tavern

Lahaina Grill   Hawaii Regional $$$

(Map p36; ☎667-5117; www.lahainagrill.com; 127 Lahainaluna Rd; mains $37-85; ⏱from 5:30pm) The windows at the Lahaina Grill frame a simple but captivating tableau: beautiful people enjoying beautiful food. Trust us (and the crowd gazing in from the side-walk) – there's something special about this restaurant. Once inside, expecta-tions are confirmed by the service and the food. The menu relies on fresh local ingredients given innovative twists and presented with artistic style.

A seafood standout is the Maui onion seared ahi with vanilla-bean jasmine rice. The finishing brush stroke? Always the triple berry pie.

Mala Ocean Tavern   Fusion $$$

(Map p46; ☎667-9394; www.malaoceantavern. com; 1307 Front St; mains brunch $8-15, lunch $15-26, dinner $19-45; ⏱11am-9:30pm Mon-Fri, 9am-9:30pm Sat, 9am-9pm Sun) A favorite of Maui's smart set, Mark Ellman's stylish bistro fuses Mediterranean and Pacific influences with sophisticated flair. Rec-ommended tapas include the Kobe beef cheeseburger slathered with caramelized onions and smoked applewood bacon, and the 'adult' mac & cheese with mush-room cream and three fancy fromages. For main meals, anything with fish is a

sure pleaser, and everyone raves over the decadent 'caramel miranda' dessert. At sunset, tiki torches on the waterfront lanai add a romantic touch.

Gerard's   French $$$

(Map p36; ☎661-8939; www.gerardsmaui.com; 174 Lahainaluna Rd; mains from $39, 8-course prix fixe per person $95; ⏱seatings 6-8pm) Where has all the romance gone? To the front porch of Gerard's, where white linens and flickering shadows are an invitation for murmurings of love. Or exclamations of culinary bliss. Chef Gerard Revers-ade, who infuses fresh Lahaina-caught seafood with flavors from the French countryside, has earned top-of-the-line accolades across Maui. The extensive wine lists are also noteworthy.

Pacific'O   Fusion $$$

(Map p36; ☎667-4341; www.pacificomaui. com; 505 Front St; lunch $14-17, dinner $29-46; ⏱11:30am-9:30pm) 🖉 Pacific Rim cuisine with contemporary bling jumps off the menu at Chef James McDonald's chic oceanside restaurant. The food is bold and innovative – where else can you try a pan-roasted spiny lobster with tobiko caviar? Lunch is a tamer affair, with island-inspired salads, sandwiches and tacos – but the same in-your-face ocean view.

I'O   Hawaii Regional $$$

(Map p36; ☎661-8422; www.iomaui.com; 505 Front St; most mains $26-44; ⏱5:30-9pm) 🖉 Oceanfront I'O is the handiwork of Maui's

Island Insights

The ahi *poke* (raw tuna) is served fresh, cheap and in numerous varieties at the Foodland (p47) grocery store seafood counter. It's one of the best culinary deals on the island. Our favorite part? The free samples! If you want a meal to-go, ask for a *poke* bowl, which comes with a hefty helping of rice. The spiced ahi *poke* is outstanding.

most acclaimed chef, James McDonald. The nouveau Hawaii cuisine includes scrumptious creations such as oven-roasted fresh catch with corn coconut sauce and slow braised short ribs from Maui Cattle Company. McDonald is so obsessed with freshness that he started a farm (p175) in Kula to grow his own veggies. There's a fierce martini menu, too.

Drinking & Nightlife

Front St is the center of the action. Check the entertainment listings in the free *MauiTime Weekly,* or just stroll the streets. In addition to places listed here, many of Lahaina's waterfront restaurants have live music at dinnertime.

Fleetwood's on Front St · Bar

(Map p36; ☑ 669-6425; www.fleetwoodson frontst.com; 744 Front St; ☻ 11am-10pm Sun-Thu, to 11pm Fri & Sat) With its comfy pillows, cushy lounges and ornate accents, this stunning rooftop oasis – owned by Fleetwood Mac drummer Mick Fleetwood – evokes Morocco. But the big views of Lanai and the rippling mountains keep you firmly rooted in Maui. At sunset, a conch-shell

blast announces a tiki-lighting ceremony that's followed by a bagpipe serenade – from a kilt-wearing Scot! It's all great fun, and it works.

Supplement the sunset ceremony with a Lime in the Coconut cocktail then stick around for island jazz. All drinks are 50% off during happy hour (3pm to 5pm). If you see the red flag flying, it means Mick is on the island.

Aloha Mixed Plate · Open-Air Restaurant

(Map p46; ☑ 661-3322; www.alohamixedplate. com; 1285 Front St; ☻ 8am-10pm; 🛜) Let the sea breeze whip through your hair while lingering over a heady mai tai – come between 2pm and 6pm and they're $3.50. After sunset, you can listen to Old Lahaina Luau's music beating next door.

Best Western Pioneer Inn · Pub

(Map p36; ☑ 661-3636; 658 Wharf St; ☻ 7am-10pm) Ahoy matey! If Captain Ahab himself strolled through the swinging doors, no one would look up from their grog. With its whaling-era atmosphere and harborfront lanai, the captain would blend right in at this century-old landmark. For

Mala Ocean Tavern

us landlubbers, the afternoon happy hour (3pm to 6pm) keeps it light on the wallet.

Spanky's Riptide — Sports Bar

(Map p36; 505 Front St; ⏰10:30am-1:30am) Yes, we understand. Don't apologize. It may be your honeymoon but you can't be expected to miss...THE game. In Lahaina, the place to watch that game is the loveably rowdy Spanky's Riptide. Follow the whoops and cheers, stroll right in, step around the dog, pick your brew, then look up at the wall of action-packed TV screens.

Lahaina Coolers — Cafe, Bar

(Map p36; ☎661-7082; www.lahainacoolers. com; 180 Dickenson St; ⏰8am-1am) This eclectic open-air cafe attracts thirty-somethings who come to mingle, munch *pupu* (snacks) and sip wine coolers. As the late-night bar favored by in-the-know locals, it's a cool place to wind down after the dance floor has emptied.

Moose McGillycuddy's — Bar

(Map p36; ☎667-7758; www.moosemcgillycuddys .com; 844 Front St; ⏰7:30am-2am) College kids? Bachelorettes? Dancing fools? Here's your party. Convivial crowds come here to drink and dance till they drop. With two dance floors, McGillycuddy's jams with live music or DJs most nights of the week. Draft beer is $1 on Tuesday and Saturday, with $5 cover, from 9pm until close.

Cheeseburger In Paradise — Open-Air Restaurant

(Map p36; ☎661-4855; www.cheeseburgerland. com; 811 Front St; ⏰8am-10pm) Perched above the sea at the corner of Lahainaluna Rd, this open-air place is a lively, and lovely, spot to watch the sunset. The music's Jimmy Buffett–style, and the setting is pure tropics, from the rattan decor to the homemade piña coladas. Live soft rock from 4:30pm nightly.

Cool Cat Cafe — Cafe

(Map p36; ☎667-0908; 658 Front St, Wharf Cinema Center; ⏰10:30am-10:30pm) Whether you're looking for fountain drinks or hard-hitting cocktails, this breezy, '50s-inspired cafe is an easygoing spot to wet your whistle as the sun sets over the harbor, just beyond the banyan tree. Live music nightly and rotating list of $4 daily cocktails.

MauiGrown Coffee — Coffee Shop

(Map p36; ☎661-2728; www.mauigrowncoffee. com; 277 Lahainaluna Rd; ⏰6:30am-5pm Mon-Sat)

The open-air decking at Cheeseburger in Paradise

Your view from the lanai at MauiGrown's historic bungalow? A sugar plantation smokestack and the cloud-capped West Maui Mountains. With 100% Maui-grown coffee, life can be good at 7am.

Entertainment

When it comes to hula and luau (Hawaiian feast), Lahaina offers the real deal. Catching a show is sure to be a highlight. You can also enjoy free hula shows at **Lahaina Cannery Mall** (Map p46; www.lahainacannery.com; 1221 Honoapi'ilani Hwy) at 7pm Tuesday and Thursday, and hula shows for the *keiki* at 1pm Saturday and Sunday.

Old Lahaina Luau
Luau

(Map p46; 667-1998, 800-248-5828; www.oldlahainaluau.com; 1251 Front St; adult/child $105/75; 5:15-8:15pm Oct-Mar, 5:45-8:45pm Apr-Sep;) From the warm aloha greeting to the extravagant feast and the mesmerizing hula dances, everything here is first rate. No other luau on Maui comes close to matching this one for its authenticity, presentation and all-around aloha. The feast is outstanding, with high-quality Hawaiian fare that includes *kalua* pork, ahi *poke, pulehu* (broiled) steak and an array of salads and sides.

It's held on the beach at the north side of town. One caveat: it often sells out a month in advance, so book ahead.

Feast at Lele
Luau

(Map p36; 667-5353, 866-244-5353; www.feastatlele.com; 505 Front St; adult/child $125/94; from 5:30pm, 6pm or 6:30pm) Food takes center stage at this intimate Polynesian luau held on the beach. Dance performances in Hawaiian, Maori, Tahitian and Samoan styles are each matched to a food course. With the Hawaiian music, you're served *kalua* pork and *pohole* ferns; with the Maori, duck salad with *poha* berry dressing. A true gourmet feast. Start time depends on the season.

'Ulalena
Dance

(Map p36; 856-7900; www.mauitheatre.com; 878 Front St, Old Lahaina Center; adult/child from $60/30; 6:30pm Mon, Tue, Thu & Fri) This Cirque du Soleil–style extravaganza has its

home at the 680-seat Maui Theatre. The theme is Hawaiian history and stories; the medium is modern dance, brilliant stage sets, acrobatics and elaborate costumes. An entertaining, high-energy performance.

Shopping

Classy boutiques, tacky souvenir shops and flashy art galleries run thick along Front St. You'll find lots of shops in one location at the **Wharf Cinema Center** (Map p36; www.thewharfcinemacenter.com; 658 Front St) and **Lahaina Cannery Mall** (Map p46; www.lahainacannery.com; 1221 Honoapi'ilani Hwy; 9:30am-9pm Mon-Sat, to 7pm Sun).

Lahaina Arts Society
Arts & Crafts

(Map p36; www.lahainaarts.com; 648 Wharf St, Old Lahaina Courthouse; 9am-5pm) A nonprofit collective representing more than 90 island artists, this extensive gallery covers two floors in the Old Lahaina Courthouse. Works range from avant-garde paintings to traditional weavings. Many of Maui's best-known artists got their start here, and there are some gems among the collection.

Village Gifts & Fine Arts
Arts & Crafts

(Map p36; www.villagegalleriesmaui.com; cnr Front & Dickenson Sts; 10am-6pm, to 9pm Fri) This one-room shop in the Masters'

Reading Room sells prints, wooden bowls and glasswork and other crafts. The shop's sister property, **Village Gallery** (Map p36; 120 Dickenson St; ⏰9am-9pm), sits in a separate building behind the store, across the parking lot.

Lahaina Printsellers   Art, Maps
(Map p36; www.printsellers.com; 764 Front St; ⏰9am-10pm) Hawaii's largest purveyor of antique maps, including fascinating originals dating back to the voyages of Captain Cook. The shop also sells affordable reproductions if you don't have a large wad of cash on you. This location shares space with **Lahaina Giclee**, a gallery selling a wide range of fine quality Hawaiian *giclée* (zhee-clay) digital prints.

Maui Hands Center   Arts & Crafts
(Map p36; www.mauihands.com; 612 Front St; ⏰10am-7:30pm Mon-Sat, to 7pm Sun) Excellent selection of island-made crafts from more than 300 fine artists, jewelers and craftspeople.

Hale Zen Home Decor & More   Homewares
(Map p36; www.halezen.com; 180 Dickenson St; ⏰10am-8pm Mon-Fri, to 9pm Sat, to 5pm Sun) The Zen is more Balinese than Hawaiian, but this inviting shop is well-stocked with candles, lotions and gifts as well as crafted furniture and cute children's clothes.

Peter Lik Gallery   Photography
(Map p36; www.lik.com/galleries/lahaina.html; 712 Front St; ⏰9am-10pm) Vibrant colors, stunning landscapes – nature is king in the stylish lair of Australian photographer Peter Lik.

Lahaina Gateway   Mall
(Map p46; www.lahainagateway.com; 305 Keawe St; ⏰9:30am-9pm) Across Hwy 30 from the Lahaina Cannery Mall is Lahaina Gateway. At this strip mall you'll find a large Barnes & Noble (www.barnesand noble.com) and a branch of Maui Dive Shop (p39).

Outlets of Maui   Mall
(Map p36; www.theoutlets ofmaui.com; ⏰9:30am-10pm) The new Outlets of Maui, just north of downtown Lahaina, opened at press time. Factory-store retailers at the open-air mall include, yawn, Banana Republic, Gap and Guess.

Diners along Front St, Lahaina
GREG ELMS/GETTY IMAGES ©

 Information

Emergency

Police (📞244-6400) For nonemergencies.

Police, Fire and Ambulance (📞911) For emergencies only.

Medical Services

The Maui Memorial Medical Center in Wailuku is the nearest hospital in case of emergencies. For serious accidents you may want to ask to be transported to O'ahu.

Longs Drugs (📞667-4390; www.cvs.com; 1221 Honoapi'ilani Hwy, Lahaina Cannery Mall; 🕐store 7am-midnight, pharmacy 8am-8pm Mon-Fri, 8am-5pm Sat & Sun)

Minit-Medical (📞667-6161; www.minit-medical.com; 305 Keawe St, Lahaina Gateway; 🕐8am-6pm Mon-Sat) Urgent care clinic. Takes walk-ins.

Money

Bank of Hawaii (www.boh.com; 130 Papalaua St, Old Lahaina Center; 🕐8:30am-4pm Mon-Thu, to 6pm Fri)

Post

Downtown Post Office Station (Map p36; 132 Papalaua St, Old Lahaina Center; 🕐10am-4pm Mon-Fri)

Tourist Information

Lahaina Visitor Center (Map p36; 📞667-9193; www.visitlahaina.com; 648 Wharf St; 🕐9am-5pm) Located inside the old courthouse.

 Getting There & Away

The Honoapi'ilani Hwy (Hwy 30) connects Lahaina with Ka'anapali and points north, with Ma'alaea to the south and Wailuku to the east. The second phase of the five-phase Lahaina Bypass opened in late 2013. The bypass swings east around downtown congestion and runs parallel to Hwy 30.

Ferries to Lana'i and Moloka'i dock at Lahaina Harbor.

 Getting Around

To/From the Airport

To get to Lahaina from the airport in Kahului, take Hwy 380 south to Honoapi'ilani Hwy (Hwy 30); the drive takes about 45 minutes. If you're not renting a car, **Executive Shuttle** (📞800-833-2303, 669-2300; www.mauishuttle.com) provides service between the airport and Lahaina, charging $47 for one person and $54 for two. From the airport to Lahaina, taxi fare is about $78.

Bus

The **Maui Bus** (📞871-4838; www.mauicounty.gov) runs between Kahului and Lahaina ($2, one hour) on the Lahaina Islander route. This bus stops at Ma'alaea Harbor. At Ma'alaea Harbor a connection can be made to Kihei via the Kihei Villager. Another route, the Ka'anapali Islander, connects Lahaina and Ka'anapali ($2, 30 minutes). Both routes depart from the Wharf Cinema Center hourly from 6:30am to 8:30pm.

Car & Motorcycle

In addition to its unique collection of sport bikes, **Maui Motorsports** (📞445-9071; www.mauisportbikerentals.com; 1429 Front St), a low-profile agency, offers various specialty vehicles at low rates, including a wild Can-Am Spyder and a sleek Mazda Miata convertible ($250 per week). Airport pickup and drop-off.

Parking

Front St has free on-street parking, but there's always a line of cruising cars competing for spots. There's one free lot on tiny Luakini St between Lahainaluna Rd and Dickenson St – but get there early, it fills fast. Your best bet is the large lot at the corner of Front and Prison Sts where there's free public parking with a three-hour limit. At private lots near downtown, you may pay as much as $5 for up to two hours and $10 for two to eight hours. Otherwise, park at one of the shopping centers and get your parking ticket validated for free by making a purchase.

Taxi

For a taxi in Lahaina, call **Maui Pleasant Taxi** (📞344-4661; www.mauipleasanttaxi.com) or **West Maui Taxi** (📞888-661-4545, 661-1122). Expect to pay $14 to $20 one-way between Lahaina and Ka'anapali.

West Maui

If you're looking for sun-kissed fun, West Maui is the place to be. Whether you want to snorkel beside lava rocks, zip-line down the mountains, thwack a golf ball, hike through the jungle or sail beneath the setting sun, the adventures are as varied as the landscape. Ka'anapali is West Maui's splashy center, a look-at-me town luring travelers with world-class golf courses, stylish resorts, oceanfront dining and a dazzling, mile-long crescent of beach.

Further north, Hawaiian history and swanky exclusivity have formed an intriguing, sometimes uneasy, alliance in Kapalua, where a luxurious hotel preens between a lush mountain watershed, a PGA golf course, an ancient burial ground and several gorgeous beaches. To escape any semblance of a 'scene,' hunker down in Kahana or Napili, lovely seaside communities known for their condos and budget-friendly prices. For off-the-grid excitement, only one adventure will do — a breezy, sometimes hair-raising, drive around the untamed northern coast.

Kapalua Bay (p78)
ROB DECAMP/GETTY IMAGES ©

West Maui Itineraries

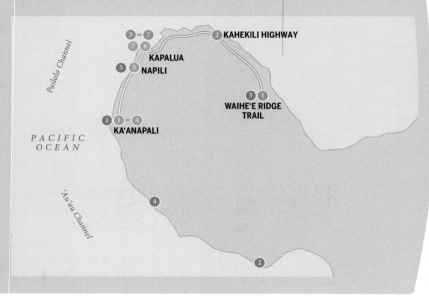

KAHEKILI HIGHWAY

KAPALUA
NAPILI

WAIHE'E RIDGE
TRAIL

KA'ANAPALI

Pailolo Channel

PACIFIC
OCEAN

'Au'au Channel

Two Days

1 Ka'anapali Beach (p66) Begin by jumping into the water at West Maui's hottest spot for sand and sun. For snorkeling, swim toward Pu'u Keka'a (Black Rock) and head for the point, home to abundant fish and colorful coral.

2 Whalers Village Museum (p67) Dry off and don your slippers for this intriguing museum, which explores West Maui's role in the whaling trade as well as the hard but exciting life of a 19th-century whaler.

3 Teralani Sailing (p68) Hop aboard a catamaran for a motor-free cruise of the coast. Teralani's open bar goes down smoothly, too.

4 Ka'anapali Beach Walk (p68) A stroll beside the lovely beach on the Ka'anapali Beach Walk is a scenic way to end the day. Watch the cliff diving and torch-lighting ceremony off Pu'u Keka'a then follow with a tropical drink at beachside Leilani's.

5 Gazebo (p77) Wake up with a splash on day two at this waterfront gem in unspoiled Napili. Macadamia nut pancakes, perhaps?

6 Kapalua (p78) Sign up for a zip-line adventure or stroll one of the trails crisscrossing the property.

7 Sansei Seafood Restaurant & Sushi Bar (p85) Slip into stylish duds for this snazzy sushi bar and restaurant tucked between Kapalua's golf courses and the Ritz-Carlton.

➡ THIS LEG: 8 MILES

Four Days

1 **Waihe'e Ridge Trail** (p90) If you have four glorious days in West Maui, plan your first two days as above. Start day three by stretching your legs on this lofty ridgeline path with misty mountain views.

2 **Kahekili Highway** (p86) After your descent, hop into the car and cruise around the rugged northern tip of the island on this serpentine highway. With one-way bridges and blind turns, this is one of West Maui's most adventurous road trips. Keep your hiking shoes on – there's a lot more than roadside views on this one.

3 **Plantation House** (p85) Start day four here with an 'Oh my gosh, I can't believe how good this is' crab cake Benedict. The backdrop for your meal? A sweeping panorama of the Ritz-Carlton, Moloka'i and, of course, the ever-present golf fiends.

4 **Kapalua Golf** (p83) Speaking of golfers, follow in the footsteps of Tiger Woods by knocking around the greens of Maui's premier golf course.

5 **Oneloa Beach** (p79) Not a golfer? Then grab your beach towel and find your way to Oneloa Beach – as uncrowded and pretty as they come.

6 **Merriman's Kapalua** (p86) In the afternoon, stroll over to the patio here for happy hour. Your reward? Six-dollar mai tais and a cliff-top perch above gorgeous Kapalua Beach.

7 **Pineapple Grill** (p86) End your West Maui adventure with top-notch Hawaiian fusion fare. And one fab view to go with it!

➡ **THIS LEG: 26 MILES**

West Maui Highlights

1 **Best Beach: Ka'anapali Beach** (p66) Snorkel beside Pu'u Keka'a (Black Rock) then strut your stuff resort-style at 'Dig-Me Beach.'

2 **Best View: Papawai Point** (p61) Thar she blows at this cliffside perch, a primo whale-watching spot.

3 **Best Hike: Waihe'e Ridge Trail** (p90) Climb into the clouds on this scenic 5-miler with sweeping north coast views.

4 **Best Water Activity: Balancing on a board** (p66) Surfing, boogie boarding and stand up paddling: everyone's catching waves.

5 **Best Hawaiian Entertainment: Masters of Hawaiian Slack Key Guitar Concert Series** (p78) These old-style jams are a cultural celebration that make everyone feel like 'ohana (family).

Hiker on the Waihe'e Ridge Trail (p90)

DAVE FLEETHAM/GETTY IMAGES ©

Discover West Maui

Lahaina to Maʻalaea

The drive between Lahaina and Ma'alaea offers fine mountain scenery, but in winter everyone is craning their necks seaward to spot humpback whales cruising just offshore. Stand up paddle surfers are also a common sight.

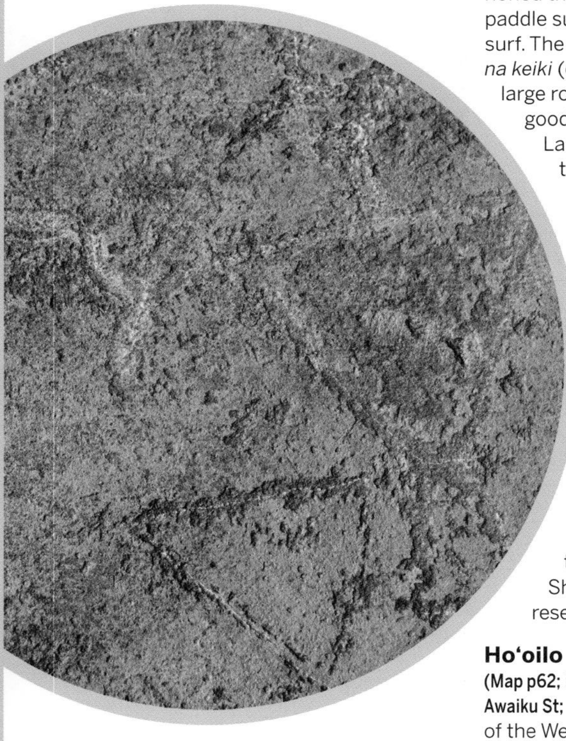

Close-up view of petroglyphs, Olowalu
QUINCY DEIN/GETTY IMAGES ©

PUAMANA BEACH PARK & LAUNIUPOKO BEACH PARK

Beaches

Launiupoko Beach Park Beach
(Map p62) Beginner and intermediate surfers head to this beach park, a popular surf spot 3 miles south of Lahaina. The southern side of the beach has small waves ideal for beginning surfers, while the northern side ratchets it up a notch for those who have honed their skills. You're also likely to see paddle surfers plying through Launiupoko's surf. The park is an ideal spot for families; *na keiki* (children) have a blast wading in the large rock-enclosed shoreline pool and good picnic facilities invite you to linger. Launiupoko is at the traffic lights at the 18-mile marker.

Puamana Beach Park Beach
(Map p62) This shady beach park, 1.5 miles south of Lahaina, is rocky but sometimes has good conditions for beginner surfers – otherwise it's mostly a quick stop for a seaside view, particularly at sunset. Not a great spot for lying out.

Sleeping

For B&Bs on Maui, remember to reserve a room ahead of time. Showing up late at night, without reservations, is strongly discouraged.

Ho'oilo House B&B **$$$**
(Map p62; ✆667-6669; www.hooilohouse.com; 138 Awaiku St; r $329; ❄📶🏊) On the slopes of the West Maui Mountains, this Zen-ful retreat is a place for relaxation. Six Asian- and Maui-themed rooms hug an A-framed community area with a sweeping view of Lana'i.

Whale-Spotting

During the winter humpback whales occasionally breach as close as 100yd from the coast, and 40 tons of leviathan suddenly exploding straight up through the water can be a real showstopper!

Beach parks and pull-offs along the road offer great vantage points for watching the action. The very best spot is **Papawai Point** (Map p98), a cliffside perch jutting into the western edge of Ma'alaea Bay, and a favored humpback nursing ground (not to mention a great place to catch a sunset). The Pacific Whale Foundation posts volunteers at the parking lot to share their knowledge and point out the whales (8am to 2pm mid-December to mid-April).

Papawai Point is midway between the 8- and 9-mile markers, about 3 miles north of Ma'alaea. Note that the road sign simply reads 'scenic point,' not the full name, but there's a turning lane into it, so slow down and you won't miss it.

Stylish furnishings differ by room – many contain Balinese imports – but all have a private lanai (veranda) and an eclectically designed outdoor shower. Breakfast includes fresh muffins and bread, cereal, granola and fruit, which is often plucked from the 2-acre property's pesticide-free orchard. There are refrigerators in all rooms. Solar panels generate 85% to 90% of the house's power, and soap products are recycled in partnership with Clean the World.

OLOWALU

The West Maui Mountains form a scenic backdrop, giving Olowalu its name, which means 'many hills.' For the moment, the tiny village is marked by the Olowalu General Store, Leoda's Kitchen & Pie shop and a juice and fruit stand. The controversial Olowalu Town Project calls for the development of 1500 housing units on land just south of the village. The good news? If completed, half of the housing will be set aside as affordable housing. The bad? Environmental groups are concerned that the project will harm Olowalu's famed coral reef at the 14-mile marker.

Beaches

Olowalu Beach   Beach
(Map p62) The coral reef of Olowalu Beach, which is popular with snorkelers, is shallow and silty, and the 'Sharks may be present' signs lining the beach are the real thing. There were three shark attacks off Olowalu between 1993 and 2002. Located at the 14-mile marker.

Sights

Olowalu Petroglyphs   Archaeological Site
(Map p62) A short walk behind the general store leads to petroglyphs (ancient Hawaiian stone carvings) dating back 200 to 300 years. To get to them, park just beyond the water tower at the back of the store. It's a quarter-mile or so walk up an open road to the petroglyph site. The road is easy to follow; just keep the cinder cone straight ahead of you as you go. Bear left at the Olowalu Cultural Reserve sign.

As with most of Maui's petroglyphs, these figures are carved into the vertical sides of cliffs (rather than on horizontal lava as they are on the Big Island). Most of the Olowalu figures have been damaged, but you can still make out some of them. Don't climb the rocks for a better look, however. And watch for falling rocks. There's a picnic table and interpretive signage at the site.

If you have mobility issues it's OK to drive to the site, instead of walking, but be respectful of neighboring landowners.

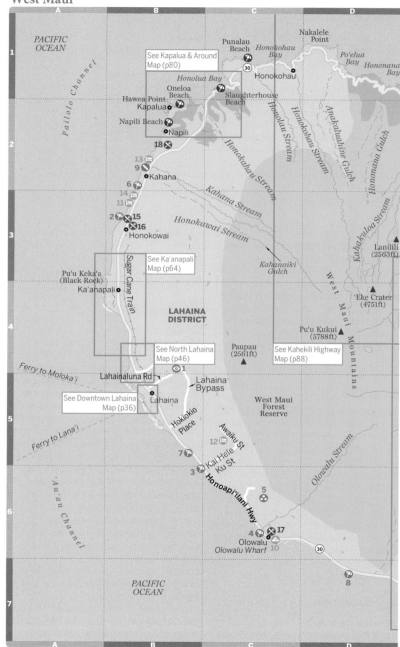

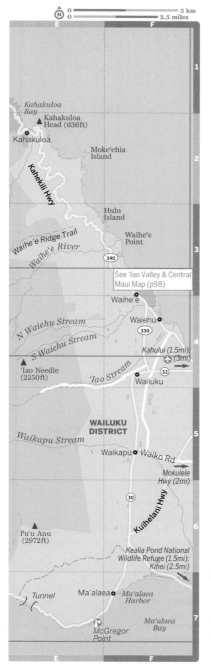

🛏 Sleeping & Eating

Camp Olowalu Campground **$**

(Map p62; ✆661-4303; www.campolowalu.com;
800 Olowalu Village Rd; campsites per adult/child
$15/5; P 🛜) Bordered by the ocean on
one side and a dense thicket of gnarled
trees on the other, the setting here is pure
Survivor. But simple amenities – cold-
water showers, outhouses, picnic tables,
drinking water – kick things up a notch.
Six rustic A-frame cabins with six cots
apiece are available for groups for $600
per night, or rent one cabin for $124
(bring your own bedding). These book up
early.

With its tightly packed sites, port-o-
johns and scruffy vibe, this place may
not work for travelers who prefer more
polished campgrounds. Enter across the
highway from the Olowalu General Store
then drive southeast beside Hwy 30 to
the campground.

Leoda's Kitchen & Pie Shop
Comfort Food $

(Map p62; ☑ 662-3600; www.leodas.com; 820 Olowalu Village Rd, on Honoapi'ilani Hwy; breakfast $7-19, lunch & dinner $6-16, dessert pies $5-9; ☺ 7am-8pm) Wear your stretchy pants to Leoda's. This simple-but-stylish new restaurant is one of the latest ventures from Chef Sheldon Simeon of Star Noodle (p48), in Lahaina, and *Top Chef* fame. Diet-busters include savory pot pies, topping-laden burgers and rich sandwiches like the 'pork, pork...mmm pork.' Save room for one of the mini dessert pies – gorgeous creations vying for attention at the front counter. Located at the 15-mile marker.

UKUMEHAME BEACH PARK & AROUND

Midway between mile markers 11 and 12 is **Papalaua Wayside Park** (Map p98; ☑ 661-4685; www.mauicounty.gov; Honoapi'ilani Hwy; permit & $5-8 fee required; ☺ no camping Wed & Thu), a lackluster county park squeezed between the road and the ocean, though it does have barbecues, portable toilets and tent camping under thorny kiawe trees. For more details about obtaining a camping permit, visit the Maui County government website (www.mauicounty.gov). Note that the place buzzes all night with traffic noise.

At the 12-mile marker is **Ukumehame Beach Park** (Map p62). Shaded by ironwood trees, this sandy beach is OK for a dip, but because of the rocky conditions most locals stick with picnicking and fishing. Dive and snorkel boats anchor offshore at **Coral Gardens**. This reef also creates **Thousand Peaks** toward its western end, with breaks favored by longboarders and beginner surfers.

The pull-off for the western end of the Lahaina Pali Trail (p116) is just south of the 11-mile marker, on the inland side of the road.

Lahaina to Ka'anapali

The stretch between Lahaina and Ka'anapali offers a couple of roadside beach parks and one very good B&B.

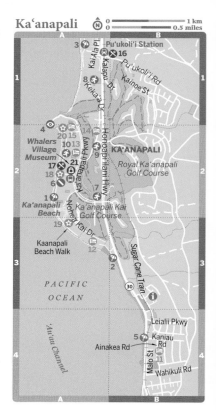

Ka'anapali

WAHIKULI WAYSIDE PARK

Two miles north of Lahaina, **Wahikuli Wayside Park** (Map p64; Honoapi'ilani Hwy) occupies a narrow strip of beach flanked by the busy highway. Although the beach is mostly backed by a black-rock retaining wall, there's a small sandy area. Swimming conditions are usually fine, and when the water's calm, you can snorkel near the lava outcrops at the park's southern end. The park has showers and restrooms.

Sleeping

Guest House
B&B $$

(Map p64; ☑ 661-8085, 800-621-8942; www.mauiguesthouse.com; 1620 Ainakea Rd; s/d incl breakfast $169/189; P ✳ @ 🛜 🏊) ⊘ The welcoming Guest House, which has been

Ka'anapali

hosting travelers for 25 years, provides amenities that put nearby resorts to shame. Every room has its own hot tub and 42in plasma TV. Stained-glass windows and rattan furnishings reflect a tropical motif, and there's an inviting salt-water pool on the front deck. Free perks include beach towels, snorkel gear, a community kitchen and a guest shower you can use before your midnight flight.

In 2012 this eco-minded B&B went 100% solar after installing a 113-panel photovoltage solar system.

Guest House is located in a residential neighborhood between Lahaina and Ka'anapali, inland of Hwy 30. The beach is just a five-minute drive away.

HANAKA'O'O BEACH PARK

The long, sandy **Hanaka'o'o Beach Park (Map p64)**, extending south from Ka'anapali Beach Resort, has a sandy bottom and water conditions that are usually safe for swimming. However, southerly swells, which sometimes develop in summer, can create powerful waves and shorebreaks, while the occasional *kona* (leeward) storm can kick up rough water conditions in winter. Snorkelers head down to the second clump of rocks on the southern side of the park, but it really doesn't compare with sites further north. The park has full facilities and is one of only two beaches on the entire West Maui coast that has a lifeguard. Hanaka'o'o Beach is also called 'Canoe Beach,' as West Maui outrigger canoe clubs practice here in the late afternoon.

A small immigrant cemetery dating from the 1850s marks the entrance.

Ka'anapali

Whether it's your honeymoon, your birthday, a family reunion or a girlfriend getaway, Ka'anapali is the place where you'll want to celebrate. Maui's flashiest resort destination welcomes guests with 3 miles of sandy beach, a dozen oceanfront hotels, two 18-hole golf courses and an ocean full of water activities. You can sit at a beachfront bar with a tropical drink, soak up the gorgeous views of Lana'i and Moloka'i across the channel and listen to guitarists strum their wiki-wacky-woo.

Beaches

Ka'anapali Beach   Beach

(Map p64) Home to West Maui's liveliest beach scene, this gorgeous stretch of sand unfurls alongside Ka'anapali's resort hotels, linking the Hyatt Regency Maui with the Sheraton Maui 1 mile north. Dubbed 'Dig-Me Beach' for all the preening, it's a vibrant spot. Surfers, boogie boarders and parasailers rip across the water, snorkelers admire the sea life and sailboats pull up on shore. Check with the hotel beach huts before jumping in, however, as water conditions vary with the season and currents are sometimes strong.

For the best snorkeling, try the underwater sights off **Pu'u Keka'a (Black Rock; Map p64)**. This lava promontory protects the beach in front of the Sheraton Maui. Novices stick to the sheltered southern side of the landmark rock – where there's still a lot to see – but the shallow coral here has been stomped to death. If you're a confident swimmer, the less-frequented horseshoe cove cut into the tip of the rock is the real prize, teeming with tropical fish, colorful coral and sea turtles. There's often a current to contend with off the point, which can make getting to the cove a bit tricky, but when it's calm you can swim right in. Pu'u Keka'a is also a popular shore-dive spot.

Kahekili Beach Park   Beach

(Map p64) To escape the look-at-me crowds clustered in front of the resorts, head to this idyllic golden-sand beach at Ka'anapali's less-frequented northern end. The swimming's better, the snorkeling's good and the park has everything you'll need for a day at the beach – showers, restrooms, a covered picnic pavilion and barbecue grills. Access is easy and there's ample free parking.

Snorkelers will find plenty of coral and marine life right in front of the beach. Sea turtle sightings are common. To go a bit further afield, swim north to **Honokowai**

Left: Kahekili Beach Park; **Below:** Historic whale products (scrimshaw and corsetry) at Whalers Village Museum

(LEFT) ANN CECIL/GETTY IMAGES ©; (BELOW) GREG ELMS/GETTY IMAGES ©

Point and then ride the mild current, which runs north to south, all the way back.

The wide beach, backed by swaying palms and flowering morning glory, is also ideal for strolling. It's a 15-minute walk south to Pu'u Keka'a. Or you could walk north along the beach for about 20 minutes to Honokowai Point and have lunch in the village.

To get to the beach from the Honoapi'ilani Hwy, turn *makai* (seaward) 0.2 miles north of the 25-mile marker onto Kai Ala Dr, then bear right.

Sights

Whalers Village Museum   Museum
(Map p64; ☎661-5992; www.whalersvillage.
com/museum.htm; 2435 Ka'anapali Pkwy,
Whalers Village; adult/child $3/1; ☺10am-4pm)
Lahaina was a popular stop for whaling ships traveling between Japan and the arctic during the Golden Age of whaling (1825–60). The ships would also restock here before the long voyage home to New England. At this small but fascinating museum the hardships and routines of life at sea are revealed in authentic period photographs, ship logs, harpoons and intriguing interpretive plaques that sound the depths of whaling history.

Particularly eye-opening is the life-size forecastle. How 20 crewmen could live for weeks in this tiny room – without coming to blows or losing their minds – is a mystery. Also worth a look is the intricate rigging on the built-to-scale replica of an 1850s-era whaling ship. Consider the skill required to maneuver such a complex vessel through rough and dangerous seas!

Interest piqued? Stick around for the humpback whale talk offered Monday, Wednesday and Friday at 11am. A full-size sperm whale skeleton welcomes guests at the front entrance to the shopping center.

67

The Best...
Outdoor Activities

1 Snorkeling, Honolua Bay (p79)

2 Hiking, Waihe'e Ridge Trail (p90)

3 Zip-lining, West Maui Mountains (p84)

4 Scrambling for a view, Nakalele Blowhole (p87)

5 Whale-watching on a cruise, off Ka'anapali Beach (p66)

6 Horseback riding, Mendes Ranch (p90)

Ka'anapali Beach Walk   Waterfront

For people-watching and a bit of exercise, take the mile-long beachfront walk that runs between the Sheraton Maui and Hyatt Regency Maui hotels. In addition to the action on the shore, both the Hyatt and the Westin Maui, located at the mid-point of the walk, are worth a detour for their dazzling garden statuary and landscaping replete with free-form pools and rushing waterfalls. At the Hyatt, pampered black African penguins love to waddle beside their four-star penguin cave, found in the rambling lobby.

At the southern end of the walk, beyond the Hyatt, the graceful 17ft-high bronze sculpture *The Acrobats*, by Australian John Robinson, makes a dramatic silhouette at sunset.

In the early evening, you'll often be treated to entertainment from the beachside restaurants.

 **Activities**

Teralani Sailing   Sailing

(Map p64; ☎661-0365; www.teralani.net; 2435 Ka'anapali Pkwy, Whalers Village; outings adult/child from $61/39; ☺hours vary) This friendly outfit offers a variety of sails on two custom-built catamarans that depart from the beach beside Whalers Village. The easygoing sunset sail offers an inspiring introduction to the gorgeous West Maui coast. Snorkel sails and whale-watching outings are additional options, but no matter which you choose, you'll find a friendly crew, refreshing cocktails and decent food.

Note the 24-hour cancellation policy and the $5 fuel charge per person.

Ka'anapali Dive Company   Diving

(Map p64; ☎661-2179; www.goscubamaui. com; Westin Maui Resort & Spa; 1-tank dive $69; ☺reservations 7am-5pm) If you've never been diving before, these are the people you want to see. The introductory dive ($99) for novices, with equipment, starts with instruction in a pool and moves on to a guided dive from the beach. It also offers beach dives for certified divers. No separate rentals. Walk up, or call to make reservations (Starwood Activities line).

Trilogy Ocean Sports   Water Sports

(Map p64; ☎661-7789; www.sailtrilogy.com; Ka'anapali Beach Walk; 2hr lesson surfing $70, SUP $89; ☺8am-5pm, later in summer) From its beach hut in front of the Ka'anapali Beach Hotel, Trilogy can get you up and riding a board with a two-hour surfing or stand up paddle boarding (SUP) lesson. Snorkel sets rent for $20 a day, and SUP boards are $25 for the first hour then $15 per hour. Don't want to work so hard? Try the sunset catamaran cruise (adult/child $69/35).

Skyline Eco-Adventures   Zip-Lining

(Map p64; ☎878-8400; www.zipline.com; 2580 Keka'a Dr, Fairway Shops; 4hr outing $150; ☺departs on the hour 7am-2pm) ✈ Got a need for speed? The Ka'anapali course takes you 2 miles up the wooded cliffsides of the West Maui Mountains and sets you off on a free-glide along eight separate lines above waterfalls, stream beds and valleys. Eco-stewardship is a mission of the company, and guides discuss local flora and fauna. If it's drizzly and windy? Hold on tight and no cannonballs!

Ka'anapali Golf Courses
Golf

(Map p64; 661-3691; www.kaanapaligolf
courses.com; 2290 Ka'anapali Pkwy; greens fee
$205-249, after 1pm $119-139; hours vary
seasonally, opens about 6:30am) The more
demanding of the two courses is the
Royal Ka'anapali Golf Course, designed by
Robert Trent Jones. It's tournament grade
with greens that emphasize putting skills.
The Ka'anapali Kai Golf Course is shorter
and more of a resort course. The setting
isn't as spectacular as the courses in
Kapalua, but it tends to be less windy and
the rates are a relative bargain.

If you're staying in a hotel or condo at
the Ka'anapali Resort, ask for the guest
rate which will save you about $70.

Tour of the Stars
Stargazing

(Map p64; 667-4727; www.maui.hyatt.com;
200 Nohea Kai Dr, Hyatt Regency Maui Resort &
Spa; guest adult/child $25/15, nonguest $30/20)
Enjoy stellar stargazing atop the Hyatt
resort. These 50-minute viewings are
limited to 14 people, use a 16in-diameter
telescope and are held at 8pm and 9pm
on clear nights. Romantic types should
opt for the couples-only viewing at
10pm Friday and Saturday, which rolls
out champagne and chocolate-covered
strawberries (guest/nonguest $40/45).

Royal Lahaina
Tennis Ranch
Tennis

(Map p64; 667-5200; www.royal-
lahaina.com/activities.cfm; 2780
Keka'a Dr; per person per day
$15; pro shop 8am-noon
daily, 2-6pm Mon-Fri, 2-5pm
Sat & Sun) Named the
2010 Facility of the Year
by the United States
Tennis Association,
this is the largest ten-
nis complex in West
Maui, with four courts
lit for night play. Rack-
ets and shoes can be
rented. Private lessons
and group clinics are
available.

Festivals & Events

Maui Onion Festival
Food

(www.whalersvillage.com/events.htm) This
popular celebration, held the first Saturday in May, highlights all that can be done
with Maui's famed Kula onions. Look for
cooking contests and an onion eating
competition. The festival celebrated its
25th anniversary in 2014.

Hula O Na Keiki
Hula

(www.kbhmaui.com; adult/child $15/6) Children
take center stage at this hula dance
competition in early to mid-November,
which features some of the best *keiki*
dancers in Hawaii. It's held at Ka'anapali
Beach Hotel.

Sleeping

The following accommodations are on the
beach or within walking distance of it. In
addition to these resorts there is one B&B
(p64) between Ka'anapali and Lahaina.

Nakalele Blowhole (p87)
KIN IMAGES/GETTY IMAGES ©

Ka'anapali Beach Hotel Resort $$

(Map p64; ☏661-0011, 800-262-8450; www.
kbhmaui.com; 2525 Ka'anapali Pkwy; r $189-266;
P✹@☎≋₩) This welcoming property
feels a bit like summer camp – but in
the best possible way. The hotel is a little
older than its neighbors and the style is
more comfy than posh, but it has its own
special charms: warm staff, nightly hula
shows, an outdoor tiki bar, tidy grounds
framed by palm trees and an enviable
location on a gorgeous stretch of beach.
Isn't this why you came to Maui?

Family-friendly activities include lei-
making and ukulele lessons. For church-
goers there's a nondenominational
outdoor service on Sunday mornings. On
your last day, bring a camera and a hankie
to your farewell lei ceremony. Parking and
wi-fi are each $10 per day.

Outrigger
Maui Eldorado Condo $$

(Map p64; ☏661-0021, 888-339-8585; www.
outrigger.com; 2661 Keka'a Dr; studio/1br/2br
from $199/225/375; P✹@☎≋) Have a
golfer in your family? Then consider this
quiet condo development bordering the
Royal Ka'anapali Golf Course. How close

are units to the fairways? One sign says it
all: 'Beware of flying golf balls in the lanai
areas.' Units are not on the beach, but the
complex isn't far from the ocean, and the
resort shuttle stops out front.

The best rooms are the large studios,
which have kitchens set apart from the
bedroom area. All units have washers and
dryers. The resort fee is $12 per day and
includes parking. There is a mandatory
cleaning charge per stay ($75 to $115).

Sheraton Maui Resort $$$

(Map p64; ☏661-0031, 866-716-8109; www.
sheraton-maui.com; 2605 Ka'anapali Pkwy; r/ste
from $349/659; P✹@☎≋₩) This sleek
resort bumps against the striking Pu'u
Keka'a (Black Rock) at the northern end
of the Ka'anapali Beach Walk. Honeymooners, families and outdoor adventurers will all find something here to brag
about on postcards and Instagram feeds:
the sunset cliff dive, whale-watching from
the room or snorkeling beside graceful
green turtles. Rooms gleam with rich
wood tones and smart Hawaiian prints.

The sprawling, 23-acre grounds have
night-lit tennis courts, a fitness center, a
lava-rock swimming pool and the spa at

Gardens and lawns at Sheraton Maui

ANN CECIL/GETTY IMAGES ©

Black Rock. The $31.25 daily resort fee includes parking, Lahaina shuttle service and wi-fi.

Hyatt Regency Maui Resort & Spa
Resort **$$$**

(Map p64; ☎661-1234; www.maui.hyatt. com; 200 Nohea Kai Dr; r/ste from $249/671; P❄@☎≋🐾) The airy lobby atrium is tricked out with exotic birds and extravagant artwork, the grounds given over to gardens and swan ponds. Kids of all ages will thrill in the water world of meandering pools, swim-through grottoes and towering water slides. As part of a $21 million renovation project, the lobby was modernized and guest rooms 'refreshed' – picture monochromatic walls, chocolate-brown furniture and bold splashes of color.

The daily resort fee of $30 includes wi-fi, but parking is a separate $14 per day.

 Eating

Don't limit yourself to Ka'anapali's restaurants as many of Maui's top chefs are just a skip down the road in Lahaina. For cheap eats, a handful of food trucks cluster on Pu'ukoli'i Rd beside the Honoapi'ilani Hwy, just north of the main entrance to Ka'anapali.

Da Shark Pit
Tacos, Burgers **$**

(Map p64; www.sharkpitmaui.com; 1 Pu'ukoli'i Rd, at Honoapi'ilani Hwy; mains $7-12; ⏰11am-4pm Mon-Sat) Da 'funked up' fish tacos come with wasabi aioli and Sriracha hot sauce – kickin'! But it's not just spicy tacos bringing appreciative lunchgoers to this no-fuss food truck, which parks off the Honoapi'ilani Hwy in northern Ka'anapali. Look for cheesy burgers and specials with an Hawaiian twist. Order at the window, sit at the picnic table and wave at the Sugar Cane Train. Da best!

Hula Grill & Barefoot Bar
Hawaii Regional **$$**

(Map p64; ☎667-6636; www.hulagrillkaanapali. com; 2435 Ka'anapali Pkwy, Whalers Village; bar lunch $13-19, bar dinner $13-20, dining room mains $24-32; ⏰bar 10:45am-10pm, dining room 4:45-9:30pm) The Barefoot Bar is your Maui

Island Insight

According to traditional Hawaiian beliefs, Pu'u Keka'a (p66), the westernmost point of Maui, is a place where the spirits of the dead leap into the unknown to be carried to their ancestral homeland. The rock is said to have been created during a scuffle between the demigod Maui and a commoner who questioned Maui's superiority. Maui chased the man to this point, froze his body into stone then cast his soul out to sea. Today, daring teens wait their turn to leap off the rock for a resounding splash into the cove below.

postcard: coconut-frond umbrellas, the sand beneath your sandals and the guy strumming the guitar. There's no better place on the beach walk to sip mai tais and nibble *pupu* (snacks) by the sea. The Kapulu Joe pork sandwich with macnut slaw (add a dash of chili water) is reliably good, and the beer-battered mahimahi tacos hit the spot too. Dinner inside at the restaurant kicks it up a notch with spicy kiawe-grilled seafood.

Japengo
Sushi, Steaks **$$$**

(Map p64; ☎661-1234; www.maui.hyatt.com; 200 Nohea Kai Dr, Hyatt Regency Maui Resort & Spa; sushi $6-24, mains $24-44; ⏰5-10pm) Got the sun-kissed tan? The windswept hair? The breezy new dress? Japengo is the place to strut your Ka'anapali glow. On the tiki-lit patio, enjoy an artist's array of tropical cocktails and delectable sushi as the sun drops behind the sea. Seafood dishes, like the grilled ahi (yellowfin tuna) with Hamakua mushrooms and wasabi butter, as well as savory steaks are prepared with Pacific Rim flair.

Roy's Ka'anapali
Hawaii Regional **$$$**

(Map p64; ☎669-6999; www.royshawaii.com; 2290 Ka'anapali Pkwy, Ka'anapali Resort; lunch $14-24, dinner $16-43; ⏰lunch 11am-2pm, bar pupu 2-5:30pm, dinner from 5:30pm) The Maui outpost of Chef Roy Yamaguchi's upscale dining empire moved from Kahana to the golf course clubhouse at the Ka'anapali Resort in 2012. Here, big-windowed views of the greens are a pleasant backdrop for the exquisitely prepared island and regional fare. Main meals include the sashimi-like blackened ahi with Chinese mustard and Roy's meatloaf with onion rings and mushroom gravy.

Drinking & Entertainment

Bars in Whalers Village and at many resorts offer live music in the evening. Luau and hula shows are also popular. Check www.mauitime.com for details.

LIVE MUSIC

Many Ka'anapali bars have live music regularly. It's typically Jimmy Buffett–style guitar tunes, occasionally spiced up with some ukulele strumming.

Leilani's   Live Music
(Map p64; ☎661-4495; www.leilanis.com; 2435 Ka'anapali Pkwy, Whalers Village; ⊙10:30am-11pm) This open-air bar and restaurant beside the beach is a pleasant place to linger over a cool drink while catching a few rays. It also has a good grill and *pupu* menu. Live music Wednesday through Sunday from 3pm to 5pm.

Longboards   Live Music
(Map p64; ☎667-8220; 100 Nohea Kai Dr, Marriott's Maui Ocean Club; ⊙5-9pm) Come here for live contemporary Hawaiian music.

Japengo   Live Music
(Map p64; ☎661-1234; www.maui.hyatt.com; 200 Nohea Kai Dr, Hyatt Regency Maui Resort & Spa; ⊙6-8pm) There's live music on the patio at Japengo from 6pm to 8pm nightly.

HULA, LUAU & THEATER
Ka'anapali Beach Hotel   Hula
(Map p64; ☎661-0011; www.kbhmaui.com; 2525 Ka'anapali Pkwy; ⊙6-9pm; ⏺) Maui's most Hawaiian hotel cheerfully entertains anyone who chances by between 6pm and 9pm with a free hula show and Hawaiian music. Enjoy mai tais and brews at the adjacent Tiki Bar, with music and dancing nightly in the Tiki Courtyard.

Sheraton Maui   Cliff Dive
(Map p64; ☎661-0031; www.sheraton-maui.com; 2605 Ka'anapali Pkwy; ⊙sunset) Everybody swings by to watch the torch-lighting and cliff-diving ceremony from Pu'u Keka'a (Black Rock) that takes place at sunset. There's also live music at the Cliff Dive Bar from 6:30pm to 8:30pm.

Drums of the Pacific   Luau
(Map p64; ☎667-4727; www.maui.hyatt.com; 200 Nohea Kai Dr, Hyatt Regency Maui Resort & Spa; adult/child from $95/49; ⊙from 5pm Oct-Mar, from 5:30pm Apr-Sep; ⏺) Ka'anapali's best luau includes an *imu* ceremony (unearthing of a roasted pig from an underground oven), an open bar, a Hawaiian-style buffet and a South Pacific dance and music show.

Whalers Village   Hula, Dance
(Map p64; ☎661-4567; www.whalersvillage. com; 2435 Ka'anapali Pkwy; ⊙7-8pm Mon, Wed & Sat) Ka'anapali's shopping center hosts Polynesian and Tahitian dance and hula performances. Check the website for a monthly calendar of all events and classes.

Shopping

You'll find more than 90 shops and restaurants at **Whalers Village** (Map p64; ☎661-4567; www.whalersvillage.com; 2435 Ka'anapali Pkwy; ⊙9:30am-10pm) shopping center.

ABC Store   Accessories
(Map p64; ☎667-9700; www.abcstores.com; Whalers Village; ⊙7am-11pm) Stop here for sunblock and great beach totes.

Crazy Shirts   Clothing
(Map p64; ☎662-8785; www.crazyshirts.com; Whalers Village) This Hawaiian company has been selling stylish T-shirts for more than 40 years.

Honolua Surf   Clothing
(Map p64; ☎661-5455; www.honoluasurf.com; Whalers Village; ⊙9am-10pm) The place to

pick up Maui-style board shorts as well as bikinis.

Lahaina Printsellers   Art, Maps
(Map p64; ☎661-7617; www.printsellers.com; Whalers Village; ☺9am-10pm) Packable Hawaiian prints and maps.

Martin & MacArthur   Arts & Crafts
(Map p64; ☎667-7422; www.martinand macarthur.com; Whalers Village; ☺9:30am-10pm) Museum-quality Hawaiian-made wood carvings, paintings and other crafts.

ⓘ Getting Around
Bus
The Maui Bus (Map p64; ☎871-4838; www. mauicounty.gov; per trip $2; ☺most routes 6am-8pm) currently connects Whalers Village shopping center in Ka'anapali with the Wharf Cinema Center in Lahaina hourly from 6am to 9pm and on the half hour between 2pm and 6pm. It also runs north up the coast to Kahana and Napili hourly from 6am to 8pm.

The free **Ka'anapali Trolley** runs between the Ka'anapali hotels, Whalers Village and the golf courses about every 20 to 30 minutes (times can vary) between 10am and 8pm. The trolley schedule is posted at the Whalers Village stop.

Car & Motorcycle
For Harley-Davidson motorcycle rentals, try **Eagle Rider** (☎662-4877; www.eaglerider.com; 30 Halawai Dr A-3; motorcycle hire per day incl helmet from $101), located just north of Ka'anapali off the Honoapi'ilani Hwy.

Parking
The resort hotels offer free beach parking to the public, but the spaces allotted are so limited they commonly fill by mid-morning. Your best bet is at the southern end of the Hyatt, which has more slots than other hotels. Another option is the pay parking lot at Whalers Village from 7am to midnight ($3 per 30 minutes; three-hour parking validation with a purchase varies by merchant).

Taxi
Cabs often line up beside the trolley and Maui Bus stop in front of Whalers Village on Ka'anapali Pkwy.

Honokowai
Condo-laden Honokowai may not have the glamour of pricier Ka'anapali to the south, but it has its virtues. It's convenient, affordable and low-rise, and the ocean views are as fine as in the upscale resorts. Another perk: in winter this is the

Beachfront condos, Honokowai

best place in West Maui to spot passing whales right from your room lanai.

The main road, which bypasses the condos, is Honoapiʻilani Hwy (Hwy 30). The shoreline road is Lower Honoapiʻilani Rd, which leads into Honokowai.

 Sights & Activities

Honokowai Beach Park
Beach

(Map p62;) The real thrills here are on land, not in the water. This family-friendly park in the center of town has cool playground facilities and makes a nice spot for a picnic. Forget swimming, though. The water is shallow and the beach is lined with a submerged rock shelf. Water conditions improve at the southern side of town, and you could continue walking along the shore down to lovely Kahekili Beach Park (p66) at the northern end of Kaʻanapali.

Boss Frog
Snorkeling

(Map p62; ☎665-1200; www.bossfrog.com; 3636 Lower Honoapiʻilani Rd; snorkel set per day from $1.50; ☺8am-5pm) Offers great prices for rental mask, snorkel and fins.

 Sleeping

Noelani
Condo $$

(Map p62; ☎800-367-6030, 669-8374; www.noelani-condo-resort.com; 4095 Lower Honoapiʻilani Rd; studio from $182, 1/2/3br from $227/329/403; ☎☒) Get to know your neighbors at the weekly mai tai party at this compact hideaway, a small condo complex that's so close to the water you can sit on your lanai and watch turtles swimming in the surf. The units range from cozy studios to three-bedroom suites, all with ocean views. Two heated pools, a Jacuzzi, a small exercise room and concierge services are additional perks.

Hale Kai
Condo $$

(Map p62; ☎800-446-7307, 669-6333; www.halekai.com; 3691 Lower Honoapiʻilani Rd; 1/2/3br $175/210/350; ☎☒) 'Glad you're here' friendliness lifts this two-story condo complex from the ho-hum into something special. The property also offers some nice Hawaiian accents, from the room decor to the lava-rock exterior. It's perched on the water's edge: step off your lanai and onto the sand. The three-bedroom corner unit has a cool loft, wraparound ocean-view windows and all the character of a Hawaiian beach house.

✗ Eating

Farmers Market Deli
Deli $

(Map p62; ☎669-7004; 3636 Lower Honoapiʻilani Rd; sandwiches & salads $6-8; ☺7am-7pm;) ✿ Stop here for healthy takeout fare. The salad bar (with free samples) includes organic goodies and hot veggie dishes. The smoothies are first-rate. The place becomes even greener on Monday, Wednesday and Friday mornings (7am to 11am),

Plate lunch at Honokowai Okazuya

when vendors sell locally grown produce in the parking lot.

Honokowai Okazuya
International $$

(Map p62; 665-0512; 3600 Lower Honoapi'ilani Rd; mains $10-18; 11am-2:30pm & 4:30-8:30pm Mon-Sat) The appeal is not immediately apparent. The place is tiny, prices are high and the choices seem weird (*kung pao chicken* and spaghetti with meatballs?). But then you nibble the piping-hot Mongolian beef. Hmm, it's OK. Chomp chomp. That's pretty interesting. Gulp gulp. What is that spice? Savor savor – until the whole darn container is empty. At this place – primarily takeout – plate lunch specialties take a delicious gourmet turn. Cash only.

Kahana

Trendy Kahana, the village north of Honokowai, boasts million-dollar homes, upscale beachfront condominiums and Maui's only microbrewery.

Sights & Activities

The sandy **beach** fronting the village offers reasonable swimming. Park at seaside **Pohaku Park (Map p62)** and walk north a couple of minutes to reach the beach. Pohaku Park itself has an offshore break called S-Turns that attracts surfers.

Maui Dive Shop
Diving, Snorkeling

(Map p62; 669-3800; www.mauidiveshop. com; 4405 Honoapi'ilani Hwy, Kahana Gateway shopping center; 2-tank dives from $140, snorkel sets per day $8; 8am-9pm) Come here for information about a full range of dives and to rent snorkel gear.

Sleeping

Kahana Village
Condo $$$

(Map p62; 669-5111, 800-824-3065; www. kahanavillage.com; 4531 Lower Honoapi'ilani Rd; 2/3br from $300/510;) With A-frame ceilings, airy lofts and oceanfront views, the 2nd-story units have a fun 'vacation' vibe. The breezy appeal of the interior is well-matched outside with lush tropical flora and weekly mai tai parties with live Hawaiian music. Some condos have views of Lana'i while others face Moloka'i. Every unit has a lanai, full kitchen, and washer and dryer.

Eating & Drinking

Hawaiian Village Coffee
Cafe $

(Map p62; 665-1114; www.hawaiianvillage coffee.com; 4405 Honoapi'ilani Hwy, Kahana Gateway shopping center; snacks & sandwiches under $10; 6am-6pm; @) Off-duty surfers shoot the breeze at this low-key coffee shop. Use one of five computers in back to surf the net (20 minutes for $3) and print documents (35¢ per page).

Maui Brewing Company
Brewery

(Map p62; 669-3474; www.mauibrewingco. com; 4405 Honoapi'ilani Hwy, Kahana Gateway shopping center; mains $12-25; 11am-10pm) From the pasta with Surfing Goat chèvre to the *kalua* pork pizza, pub grub takes a Hawaiian spin at this cavernous brewpub hunkered in the corner of Kahana Gateway shopping center. The company, which has been honored as one of Hawaii's top green businesses, implements sustainable practices where it can. The Bikini Blonde lager, Mana Wheat, Big Swell IPA and Coconut Porter are always on tap, supplemented by a wide range of seasonal and specialty brews.

Napili

Napili is a bayside oasis flanked by the posh grounds of Kapalua to the north and the hustle and bustle of Kahana and Ka'anapali to the south. For an oceanfront retreat that's a bit more affordable – but not far from the action – we highly recommend this sun-blessed center of calm.

Beaches

Napili Beach
Beach

(Map p80) The deep golden sands and gentle curves of Napili Beach offer good beachcombing at any time and excellent swimming and snorkeling when it's calm. Look for green sea turtles hanging out by

The Best...
Spot for Sunset Cocktails

1 Barefoot Bar, Hula Grill (p71)

2 Merriman's Kapalua (p86)

3 Teralani Sailing cruise (p68)

4 Sea House Restaurant

5 Cliff Dive Bar, Sheraton Maui (p72)

the rocky southern shore. Big waves occasionally make it into the bay in winter, and when they do it's time to break out the skimboards – the steep drop at the beach provides a perfect run into the surf.

 Sleeping

Napili Bay is surrounded by older condos and small, mellow resorts. Come here to escape the Ka'anapali crowds and to enjoy low-cost proximity to Kapalua. Most don't have air-conditioning but ocean breezes typically keep rooms cool.

Napili Surf Beach Resort
Condo $$

(Map p80; 888-627-4547, 669-8002; www.napilisurf.com; 50 Napili Pl; studio from $199, 1br from $305;) This friendly, well-maintained property is tucked on a gentle curve of sand on Napili Bay. One of the best deals in West Maui, a stay here includes complimentary maid service and wi-fi, not to mention tasty free mai tais at the Wednesday night mai tai party. Full kitchens are nice if you want to eat in, but the Gazebo is next door and the Sea House is a beach stroll away.

Each guest is welcomed with a fresh half-pineapple chilling in the refrigerator. Garden view units, which don't catch the

ocean breeze, can be warm on hot days. Rates start at $159 during low season.

Hale Napili
Condo $$$

(Map p80; 669-6184, 800-245-2266; www.halenapili.com; 65 Hui Dr; studio $199-295, 1br $340;) This charming place is a welcome throwback to an earlier era, when everything on Maui was small and personable. Guests receive a list of occupants, making it easier to strike up conversations, and there's a central Keurig coffee machine so you can see who's up and about. The 18 neat-as-a-pin units have tropical decor, full kitchens and oceanfront lanai. The warm aloha of the manager ensures repeat guests too.

Mauian
Condo Hotel $$$

(Map p80; 669-6205, 800-367-5034; www.mauian.com; 5441 Lower Honoapi'ilani Rd; studio with kitchen from $223, r $203;) Most Napili condos wear their age gracefully, but not the sassy Mauian, a 44-room condo/hotel hybrid kicking up her stylish heels like a teenager. Bamboo ceilings, frond prints, crisp whites and browns, Tempur-Pedic mattresses – rooms are sharp, stylish and comfortable. Enjoy the breeze from the lanai.

Units do not have TVs or phones, but both are available in the common area.

Napili Kai Beach Resort
Condo Hotel $$$

(Map p80; 800-367-5030, 669-6271; www.napilikai.com; 5900 Lower Honoapi'ilani Rd; r/studio/ste from $280/375/555;) The simple but sophisticated lobby lures visitors inside with an open-air view of the ocean. It's a gorgeous calling card for this pampering resort, which covers 10 acres at the northern end of Napili Bay. The units, which tastefully blend Polynesian decor with Asian touches, have private lanai and the condo units have kitchenettes. Don't miss the Monday 'putting party' with 50¢ cocktails on the resort's 18-hole green.

For modern style and decor, reserve a room in the Puna Point, Puna 2 or Lani 1 buildings. Some units have air-con, so check when booking. There are complimentary children's activities during holidays and in summer.

Outrigger Napili Shores
Condo $$$

(Map p80; 800-688-7444, 669-8061; www.outrigger.com; 5315 Lower Honoapi'ilani Rd; studio/1br from $245/279; [P] [@] [🛜] [🏊]) Two words: the Gazebo. West Maui's superstar breakfast joint is on the premises, giving guests a head start on the line. Freshly renovated, every unit looks new.

✖ Eating & Drinking

Gazebo
Cafe $

(Map p80; 669-5621; 5315 Lower Honoapi'ilani Rd, Outrigger Napili Shores; mains $8-12; ⊙7:30am-2pm) Locals aren't kidding when they advise you to get here early to beat the crowds. But a 7:10am arrival is worth it for this beloved open-air restaurant – literally a gazebo on the beach – with a gorgeous waterfront setting. The tiny cafe is known for its breakfasts, and those with a sweet tooth love the white chocolate macnut pancakes. Meal-size salads, hearty sandwiches and the *kalua* pig plate steal the scene at lunch. The restaurant is behind Outrigger Napili Shores.

Maui Tacos
Mexican $

(Map p62; 665-0222; www.mauitacos.com; 5095 Napilihau St, Napili Plaza; mains $5-11; ⊙9am-9pm) Mexican fare can be island-style healthy. The salsas and beans are prepared fresh daily, trans-fat-free oil replaces lard, and fresh veggies and local fish feature on the menu. Good for a quick meal.

Sea House Restaurant
Hawaii Regional $$

(Map p80; 669-1500; www.seahousemaui.com; 5900 Lower Honoapi'ilani Rd, Napili Kai Beach Resort; breakfast $9-15, lunch $10-16, dinner $24-36; ⊙7am-9pm, cocktails to 10pm) Pssst, want an $8 meal framed by a million dollar view? Sidle up to the bar at this tiki-lit favorite, order a bowl of the smoky seafood chowder then watch as the perfectly framed sun drops below the horizon in front of you. Bravo! If you stick around, and you should, seafood and steak dishes are menu highlights.

Happy hour (2pm to 5pm) draws crowds for $3 to $7 *pupu* and $5 to $8 cocktails.

Gazebo at Outrigger Napili Shores

LONELY PLANET/GETTY IMAGES ©

Napili Coffee Store
Cafe

(Map p62; 669-4170; www.coffeestorenapili.com; 5095 Napilihau St, Napili Plaza; pastries & sandwiches $2-10; ⏰6am-6pm; @ 🛜) Having a bad morning? Then try the smooth, ice-blended mocha at Napili's favorite coffee shop. It will set things right. Locals also line up for the pleasant service and the pastries, from banana bread to pumpkin-cranberry muffins and chocolate peanut butter bars. For heartier fare try a slice of quiche or a turkey sandwich with basil pesto.

You can also surf the internet on its computers ($1 per 10 minutes).

⭐ Entertainment

Masters of Hawaiian Slack Key Guitar Concert Series
Live Music

(Map p80; 669-3858; www.slackkeyshow.com; 5900 Lower Honoapi'ilani Rd, Napili Kai Beach Resort; admission $38-45; ⏰7:30pm Wed) Top slack key guitarists Ledward Kaapana and Dennis Kamakahi appear regularly at this exceptional concert series, and George Kahumoku Jr, a slack key legend in his own right, is the weekly host. As much a jam session as a concert, this is a true Hawaiian cultural gem that's worth going out of your way to experience. Reservations recommended.

Kapalua & Northern Beaches

Kapalua has long been a sacred site for Native Hawaiians. In the 1900s it was also the site of a productive pineapple plantation. Currently the home of a posh resort and two world-class golf courses, Kapalua is making an all-out effort to broaden its appeal. A revamped zip line is taking people skyward for new thrills, trails in a once-restricted forest have opened to the public, and the dining scene is among the island's best. The nightlife doesn't exactly sizzle, but the beaches – all with public access – sure do.

If you want to avoid the well-manicured glitz, swoop past the resort and take a winding drive along the rugged northern coast. The untamed views are guaranteed to replenish your soul.

If uninterrupted sunshine is your goal, note that Kapalua can be a bit rainier and windier than points south.

Slaughterhouse Beach

LONELY PLANET/GETTY IMAGES ©

Beaches

Points of interest are arranged geographically, beginning at the southwestern tip of Kapalua then heading north.

Kapalua Beach
Beach

(Map p80) For a long day on the beach, it's hard to beat this crescent-shaped strip at the southwestern tip of Kapalua. Snorkel in the morning, grab lunch at the Sea House, try stand up paddle surfing, then sip cocktails at Merriman's next door. Or simply sit on the sand and gaze across the channel at Moloka'i.

Long rocky outcrops at both ends of the bay make Kapalua Beach the safest year-round swimming spot on this coast. You'll find colorful snorkeling on the right side of the beach, with abundant tropical fish and orange slate-pencil sea urchins. There's a rental hut here for beach gear.

Take the drive immediately north of Napili Kai Beach Resort to get to the beach parking area, where there are restrooms and showers. A tunnel leads from the parking lot north to the beach. This is also a starting point for the Coastal Trail.

Oneloa Beach
Beach

(Map p80) On the Coastal Trail, this white-sand jewel is worth seeking out. Fringed by low sand dunes covered in beach morning glory, it's a fine place to soak up the rays. On calm days swimming is good close to shore, as is snorkeling in the protected area along the rocky point at the northern side of the beach. When there's any sizable surf, strong rip currents can be present.

The half-mile strand – Oneloa means 'long sand' – is backed by gated resort condos and restricted golf greens, and beach access requires a sharp eye. Turn onto Ironwood Lane and then left into the parking lot opposite the Ironwoods gate. Get here early or around lunchtime, when people are heading out.

DT Fleming Beach Park
Beach

(Map p80; Honoapi'ilani Hwy) Surrounded by ironwood trees and backed by an old one-room schoolhouse, this sandy crescent

looks like an outpost from another era. In keeping with its Hawaiian nature, the beach is the domain of wave riders. Experienced surfers and bodysurfers find good action here, especially in winter. The shorebreaks can be brutal, however, and the beach is a hot spot for injuries. The reef on the right is good for snorkeling in summer when the water is very calm.

Fleming has restrooms, showers, grills, picnic tables and a lifeguard. The access road is off Honoapi'ilani Hwy (Hwy 30), immediately north of the 31-mile marker.

The Coastal Trail ends here.

Slaughterhouse Beach & Honolua Bay
Beach

(Map p80) The narrow Kalaepiha Point separates Slaughterhouse Beach and Honolua Bay. Together they form the Honolua–Mokule'ia Bay Marine Life Conservation District, which is famed for its snorkeling and surfing.

Honolua Bay is a surfer's dream. It faces northwest and when it catches the winter swells it has some of the gnarliest surfing anywhere in the world. In summer snorkeling is excellent in both bays, thanks in part to prohibitions on fishing in the preserve. Honolua Bay is the favorite, with thriving reefs and abundant coral along its rocky edges.

Kapalua & Around

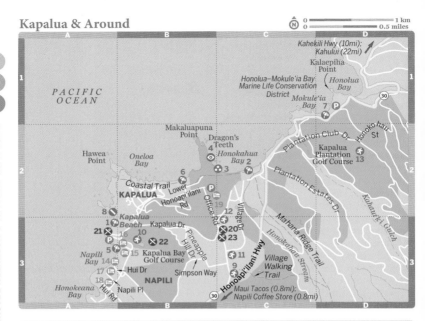

Kapalua & Around

Spinner dolphins sometimes hang near the mouth of the bays, swimming just beyond snorkelers. When it's calm, you can snorkel around Kalaepiha Point from one bay to the other, but forget it after heavy rains: Honolua Stream empties into Honolua Bay and the runoff clouds the water.

The land fronting Honolua Bay has long been owned by Maui Land & Pineapple. The company has allowed recreational access to the bay for no fee. A few families have the right to live on this land, but they cannot charge an access fee or restrict visiting hours. In 2013, with community support, the state set aside funds to purchase 280 acres beside the bay to protect them from development. See the box on p84 for more.

Once you reach the bay, read the signage about protecting the coral, then enter via the rocky coastline. Do not enter the water via the concrete boat ramp, which is very slippery and potentially hazardous.

When the waters are calm the bays offer superb kayaking. Slaughterhouse Beach is also a top-rated bodysurfing spot during the summer. Its attractive white-sand crescent is good for sunbathing and beachcombing – look for glittering green olivine crystals in the rocks at the southern end of the beach.

Just north of the 32-mile marker, there's public parking and a concrete stairway leading down the cliffs to Slaughterhouse Beach. After passing Slaughterhouse Beach, look ahead for a large parking area on the left. Here you'll find a nice view of Honolua Bay below. A half-mile past the 32-mile marker there's room for about six cars to park adjacent to the path down to Honolua Bay, plus a few spots around the bend in the road.

Sights

Makaluapuna Point   Cultural Site
(Map p80) Razor-sharp spikes crown rocky Makaluapuna Point, known informally by the nickname Dragon's Teeth. The formation does look uncannily like the mouth of an imaginary dragon. The 3ft-high spikes are the work of pounding winter waves that have ripped into the lava rock point, leaving the pointy 'teeth' behind.

Signage states that the outcropping is sacred to Native Hawaiians. Although the public is allowed access to the ocean by law, visitors are strongly discouraged from walking onto the formation out of respect for native customs. The adjacent **Honokahua burial site** (Map p80) is off-limits to the general public. These sites are of cultural significance to Native

The Best...
West Maui for Kids

1 Zip-lining (for ages 10 and up), West Maui Mountains (p84)

2 Swimming hole, Launiupoko Beach Park (p60)

3 Hula show, Ka'anapali Beach Hotel (p70)

4 Cliff divers, Pu'u Keka'a (p66)

5 Whalers Village Museum (p67)

Hawaiians and should not be inspected up close. Respect the signage. The point is also potentially hazardous. It is subject to powerful waves, particularly the northern winter swells, and covered by uneven, sometimes sharp, rocks.

For a view of Makaluapuna Point, you can skirt along the outside of the 13-acre burial site below the parking area, but don't enter areas marked 'Please Kokua,' which are easily visible islets of stones bordering the Ritz's manicured golf greens. Do not walk across the greens.

Get here by driving north to the very end of Lower Honoapi'ilani Rd, where you'll find parking and a plaque detailing the burial site. The path to the point leads down from the plaque along the northern edge of the Kapalua Bay Golf Course.

Activities

HIKING

Whether you're after an easy coastal stroll or a trek through tropical flora, Kapalua has got a trail for you.

The **Maunalei Arboretum Trail** cuts through a forest planted by DT Fleming, the arborist who developed Maui's pineapple industry. Access is strictly via a free shuttle (665-9110) that departs

WEST MAUI KAPALUA & NORTHERN BEACHES

from the **Kapalua Village Center** (Map p80; ☎ 665-4386; www.kapalua.com/adventures; 2000 Village Rd) located between the Ritz-Carlton Kapalua and the Honoapi'ilani Hwy. Shuttles depart at 9:30am, 11:30am and 1:30pm, and return from the arboretum at 9:50am, 11:50am and 1:50pm. The shuttle has limited seating so call beforehand to reserve a seat.

For a tropical hike, pick up the **Honolua Ridge Trail** (1.25 miles one-way) from the Maunalei Arboretum Trail. You'll enjoy a spectacular mountain vista along the ridge before dipping back into the jungle-like forest for a view of Pu'u Kului (5788ft), one of the wettest spots in the world, averaging 325in annually, and then a stroll through a stand of Sugi trees. From here, pick up the **Mahana Ridge Trail** (5.75 miles), which was closed in 2013 because of unsafe conditions during a nearby construction project. Stay alert for ongoing trail maintenance and nearby construction

activities. On your descent, at the sharp roadside bend after the telephone poles, turn right onto the dirt path, which leads to DT Fleming Beach, or follow the road left to return to the Kapalua Village Center.

The old Village Golf Course, now overgrown and reincarnated as the **Village Walking Trails**, offers stunning scenery as it rises up the mountain slopes. The easy **Coastal Trail** (1.75 miles) links Kapalua Beach with Oneloa Beach, then crosses below the Ritz-Carlton to end at DT Fleming Beach. During your walk, be sure to stay on the designated path to avoid disturbing nesting birds. The Coastal Trail passes ancient burial grounds and Makaluapuna Point, both located north of the Ritz-Carlton and the trail. These sites are of cultural significance to Native Hawaiians and should not be inspected up close. Respect the signage.

For maps, liability waivers and shuttle pickups, check in at the Kapalua Village Center.

GOLF

Kapalua Golf — Golf

(☎669-8044, 877-527-2582; www.golfatkapalua.
com; Bay/Plantation greens fee $208/278,
twilight (1pm) $148/178, late afternoon $98/128;
⊙1st tee around 6:40am) Kapalua boasts
two of the island's top championship golf
courses, both certified by Audubon International as sanctuaries for native plants
and animals. How's that for green greens?

The **Bay course** (Map p80; 300 Kapalua Dr)
is the tropical ocean course, meandering
across a lava peninsula. The challenging
Plantation course (Map p80; 2000 Plantation
Club Dr) sweeps over a rugged landscape
of hills and deep gorges.

Kapalua Golf Academy — Golf

(Map p80; ☎662-7740; www.golfatkapalua.com;
1000 Office Rd; 1hr private lesson $180, half-day
school $275; ⊙7am-5pm) Hawaii's top golf
academy is staffed by PGA pros.

TENNIS

Kapalua Tennis Garden — Tennis

(Map p80; ☎662-7730; www.golfatkapalua.
com/tennis.html; 100 Kapalua Dr; per person
day $14, racket rental $6; ⊙8am-6pm) Maui's
premier full-service tennis club has 10
Plexipave courts, with four lit for evening
games, and an array of clinics. If you're on
your own, give the club a ring and they'll
match you with other players for singles
or doubles games.

WATER SPORTS

Kapalua Dive Company — Diving

(Map p80; ☎669-3448; www.kapaluadive.com;
Kapalua Bay; beach dive from $85, kayak-snorkel
tour $85; ⊙8am-4:30pm) Offers a range of
water activities, including kayak-snorkel
tours and a full menu of dives. Rent a
basic snorkel set for $15 per day and a
stand up paddle board for $40 per hour;
you can use a credit card or driver's
license for rental deposit. Look for its
Beach Activities Center at the northern
end of Kapalua Beach.

Saving Honolua Bay

What do snorkelers, surfers, environmentalists and native Hawaiians have in common in West Maui? Their love for Honolua Bay, a sparkling inlet sitting about 2 miles north of Kapalua. The bay is a marine conservation area famed for its hollow, right-breaking point surf and its coral reef, which teems with marine life.

In 2007 the owner of the land surrounding the bay, Maui Land & Pineapple Company, submitted development plans to Maui County. Its vision for the property? Forty luxury homes, a golf course, a cultural area and a surf park. The Save Honolua Coalition (www.savehonolua.org) formed in response, and gathered 16,000 signatures calling for the land's preservation. Maui Land dropped its plans, but the energized community called for a more permanent protection plan. After years of negotiating, the state agreed in 2013 to allocate $20 million for the purchase of 280 acres beside the bay for use as a state park. Planning continues as regulatory requirements and eco-concerns are addressed.

ZIP-LINING

Kapalua Ziplines   Zip-Lining
(Map p80; ☎756-9147; www.kapaluaziplines. com; 500 Office Rd; 4-line zip $169, 7-line zip $189; ☺6:30am-6pm) Ready to soar across the West Maui Mountains for nearly 2 miles? On the signature tour (four hours, 15 minutes), you'll glide down seven zip lines, two of them extending a breathtaking 2000ft in length. The tour has a dual track, allowing you to zip beside a friend. Moonlight trips ($169), with headlamps and glow sticks, are offered on Monday, Wednesday and Friday.

The company, formerly known as Kapalua Adventures, is under new ownership. The office is located inside the Kapalua Village Center.

Festivals & Events

Hyundai Tournament of
Champions   Golf
(www.pgatour.com) Watch Tiger and friends tee off at the PGA Tour's season opener in early January at the Plantation course, vying for a multimillion-dollar purse.

Celebration of the Arts   Art
(www.celebrationofthearts.org) This festival held in late March at the Ritz-Carlton celebrates traditional Hawaiian culture with art, hula, music, films and cultural panels.

Kapalua Wine &
Food Festival   Food, Wine
(www.kapaluawineandfoodfestival.com) This culinary extravaganza is held over four days in mid-June at the Ritz-Carlton. It features renowned winemakers and Hawaii's hottest chefs, offering cooking demonstrations and wine tastings.

Xterra World
Championship   Sports
(www.xterraplanet.com/maui) Held mid-October, this race is a major off-road triathlon. Based out of the Ritz-Carlton, it boasts a $105,000 purse. The race moved from Makena to Kapalua in 2013.

Sleeping

Kapalua Villas   Condo $$$
(Map p80; ☎800-545-0018, 665-9170; www. outrigger.com; 2000 Village Rd; 1/2br from $205/315; P✳🌐☄) These swank condos – let's call them fortresses of luxury – are clustered into three separate compounds. The Golf Villas line the Bay Golf Course while the Bay and Ridge Villas overlook the beach. The one-bedroom units sleep up to four; the two-bedroom

units sleep six. For up-close whale-watching, try the spacious Bay Villas.

The $25 daily resort fee includes parking, wi-fi and use of the resort shuttle. The mandatory cleaning fee costs from $130 per stay. The condos are managed by Outrigger Hotels & Resorts.

Ritz-Carlton Kapalua
Resort **$$$**

(Map p80; 800-262-8440, 669-6200; www.ritzcarlton.com; 1 Ritz-Carlton Dr; r/ste from $399/849; P ✳ @ 🛜 🏊) Understated elegance attracts the exclusive golf crowd to this luxe northern outpost. On a hillside fronting the greens and the sea, the hotel has a heated multilevel swimming pool shaded by palm trees, a spa and a fitness club. Rooms dazzle with simple but sleek island style: dark-wood floors, low-key Hawaiiana and oversize marble bathrooms.

The $30 daily resort fee covers wi-fi, and use of the fitness center and resort shuttle. Self-parking is $18 per day.

🍴 Eating

Honolua Store
Plate Lunch **$**

(Map p80; 665-9105; 502 Office Rd; breakfast $5-9, lunch $6-15; store 6am-8pm) The exterior of this porch-wrapped bungalow looks much as it did when it opened in 1929 as the general store for the Honolua Pineapple Plantation. Today, the place is a nod to normalcy in the midst of lavish exclusiveness. The deli is known for its reasonable prices and fantastic plate lunches. Grab-and-go sandwiches and bento items are available in the deli case.

At the time of research, the Honolua Store was operating out of the Kapalua Village Center during a revamp and expansion of the original building. The improved digs were due to reopen in 2014.

Plantation House
Hawaii Regional **$$$**

(Map p80; 669-6299; www.theplantation-house.com; 2000 Plantation Club Dr, Plantation Golf Course Clubhouse; breakfast $9-17, lunch $11-18, dinner $28-49; 8am-3pm, dinner 5:30-9pm mid-Sep–Mar, 6-9pm rest of year) The crab cake Benedict at this open-air eatery is a fluffy, hollandaise-splashed affair that will have you kissing your plate and plotting your return. Adding to the allure are stellar views of the coast and Moloka'i, as well as the world-famous golf course below. For dinner, fresh fish and beef dishes are prepared with global flair and accompanied by Maui-grown produce.

Sansei Seafood Restaurant & Sushi Bar
Japanese **$$$**

(Map p80; 669-6286; www.sanseihawaii.com; 600 Office Rd; sushi $5-17, mains $10-44; dinner 5:30-10pm Sat-Wed, to 1am Thu & Fri) The innovative sushi menu is reason enough to dine here, but the nonsushi

Honolua Bay (p79)
KELLY FAJACK/GETTY IMAGES ©

house specials, which often blend Japanese and Pacific Rim flavors, shouldn't be overlooked. The spicy Dungeness crab ramen with truffle broth is a noteworthy prize. Order before 6pm and all food is discounted by 25%. No reservation? Queue up for one of the 12 seats at the sushi bar – folks start gathering outside about 4:50pm.

Sushi, soup and appetizers are 50% off from 10pm to 1am on Thursday and Friday nights.

Merriman's Kapalua   Hawaii Regional $$$

(Map p80; 📞 669-6400; www.merrimanshawaii.com/kapalua; 1 Bay Club Pl; happy hour menu $9-24; ⏰ happy hour 3-5pm) We especially like Merriman's at happy hour. Perched on a scenic point between Kapalua Bay and Napili Bay, the tiki- and palm-dotted Point Bar is a gorgeous place to unwind after braving the Kahekili Highway. At the acclaimed restaurant, Maui-caught fish and locally sourced meats and produce are the highlights.

Pineapple Grill   Hawaii Regional $$$

(Map p80; 📞 669-9600; www.cohnrestaurants.com; 200 Kapalua Dr, Kapalua Bay Golf Course Clubhouse; breakfast $8-16, lunch $13-24, dinner $29-40; ⏰ 8am-late) This beauty's got it all, from a sweeping hilltop view to a sleek exhibition kitchen that whips up creative fusion dishes accompanied by locally sourced vegetables. Tantalize the taste buds with the likes of lobster-coconut bisque, caramelized scallops with Tahitian vanilla brown butter, and a pork chop with Maui Gold Pineapple chutney and mashed Moloka'i sweet potatoes.

Kahekili Highway

They call this narrow, serpentine thread of pavement a highway? That's some optimistic labeling, for sure. This challenging road, which hugs the rugged northern tip of Maui, charges around hairpin turns, careens over one-lane bridges and teeters beside treacherous cliffs. It's one of Maui's most adventurous drives.

Nakalele Point

PETER FRENCH/GETTY IMAGES ©

The area is so ravishingly rural that it's hard to imagine trendy West Maui could hold such untouched countryside. The key to its preservation is the Kahekili Highway (Route 340), which narrows to the width of a driveway, keeping construction trucks and tourist buses at bay.

Not for the faint of heart, sections slow to just 5mph as the road wraps around blind curves; a lengthy stretch around the village of Kahakuloa is a mere one lane with cliffs on one side and a sheer drop on the other – if you hit oncoming traffic you may be doing your traveling in reverse! But if you can handle that, this largely overlooked route offers all sorts of adventures, with horse and hiking trails, a mighty blowhole and delicious banana bread.

Don't be fooled by car rental maps that show the road as a dotted line – it's paved and open to the public the entire way. There are no services, so gas up beforehand. Give yourself a good two hours' driving time, not counting stops.

Property between the highway and the coast is both privately and publicly owned. Trails to the shore are often uneven, rocky and slippery, and the coast is subject to dangerous waves. If you decide to explore, take appropriate precautions, and get access permission when possible.

Sights in this section are arranged in geographical order from west to east and begin after you pass Honolua Bay.

PUNALAU BEACH

Manicured golf courses and ritzy enclaves drop away and the scenery gets wilder as you drive toward the island's northern-most point. Ironwood-lined Punalau Beach, 0.7 miles after the 34-mile marker, makes a worthy stop if you're up for a solitary stroll. Swimming is a no-go though, as a rocky shelf creates unfavorable conditions for water activities.

NAKALELE POINT

Continuing on from Punalau Beach, the terrain is hilly, with rocky cattle pastures punctuated by tall sisal plants. At a number of pull-offs, you can stop and explore. Lush pastures are quite enticing,

willing you to traipse down the cliffs and out along the rugged coastline.

At the 38-mile marker, a mile-long trail leads out to a **light station** at the end of windswept Nakalele Point. Here you'll find a coastline of arches and other formations worn out of the rocks by the pounding surf. There are several worn paths leading toward the light station, but you can't really get lost – just walk toward the point. Bring water and wear a hat because there's little shade.

The **Nakalele Blowhole** roars when the surf is up but is a sleeper when the seas are calm. To check on its mood, park at the boulder-lined pull-off 0.6 miles beyond the 38-mile marker. You can glimpse the action, if there is any, a few hundred yards beyond the parking lot. It's a 15-minute scramble down a jagged moonscape of lava rocks to the blowhole, which can shoot up to 100ft. Keep a safe distance and watch your footing carefully. A tourist fell into the hole and vanished in 2011. Another died after falling from a cliff in the area in 2013. And it probably goes without saying, but don't try to sit on, or peer into, the blowhole!

Eight-tenths of a mile after the 40-mile marker look for the **Ohai Viewpoint**, on the *makai* (seaward) side of the road. The viewpoint won't be marked but there's a sign announcing the start of the Ohai Trail, a 1.2-mile loop with interpretative signage and views off the coast. For the best views, bear left from the trailhead and walk to the top of the point for a jaw-dropping coastal panorama that includes a glimpse of the Nakalele Blowhole. If you have kids, be careful – the crumbly cliff has a sudden drop of nearly 800ft!

NATURAL OCEAN BATHS & BELLSTONE

After the 42-mile post the markers change; the next marker is 16 and the numbers go down as you continue on.

One-tenth of a mile before the 16-mile marker, look seaward for a large dirt pull-off and a well-beaten path that leads 15 minutes down lava cliffs to **natural ocean baths** on the ocean's edge. Cut out of slippery lava rock and

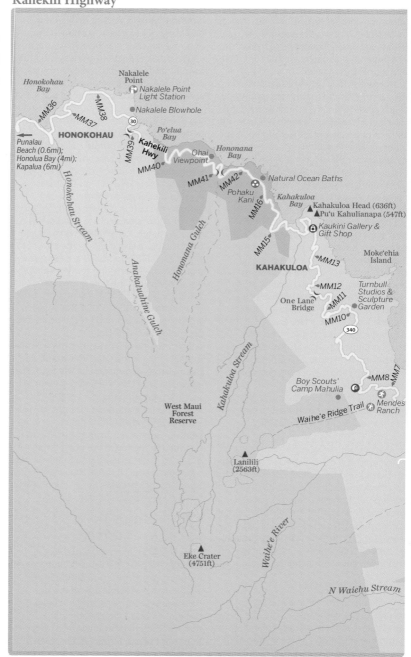

Honokohau Bay

Nakalele Point

Nakalele Point Light Station

Nakalele Blowhole

MM36
MM37
MM38
MM39
MM40

HONOKOHAU

Kahekili Hwy

Punalau Beach (0.6mi); Honolua Bay (4mi); Kapalua (6mi)

Honokohau Stream

Anakaluahine Gulch

Po'elua Bay

Ohai Viewpoint

Hononana Bay

MM41
MM42
MM16
MM15

Pohaku Kani

Natural Ocean Baths

Kahakuloa Bay

Kahakuloa Head (636ft)
Pu'u Kahulianapa (547ft)

Kaukini Gallery & Gift Shop

Moke'ehia Island

KAHAKULOA

MM13
MM12
MM11
MM10

340

Turnbull Studios & Sculpture Garden

One Lane Bridge

Hononana Gulch

Kahakuloa Stream

West Maui Forest Reserve

Boy Scouts' Camp Mahulia

MM8
MM7

Mendes Ranch

Waihe'e Ridge Trail

Lanilili (2563ft)

Waihe'e River

Eke Crater (4751ft)

N Waiehu Stream

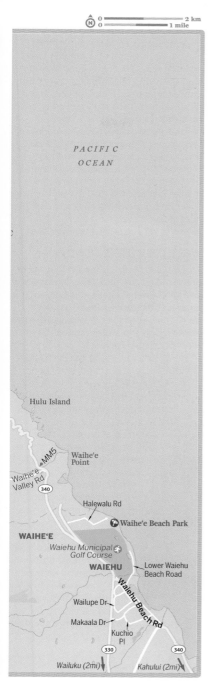

encrusted with olivine minerals, these incredibly clear pools sit in the midst of roaring surf. Some have natural steps, but if you're tempted to go in, size it up carefully – people unfamiliar with the water conditions here have been swept into the sea and drowned. If the rocks are covered in silt from recent storm runoffs, or the waves look high, forget about it – it's dangerous. Although the baths are on public land, state officials do not recommend accessing them due to the hazardous conditions, including slippery rocks, large and powerful surf, waves on ledges and strong currents.

The huge boulder with concave marks on the inland side of the road just before the pull-off is a bellstone, **Pohaku Kani**. If you hit it with a rock on the Kahakuloa side, where the deepest indentations are, you might be able to get a hollow sound. It's a bit resonant if you hit it just right, though it takes some imagination to hear it ring like a bell.

KAHAKULOA

An imposing 636ft-tall volcanic dome guards the entrance to Kahakuloa Bay like a lurking, watchful dragon. They say this photogenic landmark, known as **Kahakuloa Head**, was a favorite cliff-diving spot of Chief Kahekili. Before the road drops into the valley, there's a pull-off above town providing a bird's-eye view.

The bayside village of Kahakuloa, tucked at the bottom of a lush valley and embraced by towering sea cliffs, retains a solidly Hawaiian character. Kahakuloa's isolation has protected it from the rampant development found elsewhere on Maui. Farmers tend taro patches, dogs wander across the road, and a missionary-era Protestant church marks the village center. One of Hawaii's most accomplished ukulele players, Richard Ho'opi'i, grew up here.

You won't find stores here, but villagers set up hard-to-miss roadside stands selling fruit and snacks to day-trippers. For shave ice ($5), hit Ululani's hot-pink stand. For free samples of macadamia nuts, taro chips and *ono* (delicious) banana bread, stop at **Julia's lime-green**

89

shack (www.juliasbananabread.com; ⊙9am-5:30pm or until sold out). After one taste of the banana bread and some 'talk story' on the porch, we bet you'll buy a loaf for the road ($6). It tastes fresh for days and makes a terrific no-fuss breakfast.

KAHAKULOA TO WAIHE'E

On the outskirts of Kahakuloa, after a heart-stopping, narrow climb, you'll reach the hilltop **Kaukini Gallery & Gift Shop** (☏244-3371; www.kaukinigallery.com; ⊙10am-5pm), near the 14-mile marker. The gallery sells works by more than 120 island artists, with watercolors, jewelry, native-fiber baskets, koa boxes, vintage postcards and more. From here, it's 11 miles back to Kapalua or 13 miles onward to Wailuku.

Look for the towering giraffe statue after the 10-mile marker. It marks the entrance for **Turnbull Studios & Sculpture Garden** (☏244-0101; www.turnbullstudios.org; 5030 Kahekili Hwy; ⊙10am-5pm Mon-Fri), where you can view Bruce Turnbull's ambitious bronze and wood creations, as well as the works of other area artists...very cool stuff.

Continuing around beep-as-you-go blind turns, the highway gradually levels out atop sea cliffs. For an Eden-like scene, stop at the pull-off 0.1 miles north of the 8-mile marker and look down into the ravine below, where you'll see a cascading **waterfall** framed by double pools.

For a real *paniolo* (cowboy) experience, saddle up at **Mendes Ranch** (☏871-5222; www.mendesranch.com; 3530 Kahekili Hwy; 1½hr rides $110; ⊙rides 8:45am & 11:30pm), a working cattle ranch near the 7-mile marker, just past the road to Waihe'e Ridge Trail. The picture-perfect scenery on these rides includes everything from jungle valleys to lofty sea cliffs and waterfalls.

WAIHE'E RIDGE TRAIL

This fabulous trail has it all: tropical flora, breezy ridgelines, lush valley landscapes and lofty views of Maui's wild northern coast and the central valley. The best part? The well-defined trail is less than a 5-mile round-trip and only takes about three hours to complete.

The path is a bit steep, but it's a fairly steady climb and not overly strenuous. It's best to tackle this one before 8am in order to beat the clouds, which can obscure the view from the top later in the morning.

Starting at an elevation of 1000ft, the trail, which crosses reserve land, climbs a ridge, passing from pasture to forest. Guava trees and groves of eucalyptus are prominent, and the aroma of fallen fruit may accompany you after a rainstorm. From the 0.75-mile post, panoramic views open up, with a scene that sweeps clear down to the ocean along the **Waihe'e Gorge** and deep into pleated valleys.

Kahakuloa Head (p89)
RON DAHL/GETTY IMAGES ©

As you continue on, you'll enter ohia forest with native birds and get distant views of waterfalls cascading down the mountains. The ridge-top views are similar to those you'd see from a helicopter, and you'll probably see a handful of them dart into the adjacent valley like gnats on a mission.

There are several benches along the trail to stop and soak in the scenery and the remarkable stillness. Birdsong, chirping insects, a rushing stream, muffled bits of hiker conversation below – these are the only interruptions. The trail ends at a small clearing and picnic table on the 2563ft peak of **Lanilili**. Here you'll find awesome views in all directions. If it's foggy, wait about 10 minutes or so because it may blow off.

Solos, seniors and in-shape kids should be fine on this hike. If you have access to hiking poles, bring them. The trail gets muddy and steep in spots.

To get to the trailhead, take the one-lane paved road that starts on the inland side of the highway just south of the 7-mile marker. It's almost directly across the road from the big gate to Mendes Ranch. After passing through an entrance gate (currently open 7am to 5pm), the road climbs one mile through open pasture to the Boy Scouts' Camp Maluhia. Keep an eye out for cattle that mosey across the road. The trailhead, marked with a Na Ala Hele sign, is on the left just before the camp. Take a right for the parking lot. For complete details, visit www.hawaiitrails.org.

WAIHE'E TO WAILUKU

Soon after the Waihe'e Ridge Trail, the Kahekili Highway runs through the sleeper towns of Waihe'e and Waiehu before arriving in Wailuku. There's not much to do here, but if you're up for a round of golf, the county-run **Waiehu Municipal Golf Course** (☏243-7400; www.mauicounty.gov; 200 Halewaiu Rd; greens fee $55, optional cart $20; ⏰6:45am-5pm Mon-Fri, 6am-5pm Sat & Sun) offers an affordable and easily walkable 18 holes on the coast. On-site are a small cafe, pro-shop and public restrooms.

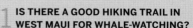

Local Knowledge

NAME: KEVIN COONEY
OCCUPATION: FORESTRY & WILDLIFE TECHNICIAN, DIVISION OF FORESTRY & WILDLIFE, DEPARTMENT OF LAND & NATURAL RESOURCES
RESIDENCE: KULA

1 IS THERE A GOOD HIKING TRAIL IN WEST MAUI FOR WHALE-WATCHING?

The Lahaina Pali Trail... If people park on the Lahaina side and then go up the beginning of the trail, even say to the first half-mile, then you get really excellent views of the ocean and the reef system. There's all kinds of whale activity.

2 WHICH WEST MAUI TRAIL IS BEST FOR AMATEUR BOTANISTS?

It's definitely not an easy trail, but the Waihe'e Ridge Trail. That's the one I always tell people to go to because there's still a great deal of native plants up on that trail and you can see what a lot of the West Maui vegetation looks like and the diversity of it.

3 ARE THERE ANY TRAILS ORIGINALLY BUILT BY NATIVE HAWAIIANS?

In the 'Ahihi-Kina'u Natural Area Reserve, which is known to everyone else as La Pérouse, there's a trail. The King's Hwy they call it. And that's the one built right through the lava flow and shows a lot of really fabulous stone work and some really amazing trail building that went on in the mid to late 19th century. Real impressive to see.

4 ANY WORDS OF ADVICE FOR HIKERS?

I would say caution first. People usually get in trouble because they're going too close to the edge, they're getting right up on top of the blowhole, they're trying too hard to get the perfect picture or they're turning their back on the ocean. Always keep one foot in reality because things can go from a perfect to dangerous situation very fast.

ʻIao Valley & Central Maui

Welcome to the flat bit. Central Maui is the isthmus connecting the West Maui Mountains to mighty Haleakalā, giving the island its distinctive three-part shape. This odd wedge of topography, Maui's most arable piece of land, was once known only for its fields of waving sugarcane, but it now boasts a potpourri of interesting attractions.

To the north, the island's commercial center, Kahului, contains windswept Kanaha Beach, action-central for water sports. Sister-city Wailuku is a funky up-and-comer with the best lunch scene, and the gateway to the extraordinary ʻIao Valley.

On the southern coast, Maʻalaea has morphed into the pleasure boating hub, your first stop for a cruise. In the middle you'll find the finest building on the island, a Frank Lloyd Wright treasure that looks as if the Mother Ship has landed. Those poor aliens: where to begin?

Pineapple plantation near Wailuku (p106)

'Iao Valley & Central Maui Itineraries

Day One

1 **'Iao Valley State Park** (p111) Start your day by embracing a beautiful tropical valley. Snap the mandatory photo of 'Iao Needle, Maui's most well-known landmark, and walk some refreshing stream-side trails; the best one goes deep into the valley itself.

2 **Kepaniwai Park & Heritage Gardens** (p111) Just beyond the park, take a pleasant and unique stroll through Hawaii's cultural heritage, in the form of architecture inspired by various immigrant groups.

3 **Wailuku** (p106) There's no better place for an island-style lunch. But should you try Sam Sato's famous noodles, join the locals at Main Street Bistro, or down a classic plate lunch from Ichiban Okazuya? In any case, follow-up with a lazy coffee at Wailuku Coffee Co, then work off your calories by poking around the town's antique shops and the historic Bailey House Museum.

4 **Kanaha Beach Park** (p96) Welcome to Kahului's water-sports mecca. Prepare to be amazed by the scores of colorful sails ripping across the late-afternoon waves. Itching to join in? Top windsurfing and kitesurfing instructors give lessons right on the beach.

5 **Maui Arts & Cultural Center** (p104) Whether it's slack key masters or ukulele virtuosos, an evening show at this state-of-the-art venue could be a highlight of your trip. Be sure to stop by the Schaefer International Gallery beforehand, where you'll find their latest art exhibition.

THIS LEG: 11 MILES

Days Two & Three

1 **Pu'unene** (p119) Begin at the end: the end of Hawaii's sugar industry, that is. The last surviving mill here is a living monument to an era now passed. The Alexander & Baldwin Sugar Museum provides the facts, while a drive around back reveals the remains of a forgotten plantation town.

2 **Maui Tropical Plantation** (p113) Touristy, yes. But there's something for everyone at this low-key, family-friendly theme park, from a good morning walk to a mountain zip line.

3 **King Kamehameha Golf Club** (p113) While the course is excellent here, the real star is the clubhouse. Prepare to be astonished by a Frank Lloyd Wright masterpiece. Is it a UFO, or a bed of clams? Whatever your answer, the greatest building on Maui is a work of art.

4 **Ma'alaea Harbor** (p114) Having crossed the island, you're ready for a whale-watching trip, a sunset cruise or a snorkeling expedition to Molokini. Having trouble choosing? The Activities Hut by the pier makes planning a breeze. If your ship hasn't come in, try harbor-watching on the porch of Ma'alaea General Store & Cafe, or visit the Story of Hawaii Museum for a fascinating tale told in maps.

5 **Maui Ocean Center** (p114) Most of Hawaii lies beneath the water, and here's your best chance to see the many unique species that live there. The glass tunnel through the shark tank will drop the kids' jaws. Yours too.

6 **Kealia Coastal Boardwalk** (p118) Surrounded by ocean, marsh and pond, Maui's longest boardwalk is a great place to take a late-afternoon walk and reflect upon a memorable day. If you're a bird-watcher, you're in heaven.

➡ THIS LEG: 11 MILES

'Iao Valley & Central Maui Highlights

1 **Best Adventure: Blue Hawaiian Helicopter tour** (p100) The trip through the West Maui Mountains to Moloka'i is unforgettable.

2 **Best Natural Wonder: 'Iao Valley State Park** (p111) A beautiful tropical valley embraces you.

3 **Best Architecture: King Kamehameha Golf Club** (p113) A stunning Frank Lloyd Wright design of global stature.

4 **Best Hostel: Banana Bungalow** (p107) Party central. Sleep optional.

5 **Best Shopping: Maui Swap Meet** (p104) Tent after tent of local arts, crafts and food.

The clubhouse at King Kamehameha Golf Club (p113)
ARCHITECT: FRANK L WRIGHT. PHOTOGRAPHER: MARK GIBSON/GETTY IMAGES ©

Discover 'Iao Valley & Central Maui

Kahului

Whether it's Lihu'e on Kaua'i, Hilo on the Big Island, or Kaunakakai on Moloka'i, most Hawaiian islands have a working town like Kahului, full of warehouses, strip malls, shopping centers and that island-wide magnet, the big box store. Like its counterparts, Kahului also contains Maui's main harbor and airport, turning it, in the eyes of many, into a transit stop. But at the same time, you'll find a great swath of local life

here, if you're willing to look beneath the surface. You can talk story with the locals at the Saturday swap meet, take in a concert on the lawn of the cultural center, join the wave-riding action at Kanaha Beach, and more. So if you are just passing through, don't forget to cherry-pick the highlights.

Beaches

Kanaha Beach Park   Beach
(Map p98) Well you can't judge a beach by its cover. Wedged between downtown Kahului and the airport, and hidden behind a strip of ironwood trees, this mile-long stretch of sand is surf city, with scores of brilliant sails zipping across the waves. Kitesurfers converge at the southwest end, known as **Kite Beach**, while windsurfers head northeast. A roped-off swimming area lies in-between. Facilities include restrooms, showers and shaded picnic tables.

There's no better place to learn how to ride the wind – or just to watch the action.

Sights

Kanaha Pond Bird Sanctuary   Nature Reserve
(Map p102; Hwy 37; ⏲sunrise-sunset) 🅿 **FREE** You wouldn't expect a wildlife sanctuary to be so close to a main road, but a short walk leaves it behind. This shallow marsh is a haven for rare Hawaiian birds, including native coots, black-crowned night herons and the ae'o (Hawaiian black-necked stilt), a graceful wading bird with long, orange legs that feeds along the pond's marshy edges.

There are only 1500 ae'o in the entire state, but you can count on spotting some here.

Windsurfers, Kanaha Beach
AEDER ERIK/GETTY IMAGES ©

Schaefer International Gallery
Museum

(Map p102; ☎242-2787; www.mauiarts.org; 1 Cameron Way; ⏰10am-5pm Tue-Sun) This art gallery at the Maui Arts & Cultural Center features six different exhibitions per year, ranging from native Hawaiian arts to contemporary local artists working in all mediums.

Kahului Harbor
Harbor

(Map p102) Kahului's large protected harbor is the island's only deep-water port, so all boat traffic, from cruise ships to cargo vessels, docks here. But it's not all business. Late afternoon you're likely to see outrigger canoe clubs like Na Kai ʻEwalu (www.nakaiewalucanoeclub.org) practicing at **Hoʻaloha Park** – a timeless scene.

Maui Nui Botanical Gardens
Gardens

(Map p102; ☎249-2798; www.mnbg.org; 150 Kanaloa Ave; adult/child $5/free, free on Sat; ⏰8am-4pm Mon-Sat) 🍃 For botanophiles interested in native Hawaiian plants, this garden on the grounds of a former zoo is a wealth of knowledge. An excellent new audio tour ($5) brings it to life. Don't expect the exotic tropicals that dominate most Hawaiian gardens; do expect dedicated staff. Staff also lead personal **guided tours** from 10am to 11:30am Tuesday to Friday (suggested donation $5).

🎿 Activities

Kanaha Beach Park is the best place to windsurf on Maui, unless you're an aspiring pro ready for Hoʻokipa. Board-and-rig rentals start at $50/315 per day/week, while two-hour introductory classes cost around $90. For more info see www.mauiwindsurfing.net.

Kitesurfing (or kiteboarding) is enormously popular in Kahului. The action centers on Kite Beach, the southwest end of Kanaha Beach Park. Here you can learn the ropes from some real pros. Expect to pay about $275 for a half-day intro course. Check out the scene live at www.kitebeachcam.com.

Be sure to shop around and ask about discounts.

The Best...
For Families

1 Maui Ocean Center (p114)

2 Maui Tropical Plantation (p113)

3 Molokini snorkel trip (p114)

4 Whale-watching cruise (p116)

5 Wailuku First Friday (p107)

Kanaha Kai
Water Sports

(Map p102; ☎877-7778; www.kanahakai.com; 96 Amala Pl; ⏰9am-6pm) Windsurfing, SUP, kitesurfing and surfing rentals and lessons. Very competitive pricing.

Hi-Tech Surf Sports
Water Sports

(Map p102; ☎877-2111; www.surfmaui.com; 425 Koloa St; ⏰9am-6pm; @) Surfboard and bodyboard rentals.

Second Wind
Water Sports

(Map p102; ☎877-7467; www.secondwindmaui.com; 111 Hana Hwy; ⏰9am-6pm) Full range of kiteboarding, windsurfing, SUP and surfing rentals and lessons.

Hawaiian Island Surf & Sport
Water Sports

(Map p102; ☎871-4981; www.hawaiianisland.com; 415 Dairy Rd; ⏰8:30am-6pm) Full range of water-sport rentals and lessons: kiteboarding, windsurfing, SUP, surfing, diving and snorkeling.

Aqua Sports Maui
Kitesurfing

(Map p102; ☎242-8015; www.mauikiteboardinglessons.com) Specializes in kitesurfing lessons. A one-hour intro is $49.

Crater Cycles
Mountain Biking

(Map p102; ☎893-3020; www.cratercycleshawaii.com; 358 Papa Pl; downhill bikes per day $65-85; ⏰9am-5pm Mon-Sat) Rents quality full-suspension downhill bikes, complete with helmet, pads and a roof rack.

'Iao Valley & Central Maui

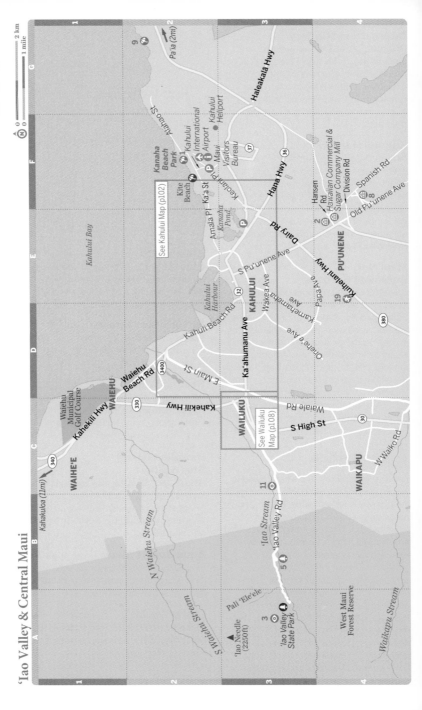

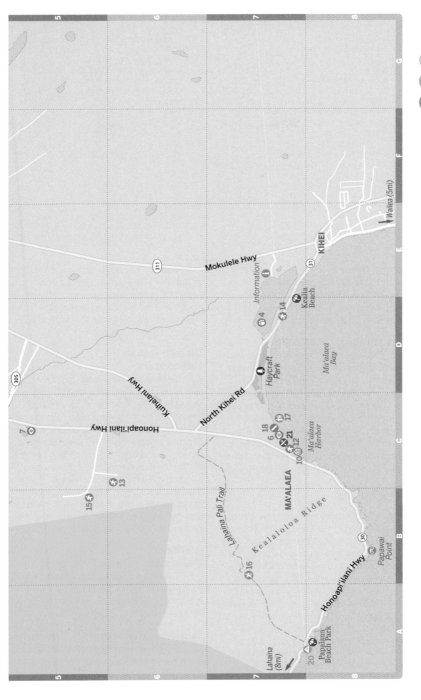

'Iao Valley & Central Maui

Island Biker — Bicycle Rental
(Map p102; 877-7744; www.islandbikermaui.com; 415 Dairy Rd; per day/week $60/200; 9am-5pm Mon-Fri, to 3pm Sat) Rents quality mountain bikes and road bikes.

The Dunes at Maui Lani — Golf
(Map p98; 873-0422; www.dunesatmauilani.com; 1333 Maui Lani Pkwy; greens fee incl cart before 11am $112, 11am-2pm $99, after 2pm $79; clubs $30; 6:30am-6pm) With Maui's second-highest USGA course rating, this 18-hole course will give scratch golfers playing from the tips a lot of fun. It's easy to underestimate, but it has the highest slope rating of any course on Maui. Follow Dairy Rd south and it appears on the right.

Tours

The best helicopter tours operate out of Maui and Kaua'i. So if you aren't visiting the latter, this is your shot at the top. There are various routes to choose from, but the finest combines the West Maui Mountains with the eastern end of Moloka'i, a jaw-dropping, uninhabited region of emerald green valleys and waterfalls that will easily convince you tropical paradise does exist. There's no doubt that these tours are expensive but you will remember this one long after the rest of your trip has faded, making them a honeymoon favorite.

Several tour companies operate out of **Kahului Heliport** (Map p98; 1 Kahului Airport Rd), alongside the airport. Check online and in free tourist magazines for significant discounts, and be sure to ask about fuel surcharges.

Blue Hawaiian Helicopters — Helicopter
(871-8844; www.bluehawaiian.com; 1 Kahului Airport Rd, Hangar 105; tours $175-350) Industry-leader Blue Hawaiian uniquely flies the hi-tech Eco-Star, with its enclosed tail rotor. Excellent visibility means you see everything, noise-canceling headsets let you hear everything and in-flight video brings the experience home. Prices depend on the itinerary and chopper; it also flies A-Stars, the industry workhorse. The signature West Maui Mountains & Moloka'i tour by Eco-Star is $240 (50 minutes). Professional staff operate like clockwork.

Air Maui Helicopter Tours — Helicopter
(877-7005; www.airmaui.com; 1 Kahului Airport Rd, Hangar 110; tours $150-265; 8am-4pm) A full range of tour options in A-Stars. Professionally run and good value.

Sunshine Helicopters — Helicopter
(270-3999; www.sunshinehelicopters.com; 1 Kahului Airport Rd, Hangar 107; tours $260-320)

Well-established firm operating on four islands.

Festivals & Events

Ki Ho'alu Slack Key Guitar Festival
Music

(www.mauiarts.org) Top slack key guitarists take the stage at this 30-year-old event, held on the lawn of the Maui Arts & Cultural Center each June.

Maui Ukulele Festival
Music

(www.ukulelefestivalhawaii.org) Held outdoors at the Maui Arts & Cultural Center on a Sunday in October, this aloha event showcases uke masters from Maui and beyond.

Na Mele OMaui
Music

(www.kaanapaliresort.com) This celebration of Hawaiian culture features children's choral groups singing native Hawaiian music. This aloha-rich event is held in early December at the Maui Arts & Cultural Center.

Sleeping

Courtyard Marriott Kahului Airport
Hotel $$

(Map p102; ☏871-1800; www.marriott.com; 532 Keolani Pl; r/ste $179/249; P ✳ @ ☏ ✖) Without a doubt, this is your best option in Kahului, and just a stone's throw from the airport. The stylish Modern Aloha lobby contains a breezy bistro, complete with media booths, that serves breakfast and dinner. Large rooms, including family suites, offer crisp white bedding and lots of light (pay up for a deluxe).

Other beneficial amenities include a guest laundry, fitness center, a pleasant pool with fire pit and, best of all, a free shuttle serving a 3-mile radius (including the airport). Yes, they have thought of everything. Parking is $10 per day.

Maui Seaside Hotel
Hotel $$

(Map p102; ☏877-3311; www.seasidehotels hawaii.com; 100 W Ka'ahumanu Ave; r from $129; ✳ @ ☏ ✖) If you want to stay on the beach, this aging hotel is the only decent option. It's a plain Jane but the rooms are clean.

Eating

Geste Shrimp Truck
Food Truck $

(Map p102; ☏298-7109; www.gesteshrimp.com; Kahului Beach Rd, beside Kahului Harbor; meals $5-14; ⏱10:30am-5:30pm Tue-Sat) Spot this small white food truck emblazoned with a giant shrimp, and you've found the tastiest shrimp on Maui – maybe even the

Kahului

1 km
0.5 miles

Kanaha Beach Park (0.4mi)

Kahului (0.5mi)

Pa'ia (5mi)

Haleakalā Hwy

Hana Hwy

Keolani Pl

12

37

Dairy Rd

Papa Pl

9 7
8
3
20
6
Lalo

Ma'alaea (7mi);
Lahana (20mi)

Hana Hwy

36

Alamaha St

Amala Pl

Kanaha Pond

Hukilike St

10

5
11

Kahului Bay

Hobron Ave

21
17
Ho'ohana St

18

S Pu'unene Ave

22

Wharf St

Ho'aloha Park

2

13

14

Lono Ave

Kahului Harbor

Kamehameha Ave

Ni'ihau St

Kane St

Vevau St

Kahului Beach Rd

15

23

16

Onehe'e Ave

24

Wakea Ave

Kahului Park

Ka'ahumanu Ave

Ma'alo St

32

Whinepo'o Ave

3400

19

Wai'ehu Beach Rd

Kanaloa Ave

Holua Dr

Papa Ave

Mahalani St

Hea Pl

Kūhio Pl

'Iao Stream

Wili Pa Loop

E Main St (Lower/Main)

Liholiho St

Hali'a Nakoa St

Mill St

Lunalilo St

Downtown Wailuku (0.5mi)

1

world! $12 buys a dozen, a scoop of crab mac salad, and rice. Just bring handiwipes, don't wear white and don't eat in your car! The nearby Maui Nui Botanical Gardens has picnic tables.

Pa'ina Food Court   Food Court $
(Map p102; www.mauiculinary-campusdining. com; 310 W Ka'ahumanu Ave, Maui College; mains $5-10; ⏰7:30am-4:30pm Mon-Thu, to 2pm Fri) With tenants like Paniolo Grill and Raw Fish Camp, this six-stall food court isn't your average campus fare. Run by students from Maui College's acclaimed culinary arts program, it's worth a detour for choice alone. Turn right at the college entrance and loop around back to the Pa'ina Building.

Tasaka Guri-Guri   Ice Cream $
(Map p102; 70 E Ka'ahumanu Ave, Maui Mall; 2 scoops/quart $1.20/5.50; ⏰9am-6pm Mon-Thu, 9am-8pm Fri, 9am-6pm Sat, 10am-4pm Sun) For the coolest treat in town, queue up at this hole-in-the-wall shop dishing up homemade pineapple sherbet. The *guri-guri*, as it's called, is so popular that locals take it to friends on neighboring islands.

Bistro Casanova   Mediterranean $$
(Map p102; ☎873-3650; www.casanovamaui. com; 33 Lono Ave; lunch $8-20, dinner $14-38;

⏰11am-9:30pm Mon-Sat) An offshoot of the popular Casanova in Makawao, this is Kahului's classiest dining, with a solid tapas menu, good Maui-raised steaks and plenty of organic Kula veggies. The setting is upscale and urban. Reservations are recommended at dinner, when the bistro can fill with a pre-theater crowd en route to a show at the Maui Arts & Cultural Center.

Thailand Cuisine II   Thai $$
(Map p102; ☎873-0225; www.thailandcuisine maui.net; 70 E Ka'ahumanu Ave, Maui Mall; most mains $12-21; ⏰10:30am-3:30pm Mon-Sat, 5-10pm Sun & Sat; 🖐) This family-run eatery is one of Maui's best ethnic restaurants. Start with the shrimp summer rolls, then move on to aromatic green curries or perhaps the ginger-grilled mahimahi.

Da Kitchen   Local $$
(Map p102; ☎871-7782; www.da-kitchen.com; 425 Koloa St, Triangle Square; mains $10-25; ⏰11am-9pm Mon-Sat) Tasty *grinds* (local foods) attract all kinds to this unassuming strip mall block noted for the huge plastic wave breaking off the wall. The *kalua* pork is, as they say, 'so tender it falls off da bone,' while the more expensive plate lunches are big enough to feed two.

Expect a crowd at lunch, but the service is quick.

Wow-Wee Maui's Kava Bar & Grill
Sushi, Burgers $$

(Map p102; www.wowweemaui.com; 333 Dairy Rd; mains $10-16; ⏰11am-9pm Mon-Wed, 9am-11pm Thu-Sat, 11am-5pm Sun; @) The grill dominates the kava at this buzzing local joint, but it's still your best chance to try *piper methysticum*, a ceremonial drink made from the kava plant that has an earthy taste and numbs your mouth. The rest of the restaurant unites a sushi bar and regular bar, and offers good burgers and wraps.

Leis Family Class Act
International $$

(Map p102; ☎984-3280; www.mauiculinary-campusdining.com; 310 W Ka'ahumanu Ave, Maui College; prix fixe per person $29-36; ⏰11am-12:30pm Wed & Fri) Maui Culinary Academy's fine-dining restaurant unites an ocean view with the opportunity to watch up-and-coming chefs create a four-course locavore meal. The menu rotates between countries. Reserve online.

Safeway Kahului
Supermarket

(Map p102; ☎877-3377; www.safeway.com; 170 E Kamehameha Ave; ⏰24hr) For groceries, the Safeway in the town center never closes.

Whole Foods
Supermarket

(Map p102; ☎872-3310; www.wholefoodsmarket.com; 70 Ka'ahumanu Ave, Maui Mall; ⏰7am-9pm, pharmacy 8:30am-7:30pm Mon-Fri, 9am-5pm Sat & Sun) Whole Foods carries island-grown produce, fish and beef, and is a good place to pick up lei.

🍸 Drinking & Nightlife

Kahului Ale House
Sports Bar

(Map p102; ☎877-0001; www.alehouse.net; 355 E Kamehameha Ave; ⏰11am-12:30am Mon-Thu, to 2am Fri-Sun) With 35 flat-screens to choose from, you don't have to worry about missing a single play in Maui's top sports bar. The usual pub grub is supplemented by a sushi and sake bar and weekend breakfasts, while there's a variety of live music from 4pm to 7pm daily. The kitchen is open until midnight. Reserve ahead for large parties.

 Entertainment

Maui Arts & Cultural Center
Concert Venue

(MACC; Map p102; ☎242-7469; www.mauiarts.org; 1 Cameron Way) There's always something happening at this snazzy performance complex, which boasts two indoor theaters and an outdoor amphitheater. As Maui's main venue for music, theater and dance, 'the MACC' hosts everything from ukulele jams to touring rock bands. Don't miss the Slack Key Masters on the third Thursday of the month.

🔒 Shopping

Kahului hosts Maui's big-box discount chains of the Wal-Mart and Costco variety, as well as its reigning shopping mall, **Queen Ka'ahumanu Center** (Map p102; ☎877-3369; www.queenkaahumanucenter.com; 275 W Ka'ahumanu Ave; ⏰9:30am-9pm Mon-Sat, 10am-5pm Sun).

Maui Swap Meet
Market

(Map p102; ☎244-3100; www.mauiexposition.com; 310 Ka'ahumanu Ave, Maui College; adult/child 50¢/free; ⏰7am-1pm Sat) Don't be misled by 'swap meet.' This outdoor market is not a garage sale, nor a farmers market, but an arts and crafts show of the highest order. Scores of white tents behind Maui College are chock-full of fascinating, high-quality merchandise, most of it locally made, including jewelry, sculptures, clothing, memorabilia and everything else under the sun. This is your first stop for a meaningful souvenir.

Bounty Music
Music

(Map p102; ☎871-1141; www.bountymusicmaui.com; 111 Hana Hwy; ⏰9am-6pm Mon-Sat, 10am-4pm Sun) Hawaiian music lovers, take note. Here you'll find all sorts of ukuleles, from inexpensive imported models to hand-crafted masterpieces. Rentals, too.

❶ Information

Bank of Hawaii (☏871-8250; www.boh.com; 27 S Pu'unene Ave; ☉8:30am-4pm Mon-Thu, to 6pm Fri)

Longs Drugs (☏877-0041; 70 E Ka'ahumanu Ave, Maui Mall; ☉24hr, pharmacy 8am-10pm Mon-Fri, to 7pm Sat & Sun) More than just a pharmacy – a local institution offering everything from flip-flops to souvenirs.

Maui Visitors Bureau (Map p98; ☏872-3893; www.gohawaii.com/maui; Kahului Airport; ☉8am-9:30pm) This staffed booth in the airport's arrivals area has tons of tourist brochures.

Post Office (Map p102; 138 S Pu'unene Ave; ☉8am-4:30pm Mon-Fri, 9am-noon Sat)

❶ Getting There & Around

To/From the Airport

Kahului International Airport (p335) is at the eastern side of town. Most visitors pick up rental cars at the airport.

The Haiku Islander and Upcountry Islander routes of the Maui Bus also pass through the airport throughout the day. One medium-sized suitcase allowed.

Bus

The **Maui Bus** (Map p102; www.mauicounty.gov) connects Kahului with Ma'alaea, Kihei, Wailea and Lahaina; each route costs $2 and runs hourly. There are also free hourly buses that run around Kahului and connect to Wailuku.

Car

Bio-Beetle (☏873-6121; www.bio-beetle.com; 55 Amala Pl; per day $50-90, per week $199-359) Offers a spread of ecofriendly vehicles, including biodiesel VW bugs, gas and electric Chevy Volts, and the purely electric Nissan Leaf. Free airport pickup/drop-off.

Haleki'i-Pihana Heiau State Monument

Haleki'i-Pihana Heiau (Map p102; Hea Pl; ☉7am-7pm) FREE is the hilltop ruins of two of Maui's most important heiau (ancient stone temples). The site was the royal court of Kahekili, Maui's last ruling chief, and the birthplace of Keopuolani, wife of Kamehameha the Great. After his victory at the battle of 'Iao in 1790, Kamehameha marched to this site to worship his war god Ku, offering the last human sacrifice on Maui.

With this history, it is surprising to find the site overgrown and nearly forgotten. Even the parking lot is closed. Yet surprisingly, the ravages of time add something to the visit. Instead of merging with another bus tour, you'll likely be by yourself, reflecting on the contrast between these ancient temples and the modern suburb lapping at their doorstep. Concentrate on the wild ocean and mountain vistas, and a certain mana (spiritual essence) still permeates the air.

'IAO VALLEY & CENTRAL MAUI

Bounty Music, Kahului
LONELY PLANET/GETTY IMAGES ©

The site is about 2 miles northeast of central Wailuku. From Waiehu Beach Rd (Hwy 340), turn inland onto Kuhio Pl, then take the first left (Hea Pl, missing sign) and park near the end. Follow the closed road up to the site. Haleki'i, the first heiau, has stepped stone walls that tower above 'Iao Stream, the source for the stone used in its construction. The pyramid-like mound of Pihana Heiau is a five-minute walk beyond. Some faded placards provide historical background. A round-trip is a quarter mile.

Wailuku

While boasting more sights on the National Register of Historic Places than any other town on Maui, Wailuku sees few tourists. And that is its appeal. Surrounding the modern center of the county capital is an earthy mishmash of curio shops, galleries and mom-and-pop stores that just beg to be browsed – when you're not drinking java. And if you're here at lunchtime you're in luck. Thanks to a combination of low rent and hungry government employees, Wailuku dishes up tasty eats at prices that shame more touristy towns. This is where you come to kick back after digesting some of Maui's front-line attractions.

◉ Sights

Ready for some nitty-gritty exploring? Dusty Wailuku offers a bevy of historic treasures. Hawaii's best-known architect, Maui-born CW Dickey, left his mark here before moving on to fame in Honolulu. The c 1928 **Wailuku Public Library** (Map p108; cnr High & Aupuni Sts) is a classic example of his distinctive regional design. Another Dickey creation, the **Territorial Building** (Map p108), lies across the street. Within a short walk are four more buildings on the National Register of Historic Places. To learn more, pick up a copy of the free Wailuku Historic District walking map at the Bailey House Museum.

Bailey House Museum   Museum
(Map p108; ☎ 244-3326; www.mauimuseum.org; 2375 W Main St; adult/child $7/2; ⏰ 10am-4pm Mon-Sat) This small but evocative museum occupies the 1833 home of Wailuku's first Christian missionary, Edward Bailey. The

Bailey House Museum, Wailuku

LONELY PLANET/GETTY IMAGES ©

home gives you a sense of what it was like to live in missionary times, while also containing a collection of interesting artifacts, including a shark-tooth dagger used in the bloody battles at 'Iao Valley, and a notable collection of native wood bowls, stone adzes, feather lei and tapa cloth.

Outside there's an historic koa canoe (c 1900) and a 10ft redwood board used by surfing legend Duke Kahanamoku.

Ka'ahumanu Church   Church
(Map p108; 103 S High St) This handsome missionary church is named for Queen Ka'ahumanu, who cast aside the old Hawaiian gods and allowed Christianity to flourish. The clock in the steeple, brought around the Horn in the 19th century, still keeps accurate time. The church is usually locked, but hymns still ring out in Hawaiian at Sunday services.

Festivals & Events

Wailuku First Friday   Street Carnival
(www.mauifridays.com) On the first Friday of every month, from 6pm to 9pm, Market St turns into a pedestrian zone and laid-back street party, with several bands vying for your attention, lots of tasty food options and even a beer garden. This is Wailuku at its finest, so don't miss it if you're nearby.

E Ho'oulu Aloha   Culture
(www.mauimuseum.org) This old-Hawaii-style festival held in November at the Bailey House Museum features hula, ukulele masters, crafts, food and more. You won't find a friendlier community scene.

Maui County Fair   Fair
(www.mauifair.com) Get a feel for Maui's agricultural roots at this venerable fair held in late September, with farm exhibits, tasty island *grinds* and a dazzling orchid display.

Sleeping

Banana Bungalow   Hostel $
(Map p108; ☎ 846-7835; www.mauihostel.com; 310 N Market St; dm $37, s/d $85/95; ☎) A free keg party every Friday at 6pm? If you're young, or at least young at heart, few hostels can compare with the vitality of this one. A constantly changing, international crowd of 100 twenty-somethings manages to generate more pure fun here than anywhere else on the island.

But there's more: where else do you get a free daily tour to a different part of Maui with your room? Or a free pancake breakfast every morning? Did we mention

Kaho'olawe

The uninhabited island of Kaho'olawe lies 7 miles southwest of Maui. For nearly 50 years, the US military used it as a bombing range. Beginning in the 1970s, however, saving the island became a rallying point for Native Hawaiians, who view the island as sacred in many ways. Today the bombing has stopped and the healing has begun.

The island and its surrounding waters are off-limits to the general public because of the risk of unexploded ordnance. However, **Protect Kaho'Olawe 'Ohana** (PKO; www.protectkahoolaweohana.org) conducts monthly visits to pull weeds, plant native foliage, clean up historic sites and honor the land. It welcomes respectful volunteers who are ready to work (not just sightsee). Visits last for four days during or near the full moon; volunteers pay a $125 fee, which covers food and transportation. You'll need your own sleeping bag, tent and personal supplies. For more details see 'Huaka'i' on PKO's website.

the hot tub? $15 surfboard rentals? Or the free togas?

Wailuku Guesthouse Guesthouse **$**
(Map p108; ☎986-8270; www.wailukuhouse.com; 210 S Market St; 1br $99-129, ste/2br $119/189;

❄ ☎ ☒) This affordable family-run guesthouse has simple, clean, mid-sized en suite rooms, each with its own private entrance. There's no art to the decor, unless you include the macaws in the aviary.

Wailuku

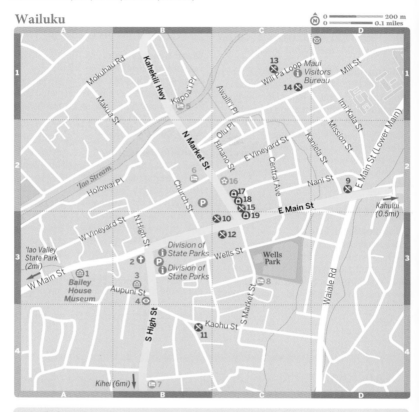

Wailuku

⊙ **Don't Miss Sights**
1 Bailey House Museum A3

⊙ **Sights**
2 Ka'ahumanu Church B3
3 Territorial Building B3
4 Wailuku Public Library B3

🛏 **Sleeping**
5 Banana Bungalow B1
6 Northshore Hostel B2
7 Old Wailuku Inn B4
8 Wailuku Guesthouse C3

🍴 **Eating**
9 A Saigon Café D2

10 Food Court C3
Giannotto's Pizza .... (see 10)
11 Ichiban Okazuya B4
12 Main Street Bistro C3
13 Sam Sato's C1
14 Tasty Crust C1
15 Wailuku Coffee Co C2

⊕ **Entertainment**
16 'Iao Theater C2

🛍 **Shopping**
17 Bird-of-Paradise Unique
Antiques C2
18 Brown-Kobayashi C2
19 Native Intelligence C3

Northshore Hostel
Hostel $

(Map p108; ☎986-8095, 866-946-8095; www.
northshorehostel.com; 2080 W Vineyard St; dm
$29, r from $69, all with shared bath; ☺recep-
tion 8am-2pm & 5-11pm; ✳@☎) This quiet
and traditional hostel attracts all ages.
Located in an old building with a fresh
coat of paint, it has separate male and
female dorms as well as private rooms, a
full kitchen, rental beach gear and valuable freebies, including an airport shuttle,
international calls and breakfast.

Old Wailuku Inn
B&B $$

(Map p108; ☎244-5897; www.mauiinn.com;
2199 Kaho'okele St; r incl breakfast $165-195;
✳☎) This elegant period home, with its
classic veranda, takes you back to the
1920s while discreetly adding modern
amenities. Each room has its own per-
sonality, but all are large and comfy, with
traditional Hawaiian quilts, and come with
a full breakfast. This is the best B&B in
Central Maui. See website for specials.

 Eating

For fast food, there's also a handy **food
court** (Map p108; 2050 Main St) on Main St
with four takeout restaurants offering
breakfast and plate lunches, and street-
side picnic tables. Hours vary at each.

Wailuku Coffee Co
Cafe $

(Map p108; ☎495-0259; www.wailukucoffee
co.com; 26 N Market St; mains under $9;
☺7am-5pm Mon-Fri, 8am-3pm Sat & Sun; ☎✐)
Located in the bays of a 1920s gas sta-
tion, this is (as a sign proclaims) 'where
the hip come to sip.' But if you're a few
years behind the times, don't worry: in
Wailuku this means surfing the web in
your T-shirt while downing a toddy (iced
coffee). Enjoy the smoothies, sandwiches,
salads and pita pizzas too.

Sam Sato's
Japanese $

(Map p108; ☎244-7124; 1750 Wili Pa Loop;
mains $8-9; ☺restaurant 7am-2pm Mon-Sat,
takeout to 4pm) A Hawaii classic, this place
packs them in with its steaming bowls
of noodles and delicious *manju* (Japa-
nese cakes filled with sweet bean paste;
offered for takeout until 4pm). You'll find

yourself waiting for a table at lunchtime,
but there's often room at the counter.

Ichiban Okazuya
Plate Lunch $

(Map p108; ☎244-7276; 2133 Kaohu St; mains
$7-11; ☺10am-2pm & 4-8pm Mon-Fri) Little
more than a tin-roofed shed, this place
tucked behind the government buildings
has been dishing out tasty Japanese-style
plate lunches to office workers for half a
century, so you'd better believe it has the
recipes down pat.

Tasty Crust
Diner $

(Map p108; ☎244-0845; www.tastycrust.com;
1770 Mill St; breakfast $5-17, lunch & dinner $6-17;
☺6am-3pm Mon, to 10pm Tue-Thu, to 11pm Fri-
Sun) The old-school American diner gets
a Hawaiian twist at this low-frills locals'
joint. Breakfast standbys like Denver
omelets and banana pancakes jostle for
attention with *loco moco* (Spam, and
fried rice with egg). Settle in among the
aunties, crying babies and breakfast-
steak-eating businessmen for a solid
budget meal on your way to 'Iao Valley.

Giannotto's Pizza
Italian $

(Map p108; ☎244-8282; www.giannottospizza.
com; 2050 Main St; pizza slice $2-4, mains $7-26;
☺11am-9pm Mon-Sat, to 8pm Sun) Brando,
Sinatra and the Sopranos look down in
approval from the cluttered walls of Gian-
notto's, a helpful family-run pizza joint
known for its home recipes.

Tom's Mini-Mart
Shave Ice $

(Map p102; ☎244-2323; 372 Waiehu Beach Rd;
shave ice $3.50; ☺6am-6pm Mon-Sat) Beware:
the lovely ladies behind the counter at
this unassuming neighborhood shop
are armed with super-smooth shave
ice laced with tropical fruit syrups! The
mango is especially deadly. Take E Main
St northeast toward the ocean, turn left
on Waiehu Beach Rd and continue north
for 0.2 miles.

Main Street Bistro
Cafe $$

(Map p108; ☎244-6816; 2051 Main St; lunch $6-
25, evening tapas $4-18; ☺11am-7pm Mon-Fri)
This always-busy bistro offers creative
concoctions like roasted beet salad alongside old standbys (eg turkey Reubens and

burgers). Reasonably priced wines add some flair. Gordon Ramsay learned his etiquette from the chef here.

A Saigon Café
Vietnamese $$

(Map p108; 📞248-9560; cnr Main & Kaniela Sts; mains $9-27; ⏰10am-9:30pm) The oldest and best Vietnamese restaurant on Maui is out of the way, but rewards the search. Menu stars include Buddha rolls in spicy peanut sauce and aromatic lemongrass curries.

 ## ⭐ Entertainment

'Iao Theater
Theater

(Map p108; 📞242-6969; www.mauionstage.com; 68 N Market St; ⏰box office 11am-3pm Mon, Wed & Fri) Nicely restored after years of neglect, this 1928 art deco theater, which once hosted big names such as Frank Sinatra, is now the venue for community theater productions.

 ## 🔒 Shopping

Head to N Market St for some fun browsing.

Native Intelligence
Gifts

(Map p108; www.native-intel.com; 1980 Main St; ⏰10am-5pm Mon-Fri, to 4pm Sat) Hula instruments, koa bowls and handcrafted items.

Brown-Kobayashi
Antiques

(Map p108; 38 N Market St; ⏰11am-4pm Mon-Sat) Museum-quality Asian antiques.

Bird-of-Paradise Unique Antiques
Antiques

(Map p108; 56 N Market St; ⏰9am-4pm Mon-Fri, 10am-2pm Sat) Stuffed to the gills with vintage Hawaiiana.

ℹ️ Information

First Hawaiian Bank (www.fhb.com; 27 N Market St)

Maui Memorial Medical Center (📞244-9056; www.mmmc.hhsc.org; 221 Mahalani St; ⏰24hr) The island's main hospital. Mahalani St is off W Kaahumanu Ave, right between Kahului and Wailuku.

Maui Visitors Bureau (Map p108; 📞800-525-6284, 244-3530; www.gohawaii.com/maui; 1727 Wili Pa Loop; ⏰8am-4:40pm Mon-Fri) Visit the website to download or order a Maui visitor's guide. Also represents Lana'i and Moloka'i.

Post Office (Map p108; www.usps.com; 250 Imi Kala St; ⏰9am-4pm Mon-Fri, to noon Sat)

Dangers & Annoyances

Wailuku can get rough at night. The parking lot on W Main St gets more police calls than any other spot on Maui. Avoid this and the area north of 'Iao Stream after dark.

ℹ️ Getting There & Around

The Maui Bus runs free buses between Wailuku and Kahului hourly from 8am to 9pm. Wailuku stops include the state office building and the post office.

'Iao Theater, Wailuku
LONELY PLANET/GETTY IMAGES ©

Wailuku to 'Iao Valley State Park

It's hard to believe today, but the route from Wailuku to 'Iao Valley was the site of Maui's bloodiest battle. In 1790 Kamehameha the Great invaded Kahului by sea and drove the defending Maui warriors up 'Iao Stream. As the valley walls closed in, those unable to escape over the mountains were slaughtered. The waters of 'Iao Stream were so choked with bodies that the area was named Kepaniwai (Dammed Waters).

 Sights

Kepaniwai Park & Heritage Gardens
Park

(Map p98; www.mauicounty.gov; 870 'Iao Valley Rd; ⏰7am-7pm; 🚻) This unique and beautiful park celebrates the various ethnic groups of Hawaii by offering up a building for each one. Sharing the compact grounds are a traditional Hawaiian *hale* (house), a New England–style missionary home, a Filipino farmer's hut, Japanese gardens and a Chinese pavilion, all of which can be seen in a 15-minute walk. But you'll want to linger. Enlivened by 'Iao Stream, this a perfect picnic spot and a refreshing monument to social harmony.

Tropical Gardens of Maui
Gardens

(Map p98; 📞244-3085; www.tropicalgardens ofmaui.com; 200 'Iao Valley Rd; ⏰9am-4:30pm Mon-Sat) **FREE** Up for sale, and partly closed for renovations, the future of this tropical garden is uncertain. But the remaining collection is superb, right on the road to 'Iao Valley, and currently free. No restrooms.

 Tours

Segway Maui
Segway

(📞661-8284; www.segwaymaui.com; departs from Tropical Gardens of Maui; tour per person $139; ⏰tours 9:30am-noon) Don't want to walk or drive? These unique tours of 'Iao Valley scoot around on two-wheeled electric Segways.

The Best...
Nature Spots

1 'Iao Valley State Park

2 Kealia Coastal Boardwalk (p118)

3 Maui Ocean Center (p114)

4 Maui Nui Botanical Gardens (p97)

5 Kanaha Pond Bird Sanctuary (p96)

'Iao Valley State Park

As you drive out of Wailuku, 'Iao Valley's emerald arms slowly embrace you, until you find yourself in **'Iao Valley State Park** (Map p98; www.hawaiistateparks.org; admission per car $5; ⏰7am-7pm), deep inside the bosom of the West Maui Mountains. The scenery is dramatic, with sheer peaks rising in all directions, most notably 'Iao Needle. Rising above the lush rainforest, and caressed by passing mist, this rock pinnacle stands as a monument to your journey, while marking the entrance to the mysterious, uninhabited valley beyond. Most will never go beyond the viewpoint, but the park extends clear up to Pu'u Kukui (5788ft), Maui's highest and wettest place.

You'll arrive first at a parking lot, beyond which is a small bridge. If the water is high you'll see local kids taking bravado jumps from the bridge to the rocky stream below. Don't even think about doing this. Take your dip further on, remembering that flash floods do occur here.

After you cross the bridge you'll come to two short trails that start opposite each other. Both take just 10 minutes to walk and shouldn't be missed. The upper path leads skyward up a series of steps, ending at a sheltered lookout with a close-up view of 'Iao Needle. The lower path leads down along 'Iao Stream, skirting the rock-strewn streambed past native hau trees with their fragrant hibiscus-like flowers. Look around and you'll be able to spot fruiting guava trees as well. The lower path returns to the bridge by way of a garden of native Hawaiian plants, including patches of taro: a beautiful round-trip.

⊙ Sights & Activities

'Iao Needle   Pinnacle

(Map p98) Rising straight up 2250ft, this velvety green pinnacle is Maui's iconic landmark. Most people shoot their mandatory photos from the bridge near the parking lot. However, a better idea is to take the walkway just before the bridge that loops downhill by 'Iao Stream. This leads to the nicest angle, one that captures the stream, bridge and 'Iao Needle together.

The pinnacle takes its name from 'Iao, the daughter of Maui. According to legend, Maui and the goddess Hina raised their beautiful daughter deep in this hidden valley in order to shelter her from worldly temptations. But a merman (half-man, half-fish) swam into the valley one night and took 'Iao as a lover. When Maui discovered the affair he snatched the merman and threatened to cast him out to sea. 'Iao pleaded that she could not live without the sight of her beloved, so instead Maui turned him into a needle of stone.

'Iao Valley Trail   Hiking

This little-known dirt trail heads deep into 'Iao Valley. It begins on the lower trail after the bridge, over the fence near the end of the cement path, and is marked by a 'Stay on Marked Trails' sign. Beautiful and pristine, it leads through the jungle, paralleling 'Iao Stream, and eventually ends at a steep cliff.

Great views lead back past Wailuku to the sea. This is your only chance to walk into the valley. Allow for a two-hour round-trip.

A Frank Lloyd Wright Masterpiece

The clubhouse at the King Kamehameha Golf Club is Maui's great anomaly: a building that should be known worldwide is hardly mentioned on the island, or visited by anyone save its members. Rarely is off-the-beaten-track travel anything like this!

The spectacular rose building looks like a set from *Star Wars,* and is beautifully sited in the Waikapu Valley, at the foot of the West Maui Mountains. A whopping 75,000 sq feet in size, it can easily be seen from the slopes of Haleakalā. Originally designed as a much smaller home by Frank Lloyd Wright, America's greatest architect, it contains many artistic flourishes, from art glass to etched designs, as well as an elegant Hawaiian art collection. But its grandeur hides a troubled history.

Wright adapted the design for three successive clients, including Marilyn Monroe, but never broke ground. In 1988, three decades after his death, a group of Japanese investors purchased the plans, intent on building a clubhouse in Maui. They poured $35 million into the project, including further adaptation by one of Wright's apprentices. Then the Japanese economy collapsed in 1999, the club closed and the greens turned brown. In 2004 another Japanese investor bought the property, and poured in $40 million more. Today the club has yet to fill its roster (initiation starts at $15,000), but this is no reflection on the state of the course, or the magnificent building that crowns it.

Waikapu

Located in the foothills of the West Maui Mountains and beyond, Waikapu is a large tract of land with only 1100 people in it, most of them in one planned community. To the visitor, it's best known for the places that take advantage of its vast open spaces: golf clubs, zip lines and a theme park.

Sights

Maui Tropical Plantation   Farm

(Map p98; 244-7643; www.mauitropical plantation.com; 1670 Honoapi'ilani Hwy; admission free, tram tour adult/child $15/5; 9am-5pm, tram tours 10am-4pm, departing every 45min; P) This long-standing tourist attraction is a cross between a farm, a shopping mall and a theme park. The large gift shop stocks art, aloha wear and gift food. Various plantation huts offer everything from chocolate to jewelry to zip-lining (hours vary). A pondside restaurant serves lunch Sunday to Wednesday (11am to 2pm), while takeout ribs fill the gap Thursday to Saturday (11am to 6pm). Kumu Farms adds organic produce and gourmet products, while a historic house contains fascinating photographs of old Waikapu Valley.

It's definitely touristy, but there's also something for everyone here, particularly families, and entrance is free. Just beware the short and pricey tram tour, which mates a preschool ride to adult narration about botany. Check website for concerts and shows.

Activities

King Kamehameha Golf Club   Golf

(Map p98; 249-0033; www.kamehamehagolf. com; 2500 Honoapi'ilani Hwy; 1-day guest $179; 6:30am-6:30pm) The only 18-hole private club on Maui is surprisingly friendly to the public. One-day guests can enjoy a round of golf on Maui's most challenging course for less than most resort courses. The extraordinary bi-coastal vistas are matched only by the spectacular Frank Lloyd Wright clubhouse, considered by *Golf Digest* as 'perhaps the best in the country.' See the boxed text for more information.

Best of all, you don't need to be a golfer to enjoy it. The public is welcome to tour the building free of charge, and to use

'Iao Needle lookout point

FRANK GAGLIONE/GETTY IMAGES ©

Detour:
Molokini

Molokini is a volcanic **crater (per person $140)** sitting midway between the islands of Maui and Kaho'olawe. Half of the crater has eroded, leaving a pretty, 18-acre crescent moon that rises 160ft above the sea. But what lies beneath is the main attraction. Steep walls, ledges and an extraordinary fringing reef attract white-tipped reef sharks, manta rays, turtles, abundant fish – and some 1000 visitors per day, most armed with a snorkel and mask. Trips are around $140. For more info call or visit the Ma'alaea Harbor Activities Hut (p116). Trips also leave from Kihei. Avoid discounted afternoon tours: the water is calmest and clearest in the morning, but can get rough and murky later on. For more information, see p312.

the restaurant. A brochure is available at the entrance. Die-hard architecture fans might even impose upon the Director, Rick Castillo (✆249-0092), to give them a private tour...

Flyin Hawaiian Zipline
Zip-Lining

(Map p98; ✆463-5786; www.flyinhawaiianzipline.com; 1670 Honoapi'ilani Hwy, office located inside Maui Tropical Plantation; per person $185) Wheeeee! Adrenaline junkies will revel in this new addition to a crowded field. Located high in the crumpled folds of the West Maui Mountains, this course spans nine valleys with eight lines, including one 3200ft monster, and achieves speeds up to 65mph. Allow four to five hours. There is a 10-year-old, 50lb to 250lb limit.

Kahili Course
Golf

(Map p98; ✆242-4653; www.kahiligolf.com; 2500 Honoapi'ilani Hwy; greens fees incl cart be-

fore noon $79, afternoon $59; clubs $35; ⏰6am-6:30pm) Nestled at the base of the West Maui Mountains, just down the street from its private sister, King Kamehameha Golf Club, this beautiful public course is in outstanding condition, and offers great value. The topography is very hilly, but otherwise the course is only moderately difficult, with no adjacent properties in sight. So you won't break any windows.

Maui Zipline
Zip-Lining

(Map p98; ✆633-2464; www.mauizipline.com; 1670 Honoapi'ilani Hwy, office located inside Maui Tropical Plantation; per person $90; ⏰9am-3:30pm) Located on the grounds of Maui Tropical Plantation, this is an extremely tame, five-line course designed for families, with a low five-year-old, 50lb limit and dual lines. The zip over a pond adds some spice. However, without any discount for kids, families pay a lot for this two-hour experience.

Ma'alaea

Wind defines Ma'alaea. Prevailing trade winds sweep from the north, funneling down between the two great rises of Haleakalā and the West Maui Mountains straight at Ma'alaea Bay. It's no coincidence that Maui's first windmill farm marches up the slopes here. By midday you'll need to hold on to your hat.

Beaches

Ma'alaea Bay
Beach

Ma'alaea Bay is fronted by a 3-mile stretch of sand, running from Ma'alaea Harbor south to Kihei. Access is from **Haycraft Park** (Map p98; www.co.maui.hi.us; 399 Hauoli St) at the end of Hauoli St in Ma'alaea and from several places along N Kihei Rd including **Kealia Beach**, which parallels the Kealia Coastal Boardwalk. Parking is limited, but the beach is mostly deserted.

Sights

Maui Ocean Center
Aquarium

(Map p98; ✆270-7000; www.mauioceancenter.com; 192 Ma'alaea Rd; adult/child $26/19;

⏱9am-5pm Sep-Jun, to 6pm Jul & Aug; 👫) This mid-size aquarium showcases Hawaii's dazzling marine life, including many species found nowhere else. The floorplan takes you on an ocean journey, beginning with nearshore reefs teeming with colorful tropical fish and ending with deep-ocean sea life. The grand finale is a 54ft glass tunnel that leads you through the center of a large tank as toothy sharks glide by. Local ordinance prevents exhibition of live cetaceans, so there's no dolphin show. The rest is family-friendly, but pricey.

Story of Hawaii Museum Museum
(Map p98; 📞242-6938; www.storyofhawaii museum.com; 300 Ma'alaea Rd, Ma'alaea Harbor Shops; suggested donation adult/child $7/5; ⏱10am-5pm) FREE This quirky new gem offers a fascinating look at the history of Hawaii as told through centuries of maps. The collection proceeds in chronological order, encompassing early explorers, the Monarchy, Territorial days, WWII, Statehood and the Golden Era of the Matson cruise line. You can also buy *giclée* prints of what you see.

To unlock the cartographic tale, the 30-minute, docent-led tour is a must. Of particular note is a map that suggests Captain Cook may not have been the first European to discover Hawaii (see boxed text, p117).

🏃 Activities

Wicked winds from the north shoot straight out toward Kaho'olawe, creating excellent windsurfing conditions that, unlike elsewhere, persist throughout the winter. The bay also has a couple of hot surfing spots. The **Ma'alaea Pipeline** (Map p98) freight-trains right and is the fastest surf break in all Hawaii. Summer's southerly swells produce huge tubes.

Swim with the Sharks

No, this is not a trip to Wall Street. We mean *real* sharks. Some 20 of them, to be exact. Blacktip reef sharks, hammerheads and, gasp, a tiger shark. And you can jump in and join them.

Shark Dive Maui (Map p98; 📞270-7075; www.mauioceancenter.com; 2hr dive $199, incl admission to aquarium for diver & viewing guest; ⏱8:15am Mon, Wed & Fri) takes intrepid divers on a daredevil's plunge into Maui Ocean Center's 750,000-gallon deep-ocean tank to swim with the toothy beasts as aquarium visitors gaze on in disbelief.

You do need to be a certified diver over 15, and since it's limited to only four divers per day, advance reservations are essential.

Aerial view of Molokini
RON DAHLQUIST/GETTY IMAGES ©

'IAO VALLEY & CENTRAL MAUI MA'ALAEA

Lahaina Pali Trail · Hiking

(Map p98; www.mauiguidebook.com/adventures/lahaina-pali-trail) This dry and rugged trail, part of the ancient King's Trail that circles Maui (see boxed text, p220), runs from Ma'alaea up over Kealaoloa Ridge (the unmissable wind farm on the edge of the West Maui Mountains), down through Uku-mehame Gulch, and on to long and sandy Papalaua Beach, where you can snorkel and picnic.

Along the way you'll enjoy great views of Kaho'olawe and Lana'i, ancient petroglyphs, and whales in season. Download the excellent trail guide first, as it explains the 16 numbered markers en route.

The 5.5-mile trail ranges 1500ft in elevation, making it strenuous, and takes about 2½ hours one-way. You'll need to drop a car at one end if you don't want to hike or hitch back. The eastern trailhead access road, marked by a Na Ala Hele sign, is on Hwy 30, just south of its intersection with N Kihei Rd. Starting early here will keep you ahead of the blistering sun. The western trailhead is also on Hwy 30, 200yd south of the 11-mile marker. For a shortened hike with excellent views, take the eastern trailhead to the wind farm and back.

Da Beach House · Water Sports

(Map p98; ☎986-8279; www.dabeachhousemaui.com; 300 Ma'alaea Rd, Ma'alaea Harbor Shops; per day surfboards $25, SUP $40, boogie boards $10; ☻10am-6pm) Rents water-sports equipment and beach chairs.

Tours

The tour operators at Ma'alaea Harbor have consolidated reservations at **Ma'alaea Harbor Activities** (Map p98; ☎280-8073; www.maalaeaharboractivities.com; Ma'alaea Harbor; ☻9am-8pm), facing Slip 47. Here you can book fishing trips, snorkeling excursions, dinner/cocktail/sunset cruises and whale-watching trips (December 15 to May 15). They're great at comparison shopping.

Pacific Whale Foundation · Boat Tour

(Map p98; ☎249-8811; www.pacificwhale.org; 300 Ma'alaea Rd, Ma'alaea Harbor Shops; adult/child from $55/35; ☻7am-6pm) Led by naturalists, these tours do it right, with onboard snorkeling lessons and wild-life talks. Snacks are provided and kids under six are free. Half-day tours concentrate on Molokini; full-day tours add Lana'i. There's also a great variety of other tours, including whale-watching, dinner and cocktail cruises, and for the explorer, raft tours to Lana'i. Prices vary.

Quicksilver · Boat Tour

(Map p98; ☎662-0075; www.frogman-maui.com; Slip 44, Ma'alaea Harbor; adult/child $85/55) If you want more of a party

Coastal views along the Lahaina Pali Trail
RANDY BARNES/GETTY IMAGES ©

Island Insights

While most historians credit Captain James Cook with the European discovery of Hawaii, there is evidence that the Spanish may have preceded him. From South America to the Philippines, the vast Pacific was once part of Spain's overseas empire. For over two centuries galleons made the trip from Mexico to Manila and back at the mercy of the winds. Is it possible that they discovered Hawaii? Conversely, is it possible that in hundreds of round-trips they did *not*? Spanish tradition contains references to the Islas del Rey, Islas de los Jardines, Islas de las Tables and Islas de las Mesas, any one of which could be Hawaii. Top candidates for Discoverer include Juan Gaytan, based on his rudimentary account of a trip outbound from New Spain in 1555, and Francisco Gauli, whose 1582 expedition went astray of the normal galleon route.

To review some of the evidence yourself, check out the fascinating Story of Hawaii Museum (p115) in Ma'alaea. Not only do they have a Spanish map showing the Islas de las Mesas, but the map was captured from the Spanish by a British warship. In other words, Captain Cook's navy had evidence of a mid-Pacific archipelago well before Cook himself. Perhaps the good Captain had a better compass than we think.

---

scene, hop aboard this sleek double-decker catamaran. Once you're done snorkeling, your crew cranks up Jimmy Buffett and breaks out a barbecue lunch.

Eating

Ma'alaea General Store & Cafe
Cafe $

(Map p98; ☑ 242-8900; www.maalaeastore. com; 132 Ma'alaea Rd; mains $8-12; ☉6am-7pm; ☕☑) Located in the only original building left from the days when Ma'alaea was a small Japanese fishing village, this friendly general store and cafe offers deli eats, fresh-baked bread, and a rare focus on veggie and gluten-free solutions.

The porch is a great place to dive into their signature Reuben while watching the world go by. A wonderfully restored reminder of the past meets the modern marina across the street.

Hula Cookies & Ice Cream
Dessert $

(Map p98; ☑ 243-2271; www.hulacookies.com; Ma'alaea Harbor Shops; cookie $1.50, ice cream $3-6; ☉10am-6pm Mon-Sat, to 5pm Sun) The fresh-baked cookies and Maui-made ice cream here are chock-full of macadamia nuts, pineapple and coconut. A perfect place to take the kids after the nearby aquarium.

Beach Bums Bar & Grill
Barbecue $$

(Map p98; ☑ 243-2286; www.beachbums hawaii.com; Ma'alaea Harbor Shops; lunch $7-12, dinner $9-24; ☉8am-9pm) If barbecue is your thing, you'll love this lively harbor-front eatery, which uses a wood-burning rotisserie smoker to grill up everything from burgers and ribs to turkey and Spam. Come here from 3pm to 6pm for $3.25 drafts, and 5pm to 8pm for a variety of live local music.

ℹ Getting There & Away

Ma'alaea has good connections to the rest of Maui's public bus system. The Maui Bus ($2) connects the Harbor Shops at Ma'alaea with Lahaina, Kahului and Kihei. Service depends on the route, but buses operate hourly from around 6am to 8pm.

Right: Waves breaking along the coast, Kahului (p96); **Below:** Photographic displays at the Alexander & Baldwin Sugar Museum, Pu'unene

(RIGHT) MICHAEL MELFORD/GETTY IMAGES ©; (BELOW) LONELY PLANET/GETTY IMAGES ©

Kealia Pond National Wildlife Refuge

A magnet for both birds and bird-watchers, this **refuge** (Map p98; ☎875-1582; www.fws.gov/refuge/kealia_pond/; Mokulele Hwy, MP 6; ⏲7:30am-4pm Mon-Fri) **FREE** harbors native waterbirds year-round and migratory birds from October to April. In the rainy winter months Kealia Pond swells to 400 acres, making it one of the largest natural ponds in Hawaii. In summer it shrinks to half that size, creating the skirt of crystalline salt that gives Kealia (meaning 'salt-encrusted place') its name.

Birding is excellent from the coastal boardwalk and the refuge's **headquarters** (Map p98; ⏲7:30am-4pm Mon-Fri) off Mokulele Hwy (Hwy 311) at the 6-mile marker, where there's a small, child-friendly visitors center. In both places,

you're almost certain to spot wading *ae'o* (Hawaiian black-necked stilts) and Hawaiian coots, two endangered species that thrive here. In winter ospreys can sometimes be seen diving for fish. The coastal marsh and dunes nestling Kealia Pond are also a nesting site for the endangered hawksbill sea turtle.

Activities

Kealia Coastal Boardwalk
Boardwalk

(Map p98; www.fws.gov/refuge/kealia_pond; Kealia Pond National Wildlife Refuge) This wonderful elevated boardwalk by Ma'alaea Bay seems to go on forever. It traverses over 2000ft of wetlands, making it a magnet for birders but also a great nature walk for anyone. Interpretive plaques and benches help along the way. In winter you may spot humpback whales. Located 0.2 miles north of the 2-mile marker on N Kihei Rd.

Pu'unene

Sugar is the lifeblood of Pu'unene. Endless fields of cane expand out from the Hawaiian Commercial & Sugar (C&S) Company's rusty old mill, the last of its kind in Hawaii. Its industrial hulk looms high overhead, belching smoke; if you smell molasses, they're boiling down sugarcane. Hidden nearby is the remains of a barely surviving plantation village, including an old schoolhouse, a long-abandoned church, and a shack that's served as a used **bookstore (Map p98;** ⏱**9am-4pm Tue-Sat)** since 1913. It's a bit musty, but still sells books for a dime!

To see all this, turn off Mokulele Hwy (Hwy 311) onto Hansen Rd and take the first right onto Old Pu'unene Ave, continuing past the old Pu'unene Meat Market building (c 1926) and the unmissable mill. Turn left after 0.6 miles, past a little bridge. Just before the pavement ends, turn right and drive behind the old school to reach the bookstore.

Sights

Alexander & Baldwin Sugar Museum
Museum

(Map p98; ☎**871-8058; www.sugarmuseum .com; 3957 Hansen Rd; adult/child $7/2;** ⏱**9:30am-4:30pm)** This homespun museum occupies the former residence of the sugar mill's superintendent. There's the usual display of industrial machinery, including a working model of a cane-crushing plant, but what lingers afterward is the human story.

The museum traces how the sons of missionaries took control of Maui's fertile valleys and dug the amazing irrigation system that made large-scale plantations viable. It also contains an early-20th-century labor contract from the Japanese Emigration Company committing laborers to work the cane fields 10 hours a day, 26 days a month, for $15.

Kihei & South Maui

Sunsets are a communal affair in South Maui – just look at the throngs crowding the beach wall at Kamaʻole Beach Park II in the late afternoon. It's a scene repeated up and down the coast here every day.

Dubbed Haole-wood for its LA-style strip malls and white-bread resorts, the region is a bit shiny and overbuilt. But dig deeper and you'll find a mixed plate of scenery and adventure, from Kihei to Wailea, Makena and beyond, that's truly unique. You can snorkel reefs teeming with turtles, kayak to remote bays or sail in an outrigger canoe.

The coral gardens are so rich you can dive from the shore. And the beaches are undeniably glorious, whether you're looking to relax beneath a resort cabana or to discover your own pocket of sand. Add reliably sunny weather, quiet coastal trails and a diverse dining scene and South Maui's a pretty irresistible place to strand yourself.

Ulua Beach (p138), Wailea

Kihei & South Maui Itineraries

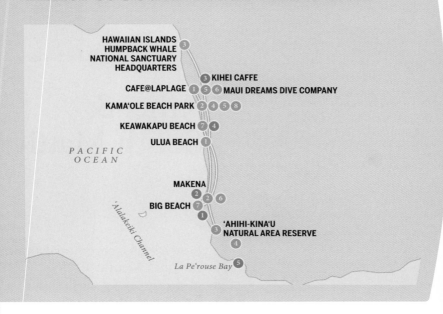

HAWAIIAN ISLANDS
HUMPBACK WHALE
NATIONAL SANCTUARY
HEADQUARTERS

KIHEI CAFFE

CAFE@LAPLAGE · MAUI DREAMS DIVE COMPANY

KAMA'OLE BEACH PARK

KEAWAKAPU BEACH

ULUA BEACH

PACIFIC
OCEAN

MAKENA

BIG BEACH

'AHIHI-KINA'U
NATURAL AREA RESERVE

'Alalakeiki Channel

La Pe'rouse Bay

Two Days

1 Ulua Beach (p138) In the morning, snorkel north to coral gardens teeming with fish at Maui's favorite snorkel spot.

2 Café O'Lei (p133) For lunch, try his stylish bistro, which serves savory Maui-centric fare. The blackened mahimahi with fresh salsa is always a tasty choice.

3 Hawaiian Islands Humpback Whale National Sanctuary Headquarters (p126) Showcasing Maui's marine life and its famous annual visitors, the humpback whales. Next door at Kalepolepo Beach Park, splash beside an ancient Hawaiian fishpond on a kid-friendly beach.

4 Kama'ole Beach Park II (p125) Join the crowds for a gorgeous sunset.

5 808 Bistro (p135) Stroll to the patio for gourmet comfort food and cap the night with dancing at South Shore Tiki Lounge.

6 Makena Landing (p144) Start your second day kayaking south through water thick with green sea turtles. On land, the nearby Keawala'i Congregational Church offers a glimpse into Makena's *paniolo* (Hawaiian cowboy) past.

7 Big Beach (Oneloa; p146) This magnificent stretch of sand and surf in Makena State Park is untouched by development. Bathing suit feeling restrictive? You can always climb the hill to Little Beach where some folks think beachwear is overrated.

THIS LEG: 30 MILES

Four Days

1 **Cafe@LaPlage** (p132) If you have four days in South Maui, plan your first two as above. On day three, fuel up with coffee and a breakfast bagel at this south Kihei spot.

2 **Malu'aka Beach** (p144) Before the wind picks up, head south to this pretty strand. Nicknamed Turtle Beach, it's the best place on Maui to swim among green sea turtles. For lunch, Jawz Fish Tacos just south serves tasty food truck fare.

3 **'Ahihi-Kina'u Natural Area Reserve** (p148) Cruise through a lava wonderland – and enjoy more snorkeling.

4 **Makena Stables** (p149) Giddy up for a sunset ride up the slopes of 'Ulupalakua Ranch with a Maui-born cowboy whose stories are as fascinating as the terrain.

5 **Kihei Caffe** (p132) In the morning, enjoy a veggie scramble, a big cup of coffee and a side of people-watching on the bustling patio at this cafe in Kihei Kalama Village, aka the Triangle.

6 **Maui Dreams Dive Company** (p127) Take the plunge with this personable bunch of folks specializing in shore dives.

7 **Keawakapu Beach** (p125) On your last evening, pack a towel and relax on Kihei's loveliest strand.

8 **Da Kitchen Express** (p133) End the day with the flavors of Maui: a hearty helping of *kalua* pork and two scoops of rice followed by a rainbow-bright Big Baby from Local Boys Shave Ice.

⊙ **THIS LEG: 35 MILES**

Kihei & South Maui Highlights

1 **Best Beach: Big Beach** (p146) Gleaming sands, wild forests, blue water – aloha from the heart of Makena State Park.

2 **Best Snorkeling: Malu'aka Beach** (p144) Green sea turtles here, green sea turtles there – at Turtle Beach these graceful beasts are everywhere.

3 **Best Breakfast Scene: Kihei Caffe** (p132) Imagine your favorite hometown diner but outdoors and with papaya and *loco moco* on the menu.

4 **Best Sunset: Keawakapu Beach** (p125) Bring a chair – sunsets at this soft-sand crescent are a nightly performance.

5 **Best Lava Landscape: La Pe'rouse Bay** (p148) Eerie yet beautiful, this craggy black lawn feels like the dark side of the moon.

Beach volleyball, Keawakapu Beach (p125)
LONELY PLANET/GETTY IMAGES ©

Discover Kihei & South Maui

Kihei

This energetic community is a good choice for short-trip vacationers who want to maximize their beach time and their budgets – and throw in an adventure or two. Yes, it's overrun with strip malls, but with 6 miles of sunny beaches, loads of affordable accommodations and a variety of dining options, it offers everything you need for an enjoyable seaside vacation.

Lifeguard post along Kama'ole Beach
MICHELE FALZONE/GETTY IMAGES ©

To zip from one end of Kihei to the other, take the Pi'ilani Hwy (Hwy 31). It runs parallel to and bypasses the stop-start traffic of S Kihei Rd. Well-marked crossroads connect these two routes.

Beaches

The further south you travel, the better the beaches. At the northern end of Kihei, swimming is not advised, but kayaking is good in the morning and windsurfers set off in the afternoon. The beaches below are listed from north to south. For a list of facilities at each beach, visit www.co.maui.hi.us.

Mai Poina 'Oe la'u Beach Park   Beach
(Map p129) This long sandy beach at the northern end of Kihei is a popular morning launch for outrigger canoes and kayaks. After the wind picks up in the afternoon, it's South Maui's main venue for windsurfing.

Kalepolepo Beach Park   Beach
(Map p129; 👫) Adjacent to the headquarters for the Humpback Whale National Marine Sanctuary, this compact park is a nice spot for families with younger kids. A grassy lawn is fronted by the ancient **Ko'ie'ie Fishpond** (Map p129), whose stone walls create a shallow swimming pool with calm waters perfect for wading. There are also picnic tables, a grill and an outdoor shower.

Punahoa Beach   Beach
(Map p126) This discreet postage-stamp-sized beach, embraced by a rocky lava shoreline, is Kihei's best bet for swimming with turtles. Forget it, however, if it's not a calm day. The beach is reached via shoreline access at the northern side of Punahoa condos.

Charley Young Beach
Beach

(Map p126; 2200 S Kihei Rd) On a side street, out of view of the main drag, this neighborhood beach is the least-touristed strand in Kihei. It's a real jewel in the rough: broad and sandy, and backed by swaying coconut palms. You're apt to find fishers casting their lines, families playing volleyball and someone strumming a guitar. It also has some of the better bodysurfing waves in Kihei.

Beach parking is on the corner of S Kihei Rd and Kaia'u Pl. To get to the beach, walk to the end of Kaia'u Pl.

Kama'ole Beach Parks
Beach

(S Kihei Rd) Kama'ole Beach is having so much fun, it just keeps rolling along. And along. And along. Divided into three sections by rocky points, these popular strands are known locally as **Kam I (Map p126; 2400 S Kihei Rd), Kam II (Map p126; 2550 S Kihei Rd)** and **Kam III (Map p126; 2800 S Kihei Rd)**. All three are pretty, golden-sand beaches with full facilities and lifeguards. There's a volleyball court at Kam I and parking lots at Kam I and III.

Travelers with disabilities can access the ocean at Kam I using a sand beach chair. For details about ADA accessibility and the sand beach chair, check the Kamaole I listing at www.co.maui.hi.us or call ☏270-6136.

Water conditions vary with the weather, but swimming is usually good. For the most part, these beaches have sandy bottoms with a fairly steep drop, which tends to create good conditions for bodysurfing, especially in winter.

For snorkeling, the southern end of Kama'ole Beach Park III has some nearshore rocks harboring a bit of coral and a few colorful fish, though it pales in comparison to the snorkeling at beaches further south.

Keawakapu Beach
Beach

(Map p126) From break of day to twilight, this sparkling stretch of sand is a show-stopper. Extending from south Kihei to Wailea's Mokapu Beach, Keawakapu is set back from the main road and is less visible than Kihei's main roadside beaches

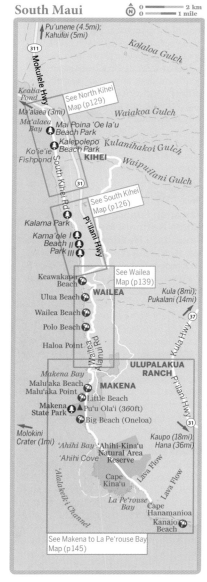

just north. It's also less crowded, and is a great place to watch the sunset.

With its cushiony soft sand, Keawakapu is also a favorite for sunrise yoga and wake-up strolls and is the perfect spot for an end-of-day swim. Mornings are best for snorkeling: head to the rocky outcrops that form the northern and southern ends of the beach. During winter look for humpback whales, which come remarkably close to shore here.

There are three beach access points, all with outdoor showers. To get to the southern end, drive south on S Kihei Rd until it dead-ends at a beach parking lot. Near the middle of the beach, there's a parking lot at the corner of Kilohana Dr and S Kihei Rd. At the northern end, beach parking can be found in a large unpaved access lot north of the Days Inn.

◎ Sights

Hawaiian Islands Humpback Whale National Marine Sanctuary Headquarters Museum

(Map p129; ☎879-2818, 800-831-4888; www.hawaiihumpbackwhale.noaa.gov; 726 S Kihei Rd; ☉10am-3pm Mon-Fri, plus 10am-1pm Sat early Jan-Mar;) FREE The newly revamped marine sanctuary headquarters overlooks the ancient Koʻieʻie Fishpond, and its oceanfront lookout is ideal for viewing the humpback whales that frequent the bay during winter. Free scopes are set up for viewing. Inside, displays and videos provide background, and there are lots of informative brochures about whales and other Hawaiian wildlife. Swing by at 11am on Tuesday or Thursday for the free '45-Ton Talks' about whales.

David Malo's Church Church

(Map p129; www.trinitybts.org; 100 Kulanihakoʻi St) Philosopher David Malo, who built this church in 1852, was the first Hawaiian ordained to the Christian ministry. He was also co-author of Hawaii's first Constitution and an early spokesperson for Hawaiian rights. While most of Malo's original church has been dismantled, a 3ft-high section of the wall still stands beside a palm grove. Pews are lined up inside the stone walls. It's really quite beautiful.

Open-air services are held at 9am on Sunday by Trinity Episcopal Church-by-the-Sea. All are welcome.

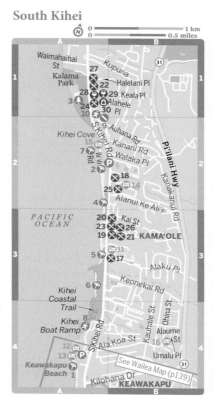

South Kihei

Kalama Park Park

(Map p126; 1900 S Kihei Rd;) Athletes, skate rats and fidgety toddlers will appreciate this expansive seaside park which has tennis and basketball courts, ball fields and a skate park. Also on-site are a playground, picnic pavilions, restrooms and showers. Although there is a small beach, behind a whale statue, a runoff ditch carries wastewater here after heavy rains so it's best to swim elsewhere.

The park is across Kihei Rd from the busy bar and restaurant scene at Kihei Kalama Village.

Kihei Coastal Trail Waterfront

This short trail meanders along coastal bluffs ideal for whale-watching and quiet meditation. You might even see an outrigger canoe glide past. At the start of the trail look for the burrows of ʻuaʻu kani

South Kihei

(wedge-tailed shearwaters), ground-nesting seabirds that return to the same sites each spring. The birds lay a single egg and remain until November, when the fledglings are large enough to head out to sea. The trail starts beyond the grassy lawn at the southern end of Kama'ole Beach Park III and winds half a mile south to Kihei Surfside condos, just beyond the Kihei Boat Ramp.

The path is made of packed gray gravel outlined in white coral. Curiously, when the trail was being built, a storm washed hundreds of yards of bleached coral onto the shore here. The coral was not originally planned for the trail construction, but the volunteers building the trail consulted with a Hawaiian kahuna (priest) and were told ancient trails were often outlined in white coral so they could be followed at night. The Hawaiian gods were thanked for the gift of coral, which was then incorporated into the trail.

◎ Activities

South Maui's top activities are water-based. Stand up paddle surfing (SUP) looks easy, and it is a learnable sport, but currents off Maui can carry you down the coast very quickly. Best to start with a lesson before renting a board.

Maui Dreams Dive Co
Diving, Snorkeling

(Map p126; ☎874-5332; www.mauidreamsdive co.com; 1993 S Kihei Rd; shore dives $69-129, boat dives $129; ◷7am-6pm) Maui Dreams is a first-rate, five-star PADI operation specializing in shore dives. With this family-run outfit, a dive trip is like going out with friends. Nondivers, ask about the introductory dive ($89), and to zoom around underwater, check out its scooter dive ($99 to $129).

South Pacific Kayaks & Outfitters
Kayaking

(☎875-4848; www.southpacifickayaks.com; kay-ak rental/tour from $45/69; ◷rentals 6:45-11am, reservations 6am-8pm) This top-notch opera-tion leads kayak-and-snorkel tours. It also rents kayaks for those who want to go off on their own, and will deliver them to Mak-ena Landing by reservation. Surfing and SUP lessons are also available, as well as hiking trips. The company also rents stand up paddle boards, surfboards and kayaks (reservations strongly recommended) across from Kalama Park, near the 76 Gas Station, from 7:30am to 11:30am.

Stand Up Paddle Surf School
Paddle Boarding

(📞 579-9231; www.standuppaddlesurfschool.com; 90min lesson $165) This SUP school is owned by Maria Souza, the first woman surfer to tow into the monster waves at Jaws, Maui's famous big-wave surfing spot, and a champion paddle-surfer. Small classes and safety are priorities, and the paddling location is determined by weather and water conditions. Classes fill quickly, so call a few days – or a week – ahead.

Blue Water Rafting
Rafting, Snorkeling

(Map p126; 📞 879-7238; www.bluewaterrafting.com; tours $39-135) In a hurry? Try the Molokini Express trip if you want to zip out to the crater, snorkel and be back within two hours. An adventurous half-day trip heads southward on a motorized raft for snorkeling among sea turtles and dolphins at remote coves along Maui's lava-rock coast, which is beyond La Pe'rouse Bay. Trips depart from the Kihei Boat Ramp.

Maui Dive Shop
Diving, Snorkeling

(Map p129; 📞 879-3388; www.mauidiveshop.com; 1455 S Kihei Rd; 2-tank dives $140-150, snorkel rentals per day $6-8; 🕐 7am-9pm) This is a good spot to rent or buy water-sports gear, including boogie boards, snorkels and wetsuits. Also rents Jeep Wranglers.

South Maui Bicycles
Bicycle Rental

(Map p126; 📞 874-0068; www.southmauibicycles.com; 1993 S Kihei Rd, Island Surf Bldg; per day $22-60, per week $99-250; 🕐 10am-6pm Mon-Sat) Rents top-of-the-line Trek and Gary Fisher road bicycles, as well as basic around-town bikes. Bike lanes run along both the Pi'ilani Hwy and S Kihei Rd, but cyclists need to be cautious of inattentive drivers making sudden turns across lanes.

🎊 Festivals & Events

World Whale Day
Outdoor Festival

(www.mauiwhalefestival.org) Organized by the Pacific Whale Foundation, this family-friendly bash celebrates Maui's humpback whales with a parade, crafts, live music, food booths and environmental displays. It's held at Kalama Park on a Saturday in mid-February.

Kihei First Friday
Street Carnival

(www.mauifridays.com) On the fourth Friday night of the month, between 6pm and 9pm, make your way to Azeka Mauka II for arts, crafts, live music, kiddie events and food trucks.

Sleeping

Condos are plentiful in Kihei, while hotels and B&Bs are few. Some condominium complexes maintain a front desk that handles bookings, but others are booked via rental agents. Be sure to ask about reservation fees, cleaning fees and cancellation policies, which vary. Traffic along S Kihei Rd can be noisy, so avoid rooms close to the road. Prices drop dramatically in the low season, which is typically April to mid-December.

Pineapple Inn Maui
Inn $$

(Map p139; 📞 877-212-6284, 298-4403; www.pineappleinnmaui.com; 3170 Akala Dr; r $159-169, cottages $255; ❄ 🛜 🏊) For style with a personal touch, consider this inviting, nicely priced boutique inn that's less than a mile from the beach. Rooms, which have ocean-view lanai (verandas) and private entrances, are as attractive as those at the exclusive resorts, but at a fraction of the cost. You can watch the sunset from the pool. Rooms have kitchenettes, and the two-bedroom cottage comes with a full kitchen. The inn is at the southern end of Kihei, bordering Wailea.

Ocean Breeze Hideaway
B&B $$

(Map p129; 📞 888-463-6687, 879-0657; www.hawaiibednbreakfast.com; 435 Kalalau Pl; r incl breakfast from $99; @ 🛜) This welcoming B&B, in a residential neighborhood, is one of the best deals in Kihei. Owners Bob and Sande have run Ocean Breeze for 14 years and are a treasure trove of insider tips. Their low-key home has two comfortable guest rooms, one with a queen bed and ceiling fans, the other with a king bed

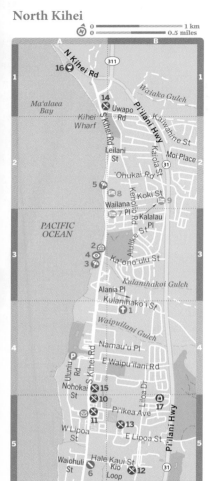

ing with whimsical maritime imagery. The Poolside Sweet, with its sunset colors and in-room guitar, might inspire your own inner songwriter. Organic island fruit is provided for breakfast. Both units have kitchenettes, and the Ocean Ohana suite has air-con. Families are welcome.

Formerly known as Two Mermaids, the new name reflects the owners' status as *tutus* – or grandmothers.

Kihei Kai Nani
Condo $$

(Map p126; ☏879-9088, 800-473-1493; www.kiheikainani.com; 2495 S Kihei Rd; 1br $168; 🛜⊠) Rooms and decor may be a little dated, but when it comes to amenities, this inviting low-rise condo is on par with more expensive properties. On-site are a large pool, a laundry room, shuffleboard, barbecue grills and picnic tables – all fringed by colorful tropical landscaping. All units but one have air-con. Kama'ole Beach Park II is across the street.

and air-con. Both have a private entrance and a refrigerator. The couple also rents a two-bedroom oceanfront condo (from $210 per night; no breakfast).

Tutu Mermaids
on Maui B&B
B&B $$

(Map p126; ☏874-8687, 800-598-9550; www.twomermaids.com; 2840 Umalu Pl; d incl breakfast $180-200; @🛜⊠👪) I'd like to be, under the sea... Yep, the happy-go-lucky Beatles tune springs to mind inside the Ocean Ohana suite, a bright space swirl-

Island Insights

In ancient Hawaii, coastal fishponds were built to provide a ready source of fish for royal families. The most intact fishpond remaining on Maui is the 3-acre Koʻieʻie Fishpond (p124), now on the National Register of Historic Places. This fascinating place borders both Kalepolepo Beach Park and the Hawaiian Islands Humpback Whale National Marine Sanctuary Headquarters.

With about 160 rentable units, give these helpful folks a call if you've landed in Maui without reservations. They may have room or can suggest alternatives.

Nona Lani Cottages   Cottages **$$**
(Map p129; ☎879-2497; www.nonalanicottages. com; 455 S Kihei Rd; cottages $195; ❄ 🛜)

Wooden cottages, lazy hammocks, picnic tables, swaying palms – this place looks like the tropical version of Camp Minnehaha. The eight retro cottages are compact but squeeze in a full kitchen, private lanai, living room with daybed and a bedroom with a queen bed, plus cable TV. Also offers hotel-like suites ($165 per night), which aren't shown on the website. Wi-fi is available in the lobby area.

Kihei Surfside Resort   Condo **$$**
(Map p126; www.kiheisurfsideresort.com; 2936 S Kihei Rd; 1br/2br from $180/360; 🏊) Tucked between the Kihei Coastal Trail and Keawakapu Beach, this six-story condo complex sports a bit of natty style – just look at that crisp, green lawn. Units are managed by a variety of management companies, and some individual owners. Photos, rates and contact information for each unit are on the Kihei Surfside website. All have full kitchens, and the grounds include a heated oceanside pool and a putting green.

Punahoa Condo $$$

(Map p126; ☏ 879-2720, 800-564-4380; www.punahoabeach. com; 2142 Iliʻili Rd; studio $189, 1br $269-294, 2br $299; 🛜) Sip coffee, scan for whales, savor sunsets – it's hard to leave your lanai at Punahoa, a classy boutique condo where every unit has a clear-on ocean view. Tucked on a quiet side street, this 15-unit complex offers privacy and warm alohas. It's also next to a gorgeous strand of sand, Punahoa Beach, that's a favorite of turtles and surfers. Penthouse units have air-conditioning. Cleaning fees from $90 per visit.

Mana Kai Maui Condo $$$

(Map p126; ☏ 800-525-2025, 879-1561; www. manakaimaui.com; 2960 S Kihei Rd; r/1br/2br from $298/473/547; ❄🛜🏊) From her throne overlooking Keawakapu Beach, Mana Kai Maui has much to admire in her small seaside kingdom. The sunset views from the beach are some of the best in Kihei, and guests can swim and snorkel in the ocean right outside the door. The on-site rental company, with a front desk, manages hotel rooms (with microwaves and mini-refrigerators) and one- and two-bedroom condos. Decor varies.

Request an upper floor for the best views. The full-service restaurant here, Five Palms (p136), is famous for its sunset happy hour.

Maui Coast Hotel Hotel $$$

(Map p126; ☏ 800-895-6284, 874-6284; www.mauicoasthotel.com; 2259 S Kihei Rd; r $300-349, ste $325-379; 🅿❄@🛜🏊) The snazzy Maui Coast has a lot going for it – sharp, modern rooms and a fun poolside bar – but the daily resort fee of $17.50 is off-putting. The property is not on the beach, and it's more hotel than tradi-tional resort. The included local shuttle service is a nice touch. Overall, it's clean and comfortable, and its location back from the road keeps it quieter than other places on the strip.

131

The Best...
South Maui for Kids

1 Ulua Beach (p138)

2 Hawaiian Sailing Canoe Adventures (p140)

3 Kama'ole Beach Park III (p125)

4 Local Boys Shave Ice

5 Hawaiian Islands Humpback Whale National Marine Sanctuary Headquarters (p126)

The resort fee also includes parking and wi-fi (but iPad users may have problems connecting).

Maui Sunseeker   Hotel $$$

(Map p129; ☎ 800-532-6284, 879-1261; www.mauisunseeker.com; 551 S Kihei Rd; r $239, ste $289-349; ❄ @ 🛜) After a no-holds-barred makeover on the Travel Channel's reality show *Hotel Impossible*, the Maui Sunseeker emerged sleeker, smarter and, dare we say, a bit more fun. Catering to gays and lesbians this breezy boutique hotel sprawls across five buildings in north Kihei, across the street from Mai Poina 'Oela'u Beach. The revamp is ongoing, but the low-key tropical decor outshines other places in this price range.

Watch for a new reception area and cafe. The clothing optional rooftop deck is still open. The property is adults only.

 Eating

808 Deli   Cafe $

(Map p126; ☎ 879-1111; www.808deli.net; 2511 S Kihei Rd, Suite 102; breakfast $5-7, lunch $6-8; ⏱ 9am-5pm) As Subway wept and Quizno's cried, 808 Deli tap-danced its way into our sandwich-loving hearts. With fresh breads, gourmet spreads and 19 different sandwiches and paninis, this tiny gourmet sandwich shop across from Kam II is the place to grab a picnic lunch. For a spicy kick, try the roast beef with pepper jack and wasabi aioli.

Kihei Caffe   Cafe $

(Map p126; www.kiheicaffe.net; 1945 S Kihei Rd, Kihei Kalama Village; mains $6-13; ⏱ 5am-2pm) Solos, couples, families – everybody's here or on the way. If you're a Kihei Caffe newbie, here's the deal: step to the side to review the menu before joining the queue. The cashier is chatty, but he keeps that long line moving. Next, fill your coffee cup at the thermos, snag a table on the patio then watch the breakfast burritos, veggie scrambles and *loco moco* (rice, hamburger patty and fried egg) flash by. Keep an eye on those sneaky birds on the patio. Cash only.

Local Boys Shave Ice   Shave Ice $

(Map p126; www.localboysshaveice.com; 1941 S Kihei Rd, Kihei Kalama Village; shave ice from $4.50; ⏱ 10am-9pm) Local Boys dishes up soft shaved ice drenched in a rainbow of sweet syrups. We like it tropical (banana, mango and 'shark's blood') with ice cream, *kauai* cream and azuki beans. Load up on napkins, these babies are messy! Cash only.

Cafe@LaPlage   Cafe $

(Map p126; www.cafe-maui.com; 2395 S Kihei Rd, Dolphin Plaza; sandwiches $4-12; ⏱ 6:30am-5pm Mon-Sat, to 3pm Sun; 🛜) They stack the sandwiches high at this small cafe and coffee shop. At breakfast, choose from five different bagel sandwiches or get your bagel with a simple slather of cinnamon-honey butter. Lunchtime paninis include the Maui Melt, with turkey, bacon, pepper jack, avocados and jalapeños. Wi-fi is free, and there are computers in the front ($3 for the first 15 minutes, then 15¢ per minute).

Amigo's   Mexican $

(Map p129; ☎ 879-9952; www.amigosmaui.com; 1215 S Kihei Rd; breakfast $6-12, most mains lunch & dinner $6-16; ⏱ 8am-9pm Sun-Thu, 9am-10pm Fri & Sat) On Tuesday burritos are only $7 at this family-run Mexican restaurant that's part of a small island-wide chain.

Come here for huevos rancheros, sizzling fajitas and combo plates. Staff is attentive, and the salsa bar is a can't miss if you like to spice it up.

Café O'Lei
Hawaii Regional **$$**

(Map p126; ☎891-1368; www.cafeoleimaui.com; 2439 S Kihei Rd, Rainbow Mall; lunch $8-16, dinner $17-27; ⏰10:30am-3:30pm & 4:30-9:30pm) This strip mall bistro looks rather ho-hum at first blush. But step inside. The sophisticated atmosphere, innovative Hawaii Regional cuisine, honest prices and excellent service knock Café O'Lei into the fine-dining big leagues. For a tangy treat, order the blackened mahimahi with fresh papaya salsa. Look for unbeatable lunch mains, with salads, for under $10, and a sushi chef after 4:30pm. Famous martinis, too.

Da Kitchen Express
Hawaii Regional **$$**

(Map p126; www.da-kitchen.com; 2439 S Kihei Rd, Rainbow Mall; breakfast $9-13, lunch & dinner $9-18.50; ⏰9am-9pm) Tucked at the back of anvil-shaped Rainbow Mall, this no-frills eatery is all about Hawaiian plate lunches. The local favorite is Da Lau Lau Plate (with steamed pork wrapped in taro leaves), but you won't go wrong with any choice, from charbroiled teriyaki chicken to the gravy-laden *loco moco*. We particularly liked the spicy *kalua* pork.

Fabiani's Bakery & Pizza
Italian **$$**

(Map p129; ☎874-1234; www.fabianis.com; 95 E Lipoa St; breakfast $3-9, lunch $8-14, dinner $11-17; ⏰7am-10pm) What puts the fab in Fabiani's? Definitely the prosciutto, mozzarella and arugula pizza with truffle oil. Or wait, maybe it's the linguini with sautéed clams. Or the chef-made pastries preening like celebrities

as you walk in the door. Whatever your choice, you'll surely feel fabulous nibbling your meal inside this sparkling Italian eatery and pastry shop. There's also a rather nice bar.

Kina'ole Grill
Food Truck **$$**

(Map p126; www.facebook.com/kinaolegrillfoodtruck; 11 Alanui Keali'i Dr; $12-14; ⏰11am-8pm) Hawaiian-style fish and seafood plates are the tasty specialties at this tropically bright food truck that parks on Alanui Keali'i Rd, not far from Kama'ole Beach Park I. The coconut shrimp comes with sweet Thai chili sauce. Cash only.

Coconut's Fish Cafe
Seafood **$$**

(Map p129; ☎875-9979; www.coconutsfishcafe.com; 1279 S Kihei Rd, Azeka Mauka II; mains $12-17; ⏰11am-9pm; 👪) This breezy spot is Kihei's go-to spot for fresh, healthily prepared seafood. Order at the counter – we recommend the fish tacos – then settle in at one of the surfboard tables. All the fish is grilled, all ingredients are homemade (except the catsup), and the staff is welcoming.

Children at Local Boys Shave Ice, Kihei
LONELY PLANET/GETTY IMAGES ©

With its quick service, children's menu and low-fuss decor, Coconut's is a great choice for families with younger kids.

Sansei Seafood Restaurant & Sushi Bar
Japanese $$

(Map p126; 879-0004; www.sanseihawaii.com; 1881 S Kihei Rd, Kihei Town Center; appetizers $3-15, mains $10-48; 5:30-10pm, to 1am Thu-Sat) Maui is laid-back, but sometime you have to plan ahead. Dinner at Sansei is one of those times – make a reservation or queue early for the sushi bar. The creative appetizer menu offers everything from a shrimp cake with ginger-lime chili butter to lobster-and-blue-crab ravioli. Fusion dishes include Japanese jerk chicken with garlic mashed potatoes and herb beurre fondue.

Between 5:30pm and 6pm all food is discounted 25%, and sushi is discounted 50% from 10pm to 1am Thursday through Saturday.

Eskimo Candy
Seafood $$

(Map p129; 891-8898; www.eskimocandy.com; 2665 Wai Wai Pl; most mains $8-14; 10:30am-7pm Mon-Fri;) Tucked on a side street, Eskimo Candy is a fish market with a takeout counter and a few tables. Fresh-fish fanatics should key in on the *poke* (cubed, marinated raw fish), ahi (yellowfin tuna) wraps and fish tacos.

Parents will appreciate the under $8 kids' menu.

Maui Thai Bistro
Thai $$

(Map p126; www.mauithaibistro.com; 2439 S Kihei Rd, Rainbow Mall; lunch $12-16, dinner $12-19; 5-9pm daily, 11:30am-2:30pm Tue-Sun) Chef Prakong Tongsod was one half of the famed 'Thai by Prakong/Thai by Pranee' eatery in Hana, known for its fresh and savory Thai fare. In 2013, she moved her kitchen to Kihei. This new venture serves authentic Thai dishes, with seasonal menu changes.

As for service, the bistro may still be working out a kink or two, but the noodles and curries are spiced just right.

Pita Paradise
Mediterranean $$

(Map p126; 875-7679; www.pitaparadisehawaii.com; 1913 S Kihei Rd, Kihei Kalama Village; mains $8-20; 11am-9:30pm) Aloha. *Yassou*. And dig in. Enjoy gyros and kabobs at this low-key Greek favorite in the Triangle. Place you order at the counter.

Roadside farmers market, Kihei

808 Bistro

Bistro $$$

(Map p126; ☎879-8008; www.808bistro.com; 2511 S Kihei Rd; breakfast $7-15, dinner $15-24; ⏰7am-noon & 5-9pm) This open-air eatery showcases comfort foods prepared with a gourmet spin – think short-rib pot pie and gorgonzola alfredo with shrimp. Kiss your diet good-bye at breakfast with the decadent whale pie with ham, hash browns, egg, cheese and gravy.

The restaurant, owned by the maestro's behind 808 Deli, is BYOB with a $5 corkage fee.

'ami 'ami Bar & Grill

Seafood, Steakhouse $$$

(Map p126; ☎875-7522; www.mauicoasthotel.com; 2259 S Kihei Rd, Maui Coast Hotel; breakfast $6-13, dinner $17-44; ⏰7-11am & 5-9pm) Your first thought as you cruise past the chic and sultry glow of 'ami 'ami? Hey baby, you're looking fine tonight. Things are even more fine inside this latest venture from the folks behind ever-popular Café O'Lei. With an easy indoor-outdoor flow, hospitable service and a short but satisfying menu of steaks and seafood dishes, it's a stylish place to unwind.

At breakfast, enjoy lip-smacking fare like the chorizo and jack cheese omelet, *kalua* pork hash and eggs, and bananas foster pancakes.

Foodland

Supermarket

(Map p126; ☎879-9350; www.foodland.com; 1881 S Kihei Rd, Kihei Town Center; ⏰24hr) Handy 24-hour supermarket.

Safeway

Supermarket

(Map p129; ☎891-9120; www.safeway.com; 277 Pi'ikea Ave, Pi'ilani Village; ⏰24hr) Twenty-four-hour supermarket.

Hawaiian Moons Natural Foods

Supermarket

(Map p129; ☎875-4356; www.hawaiianmoons.com; 2411 S Kihei Rd, Kama'ole Beach Center; ⏰8am-9pm;) Pack a healthy picnic lunch or build a masterpiece at the salad bar.

The Best...
Bars

1 Monkeypod Kitchen (p142)

2 Dog & Duck

3 South Shore Tiki Lounge (p136)

4 Red Bar at Gannon's (p143)

5 Five Palms (p136)

Kihei Farmers Market

Market

(Map p129; 61 S Kihei Rd; ⏰8am-4pm Mon-Thu, to 5pm Fri) Sells island-grown fruits and vegetables – a bit pricey but fresh.

Yee's Orchard

Fruit Stand

(Map p129; 1165 S Kihei Rd; ⏰11am-5pm Tue-Thu, Sat & Sun) For out-of-this-world mangoes from May through summer, pull over for this 60-year-old fruit stand just north of Long's Drugs.

Drinking & Nightlife

Most bars in Kihei are across the street from the beach and have nightly entertainment. Kihei Kalama Village, aka the Bar-muda Triangle (or just the Triangle), is crammed tight with buzzy watering holes.

Dog & Duck

Pub

(Map p126; ☎875-9669; www.theworldfamous doganddduck.com; 1913 S Kihei Rd, Kihei Kalama Village; ⏰11am-2am Mon-Fri, 8am-2am Sat & Sun) This lively Irish pub with a welcoming vibe attracts a younger crowd. And yes, it has sports on TV, but it's not blaring from every corner.

Decent spuds and pub grub go along with the heady Guinness draft.

South Shore Tiki Lounge Bar

(Map p126; www.southshoretikilounge.com; 1913 S Kihei Rd, Kihei Kalama Village; ⏱11am-2am; 📶) This cozy tropical shack has a heart as big as its lanai. The drink maestros here regularly win annual *MauiTime Weekly* awards for best female and male bartenders. It's good for dancing too.

Five Palms Cocktail Bar

(Map p126; www.5palmsrestaurant.com; 2960 S Kihei Rd, Mana Kai Maui; ⏱8am-11pm, happy hour 3-7pm & 9-11pm) For sunset cocktails beside the beach, this is the place. Arrive an hour before the sun goes down because the patio, just steps from stunning Keawakapu Beach, fills quickly. Sushi and *pupu* (snacks) are half price during happy hour.

Ambrosia Martini Lounge Bar

(Map p126; www.ambrosiamaui.com; 1913 S Kihei Rd, Kihei Kalama Village; ⏱8pm-1:30am Mon-Wed, 7pm-2am Thu-Sun, happy hour 7-9pm Thu-Sat & all night Sun) Nicknamed 'Amnesia' by locals, this compact martini bar brings a hint of nightclub style to Kihei – but without the pretension. Look for live music or a DJ nightly. Two-for-one martinis during happy hour.

Dina's Sandwitch Pub

(Map p129; www.dinassandwitch.com; 145 N Kihei Rd, Sugar Beach Resort; ⏱11am-late) The mai tais are handcrafted at Dina's, a convivial, come-as-you-are locals' joint in north Kihei. For something decadent, try the Nutty Witches Tit – a scoop of mac-nut ice cream with Myers rum, vodka and banana liqueur. The walls are covered with $1 bills – $18,000 worth they say.

Diamonds Ice Bar Bar

(Map p129; www.diamondsicebar.com; 1279 S Kihei Rd, Azeka Mauka II; ⏱11am-2am Mon-Sat, 7am-2am Sun) We're not sure where the bar's cheesy name originated, but we can tell you this – Diamonds Ice loves its Jagermeister. So slurp your cold shot, get woozy, play a little pool then wait and see who's lured in by the bright neon lights. Check the Facebook page to see who's playing or spinning on the weekends.

🛍 Shopping

Pi'ilani Village Mall

(Map p129; 225 Pi'ikea Ave) Kihei's largest shopping center has a wide range of stores. Flip through women's swimsuits at **Maui Waterwear** (www.mauiclothingcompany.com/mww.html) and Hawaiian-themed gifts at **Hilo Hattie** (www.hilohattie.com).

Kihei Kalama Village Market

(Map p126; 1941 S Kihei Rd; ⏱pavilion shops 10am-7:30pm) More than 40 shops and stalls are clustered at this central shopping arcade. For fashionable women's beachwear pop into **Mahina** (www.mahina-maui.com). For unique T-shirts and hoodies check out **808 Clothing Store** (www.the-808clothingcompany.com), with two locations at Kalama Village. Made-in-Hawaii jams and jellies are for sale in **Tutu's Pantry** (www.tutuspantry.com).

ℹ Information

Bank of Hawaii (📞879-5844; www.boh.com; 1279 S Kihei Rd, Azeka Mauka II; ⏱8:30am-4pm Mon-Thu, to 6pm Fri)

Kihei Police District Station (📞244-6400; 1881 S Kihei Rd, Kihei Town Center; ⏱7am-4pm Mon-Fri)

Longs Drugs (📞879-2033; www.cvs.com; 1215 S Kihei Rd; ⏱24hr) This convenience store, with a pharmacy (8am to 10pm Monday to Friday, until 7pm Saturday and Sunday), has one aisle loaded up with slippers (flip flops, yo').

Post Office (Map p129; 📞879-1987; www.usps.com; 1254 S Kihei Rd; ⏱8:30am-4:30pm Mon-Fri, 9am-1pm Sat)

Urgent Care Maui Physicians (📞879-7781; 1325 S Kihei Rd; ⏱7am-9pm) This clinic accepts walk-in patients.

ℹ Getting There & Around

To/From the Airport

Almost everyone rents a car at the airport in Kahului. Otherwise, expect to pay about $26 to $32 for shuttle service or $30 to $55 for a taxi depending on your South Maui location.

Beach volleyball on Charley Young Beach (p125)

Bus

The **Maui Bus** (www.mauicounty.gov) serves Kihei with two routes. One route, the Kihei Islander, connects Kihei with Wailea and Kahalui; stops include Kama'ole Beach Park III, Pi'ilani Village shopping center, and Uwapo and S Kihei Rds. The other route, the Kihei Villager, primarily serves the northern half of Kihei, with a half-dozen stops along S Kihei Rd and stops at Pi'ilani Village shopping center and Ma'alaea. Both routes operate hourly from around 6am to 8pm and cost $2.

Car & Motorcycle

Kihei Rent A Car (☏800-251-5288, 879-7257; www.kiheirentacar.com; 96 Kio Loop; per day/week from $35/175) This family-owned company rents cars and 4WDs to those aged 21 and over, and includes free mileage. For the lowest rates consider one of the older model cars (which can be well-worn!). Provides Kahului Airport shuttle pickup for rentals over five days.

Wailea

With its tidy golf courses, protective privacy walls and discreet signage, Wailea looks like a members-only country club. Wailea is South Maui's most elite haunt,

and it stands in sharp contrast to Kihei. Don't bother looking for gas stations or fast-food joints; this exclusive community is all about swank beachfront resorts and low-rise condo villas, with all the glitzy accessories.

One look at the beaches and it's easy to see why it's become such hot real estate. The golden-sand jewels sparkling along the Wailea coast are postcard material, offering phenomenal swimming, snorkeling and sunbathing. If you're not staying here, say a loud *mahalo* (thank you) for Hawaii's beach-access laws that allow you to visit anyway, with dedicated parking lots.

From Lahaina or Kahului, take the Pi'ilani Hwy (Hwy 31) to Wailea instead of taking S Kihei Rd, which is Kihei's stop-and-go main road. Once in Wailea, Wailea Ala-nui Dr turns into Makena Alanui Dr after Polo Beach and continues to Makena.

Beaches

Wailea's fabulous beaches begin with the southern end of Keawakapu Beach in Kihei and continue south toward Makena. All of the beaches that are backed by resorts have public access, with free parking, showers and restrooms. The beaches in this section are listed from north to south.

Mokapu & Ulua Beaches   Beach

These two beaches are separated by a small point. The lovely **Mokapu Beach** (Map p139) is on the northern side of the point, behind the new Andaz Maui resort hotel. Snorkelers should head straight for **Ulua Beach** (Map p139) to the south. The coral at the rocky outcrop on the right side of Ulua Beach offers Wailea's best easy-access snorkeling. Not only is it teeming with brilliant tropical fish, but it's also one of the best spots for hearing humpbacks sing as they pass offshore.

Snorkeling is best in the morning before the winds pick up and the masses arrive. When the surf's up, forget snorkeling – go bodysurfing instead. Beach access is just south of the new Andaz Maui.

The opening of the Andaz has brought resort crowds and ongoing construction to these two idyllic beaches. One bonus?

A larger public parking lot (which may be bad news for snorkelers looking to escape the crowds).

Wailea Beach   Beach

(Map p139) To strut your stuff celebrity-style, make a beeline to this sparkling strand, which fronts the Grand Wailea and Four Seasons resorts and offers a full menu of water activities. The beach slopes gradually, making it a good swimming spot. When it's calm, there's decent snorkeling around the rocky point on the southern end. Most afternoons there's a gentle shorebreak suitable for bodysurfing. Divers entering the water at Wailea Beach can follow an offshore reef that runs down to Polo Beach. The beach access road is between the Grand Wailea and Four Seasons resorts.

Polo Beach   Beach

(Map p139) In front of the Fairmont Kea Lani, Polo Beach is seldom crowded. When there's wave action, boogie boarders and bodysurfers usually find good shorebreaks here. When calm, the rocks at the northern end of the beach provide good snorkeling. At low tide, the lava outcropping at the southern end holds tide pools harboring spiny sea urchins and small fish. To find it, turn down Kaukahi St after the Fairmont Kea Lani and look for the parking lot on the right.

Poʻolenalena Beach   Beach

(Map p139) This long crescent-shaped beach is favored by local families on weekends. South of the resorts, it's rarely crowded, and the shallow, sandy bottom and calm waters make for excellent swimming. There's good snorkeling off both the southern and northern lava points. The parking lot is on Makena Alanui Rd,

The Gold course at Wailea Golf Club
RON DAHLQUIST/GETTY IMAGES ©

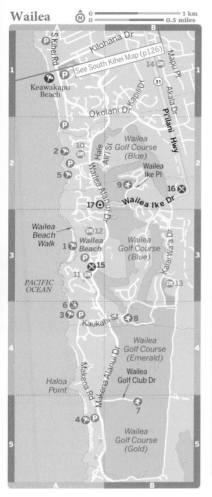

a half-mile south of its intersection with Makena Rd.

🏃 Activities

Wailea Golf Club   Golf
(☎875-7450; www.waileagolf.com; 100 Wailea Golf Club Dr; greens fee $140-235; ☉7am-5pm) There are three championship courses in Wailea. The **Emerald course** is a tropical garden that consistently ranks at the top; the rugged **Gold course** takes advantage of volcanic landscapes; and the **Old Blue**

course (120 Kaukahi St) is marked by an open fairway and challenging greens.

For the cheapest fees, tee off in the afternoon (check times), when 'twilight' rates are in effect.

Wailea Beach Walk   Walking
For the perfect sunset stroll, take the 1.3-mile shoreline path that connects Wailea's beaches and the resort hotels that front them. The undulating path winds above jagged lava points and back down to the sandy shore.

In winter this is one of the best places in all of Maui for spotting humpback whales. On a good day you may be able to see more than a dozen of them frolicking offshore.

Some of the luxury hotels you'll pass along the walk are worth strolling through as well, most notably the Grand Wailea Resort, which is adorned with $30 million worth of artwork. In front of the Wailea Point condos you'll find the foundations of three Hawaiian house sites dating to AD 1300; this is also a fine spot to watch the sun drop into the sea.

Maui Ocean Activities Water Sports
(Map p139; ☎357-8989; www.mauioceanactivities.com; 3850 Wailea Alanui Dr, Grand Wailea Resort; snorkel/boogie boards/kayak/stand up paddle board per hr $10/10/30/40; ☺8am-3pm) On the beach behind the Grand Wailea, Maui Ocean rents everything you need for watery fun.

Wailea Tennis Club Tennis
(Map p139; ☎879-1958; www.waileatennis.com; 131 Wailea Ike Pl; per person $20, racket rental per day $10; ☺7am-6pm Mon-Fri, to 5pm Sat & Sun) Nicknamed 'Wimbledon West,' this award-winning complex has 11 Plexi-pave courts. Ninety-minute lessons are also available (clinic/private $35/140).

Tours

Hawaiian Sailing Canoe Adventures Canoeing
(Map p139; ☎281-9301; www.mauisailingcanoe.com; adult/child $99/79; ☺tours 8am & 10am) Learn about native traditions on two-hour trips aboard a Hawaiian-style outrigger canoe. With a maximum of six passengers, it's able to accommodate requests – including stopping to snorkel with turtles. Tours depart from Polo Beach.

Festivals & Events

Maui Film Festival
Film

(www.mauifilmfestival.com) Hollywood celebs swoop in for this five-day extravaganza in mid-June. Join the stars under the stars at various Wailea locations, including the open-air 'Celestial Theater' on a nearby golf course.

Sleeping

Four Season Maui at Wailea
Resort $$$

(Map p139; ☎874-8000, 800-311-0630; www.fourseasons.com/maui; 3900 Wailea Alanui Dr; r/ste from $899/1549; ▣❋@🛜🏊🏃) As you sip your complimentary ginger-mint lemonade in the lobby, it's hard not to be impressed by the Four Season's sophisticated charm. From the plush lobby lounge with its framed ocean views to the accommodating staff to the inclusive pricing (no resort fee), the joy is in the details and the warm aloha spirit. Standard rooms are midsized and furnished with

understated tropical elegance, slightly more comfy than sophisticated. Marble-floored bathrooms have lots of counter space and a choice of piped-in music.

Children are welcome – there are pools plus the Kids for All Seasons program – but the resort feels more low-key than its neighbors. To relax, float in the adults-only serenity pool or enjoy a Hawaiian heated stone massage overlooking the sea. Parking is $25 per day.

Andaz Maui
Resort $$$

(Map p139; ☎573-1234; www.maui.andaz.hyatt.com; 3550 Wailea Alanui Dr; r/ste from $489/1139; 🛜🏊) iPad-carrying attendants emerge like modern-day beach nymphs as you enter the sensually chic lobby at the new Andaz Maui, ready to grant your every wish. And the rooms? Low beds, simple wooden furniture, plantation shutters: it's base camp for your cushy tropical expedition. On-site, take a cultural tour, attend a lei-making class, paddle an outrigger canoe or craft your own lotion at 'Awili Spa & Salon's apothecary lounge.

The resort is also home to the Japanese restaurant Morimoto Maui, the latest venture from Iron Chef Masaharu Morimoto. There is no resort fee, but parking is valet only and $30 per night.

Grand Wailea Resort Hotel & Spa
Resort $$$

(Map p139; ☎800-888-6100, 875-1234; www.grandwailea.com; 3850 Wailea Alanui Dr; r/ste from $299/499; ❄@🛜☁👶) The Grand Wailea's unbridled extravagance, from the million-dollar artwork in the lobby to the guest rooms decked out in Italian marble, is a wonder. But it's not all highbrow. The resort, part of the Hilton's Waldorf-Astoria line, boasts the most elaborate water-world wonders in Hawaii, an awesome series of nine interconnected pools with swim-through grottoes and towering water slides. This is a place for exuberant, join-the-crowd fun. The $25 resort fee includes wi-fi, yoga classes, scuba clinics, and art and garden tours. Parking is valet only, and an extra $30 per day.

Hotel Wailea
Hotel $$$

(Map p139; ☎874-0500, 866-970-4167; www.hotelwailea.com; 555 Kaukahi St; ste from $299; ❄🛜☁) With its hilltop perch, lush grounds and stove-pipe lobby, the Hotel Wailea just needs a frame for artistic completion. The all-suites hotel, which formerly catered to Japanese business-men, is under new ownership and units are benefiting from a stylish, ongoing revamp. Rooms come with microwaves and mini-refrigerators. Morning yoga is offered four days a week.

The hotel is not on the ocean, but the $25 resort fee includes wi-fi, parking and a shuttle to Wailea Beach, where you can charge food and drinks at the Grand Wailea to your suite.

Eating

Waterfront Deli
Deli $

(Map p139; ☎891-2039; 3750 Wailea Alanui Dr, Shops at Wailea; sandwiches $7; ⏱store 7am-10:30pm, deli 7am-8pm) For a quick, inexpensive meal to-go, visit this deli inside the Whalers General Store at the back of the Shops at Wailea.

Monkeypod Kitchen
Gastropub $$

(Map p139; ☎891-2322; www.monkeypodkitchen.com; 10 Wailea Gateway Pl, Wailea Gateway Center; lunch $13-25, dinner $14-36; ⏱11:30am-11pm,

Landscaped garden and pool area, Grand Wailea Resort Hotel & Spa

happy hour 3-5:30pm & 9-11pm) 🌿 At first glance, chef Peter Merriman's latest venture seems a little too hip and a little too glossy for laid-back Maui. But then you take a seat at the chattering bar. There, the staff, your fellow drinkers and the 36 beers on tap keep the alohas real.

The restaurant strives to maintain an organic and sustainable menu, evidenced by the Maui Cattle burgers and Upcountry veggies. Wood-fired pizzas are $9 during happy hour – mmm, Hamakua wild mushroom.

Pita Paradise   Mediterranean $$
(Map p139; ☎879-7177; www.pitaparadisehawaii.com; 34 Wailea Gateway Pl, Wailea Gateway Center; lunch $9-18, dinner $16-30; ⏱11am-9:30pm) Although this Greek taverna sits in a strip mall lacking ocean views, the inviting patio, the townscape mural and the tiny white lights – not to mention the succulent Mediterranean chicken pita – banish any locational regrets. Owner John Arabatzis catches his own fish, which is served in everything from pita sandwiches at lunch to grilled kabobs at dinner.

Ferraro's   Italian $$$
(Map p139; ☎874-8000; www.fourseasons.com/maui; 3900 Wailea Alanui Dr, Four Seasons Maui at Wailea; lunch $19-26, dinner $35-56; ⏱11:30am-9pm) No other place in Wailea comes close to this breezy restaurant for romantic seaside dining. Lunch strays into fun selections such as the seared ahi wrap with avocado and a lobster salad sandwich with garlic aioli. Dinner gets more serious, showcasing a rustic Italian menu.

🍷 Drinking & Entertainment

All the Wailea hotels have some sort of live music, most often jazz or Hawaiian, in the evening.

Red Bar at Gannon's   Cocktail Bar
(Map p139; www.gannonsrestaurant.com; 100 Wailea Golf Club Dr; ⏱8:30am-9pm, happy hour 3-6pm) Everyone looks sexier when they're swathed in a sultry red glow. Come to this chic spot at happy hour for impressive food and drink specials, as well as atten-

tive bartenders and stellar sunsets. The bar is located inside Gannon's, Bev Gannon's restaurant at the Gold and Emerald courses' clubhouse.

Mulligan's on the Blue   Pub
(Map p139; www.mulligansontheblue.com; 100 Kaukahi St; ⏱11am-1am Mon-Fri, 8:30am-1am Sat & Sun) Rising above the golf course, Mulligan's offers entertainment nightly, with anything from Hawaiian steel guitar to a lively magician. It's also a good place to quaff an ale while enjoying the distant ocean view, or catching a game on the 10 TVs.

Four Seasons Maui at Wailea   Live Music
(Map p139; 3900 Wailea Alanui Dr; ⏱5-11:30pm) The lobby lounge has Hawaiian music and hula performances from 5:30pm to 7:30pm nightly, and jazz or slack key guitar later in the evening.

🛍 Shopping

Shops at Wailea   Mall
(Map p139; www.shopsatwailea.com; 3750 Wailea Alanui Dr; ⏱9:30am-9pm) This outdoor mall has dozens of stores, most flashing designer labels such as Louis Vuitton and Gucci, but there are some solid island choices, too. Store hours may vary slightly from mall hours.

Blue Ginger   Women's Clothing
(Map p139; www.blueginger.com; 3750 Wailea Alanui Dr, Shops at Wailea) Women's clothing in cheery colors and tropical motifs.

Honolua Surf Co   Clothing
(Map p139; www.honoluasurf.com; 3750 Wailea Alanui Dr, Shops at Wailea) Hip surfer-motif T-shirts, board shorts and aloha shirts.

Martin & MacArthur   Arts & Crafts
(Map p139; www.martinandmacarthur.com; 3750 Wailea Alanui Dr, Shops at Wailea) Museum-quality Hawaiian-made koa (Hawaiian timber tree) woodwork and other crafts.

Maui Waterwear   Clothing
(Map p139; ☎891-8669; www.mauiclothingcompany.com; 3750 Wailea Alanui Dr, Shops at Wailea) Tropical swimwear you'll love to flaunt.

Sunset Drum Circle at Little Beach

One of the worst kept secrets in Makena is the sunset drum circle on Sunday nights at Little Beach. How badly kept? Let's just say there's lots of online footage – and a photo from ABC News – of Aerosmith's Steven Tyler banging a drum on the sand here. He has a house nearby. The scene is pretty chill, but be warned: about 10% of the crowd is walking around naked. But most everyone is there for the same things: the surf, the sand and the sunset. And maybe some pot brownies. The fire dancing starts after the sun goes down. If you're feeling groovy, check it out. And bring a headlamp. The trail back, which twists over a lava outcrop, is short but it's also steep and rocky. So far, state authorities have kept a distance, but they could shut it all down at anytime. Sweet emotion...

ℹ Information

Shops at Wailea (www.shopsatwailea.com; 3750 Wailea Alanui Dr; ⏰9:30am-9pm) This outdoor mall has an ATM and public restrooms.

ℹ Getting There & Around

The **Maui Bus** (www.mauicounty.gov) operates the Kihei Islander between Wailea and Kahului hourly until 8:27pm. The first bus picks up passengers on Wailea Ike Dr (just east of the Shops at Wailea) at 6:27am, and runs north along S Kihei Rd before heading to the Pi'ilani Village shopping center and then to Kahului, with a final stop at Queen Ka'ahumanu Center. For Lahaina, pick up the Kihei Villager at Pi'ilani Village, which travels to Ma'alaea. There, transfer to the Lahaina Islander.

Makena

Makena may be home to an oceanfront resort and a well-manicured golf course, but the region still feels wild, like a territorial outpost that hasn't quite been tamed. It's a perfect setting for aquatic adventurers who want to escape the crowds, offering primo snorkeling, kayaking and bodysurfing, plus pristine coral, reef sharks, dolphins and sea turtles galore.

The beaches are magnificent. The king of them all, Big Beach (Oneloa Beach), is an immense sweep of glistening sand and a prime sunset-viewing locale. The secluded cove at neighboring Little Beach is Maui's most popular nude beach –

you *will* see bare buns. Together these beaches form Makena State Park, but don't be misled by the term 'park,' as they remain in a natural state, with no facilities except for a couple of pit toilets and picnic tables. And those rumors about the nude Sunday evening drum circle? Well...

🏖 Beaches

The beaches here are listed from north to south.

Makena Bay   Beach
Paniolo (Hawaiian cowboys) used to herd cattle onto boats bound for Honolulu at this low-key bay, once a busy port for livestock, pineapples and people. Today, there's no better place on Maui for kayaking, and when seas are calm, snorkeling is good along the rocks at the southern side of **Makena Landing**, the boat launch that's the center of the action. Makena Bay is also a good place for shore dives; divers should head to the north side of the bay.

Kayakers should paddle south along the lava coastline to Malu'aka Beach, where green sea turtles abound. Kayak-snorkel tour operators meet just south of the landing for trips. South Pacific Kayaks (p127) will deliver pre-reserved kayaks here for rental. There are no shops on-site.

Malu'aka Beach   Beach
(Map p145) Dubbed 'Turtle Beach,' this golden swath of sand behind Makena Beach &

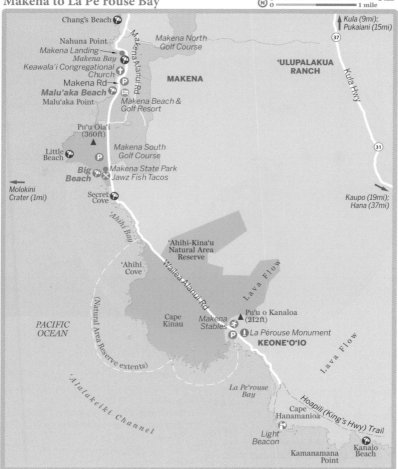

Golf Resort is popular with snorkelers and kayakers hoping to glimpse the surprisingly graceful sea turtles that feed along the coral here and swim within a few feet of snorkelers. You'll find terrific coral about 100yd out, and the best action is at the southern end of the beach. Come on a calm day – this one kicks up with a little wind, and when it's choppy you won't see anything. Parking lots, restrooms and showers are at both ends of the beach. On the northern side, park at the lot opposite Keawala'i Congregational Church then follow the road a short distance south. If that lot is full, take the first right after the resort, where there's additional parking for about 60 cars.

Little Beach   Beach
(Pu'u Ola'i Beach; Map p145; www.hawaii
stateparks.org) Those folks with the coolers and umbrellas, walking north from the sandy entrance to Big Beach? They're heading to Little Beach, which is part of Makena State Park. Also known as Pu'u Ola'i Beach, this cozy strand is *au naturel*.

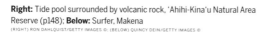
KIHEI & SOUTH MAUI MAKENA

Nudity is officially illegal, though enforcement is at the political whim of the day. The beach is hidden by a rocky outcrop that juts out from Pu'u Ola'i, the cinder hill that marks the northern end of Big Beach. Take the short, steep trail over the outcrop and bam, there it is, bare buns city.

Little Beach fronts a sandy cove that usually has a gentle shorebreak ideal for bodysurfing and boogie boarding. When the surf's up, you'll find plenty of local surfers here as well. When the water's calm, snorkeling is good along the rocky point. Park at the northern lot at Big Beach.

Big Beach   Beach
(Oneloa Beach; Map p145; www.hawaiistateparks. org) The crowning glory of Makena State Park, this untouched beach is arguably the finest on Maui. In Hawaiian it's called, literally, 'Long Sand.' And indeed the golden sands stretch for the better part of a mile and are as broad as they come. The waters are a beautiful turquoise. When

they're calm you'll find kids boogie boarding here, but at other times the breaks belong to experienced bodysurfers, who get tossed wildly in the transparent waves. There is a lifeguard station here.

In the late 1960s this was the site of an alternative-lifestyle encampment nicknamed 'Hippie Beach.' The tent city lasted until 1972, when police finally evicted everyone. For a sweeping view of the shore, climb the short trail to the rocky outcrop just north, which divides Big Beach from Little Beach.

The turnoff to the main parking area is a mile beyond the Makena Beach & Golf Resort. There's a port-o-john here. A second parking area lies a quarter of a mile to the south. Thefts and broken windshields are a possibility, so don't leave valuables in your car in either lot.

Secret Cove   Beach
(Map p145) This lovely, postcard-size swath of sand, with a straight-on view of Kaho'olawe, is worth a peek – although

it's no longer much of a secret. The cove is a quarter-mile after the southernmost Makena State Park parking lot. The entrance is through an opening in a lava-rock wall just south of house No 6900.

 Activities

Makena Landing is a popular starting point for kayak tours. For golfers, the course at Makena Beach & Golf Resort, which was designed by Robert Trent Jones Jr, has been closed for renovations. At press time it was scheduled to reopen in 2014, but as a private course.

Aloha Kayaks   Kayaking

(✆270-3318; www.alohakayaksmaui.com; adult/child $75/55; ⏱tours 7:15am) 🏄 For an eco-minded snorkel-kayak trip with an enthusiastic team of owner-operators, take a paddle with Aloha Kayaks. The owners, Griff and Peter, have about 10 years of guiding experience apiece. Their mission? To educate guests about the environment and to keep their operations sustainable –

and to make sure you see marine life. Trips depart from Makena Landing. Wear a swimsuit and sandals.

Check the website for details about the company's Green Paddling Blue Water Campaign, which describes how Aloha Kayaks keeps things green.

 Sleeping

Makena Beach & Golf Resort   Resort $$$

(Map p145; ✆800-321-6284, 874-1111; www.mak enaresortmaui.com; 5400 Makena Alanui Dr; r/ste from $325/575; P❄@🛜🏊) This striking place is our favorite resort in South Maui. Its fortresslike exterior isn't particularly appealing, but the aloha of the staff and the stunning Malu'aka Beach, which is just out back, vault this secluded retreat to the top of the heap. Rooms, revamped in 2012, shine with simple but sophisti-cated style: white bedspreads, subdued tropical throws, granite countertops and cherrywood furniture. The kicker? No resort fee or parking fee.

Paniolo Roots

Sitting beneath the slopes of Upcountry's 'Ulupalakua Ranch, Makena was once a *paniolo* (Hawaiian cowboy) village, home to Hawaiian cowboys who corralled cattle at the landing and loaded them onto barges bound for Honolulu slaughterhouses. To catch a glimpse of Makena's roots, stop at the **Keawala'i Congregational Church (Map p145)**, just south of Makena Landing. One of Maui's earliest missionary churches, its 3ft-thick walls were constructed of burnt coral rock. In the seaside churchyard take a look at the old tombstones adorned with cameo photographs of the Hawaiian cowboys laid to rest a century ago.

The beach is a top launch pad for snorkelers and kayakers hoping to spy a green sea turtle or two.

 Eating

Vendors with cold coconuts, pineapples and other fruit are sometimes found along Makena Alanui Dr opposite Big Beach.

Jawz Fish Tacos　Food Truck **$**
(Map p145; www.jawzfishtacos.com; Makena State Park; snacks $6-11; ⏲11am-4pm) Get your beach snacks – tacos, burritos, shave ice – at this food truck beside the northernmost Big Beach parking lot.

Beyond Makena

Makena Rd turns adventurous after Makena State Park, continuing for three narrow miles through the lava flows of 'Ahihi-Kina'u Natural Area Reserve before dead-ending at La Pe'rouse Bay.

'AHIHI-KINA'U NATURAL AREA RESERVE

Scientists haven't been able to pinpoint the exact date, but it is believed that Maui's last lava flow spilled down to the sea here between AD 1480 and 1600, shaping 'Ahihi Bay and Cape Kina'u. The jagged lava coastline and the pristine waters fringing it have been designated a reserve because of its unique marine habitat.

Thanks in part to the prohibition on fishing here, the snorkeling is incredible. Just about everyone heads to the little roadside cove 0.1 miles south of the first reserve sign – granted, it offers good snorkeling, but there are better (and less-crowded) options. Instead, drive 0.2 miles past the cove and look for a large clearing on the right. Park here and follow the coastal footpath south for five minutes to a black-sand beach with fantastic coral, clear water and few visitors. Enter the water from the left side of the beach where access is easy; snorkel in a northerly direction and you'll immediately be over coral gardens teeming with an amazing variety of fish. Huge rainbow parrot fish abound here, and it's not unusual to see turtles and the occasional reef shark.

Large sections of the 1238-acre reserve are closed to visitors until July 31, 2014, which will allow the Department of Land and Resource Management (www.dlnr.hawaii.gov) to protect the fragile environment from tourist wear-and-tear and to develop a long-term protection plan. Visitation in the north is still permitted between 5:30am and 7:30pm.

LA PE'ROUSE BAY

Earth and ocean merge at La Pe'rouse Bay with a raw desolate beauty that's almost eerie. Historians originally thought that Maui's last volcano eruption occurred in 1790, but more recent analysis indicates that the lava flow occurred about 200 to 300 years earlier. Before the blast, the ancient Hawaiian village of Keone'o'io flourished here, and its remains – mainly house and heiau platforms – can be seen scattered among the lava patches.

In May 1786 the renowned French explorer Jean François de Galaup La Pérouse became the first Westerner to land on Maui. As he sailed into the bay that now bears his name, scores of Hawaiian canoes came out to greet him. A monument to the explorer is located at the end of the road at La Pe'rouse Bay.

From the volcanic shoreline look for pods of spinner dolphins, which commonly come into the bay during the early part of the day. The combination of strong offshore winds and rough waters rules out swimming, but it's an interesting place to explore on land.

 Activities

Makena Stables   Horseback Riding
(Map p145; ☏879-0244; www.makenastables. com; Makena Rd; 2½-3hr trail rides $155-180; ◷8am-6pm) Located just before the road ends, this place offers morning and sunset horseback rides across the lava flows, with the sunset tour traveling up the scenic slopes of 'Ulupalakua Ranch.

Hoapili Trail   Hiking
From La Pe'rouse Bay, this section of the ancient King's Trail (see p220) follows the coastline across jagged lava flows. The first part of the trail is along the sandy beach at La Pe'rouse Bay. Be prepared: wear hiking boots, bring plenty to drink, start early and tell someone where you're going. It's a dry area with no water and little vegetation, so it can get very hot.

Right after the trail emerges onto the lava fields, it's possible to take a spur trail for three-quarters of a mile down to the light beacon at the tip of Cape Hanamanioa. Alternatively, walk inland to the Na Ala Hele sign and turn right onto the King's Hwy as it climbs through rough 'a'a lava inland for the next 2 miles before coming back to the coast to an older lava flow at Kanaio Beach. Although the trail continues, it becomes harder to follow and Kanaio Beach is the recommended turn around point. If you don't include the lighthouse spur, the round-trip distance to Kanaio Beach is about 4 miles. For details and a basic map, visit www.hawaiitrails.org.

Local Knowledge

NAME: PETER HAMILTON AND GRIFF DEMPSEY

OCCUPATION: OWNER-OPERATORS ALOHA KAYAKS

RESIDENCE: KIHEI, MAKAWAO

1 ANY GOOD SPOTS FOR OFFSHORE SNORKELING IN SOUTH MAUI?
Griff: Makena Landing. It has a parking lot.
Peter: Down south of Makena is 'Ahihi-Kina'u. That's a really nice spot, 'The Dumps' there. That's part of a marine conservation district. The only thing about that area is there are no bathrooms, there are no lifeguards. It's kind of remote, but it's a pretty good snorkeling area.

2 ANY TIPS FOR ENVIRONMENTALLY FRIENDLY SNORKELING?
Griff: Don't walk on the coral. Don't touch the turtles. And don't feed the fish. Those are the three big ones.

3 WHEN SHOULD SNORKELERS AVOID GOING INTO THE WATER?
Peter: High wind or big waves – I usually say stay out of the water. Big waves stir up the sand, which causes bad visibility which causes the potential for a shark to take a bite. With bad visibility, first off, you're not going to see much. Two, you might go on the coral reef if you don't see it. I would say, in terms of being safe, morning time is usually best.

4 ANY TRAVEL TIPS FOR VISITORS?
Peter: Do your early morning activities the first couple of days on the island. Do your late night luau, boat trip, sunset trip – do that in the last couple of days of your tour. The first day you get here, you're going to be up at 4am and face-planting at 8 o'clock at night. Tired. But your last day on the island, you've adjusted.

5 DO YOU HAVE ANY RESTAURANTS TO RECOMMEND FOR A POST-SNORKEL LUNCH OR DRINK?
Peter: Café O'Lei is a really cool lunch spot right here in Kihei. They have great food and a good little happy hour. Monkeypod's has got a good happy hour.

North Shore & Upcountry

Maui's greatest treasure is its extraordinary concentration of variety, and here you'll find that in spades. In a half-hour drive, you can ascend from the beaches of the North Shore (including the world's windsurfing capital) through the jungle of the lower slopes, and break out into open Upcountry hills, where cowboys still roam the range, and farmers work the island's Garden Belt.

Communities change accordingly. The hip surfer town of Pa'ia gives way to Makawao's Old West architecture, which dissolves into a handful of stores in mud-on-boots Keokea, after which the road passes on to eternity.

All of this begs for a lazy country drive, taking in athletic surfers, artsy shops, forest trails, mountain views and organic cafes at your own rate. For the adventurous, there's plenty of zip-lining, paragliding and mountain biking too.

Upcountry scenery near 'Ulupalakua (p180)
RON DAHLQUIST/GETTY IMAGES ©

North Shore & Upcountry Itineraries

Day One

1 **HA Baldwin Beach Park** (p154) Start off this elevating day at sea level, on one of Maui's classic beaches.

2 **Pa'ia** (p154) Explore the main street of this funky town, starting with a java at Pa'ia Bay Coffee and ending with the Asian exotica at Indigo.

3 **Makawao** (p166) A straight shot up Baldwin Ave takes you to art central. Check out the Hui No'eau Visual Arts Center first, then explore the town's many galleries, including the wide-ranging Maui Hands and the amazing Andreas Nottebohm works at Wertheim Contemporary. Lunch at Market Fresh Bistro or Makawao Garden Café.

4 **Makawao Forest Reserve Trails** (p167) Time to walk off lunch. How about a stroll through a beautiful forest? Just look out for the mountain bikers.

5 **Pi'iholo & Olinda Roads** (p168) This steep and twisty loop – up Pi'iholo Rd to the very top and then back to town via Olinda Rd – passes by some of Upcountry's finest views and addresses.

6 **Ha'iku** (p163) Wind through backroads to this hidden town. Act like an insider, and visit the Booch for some kombucha.

7 **Ho'okipa Beach Park** (p154) It's afternoon, and the world's greatest windsurfing beach is in high gear. Have a look from the viewpoint at the east end.

8 **Pa'ia** (p154) Back where you started, the world is your oyster. You can dine at Pa'ia Fish Market or upscale Mama's Fish House, then head to Charley's or Café des Amis for dessert and live music.

➡ THIS LEG: 29 MILES

Day Two

1 **La Provence** (p177) Start your morning right with some amazing pastries from this hidden bakery.

2 **Ali'i Kula Lavender** (p173) Soak up the fragrant scents on a stroll through this lavender garden at the foot of a dreamy cloud forest. Tea and scones on the deck are mandatory.

3 **Polipoli Spring State Recreation Area** (p178) Wow, what an amazing drive! Once you reach the end of twisty and misty Waipoli Rd, stretch your legs on the Polipoli Hiking Circuit, which leads through towering trees.

4 **Kula Bistro** (p177) Now that you're hungry, it's time for the best lunch this side of Makawao. A simple pizza is a work of art here.

5 **Worcester Glassworks** (p173) This family of glassblowing pros will blow your mind with their sandblasted art glass. You're welcome to watch them at work.

6 **Grandma's Coffee House** (p180) This island icon is the perfect stop for a quick break on your scenic Upcountry drive. Folks here have been growing top-rate beans since Grandma's days and they have the deckside coffee trees to prove it.

7 **Maui's Winery** (p180) Having reached the border of Upcountry, you've earned an excellent wine tasting, and a chance to toast whoever put such an excellent vineyard this far from anywhere.

8 **Kula Marketplace** (p177) Time to buy a few souvenirs for the folks back home. In this broad selection drawn from 80 local vendors, there's something for everyone.

9 **Kula Lodge Restaurant** (p176) The perfect end to an Upcountry day: a sunset dinner with a jaw-dropping view. Build your own pizza from the brick ovens outside, or choose from the farm-to-table menu within.

➡ **THIS LEG: 44.9 MILES**

North Shore & Upcountry Highlights

1 **Best Beach: HA Baldwin Beach Park** (p154) This wide sandy strand is the North Shore's finest.

2 **Best Hiking: Polipoli Spring State Recreation Area** (p178) Lightly trodden trails in a unique cloud forest.

3 **Best New Restaurant: Nuka** (p165) Traditional Japanese meets contemporary flair.

4 **Best Garden: Ali'i Kula Lavender** (p173) Heady scents and sweeping views at this Upcountry favorite.

5 **Best Place to Toast: Maui's Winery** (p180) A fun vineyard on a far-out ranch.

HA Baldwin Beach Park (p154)
LONELY PLANET/GETTY IMAGES ©

Discover North Shore & Upcountry

Pa'ia

Home to an eclectic mix of surfers and soul-seekers, Pa'ia is Maui's hippest burg. Once a thriving plantation town of 10,000 residents, it fell into decline during the 1950s when the local sugar mill closed. Shops were shuttered and residents moved to Kahului. Then, like some other well-known sugar towns (eg Hanapepe on Kaua'i, and Honoka'a on the Big Island), Pa'ia successfully reinvented itself. First came a wave of paradise-seeking hippies attracted by low rents. Next came a wave of windsurfers attracted by Ho'okipa Beach. Then came the tourists. Today the town's aging wooden storefronts, splashed in bright colors, house a broad array of shops facing a constant stream of traffic. It still feels like a dusty outpost at times, but that's all part of the vibe.

Beaches

Ho'okipa Beach Park   Beach

(Map p156; ⏰5:30am-7pm) Ho'okipa is to daredevil windsurfers what Everest is to climbers. It reigns supreme as the world's premier windsurfing beach, with strong currents, dangerous shorebreaks and razor-sharp coral offering the ultimate challenge. This is also one of Maui's prime surfing spots. Winter sees the biggest waves for board surfers, while summer has the most consistent winds for windsurfers. To prevent turf battles, surfers typically hit the waves in the morning and windsurfers in the afternoon. While the action in the water is only suitable for pros, a lookout point on the eastern side of the park offers spectators a great bird's-eye view. In the fall the action includes green sea turtles laying eggs on the beach at dusk. Ho'okipa is just before the 9-mile marker.

HA Baldwin Beach Park   Beach

(Map p156; ⏰7am-7pm) Bodyboarders and bodysurfers take to the waves at this palm-lined county park about a mile west of Pa'ia, at the 6-mile marker. The wide sandy beach drops off quickly, and when the shorebreak is big, swimmers should beware of getting slammed. Calmer waters can be found at the eastern end, where there's a little cove

Kitesurfer, Sprecklesville Beach
RON DAHLQUIST/GETTY IMAGES ©

Maui Downhill

Cycling from the summit of Haleakalā all the way down to seaside Pa'ia has become an island rite of passage. The 25-mile journey, a 10,000ft drop in elevation, offers tremendous views, a thrilling ride and Upcountry sightseeing, including Makawao. It's also dead easy – the bikes only have one gear – although you have to be careful to keep your speed down around some seriously sharp corners (yes, there have been accidents).

There are two companies in Pa'ia that do this well, albeit differently:

Maui Sunriders (Map p158; ☎579-8970; www.mauibikeride.com; 71 Baldwin Ave, Suite C1; online price per person $90; ⏱3am-4:30pm Mon-Fri) Offers a daily self-guided tour that begins in the wee hours (around 3:15am) with a van ride to the summit. After a beautiful sunrise, you're given a new Trek mountain bike, and off you go. You don't have to return the bike until 4:30pm, so you can sightsee at your own rate and make a day of it.

Maui Easy Riders (Map p156; ☎344-9489; www.mauieasyriders.com; Baldwin Beach Park; per person $99) Offers a four-hour tour for groups of eight or less on comfy cruisers. Stops include Makawao and Pa'ia. Departs 9am and 1:30pm Monday to Friday.

Tip: if you rent a bike for the day at Maui Sunriders ($30), the price includes a bike rack. Thus a travel companion could drop you and others off at the summit, saving $60 each.

shaded by ironwood trees. Showers, restrooms, picnic tables and well-used sports fields round out the facilities. The park has a reputation for rowdy behavior after sunset, but it's fine in the daytime when there's a lifeguard on duty.

Spreckelsville Beach
Beach

(Map p98; 👫) Extending west from HA Baldwin Beach, this 2-mile stretch of sand is a good walking beach. Its near-shore reef makes it less ideal for swimming, but it does provide protection for young kids. If you walk toward the center of the beach, you'll soon come to a section dubbed 'Baby Beach.' There are no facilities. At the 5-mile marker, turn toward the ocean on Nonohe Pl, then left on Kealakai Pl just before the Maui Country Club.

Tavares Beach
Beach

(Map p156) This unmarked sandy beach is quiet during the week but livens up on weekends when local families come here toting picnics, guitars, dogs and kids. A submerged lava shelf runs parallel to the beach about 25ft from the shore, shallow enough for swimmers to scrape over. Once you know it's there, however, the rocks are easy to avoid, so take a look before jumping in. The beach parking lot is at the first shoreline access sign on the Hana side of the 7-mile marker. There are no facilities.

◎ Sights & Activities

Maui Dharma Center
Buddhist

(Map p158; ☎579-8076; www.mauidharma-center.com; 81 Baldwin Ave; ⏱6:30am-6:30pm) Marked by its roadside stupa, this Tibetan Buddhist center offers daily, weekly and monthly prayer and meditation sessions, retreats and Dharma talks. Or just take a stroll around the stupa's prayer wheel.

Simmer
Windsurfing

(Map p158; ☎579-8484; www.simmerhawaii.com; 137 Hana Hwy; sailboards per day $50; ⏱10am-7pm) This windsurfing center handles everything from repairs to top-of-the-line gear rentals.

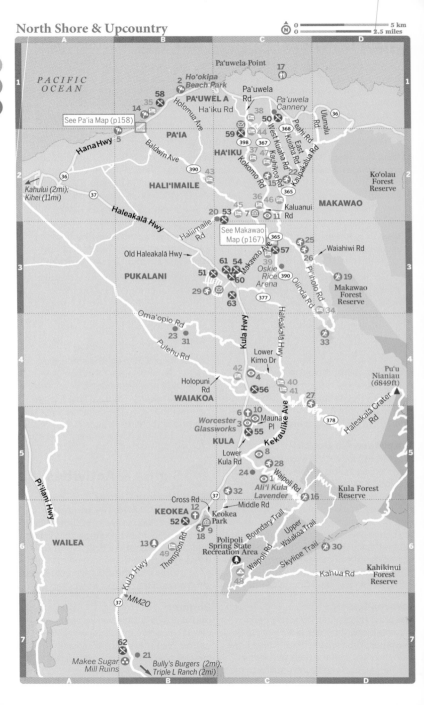

North Shore & Upcountry map

0 — 5 km
0 — 2.5 miles

PACIFIC OCEAN

Pa'uwela Point

Ho'okipa Beach Park

PA'UWELA

Pa'uwela

Pa'uwela Rd

Pa'uwela Cannery

See Pa'ia Map (p158)

Holomua Ave

Ha'iku Rd

West Kuiaha Rd

East Kuiaha Rd

Peahi Rd

Ulumalu Rd

PA'IA

Hana Hwy

Baldwin Ave

HA'IKU

Kokomo Rd

Kauhikoa Rd

Kaupakalua Rd

Ko'olau Forest Reserve

Kahului (2mi);
Kihei (11mi)

HALI'IMAILE

Haleakalā Hwy

Hali'imaile Rd

Kaluanui Rd

MAKAWAO

See Makawao Map (p167)

Makawao Ave

Waiahiwi Rd

PUKALANI

Old Haleakalā Hwy

Oskie Rice Arena

Piʻiholo Rd

Olinda Rd

Makawao Forest Reserve

Oma'opio Rd

Pulehu Rd

Kula Hwy

Lower Kimo Dr

Haleakalā Hwy

Pu'u Nianiau (6849ft)

Holopuni Rd

WAIAKOA

Haleakalā Crater Rd

Worcester Glassworks

Mauna Pl

KULA

Kekaulike Ave

Lower Kula Rd

Ali'i Kula Lavender

Waipoli Rd

Kula Forest Reserve

Pi'ilani Hwy

WAILEA

Cross Rd

KEOKEA

Middle Rd

Keokea Park

Thompson Rd

Polipoli Spring State Recreation Area

Boundary Trail

Upper Waiakoa Trail

Skyline Trail

Waipoli Rd

Kahua Rd

Kahikinui Forest Reserve

Kula Hwy

MM20

Makee Sugar Mill Ruins

Bully's Burgers (2mi);
Triple L Ranch (2mi)

North Shore & Upcountry

Festivals & Events

Ergo/High-Tech /Lopez Surfbash
Surf Meet

(www.mauisurfohana.org) This weekend surf contest takes place at Ho'okipa Beach around mid-November with competing short-boarders, long-boarders and body-boarders.

Sleeping

Nalu Kai Lodge
Hotel $$

(Map p158; ☏ 385-4344; www.nalukailodge. com; 95 Nalu Pl; r $125; ❄ ☎) Squeezed into a jungle-like block near downtown, this throwback to 1960s Hawaii kitsch offers a dozen cute but tight rooms without much privacy. Interior bathrooms are closed off with a curtain; exterior ones belong

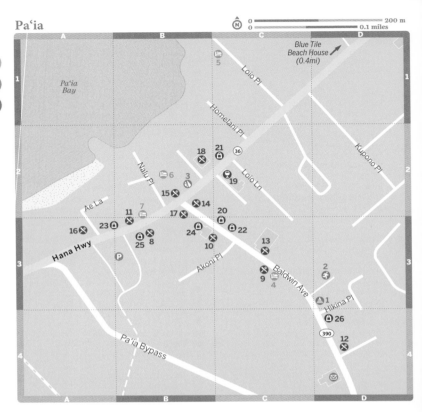

to adjacent shops. A stockade bamboo fence conceals a small garden, a lonely tiki bar, and a waterfall so fake it fits right in. Some rooms have air-con.

Blue Tile Beach House
B&B $$
(Map p156; ☑ 579-6446; www.beachvacation maui.com; 459 Hana Hwy; r $110-165, ste $250, $30 charge for under 3 nights; 🛜) Slide into your bathing suit, step out the door of this exclusive oceanfront estate and you're literally on Tavares Beach. Sleeping options range from a small straight-forward room to a spacious honeymoon suite with wraparound ocean-view windows and a four-poster bed. All six rooms share a living room and a kitchen.

Lumeria Maui
Resort $$$
(Map p156; ☑ 855-579-8877; www.lumeriamaui. com; 1813 Baldwin Ave; r/ste incl breakfast $329/489; 🛜 🏊) This spa for the soul starts working its magic the moment you pull into the hibiscus-lined drive. Set on tidy, garden-filled grounds on an upcountry slope above Pa'ia, Lumeria is a gorgeous place to nourish both mind and body. Farm-to-table breakfasts prime the spirit before days filled with yoga, garden strolls, hot stone massages and aromatherapy.

At night guests retreat to minimalist, Asian-inspired cottages that once served as dorms for plantation workers. A daily $25 resort fee covers a range of classes.

Pa'ia Inn
Boutique Hotel $$$
(Map p158; ☑ 579-6000; www.paiainn.com; 93 Hana Hwy; r $189-349, ste $259-899; ❄ @ 🛜) This classy boutique hotel in a historic building offers the ultimate Pa'ia immersion: step out the front and the town is on your doorstep; step out the

back and you're on a path to the beach. With 15 appealing rooms in five different categories, you'll find something to your liking, particularly the captivating three-bedroom oceanfront beach house ($900 to $2000). A new bar/restaurant should be complete by publication.

Makani Akau   Vacation Rental **$$$**
(Map p158; ☎575-9228; www.maui.cc/ MakaniAkau-Maui.html; 55 Loio Pl; per night $800, 7-night minimum, cleaning fee $500; 🖘) With sweeping views of Pa'ia Bay, this five-bedroom home is a contemporary classic. Folding glass doors bring all the surfing action into the living room. A 55ft pool fronts the sea. A huge kitchen, comfy leather couches and beautiful teak furniture complement the private setting. Walk into town or never leave.

Inn at Mama's   Inn **$$$**
(Map p156; ☎579-9764; www.mamasfishhouse. com; 799 Poho Pl; cottage $175-575, ste $325; ❄🖘) Maui's most famous seafood restaurant has a dozen accommodations divided between cottages (studio, one bedroom, two bedrooms) and luxurious junior suites (adults only). Four of the cottages are beachfront, the rest garden, while the spacious junior suites have an outdoor courtyard. All are uniquely designed and extremely well-done, with the beachfront cottages enjoying idyllic

views. One caveat: ever-popular Mama's is not always the quietest of places.

Eating

Pa'ia Bay Coffee   Cafe **$**
(Map p158; ☎579-3111; 43 Hana Hwy; sandwiches $6-10; ⊙6:30am-5:30pm Mon-Sat, 7am-5:30pm Sun; 🖘) Hidden across the street from the town parking lot, this cool and trendy coffee shop offers a lovely shaded garden, a sanctuary on a hot day. Creativity extends beyond the fresh gourmet sandwiches to the scrambled eggs cooked in the espresso machine. Yes, that really works.

Mana Foods   Bakery, Deli **$**
(Map p158; ☎579-8078; www.manafoods maui.com; 49 Baldwin Ave; deli items under $10; ⊙8am-8:30pm; 🖉) Dreadlocked, Birkenstocked or just needing to stock up – everyone rubs shoulders at Mana, a health food store, bakery and deli all wrapped into one. Once past the unassuming entrance, you'll find narrow aisles bursting with rare goodies, coffee galore, a great salad bar and hot food to go. The mind of Pa'ia made visible.

Fresh Mint   Vietnamese **$**
(Map p158; ☎579-9144; 115 Baldwin Ave; mains $10-13; ⊙5-9pm Mon & Tue, 11am-9pm Wed-Sun; 🖉) The chef/owner here takes pride in

Castaway Chic

Pa'ia's iconic Mama's Fish House (p162) is known for its unique, ever-evolving building, which doubles as a work of art. Enter beneath a banyan tree, past a whaling ship boiler and through a fishing shack; find yourself in rooms upheld by sugar mill equipment, with fishing rod canopies, canoe beams and real plantation-cottage walls. Sound like a junk yard? It isn't. A permanent construction crew works after hours to integrate everything by hand, while a local artist ensures a tasteful result, forming a style best termed 'castaway chic'. No wonder that when the 2011 Japanese tsunami reached Hawaii, regulars report getting concerned calls from the mainland: 'Is Mama's OK?'

Vietnamese vegetarian dishes, artfully presented. Even meat eaters will be amazed at how soy takes on the flavors and texture of the foods it substitutes. In doubt? Try the spicy ginger soy beef. Lunch in high season.

Tortillas
Burrito Company   Mexican $

(Map p158; ☎579-8269; 149 Hana Hwy; burrito $8; ⏱7:30am-8pm Mon-Sat, to 7pm Sun) This build-your-own-burrito shop uses fresh ingredients and serves large portions. The fish tacos are also a local favorite.

Anthony's Coffee Company   Cafe $

(Map p158; ☎579-8340; www.anthonyscoffee.com; 90 Hana Hwy; breakfast $5-13, lunch $7-12; ⏱5:30am-6pm; 🛜) For fresh-ground organic coffee, a variety of goodies from pastries to lox Benedict, and picnic boxes for the drive to Hana.

Ono Gelato   Dessert $

(Map p158; www.onogelatocompany.com; 115 Hana Hwy; cones $5; ⏱11am-10pm) Dishes up Maui-made organic gelato in island flavors such

Left: Cane fields and historic sugar mill near Pa'ia (p154);
Below: Surfer, Ho'okipa Beach (p154)

(LEFT) RAY MAINS/GETTY IMAGES ©. (BELOW) LASZLO PODOR/GETTY IMAGES ©

as guava, mango and Kula strawberry. For the ultimate treat, order the *liliko'i* quark, combining passion fruit and goat cheese.

Pa'ia Fish Market Restaurant — Seafood $$

(Map p158; 📞579-8030; www.paiafishmarket. com; 110 Baldwin Ave; mains $9-19; ⏰11am-9:30pm) It's all about the fish here: fresh, tasty and affordable. The local favorite is *ono* fish and chips, but the menu includes plenty of other temptations, including charbroiled mahi, Cajun-style snapper and a Hawaii classic, blackened ahi sashimi. Little wonder the tables here are packed like sardines.

Café des Amis — Cafe $$

(Map p158; 📞579-6323; www.cdamaui.com; 42 Baldwin Ave; breakfast $5-11, lunch & dinner $9-18; ⏰8:30am-8:30pm) Grab a seat in the breezy courtyard to dine on the best cafe fare in Pa'ia. It's not always fast, but it's done right. The savory options include spicy Indian curry wraps with mango

chutney, and mouthwatering crepes. You'll also find vegetarian offerings, creative breakfasts and a tempting array of drinks from fruit smoothies to fine wines.

There's live music in the evenings Monday to Wednesday and Saturday.

Milagros Food Company — Cafe $$

(Map p158; 📞579-8755; www.milagrosfoodcom pany.com; 3 Baldwin Ave; mains $10-16; ⏰11am-10pm) With sidewalk tables perched on Pa'ia's busiest corner, an island-style Tex-Mex menu and some excellent craft beers, this bar/restaurant is the perfect spot for a late-afternoon pit stop. Happy hour (inside only) is from 1pm to 5pm.

Café Mambo — Cafe $$

(Map p158; 📞579-8021; www.cafemambomaui. com; 30 Baldwin Ave; mains $10-20; ⏰8am-9pm) You can't walk by this upbeat, arty cafe without being pulled in by the aromatic scents wafting out the door. Choose from fragrant Moroccan stews, mouthwatering

161

crispy duck fajitas and creative vegetarian fare. Mambo also packs box lunches ($8.50) in coolers for the road to Hana.

Flatbread Company Pizzeria $$
(Map p158; 579-8989; www.flatbreadcompany. com; 89 Hana Hwy; pizzas $12-22; 11am-10pm)
Wood-fired pizzas made with organic sauces, nitrate-free pepperoni, Kula onions – you'll never stop at a chain pizza house again. Fun combinations abound, from pure vegan to *kalua* pork with goat cheese.

Mama's Fish House Seafood $$$
(Map p156; 579-8488; www.mamasfishhouse. com; 799 Poho Pl; mains $36-75; 11am-2:30pm & 4:15-9pm) Mama's isn't just a restaurant, it's a South Seas dream. Located on a beautiful cove with swaying palms, it manages to achieve the impossible: fine dining meets Gilligan's Island. The fish is literally fresh off the boat – they'll even tell you who caught it – while the Robinson Crusoe building successfully integrates everything from driftwood to sugarcane machinery.

When the beachside tiki torches are lit at dinnertime, you'll swear you've entered a poster from *South Pacific*. The only drawback is the eye-popping prices, which match the island's most expensive resorts. Ever had a $28 cocktail or a $75 entree? Yet no one seems to care. This is a magnet for honeymooners, or for anyone else looking for that once-in-a-lifetime Hawaii experience. Located on Hana Hwy, 1.5 miles east of Pa'ia town. Reservations essential; holidays book out three months ahead.

Drinking & Nightlife

Charley's Bar
(Map p158; 579-8085; www.charleysmaui.com; 142 Hana Hwy; 7am-10pm Sun-Thu, to 2am Fri & Sat) Pa'ia's legendary saloon has been slingin' suds and pub grub since 1969. In its heyday it was a magnet for visiting rock stars, who were known to take to the stage. While that scene has moved on (OK, there's a slim chance part-time resident Willie Nelson may pop in), this is still the town's main music venue.

There's dinner music Tuesday to Thursday, DJs and bands Friday and Saturday, and open mic night Monday. Check the website for the schedule.

Shopping

Indigo Carpets, Crafts
(Map p158; www.indigopaia.com; 149 Hana Hwy; 10am-6pm) Step into this inviting boutique for a shopping trip through Central and Southwest Asia. The handcrafted rugs, one-of-a-kind furnishings and traditional crafts were collected by the owners, Daniel Sullivan and Caramiya Davies-Reid. Sullivan also sells vibrant photographs taken during his travels, while Davies-Reid designs breezy dresses and custom bathing suits.

Maui Crafts Guild Arts & Crafts
(Map p158; www.mauicraftsguild.com; 69 Hana Hwy; 10am-6pm) This long-standing artist's co-op sells everything from pottery and jewelry to hand-painted silks and natural-fiber baskets at reasonable prices.

Na Kani O Hula Hula Supplies
(Map p158; www.nakaniohula.com; 115 Baldwin Ave; 6am-2pm) Hula *halau* (troupes) come here for *'uli'uli* (feather-decorated gourd rattles), bamboo nose flutes and other traditional dance and music crafts,

Island Insights

For a surfer town bursting with healthy bodies, Pa'ia sure has some clogged arteries. Roads, that is. If you're heading Upcountry from Kahului, avoid the main intersection at Baldwin Ave by taking the bypass. If you're staying awhile, head for the town lot first, as parking is a problem. And if you're heading on to Hana, check your gas gauge. Pa'ia has the last filling station on the highway, and Hana's has been known to run dry.

any of which would make for a fascinating souvenir.

Maui Hands – Pa'ia
Arts & Crafts

(Map p158; www.mauihands.com; 84 Hana Hwy; ⏰10am-7pm Mon-Sat, to 6pm Sun) Top-end koa bowls, pottery and Maui-themed paintings.

Mandala Ethnic Arts
Clothing

(Map p158; 29 Baldwin Ave; ⏰9:30am-7:30pm) Lightweight cotton and silk clothing, Buddhas and Asian crafts.

Maui Girl
Women's Clothing

(Map p158; www.maui-girl.com; 12 Baldwin Ave; ⏰9am-6pm) Get your itty-bitty bikinis here.

Alice in Hulaland
Gifts

(Map p158; www.aliceinhulaland.com; 19 Baldwin Ave; ⏰9am-8pm) Kitschy but fun souvenirs.

ℹ️ Information

Bank of Hawaii (www.boh.com; 35 Baldwin Ave; ⏰8:30am-4pm Mon-Thu, to 6pm Fri)

Post Office (Map p158; ☎579-8866; www.usps.com; 120 Baldwin Ave; ⏰8:30-11am & noon-4:30pm Mon-Fri, 10:30am-12:30pm)

ℹ️ Getting There & Around

The Maui Bus operates between Kahului and Pa'ia ($2) every 90 minutes from 5:30am to 8:30pm. The stop is on Hana Hwy near Baldwin Ave intersection.

....

Ha'iku

This little town is like Pa'ia just before tourism took hold. Ha'iku also has its roots in sugarcane – Maui's first 12 acres of the sweet stuff were planted here in 1869, and the village once had both a sugar mill and pineapple canneries. Thanks to its affordability and proximity to Ho'okipa Beach, it's also a haunt of pro surfers, who've helped rejuvenate the town. Now visitation is rising, as seen in the expanded listings below. Nestled in greenery, this is a low-key place to stay, with many excellent accommodations and restaurants for its size.

 Activities

North Shore Zipline
Zip-Lining

(Map p156; ☎269-0671; www.nszipline.com; 2065 Kauhikoa Rd; canopy tour $100; ⏰8am-4:30pm Mon-Sat) Whizzing through giant eucalyptus, this canopy tour offers seven zip lines connected by bridges and platforms. With its medium speeds and fairly short lines, newbies might benefit most. The minimum age is five years old; the minimum weight is 40lb, maximum 270lb. Allow two hours.

Fourth Marine Division Memorial Park
Park

(Map p156; www.mauicounty.gov; Kokomo Rd, 2-mile marker) The jungle gym at this county park – complete with turrets, boardwalks and slides – is great for kids.

Surfboard fence, Ha'iku
TRINA DOPP/GETTY IMAGES ©

Rental Properties

The North Shore and Upcountry are awash in rental properties. Some of the best are reviewed here. But if you're still stuck see **Maui Vacation Properties** (Map p156; 575-9228; www.mauivacationproperties.com; 771 Ha'iku Rd; 8:30am-4:30pm), **Ho'okipa Haven Vacation Services** (Map p158; 579-8282; www.hookipa.com; 62 Baldwin Ave; 9am-4pm Mon-Fri) or **VRBO** (www.vrbo.com).

Sleeping

Ha'iku Plantation Inn   B&B $$

(Map p156; 575-7500; www.haikuleana.net; 555 Ha'iku Rd; r $129-159) Set in verdant surroundings on the edge of town, this large and lovingly restored plantation house, the former company doctor's residence, offers four rooms with private baths, high ceilings, clawfoot tubs, hardwood floors and oodles of charm, all at a reasonable price. Several acres loaded with tropical fruit trees ensure privacy when lounging on the classic porch. Gin, m'dear?

Pilialoha   Cottage $$

(Map p156; 572-1440; www.pilialoha.com; 2512 Kaupakalua Rd; d $145; 📶) Pilialoha blends countryside charm with all the comforts of a home away from home. The sunny split-level cottage has one pretty setting, nestled in a eucalyptus grove. Everything inside is pretty, too. But it's the warm hospitality and attention to detail – from the fresh-cut roses on the table to the Hawaiian music collection and cozy quilts on the beds – that shine brightest. Breakfast goodies for your first morning and coffee for the entire stay are provided. Other perks include laundry facilities and fleece jackets for that Haleakalā sunrise.

Haiku Cannery Inn B&B   B&B $$

(Map p156; 283-1274; www.haikucanneryinn.com; 1061 Kokomo Rd; r incl breakfast $115-145) Down a winding dirt road, surrounded by banana and breadfruit trees, this 1920s plantation house beams with character. High ceilings, hardwood floors and period decor reflect the place's century-old history. In addition to the rooms in the main

Inside Alice in Hulaland (p163), Pa'ia

house, there's a roomy two-bedroom detached cottage for $190.

Pililani
Vacation Rental $$$

(Map p156; ☎575-9228; www.maui.cc/Pili/Pililani-welcome.html; 110 Kane Rd; depending on occupancy $500-800, 7-night minimum, cleaning fee $500; 🛜) Looking for your own Balinese resort? Connected by glass hallways, these three hardwood chalets on four manicured acres with swaying palms, stone pool deck, sauna and tennis courts certainly fit the bill. The main house even sits over a stream. Perfect for families.

Eating

Baked on Maui
Bakery, Cafe $

(Map p156; 375 W Kuiaha; sandwiches $6-9; ⏰6:30am-5pm) Delicious homemade food, including fresh baked bread, a full breakfast menu and great sandwiches, makes this *the* local stop prior to tackling the road to Hana. From Pa'ia turn right on West Kuiaha and continue on until you reach the huge Pa'uwela Cannery building, now office space.

Veg Out
Vegetarian $

(Map p156; ☎575-5320; www.veg-out.com; 810 Kokomo Rd, Ha'iku Town Center; mains $6-10, pizza $7-17; ⏰10:30am-7:30pm Mon-Fri, 11:30am-7:30pm Sat & Sun; 🍴) Tucked inside a former warehouse, this rasta-casual vegetarian eatery serves up a dynamite burrito loaded with beans, hot tofu and jalapeños. Also right on the mark are the taro cheeseburgers and pesto-chèvre pizza.

Nuka
Japanese $$

(Map p156; ☎575-2939; www.nukamaui.com; 780 Ha'iku Rd; rolls $7-18; ⏰4:30-10pm Tue-Sun) This newcomer has already become one of Maui's best dining options. The marriage of a traditional Japanese restaurant with a jazzy cafe, it offers the classics, like sushi and tempura, alongside exotic rolls and *otsumami* (tapas). From the menus to the decor to the website, everything is presented with sophistication, and without inflated prices. And oh, that Nuka Roll...

Colleen's
American $$

(Map p156; ☎575-9211; www.colleensinhaiku.com; 810 Ha'iku Rd, Ha'iku Marketplace; breakfast $8-13, lunch $6-15, dinner $11-30; ⏰6am-9:30pm) 🌿 From morning to evening, this boisterous bistro is the Ha'iku hangout, for locals and visitors alike. Menu choices are straightforward – burgers, salads and build-your-own pizzas among them – but cooked to perfection, and supported by a wide range of craft beers. Excellent coffee and big breakfasts drag 'em in early.

Ha'iku Grocery Store
Supermarket

(Map p156; 810 Ha'iku Rd; ⏰7am-9pm) You'll find bento boxes and hot food here in addition to the usuals.

Drinking & Nightlife

Maui Kombucha
Teahouse

(Map p156; www.mauikombucha.com; 810 Kokomo Rd, Ha'iku Town Center; lunch $7-10, dinner $9-12; ⏰8am-8pm) 🌿 Welcome to 'The Booch', home of Ha'iku's alternative drink, kombucha. Hidden behind the back of a strip mall, this hip hole-in-the-wall overflows with fermented tea (with bubbles!) and a lively crowd. The veggie fare changes daily, but expect pizza, salads and lots of fun. Located behind Ha'iku Town Center.

Entertainment

Hana Hou Cafe
Live Music

(Map p156; ☎575-2661; www.hanahoucafe.com; 810 Ha'iku Rd; ⏰11am-9pm) While offering an interesting fusion of Hawaiian, Thai and French cuisine, this newcomer has rapidly become popular for high-quality live music (6pm to 9pm Monday, Wednesday and Saturday), particularly with more mature visitors, who also appreciate the indoor/outdoor seating. Whether it's folk, blues, slack key or lounge, there's something for everyone. Reserve ahead Monday and Wednesday.

❶ Information

Haiku has two gas stations, so you *don't* have to drive all the way back to Pa'ia.

Island Insights

The North Shore harbors Maui's most famous big-wave surfing spot: **Jaws** (Pe'ahi; Map p156). When present, the mammoth swell reaches as high as a seven-story building. Surfers are towed in or even dropped by helicopter. Unfortunately for onlookers, there's no legitimate public access to the cliffs above, as the path crosses private land.

Post Office (Map p156; 575-2614; www.usps. com; 770 Ha'iku Rd; ⊙9am-3pm Mon-Fri, to 11am Sat)

Hali'imaile

The tiny pineapple town of Hali'imaile offers two ripe fruit and one past its prime.

Tours

Maui Gold Pineapple Tour   Tour
(Map p156; ✓665-5491; www.mauipineappletour. com; 875 Hali'imaile Rd; adult/child $65/55, with lunch $80/70; ⊙tours 9:30am & 11:45am) This underwhelming tour centers on eating pineapple in the fields. The tour includes the adjacent processing plant – even when it's not operating. Pass.

Sleeping & Eating

Peace of Maui   Guesthouse $
(Map p156; ✓572-5045; www.peaceofmaui. com; 1290 Hali'imaile Rd; r with shared bath from $85, cottage $185; @ 🛜) Upcountry's top budget sleep is in the middle of nowhere yet within an hour's drive of nearly everywhere, making it a central base for exploring the island. Spotlessly clean rooms are small but comfortable, with refrigerator and shared bath. There's also a guest kitchen and hot tub. A separate two-bedroom, one-bath cottage offers a covered deck with beautiful mountain views and extra room for kids.

**Hali'imaile
General Store**   Hawaii Regional $$$
(Map p156; ✓572-2666; www.bevgannonrestau rants.com; 900 Hali'imaile Rd; lunch $16-22, dinner $20-42; ⊙11am-2:30pm Mon-Fri, 5:30-9:30pm daily; ✦) Chef Bev Gannon was one of the original forces behind the Hawaii Regional cuisine movement and a steady flow of in-the-know diners beat a track to this culinary outpost to feast on her inspired creations, such as sashimi pizza and Asian pear duck tostadas. The atmospheric plantation-era decor sets the mood.

Makawao

Makawao is an attractive mélange of art haven and *paniolo* (Hawaiian cowboy) culture, with a twist of New Age sensibility. A ranching town since the 1800s, its false-front buildings and hitching posts look transported from the Old West. Today the surrounding hills still contain cattle pastures and the weekend rodeo, but also some expensive homes, as these cool and quiet uplands have become a choice residential area. Meanwhile, the town below has filled with attractive galleries and cafes, making it a magnet for visitors. The main action is at the intersection of Baldwin Ave and Makawao Ave, where you can enjoy a few hours of browsing and a fine meal.

Sights

**Hui No'eau Visual
Arts Center**   Gallery
(Map p156; ✓572-6560; www.huinoeau. com; 2841 Baldwin Ave; ⊙10am-4pm) FREE Occupying the former estate of sugar magnates Harry and Ethel Baldwin, Hui No'eau is a regal setting for a community arts center. The main plantation house was designed by famed architect CW Dickey in 1917 and showcases the Hawaiian Regional architectural style he pioneered. The prestigious arts club founded here in the 1930s still offers classes in printmaking, pottery, metalsmithing and other visual arts.

You're welcome to visit the galleries, which exhibit the diverse works of island

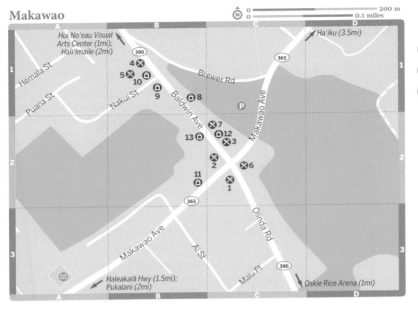

Makawao

Makawao

 Eating
Casanova Deli	(see 1)
1 Casanova Restaurant	C2
2 Komoda Store & Bakery	C2
3 Makawao Garden Café	C2
4 Makawao Steak House	B1
5 Market Fresh Bistro	B1
6 Polli's	C2
7 Rodeo General Store	C2

Shopping
8 Aloha Cowboy	B1
9 Designing Wahine Emporium	B1
10 Hot Island Glass	B1
11 Maui Hands	B2
12 Sherri Reeve Gallery	C2
Viewpoints Gallery	(see 10)
13 Wertheim Contemporary	B2

artists, and walk around the grounds, where you'll find stables converted into art studios. The gift shop sells quality ceramics, glassware and prints created on-site. Pick up a walking-tour map at the front desk. The center is just north of the 5-mile marker.

Sacred Garden of Maliko   Gardens
(Map p156; ☎ 573-7700; www.sacredgardenmaui.com; 460 Kaluanui Rd; ⊙10am-5pm) FREE Up for a meditative moment? The Sacred Garden of Maliko, a self-described healing sanctuary, has a pair of rock-garden labyrinth walks guaranteed to reset the harmony gauge. One's in an orchid greenhouse; the other's in a *kukui* (candlenut

tree) grove beside Maliko Stream. It's a truly peaceful place to spend some time.

To get there, turn east off Baldwin Ave onto Kaluanui Rd. After 0.8 miles you'll cross a one-lane bridge; 0.2 miles further look for a low stone wall – the garden is on the right just before a sharp S-curve in the road.

🏃 Activities

Makawao Forest
Reserve Trails   Outdoors
(Map p156; Kahakapao Rd, Makawao Forest Reserve; ⊙7am-7pm) The Makawao Forest Reserve has two trails popular with hikers and mountain bikers alike. The first

167

Island Insights

For a steep scenic drive with plenty of twists and turns, head into the hills above Makawao along Olinda Rd, which picks up in town where Baldwin Ave leaves off. Turn left onto Pi'iholo Rd near the top, and wind back down into town. The whole crazy loop takes about half an hour. Combine with Waihou Spring Trail (p168) for a cool midway break.

begins at the small parking area at the second (severe) dip in Kahakapao Rd, and is a peaceful and easy forest walk that goes on for several miles. You must return the same way. The second begins 100m further on.

Walk to the second parking area if your vehicle can't navigate the dip. Signs lead on to the 5-mile Kahakapao Loop Trail, which parallels a ravine before arcing back through cool upland forest. If dry, this is also a great running trail. To reach Kahakapao Rd, head up Pi'iholo Rd for 1.5 miles, turn left on Waiahiwi Rd, and turn right after 0.4 miles.

Pi'iholo Ranch Zipline   Zip-Lining
(Map p156; ☎572-1717; www.piiholozipline.com; Pi'iholo Rd; zip tours $146-198, canopy tours $94-172; ☺8am-3pm) This well-done operation offers two options: a standard dual-line course of four or five lines ($140/190), the latter with a 2800ft finale that hits 600ft in altitude, and a three-, six- or nine-line canopy course ($90/135/165). Allow one to three hours depending on length. Ages eight to 12 go free on the nine-liner. There's a 60lb minimum weight. GoPro cams available.

Waihou Spring Trail   Hiking
(Map p156) For a quiet walk in deep woods, take this cool, tranquil and easy trail, which begins 4.75 miles up Olinda Rd from central Makawao. A half-mile in you'll reach a loop trail, which brings you back where you started. A steep (and potentially muddy) offshoot descends to Waihou Spring, but for most the loop will be enough.

Pi'iholo Ranch Stables   Horseback Riding
(Map p156; ☎270-8750; www.piiholo. com; 325 Waiahiwi Rd; per person 1hr $75, 2hr $120; ☺Mon-Sat) Located in a secluded glen, high up on the edge of a rainforest, this family-run cattle ranch, now six generations old, offers group rides for up to six people with mountain, valley and pasture views galore. One-hour rides depart 8:30am and noon; two-hour rides depart 9am and 10:30am. There's also pony rides for children as young as three.

Cowboy at Makawao Rodeo
QUINCY DEIN/GETTY IMAGES ©

Festivals & Events

Makawao
Third Friday
Street Carnival

(www.mauifridays.com) On the third Friday of every month the center of Makawao turns into a pedestrian zone and laid-back street party from 6pm to 9pm, with food and live music. If there's a good musician playing (like Makana) you're in luck.

Upcountry Ag
& Farm Fair
Agricultural Fair

(☏572-3545; ⏲8am-4pm Sat & Sun) Traditional agricultural fair with a farmers market, arts and crafts, chili cookoff, *keiki* (children's) games and good ol' country music. It's held on the second weekend in June at the Eddie Tam Complex.

Makawao Rodeo
Rodeo

Hundreds of *paniolo* show up at the Oskie Rice Arena on the weekend closest to Independence Day for Hawaii's premier rodeo. Qualifying roping and riding events occur all day on Thursday and Friday prior to the big prizes over the weekend. For thrills on Friday night, head up to the arena to see the bull-riding bash.

Paniolo Parade
Parade

Held on the Saturday morning closest to July 4, this festive parade goes right through the heart of Makawao; park at Oskie Rice Arena and take the free shuttle to the town center.

Maui Polo Club
Polo

(www.mauipoloclub.com; adult/child $5/free; ⏲1:30pm, gates open 12:30pm) A friendly tailgating party surrounds these Sunday matches held behind Oskie Rice Arena, 1 mile above town on Olinda Rd, early September through mid-November; and at the Manduke Baldwin Polo Arena, 1.7 miles up Haleakalā Hwy from Makawao Ave, from April 3 to June 26. Dress is casual to island dressy (ie your best aloha shirt).

 # Sleeping

Aloha Cottage
Cottage $$

(Map p156; ☏575-9228; www.maui.cc/Aloha Cottage.html; 1875 Olinda Rd; cottage $199-299, 4-night minimum, cleaning fee $100; 🛜) Honeymooners, take note! This gated love nest, an octagonal cottage with one large room, sits on a bluff way up steep Olinda Rd, about 10 minutes from town. Surrounded by greenery, it assures privacy. There's a full kitchen, laundry, vaulted ceiling, king bed and a large lanai (veranda) with hot tub. A perfect retreat.

Ginger Falls
Studio $$

(Map p156; ☏573-1173; www.wildgingerfalls. com; 355 Kaluanui Rd; d $185, 3-night minimum; 🛜) Uniquely sited in a jungle gulch with 40ft walls of rock, ancient petroglyphs, running stream and massive banyan tree, this exquisitely decorated and very private room, with its own enormous lanai and hot tub, transports you to another world. Once a workshop for the main residence, it has been renovated into a model of creative design. Nice touches like a glass-roof shower, a wicker ceiling fan and a wall tapestry are found throughout. Oh, if they were only all like this.

Hale Ho'okipa Inn
B&B $$

(Map p156; ☏572-6698; www.maui-bed-and-breakfast.com; 32 Pakani Pl; r incl breakfast $145-185; 🛜) A short walk from the town center, this Craftsman-style house built in 1924 offers four sunny guest rooms furnished with antiques. It's all very casual and homey with country-style furnishings in the rooms and organic fruit from the yard on the breakfast table.

 # Eating

Makawao Garden Café
Cafe $

(Map p167; ☏573-9065; www.makawaogarden cafe.com; 3669 Baldwin Ave; mains $5-10; ⏲11am-3pm Mon-Sat) On a sunny day there's no better place in town for lunch than this outdoor cafe tucked into a courtyard at the northern end of Baldwin Ave. It's strictly sandwiches and salads, but everything's fresh, generous and made to order by the owner herself.

Komoda Store & Bakery
Bakery $

(Map p167; 3674 Baldwin Ave; ⏲7am-5pm Mon & Wed-Fri, to 2pm Sat) This homespun bakery, legendary for its mouthwatering cream puffs and guava-filled *malasadas* (Portuguese fried doughnuts), has been a Makawao landmark since 1916. Arrive early, as it often sells out by noon.

Casanova Deli
Deli $

(Map p167; ☎572-0220; www.casanovamakawao. com; 1188 Makawao Ave; breakfast $2-9, sandwiches $7-13; ⏰7:30am-5:30pm Mon-Sat, 8:30am-5:30pm Sun) Makawao's hippest haunt brews heady espressos and buzzes all day with folks munching on buttery croissants, thick Italian sandwiches and hearty Greek salads. Take it all out to the roadside deck for the town's best people-watching.

Rodeo General Store
Deli $

(Map p167; 3661 Baldwin Ave; meals under $8; ⏰6:30am-10pm Mon-Sat, to 9pm Sun) Stop here to grab a tasty takeout meal. The deli counter sells everything from fresh salads and Hawaiian *poke* (marinated raw fish) to hot teriyaki chicken and plate lunches ready to go. Everything is made from scratch.

Makawao Farmers Market
Market $

(Map p156; ☎280-5516; www.makawaofarmers market.org; 200 Olinda Rd; ⏰9am-2pm Wed) Upcountry gardeners gather to sell their homegrown veggies and fruit once a week at this small open-air market next to Po'okela Church.

Casanova Restaurant
Italian $$

(Map p167; ☎572-0220; www.casanovamakawao. com; 1188 Makawao Ave; lunch $10-20, dinner $12-38; ⏰11:30am-2pm Mon-Sat, 5-9pm daily) The one Makawao restaurant that lures diners up the mountain, Casanova offers reliably good Italian fare. The crispy innovative pizzas cooked in a kiawe-fired oven are as good as they get. Juicy Maui-raised steaks and classic Italian dishes shore up the rest of the menu. Casanova also doubles as the Upcountry's top entertainment venue, with a happening dance floor and live music several nights a week.

Market Fresh Bistro
International $$

(Map p167; ☎572-4877; marketfreshbistro.com; 3620 Baldwin Ave; breakfast $10-13, lunch $10-18; ⏰9am-3pm Tue-Sun, 6-8:30pm Thu) Foodies love the sophisticated tastes at this relaxing farm-to-table cafe, whose philosophy of 'global influence, local ingredients', has rapidly made it one of Makawao's best dining options. Insiders descend here Thursday evenings at 6pm for a special prix-fixe dinner ($60). Located inside the Shops at the Courtyard.

Polli's
Mexican $$

(Map p167; ☎572-7808; www.pollismexican restaurant.com; 1202 Makawao Ave; mains $11-23; ⏰11am-10pm) Locals and visitors alike flock to this friendly and reliable Tex-Mex restaurant. Have a cerveza at the small bar, or tackle some sizzling fajitas in the nearby booths.

Makawao Steak House
Steakhouse $$$

(Map p167; ☎572-8711; www.cafeoleimaui.com; 3612 Baldwin Ave; mains $17-42; ⏰4:30-9:30pm Tue-Sun) What's a cowboy town without a steakhouse? Or a saloon? You get both here, along with a warm Upcountry atmosphere. Recently purchased by the Cafe Olei franchise, the variety menu offers something for everyone, including the kids.

🔒 Shopping

Wertheim Contemporary
Gallery

(Map p167; ☎573-5972; www.wertheimcontem porary.com; 3660 Baldwin Ave; ⏰11am-5pm) Showcases the extraordinary art of Andreas Nottebohm, who etches flat sheets of aluminum to create an illusion of depth. You won't believe your eyes.

Maui Hands
Gallery

(Map p167; ☎572-2008; www.mauihands.com; 1169 Makawao Ave; ⏰10am-6pm Mon-Sat, to 5pm Sun) A fascinating collection of high-quality Hawaii art, primarily from Maui, including photography, koa, ceramics, and a mix of traditional and contemporary paintings. Don't miss the Cook Islands pine vase.

Hot Island Glass
Glass

(Map p167; www.hotislandglass.com; 3620 Baldwin Ave; ⏰9am-5pm) Maui's oldest hand-blown glass studio offers the opportunity to see the artists in action from 10:30am

An Old West Tale

Many visitors to Hawaii are surprised to discover that tropical paradise contains a strong dose of the Old West. Towns like Makawao, with their original false-front buildings, look primed for a shootout, while Hawaiian cowboys, known as *paniolo* hereabouts, still ride down the main street. Now, how the heck did that happen?

Actually, it's two different stories. The false-front architecture in both Hawaii *and* the western US came from immigrant Asian labor, while the cowboys came from Latin America – a half-century or so before their mainland counterparts rose to prominence. Hence the word 'paniolo', a corruption of 'españoles', meaning Spaniards.

to 4pm. Everything from paperweights with ocean themes to high-art decorative pieces are available.

Viewpoints Gallery   Gallery
(Map p167; ☎572-5979; www.viewpointsgallery maui.com; 3620 Baldwin Ave; ☺10:30am-5pm) This classy gallery hosts a dozen of the island's finest artists, and feels like a museum.

Designing Wahine Emporium   Gifts
(Map p167; ☎573-0990; www.designingwahine. com; 3640 Baldwin Ave; ☺10am-6pm Mon-Sat, 11am-5pm Sun) Quality gifts, classic aloha shirts, hand-dyed Ts with *paniolo* themes, and much else fills this classic plantation cottage.

Aloha Cowboy   Clothing
(Map p167; ☎573-8190; www.alohacowboy.net; 3643 Baldwin Ave; ☺9:30am-6pm Mon-Sat, 10am-5pm Sun) Get your cowboy-themed retro lunch pails and rhinestone-studded leather bags here.

Sherri Reeve Gallery   Gallery
(Map p167; www.sreeve.com; 3669 Baldwin Ave; ☺9am-5pm Mon-Fri, 10am-4pm Sat & Sun) Floral watercolors in a jewel-toned palette on everything from T-shirts to full-size canvasses. Artist is generally present.

ⓘ Information

Minit Stop (☎572-6350; www.minitstop.com; 1100 Makawao Ave; ☺5am-11pm) There's no

bank in town, but this convenience store has gas and an ATM. It also serves legendary fried chicken: your budget lunch.

Post Office (Map p167; ☎572-0019; www.usps. com; 1075 Makawao Ave; ☺9am-4:30pm Mon-Fri, to 11am Sat)

Pukalani & Around

True to its name, which means Heavenly Gate, Pukalani is the gateway to the lush Upcountry. Most visitors just drive past Pukalani on the way to Kula and Haleakalā, unless they need food or gas (the last before the park).

To reach the business part of town, get off Haleakalā Hwy (Hwy 37) at the Old Haleakalā Hwy exit, which becomes Pukalani's main street.

Activities

Pukalani Country Club   Golf
(Map p156; ☎572-1314; www.pukalanigolf.com; 360 Pukalani St; greens fee with cart $61, with clubs $81; ☺7am-dusk) With its clubhouse in a mobile home, and its restaurant boarded up from a fire years ago, the Pukalani Golf Club doesn't present a pretty face, but the course is in excellent condition and one of the best deals on the island. Come after 2:30pm and golf the rest of the day for just $35 – cart included.

Tours

Surfing Goat Dairy
Farm Tour

(Map p156; ☎878-2870; www.surfinggoatdairy.com; 3651 Oma'opio Rd; ☺store 9am-5pm Mon-Sat, to 2pm Sun) 'Feta mo betta' is the motto at this 42-acre farm, the source of all that luscious chèvre adorning the menus of Maui's top restaurants. There's a well-stocked store and various child-friendly 'ag tours,' including a frequent 20-minute dairy tour (10am to 3:30pm Monday to Saturday, to 1pm Sunday; adult/child $10/7), an 'evening chores & milking' tour (3:15pm Monday to Saturday; adult/child $15/12; reserve ahead) and the two-hour 'grand dairy' tour (9am Saturday; $25; call for dates). Children under 11 free.

Ocean Vodka Organic Farm & Distillery
Distillery Tour

(Map p156; ☎877-0009; www.oceanvodka.com; 4051 Oma'opio Rd; adult/child $10/free; ☺tours 9:30am-3:30pm) This family-run start-up vodka distillery adds a unique new ag tour to Maui. Passionate guides tell an interesting story about the organic roots of vodka production, and a sampling is provided for the eligible. Reasonably priced, too. Combine with nearby Surfing Goat Dairy.

 # Eating

Kojima's
Japanese $$

(Map p156; www.kojimassushi.com; 81 Makawao Ave; lunch $8-16, dinner $15-18; ☺11:30am-2pm & 5-9pm Mon-Fri, 5-9pm Sat) The real deal. This cafe and sushi bar with outdoor porch showcases the talents of Chef Kojima, who has been cooking traditional Japanese cuisine for over three decades in Japan and the US. Try the rock 'n' roll, a crab and avocado roll topped with unagi glaze. BYO alcohol.

Serpico's
Italian $$

(Map p156; ☎572-8498; www.serpicosmaui.com; cnr Aewa Pl & Old Haleakalā Hwy; mains $8-19, pizza $13-23; ☺11am-10pm; ♿) In the center of Pukalani, opposite McDonald's, this casual Italian eatery makes New York–style pizzas and pasta dishes, and it makes them well. If you're in a hurry, there are sandwiches and inexpensive lunch specials, as well as a $6 to $7 kids' menu.

Ali'i Kula Lavender, Kula

Upcountry Farmers Market   Market

(Map p156; www.upcountryfarmersmarket.com;
55 Kiopaa St; ⏰7am-noon Sat) More than
40 local farmers – and a food truck or
two – share fruit, vegetables and locally
prepared fare at this market in the parking lot of Longs Drugs at the Kulamalu
Shopping Center. Arrive by 9:30am for
the best choices.

Pukalani Superette   Supermarket

(Map p156; www.pukalanisuperette.com; 15
Makawao Ave; prepared meals $5-10; ⏰5:30am-
9pm Mon-Fri, 6:30am-9pm Sat, 7am-8pm Sun) A
popular choice for prepared hot meals –
kalua pork, chicken long rice, Spam
musubi (Spam with rice and nori) etc.

Foodland   Supermarket

(Map p156; cnr Old Haleakalā Hwy & Pukalani St;
⏰24hr) Located in the Pukalani Terrace
Center, this always-open supermarket is a
convenient pit stop for people heading up
and down the mountain.

Information

Bank of Hawaii (www.boh.com; cnr Old
Haleakalā Hwy & Pukalani St, Pukalani Terrace
Center) The last bank and ATM before reaching
Kula and Haleakala National Park.

Post Office (Map p156; www.usps.com; cnr Old
Haleakalā Hwy & Pukalani St, Pukalani Terrace
Center)

Kula

It's cooler in Kula – refreshingly so. Think
of this Upcountry heartland as one big
garden, and you won't be far off. So
bountiful is Kula's soil, it produces most
of the onions, lettuce and strawberries
grown in Hawaii and almost all of the
commercially grown protea. The latest
addition, sweet-scented lavender, is
finding its niche, too. The magic is in the
elevation.

At 3000ft, Kula's cool nights and sunny
days are ideal for growing all sorts of
crops – making Kula synonymous with
fresh veggies on any Maui menu.

The Best...
Activities for Kids

1 Farm tour, Surfing Goat Dairy (p172)

2 Pony rides, Pi'iholo Ranch
Stables (p168)

3 Spreckelsville Beach (p155)

4 Watching glassblowers,
Hot Island Glass (p170)

Sights

Ali'i Kula Lavender   Gardens

(Map p156; ☏878-3004; www.aklmaui.com;
1100 Waipoli Rd; parking $3; ⏰9am-4pm) Oc-
cupying a gorgeous hillside location with
panoramic views toward the West Maui
Mountains, this charming lavender farm
offers fragrant pathways, a gift shop with
a variety of lavender products and, best of
all, a lanai with sweeping views where you
can enjoy a scone and a cup of lavender
tea. To reach the parking area, proceed
through the Kula Forest Reserve gates and
follow the signs around the loop.

Worcester Glassworks   Glassblowing

(Map p156; ☏878-4000; www.worcesterglass
works.com; 4626 Lower Kula Rd; ⏰10am-5pm
Mon-Sat) This family-run working studio
and gallery produces some amazing
pieces, particularly the sand-blasted
glass in natural forms (eg seashells).
Visitors are welcome to watch the artists
and their solar-powered furnaces at work.
The adjacent store offers seconds from
$20 to $3500.

Enchanting
Floral Gardens   Gardens

(Map p156; ☏878-2531; www.enchantingfloral
gardens.com; 2505 Kula Hwy; adult/child $10/5;
⏰9am-3pm Wed-Sun) 🌿 This huge garden
occupies a narrow zone where tropical,

temperate and desert vegetation all thrive, producing an amazing variety of plants, from flamboyant proteas and orchids to orange trees and kava. A garden stroll ends with a sampling of fruits, and perhaps a sandwich and smoothie in the cafe.

NORTH SHORE & UPCOUNTRY KULA

Kula Botanical Garden
Gardens

(Map p156; ☎878-1715; www.kulabotanical garden.com; 638 Kekaulike Ave; adult/child $10/3; ☻9am-4pm) 🖉 Well-kept and shady, this mature 9-acre garden has paths that wind through acres of theme plantings, including native Hawaiian specimens and a 'taboo garden' of poisonous plants. Because a stream runs through it, the garden supports water-thirsty plants you won't find in other Kula gardens. After rain the place is an explosion of color.

Maui Agricultural Research Center
Gardens

(Map p156; ☎878-1213; www.ctahr.hawaii.edu; 424 Mauna Pl; ☻7:30am-3:30pm Mon-Thu) **FREE** It was in this garden operated by the University of Hawai'i that the state's first proteas were planted in 1965. Today you can walk through row after row of their colorful descendants. Named for the Greek god Proteus, who was noted for his ability to change form, the varieties are amazingly diverse – some look like oversize pincushions, others like spiny feathers.

Nursery cuttings from the plants here are distributed to protea farms across Hawaii, which in turn supply florists as far away as Europe. To get here, take Copp Rd (between the 12- and 13-mile markers on Hwy 37) for half a mile and turn left on Mauna Pl. Best to call ahead.

Holy Ghost Church
Church

(Map p156; 4300 Lower Kula Rd; ☻8am-6pm) Waiakoa's hillside landmark, the octagonal Holy Ghost Church, was built in 1895 by Portuguese immigrants. It features a beautifully ornate interior that looks like it came right out of the Old World, as indeed much of it did. The gilded altar was carved by renowned Austrian woodcarver Ferdinand Stuflesser and shipped in pieces around the Cape of Good Hope.

🏃 Activities

Pony Express and Skyline Eco-Adventures operate on land belonging to Haleakalā Ranch, a working cattle ranch that sprawls across the slopes beneath Haleakalā National Park. The businesses are adjacent to each other on Hwy 378, 2.5 miles up from Hwy 377, next to Maui Lavender.

Pony Express
Tour

(Map p156; ☎667-2200; www.ponyexpresstours. com; Haleakalā Crater Rd; ☻reservations 7am-9pm) Offers a two-hour ride through the cattle country of Haleakala Ranch ($110, 8am check-in), and a 1½-hour 'mauka ride' ($95, 11am and 1:30pm check-in), both with great

Hot Island Glass (p170), Makawao
LONELY PLANET/GETTY IMAGES ©

views from 4000ft. The real prize is a four-hour ride down Sliding Sands Trail into Haleakalā's lunar-like crater, a 2500ft descent ($188, includes lunch). Check website for discounts and reservations.

Skyline Eco-Adventures Zip-Lining
(Map p156; ☏878-8400; www.zipline.
com; Haleakalā Crater Rd; zip-line tour $119;
◷8:30am-3:30pm) Maui's first zip line has a prime location on the slopes of Haleakalā. The five lines are relatively short compared with the competition (100–850ft), although a unique 'pendulum zip' adds some spice at the end. Good for newbies.

Proflyght Paragliding Paragliding
(Map p156; ☏874-5433; www.paraglidemaui.
com; Waipoli Rd; 1000ft paraglide $95, 3000ft
$185; ◷office 7am-7pm, flights 2 hours after sunrise) Strap into a tandem paraglider with a certified instructor and take a leap off the cliffs beneath Polipoli Spring State Recreation Area. The term 'bird's-eye view' will never be the same. Must be under 230lb.

 Tours

Oʻo Farm Farm Tour
(Map p156; ☏667-4341; www.oofarm.com;
Waipoli Rd; lunch tour adult/child $50/25;
◷10:30am-2pm Mon-Thu) Whether you're a gardener or a gourmet, you're going to love a tour of famed Lahaina chef James McDonald's organic Upcountry farm. Where else can you help harvest your own meal, turn the goodies over to a gourmet chef and feast on the bounty? BYO wine.

 Festivals & Events

Holy Ghost Feast Festival
(www.kulacatholiccommunity.org) Enjoy the aloha of Upcountry folks at this festival celebrating Kula's Portuguese heritage. Held at the Holy Ghost Church on the fourth Saturday and Sunday in May, it's a family event with games, craft booths, a farmers market and a free Hawaiian-Portuguese lunch on Sunday.

1 **YOU MUST GIVE ADVICE TO TRAVELERS EVERY DAY – WHAT ARE THE TOP THREE QUESTIONS PEOPLE ASK?**
First, they want to know where to go to the beach. For swimming it's Baldwin. It has a sandy beach, lifeguards and an area for kids. For surfing or windsurfing it's Hoʻokipa – even if you're just watching. And for kiteboarding it's Kanaha, by the airport. If you want to snorkel, it's best to go to the south or west side of Maui, not the North Shore.

2 **AND THE SECOND QUESTION?**
Where to swim beneath a waterfall! If you want easy access, the answer is Twin Falls. Just expect a crowd. If you're more athletic I'd recommend the Bamboo Trail. Not as many people know about that yet and it's a real adventure.

3 **QUESTION THREE?**
The best hike. I have two favorites. One is Polipoli, which is remote, uncrowded and forested, with lots of birds, deer and owls. Then there's the little-known hike that heads deep into ʻIao Valley, off the main trail. It's old Hawaii – beautiful and pristine.

4 **ANY OTHER COMMON QUESTIONS?**
The best restaurant, which I think is Paʻia Fish Market. Great food, inexpensive and bursting with local color. The best sunset is the lookout point at Hoʻokipa. And the best Hawaiian music is Monday night at Hana Hou, Haʻiku.

 Sleeping

Kula Lodge Cabin $$
(Map p156; ☏878-1535; www.kulalodge.com;
15200 Haleakalā Hwy; cabins $150-220; ☏)
These five rustic cabins are about 45 minutes from the summit of Haleakalā. All

Right: Fog settles over the countryside near Kula;
Below: Protea flower at Kula Botanical Garden (p174)

units come with lanai, coffeemakers and extra blankets, but no TVs or kitchenettes. Four have open lofts, which are great for kids, but offer no privacy. Wi-fi is available at the on-site restaurant.

Kula Sandalwoods
Inn **$$**

(Map p156; 878-3523; www.kulasandal woods.com; 15427 Haleakalā Hwy; r $141-159; restaurant 7am-3pm Mon-Sat, to noon Sun;) Conveniently located on the doorstep of Haleakalā National Park, these six rustic cottages offer sweeping views at a bargain price. The adjacent restaurant (mains $9 to $15) has classic breakfasts, including its signature eggs Benedict, and lunch featuring heaping Hawaiian pork.

Kula View Bed & Breakfast
B&B **$$**

(Map p156; 878-6736; www.kulaview.com; 600 Holopuni Rd; studio incl breakfast $115) This simple studio unit sits atop a country home and offers sunset ocean views.

Breakfast includes fruit from the backyard and home-made muffins. A bit tattered around the edges, but priced accordingly.

Eating

Maui Lavender
Burgers **$**

(Map p156; 250-2284; www.mauilavender.com; 18303 Haleakalā Hwy; breakfast $4-13, lunch $8-11; 7am-4pm) Occupying a beautiful hill-side location on the way to the summit, this informal restaurant (burgers, tacos, pizza etc) also offers the chance to walk the grounds of a lavender farm, including a charming gazebo with fall-away view.

Kula Lodge Restaurant
Hawaii Regional **$$**

(878-1535; www.kulalodge.com; 15200 Haleakalā Hwy; lunch $14-20, dinner $15-36; 7am-8:30pm) Assisted by its stagger-ing view, perhaps the best of any Maui restaurant, Kula Lodge has reinvented itself to great effect. Inside, veteran chef Casey Webster has the kitchen humming

to a farm-to-table variety menu. Outside, brick ovens provide build-your-own pizzas served under attractive cabanas. A spectacular sunset here is the perfect ending to a day on the summit.

Jazz from 6pm to 8pm every Friday and Saturday is another nice touch. Reserve on holidays.

Kula Bistro
Italian $$

(Map p156; 871-2960; www.kulabistro.com; 4566 Lower Kula Rd; breakfast $7-15, lunch & dinner $9-25; 7:30am-8:30pm) This superb family-owned bistro offers a magic recipe: a friendly dining room, sparkling service and delicious home cooking, including fabulous pizza and huge servings of coconut cream pie (enough for two). You'll be surprised to find food of this quality so high up the mountain.

BYO wine from Morihara Store across the street.

La Provence
Cafe $$

(Map p156; 878-1313; www.laprovencekula. com; 3158 Lower Kula Rd, Waiakoa; pastries $2-5, lunch $11-13, crepes $4-13; 7am-9pm Wed-Sun) One of Kula's best-kept secrets, this little courtyard restaurant in the middle of nowhere is the domain of Maui's finest pastry chef. Popular offerings include ham-and-cheese croissants, chocolate-filled pastries and filled crepes. Weekends offer a brunch menu that draws patrons from far and wide. Try the warm goat cheese and Kula greens salad.

Shopping

Kula Marketplace
Gifts

(Map p156; www.kulamarketplace.com; 15200 Haleakalā Hwy/Hwy 377; 7am-7pm) This rustic market perched on the side of the volcano acts as a clearinghouse for over 80 local vendors, evenly divided between food and arts and crafts. Gourmet selections include wine, chocolate and homemade jams. Great for gifts.

There's also fast food available if you've forgotten to load up.

Polipoli Spring State Park

This misty **cloud forest** (Map p156; www.hawaiistateparks.org) on the western slope of Haleakalā takes you deep off the beaten path. Crisscrossed with lightly trodden trails, it offers cool, shady and refreshing hikes amid tall redwoods, where a profound stillness prevails.

Half the fun is just getting here. Access is via spectacular Waipoli Rd, off Hwy 377, just under 0.5 miles before its southern intersection with the Kula Hwy (Hwy 37). This narrow ribbon twists back and forth for miles, never seeming to end. And given the views, you won't want it to. Layers of clouds drift in and out, revealing panoramic vistas across green rolling hills to the islands of Lana'i and Kaho'olawe.

The road has some soft shoulders, but the first 6 miles are paved. It becomes dirt after entering the Kula Forest Reserve. If mud prevails, the final 4 miles to the campground could require a 4WD vehicle. Otherwise you can crawl slowly to the finish line. The park is open 6am to 6pm.

Activities

To make a trip to Polipoli worthwhile, you should bring a picnic and spend some time hiking the trails. Two trails, the 0.6-mile Polipoli Trail and the 1.7-mile Redwood Trail, leave from the campground and connect with others, forming a complex system. There is a trail map at the campground, and signage en route.

Polipoli Hiking Circuit   Hiking

From the Polipoli campground parking area, the Redwood, Plum, Haleakalā Ridge and Polipoli Trails form a worthwhile 3.5-mile loop. Proceeding counterclockwise, the Redwood Trail leads from the right of the parking area to the ranger cabin and beyond. From there you'll descend into a towering redwood forest that feels more like California than Hawaii. After climbing back out to a ridgeline, you'll find spurs affording excellent views. Allow 2½ hours.

Waiakoa Loop Trail   Hiking

This two-hour, 3-mile loop passes through pine forest, eucalyptus stands and scrub scored with feral pig trails. It's fairly easy and fun on a mountain bike. The trailhead is at the **hunter check station** (Map p156), 5 miles up Waipoli Rd. Walk three-quarters of a mile down the grassy spur road on the left to a gate.

Boundary Trail   Hiking

This 3.8-mile trail begins about 200yd beyond the end of the paved section of Waipoli Rd. Park to the right of the cattle grate that marks the boundary of the Kula Forest Reserve. It's a steep downhill walk that crosses gulches and drops deep into woods of eucalyptus, pine and cedar, as well as a bit of native forest. In the afternoon the fog rolls in and visibility fades.

Skyline Trail   Hiking

(Map p156) The rugged Skyline Trail begins near the summit of Haleakalā National Park and drops more than 3000ft, passing cinder cones and craters, and offering clear-on views of West Maui and the islands of Hawai'i, Kaho'olawe and Lana'i before descending into the forest of Polipoli Spring State Recreation Area.

Sleeping

Polipoli Spring State Park Campground   Campground $

(Map p156) You'll rough it here. Facilities include picnic tables and toilets but no showers or drinking water. Fellow campers are likely to be pig hunters. Otherwise the place can be eerily deserted. It's also a fog zone, so expect damp weather. In winter temperatures frequently drop below freezing at night. Tenting requires a state permit (p326).

Polipoli Cabin   Cabin $

(Map p156; 984-8109; www.hawaiistateparks.org/camping/maui.cfm; Polipoli Spring State Recreation Area campground; cabin per night $90) Polipoli Spring State Recreation Area has one cabin for rent, which sleeps eight. Located adjacent to the campground at the very end of Waipoli Rd, it has gas lanterns and a wood-burning stove, but no electricity, refrigeration or linens.

Keokea

Modest as it may be, Keokea is the last real town before Hana if you're swinging around the southern part of the island. The sum total of the town center consists of a coffee shop, an art gallery, a gas station and two small stores, the Ching Store and the Fong Store. The last two announce one of Hawaii's many immigrant populations. Drawn by rich soil, Hakka Chinese farmers migrated to this remote corner of Kula at the turn of the 20th century. Their influence is still found throughout the village.

Sights

Sun Yat-sen Park　　　　　Park
(Map p156) For a time Sun Yat-sen, father of the Chinese nationalist movement, lived in Keokea. He's honored at Sun Yat-sen Park, found along the Kula Hwy (Hwy 37), 1.7 miles beyond Grandma's Coffee House. The park has picnic tables and is a great place to soak up the broad vistas that stretch clear across to West Maui.

Kwock Hing Society　　　Historic Building
(Map p156; Middle Rd) This colorful two-story building (1907) was originally built to provide services to immigrant Chinese workers. Now on the National Register of Historic Places, it's one of two such halls surviving on Maui, and contains an interesting photo collection on Chinese immigrants. It's generally locked, but Richard Shim (☎264-1186) will let you in. Speak loudly.

St John's Episcopal Church　　　Church
(Map p156; ☺services 8:30am Wed, 7:30am & 9:30am Sun) Built c 1907,

this local landmark still bears its name in Chinese characters.

Activities

Thompson Ranch　　Horseback Riding
(Map p156; ☎878-1910; www.thompsonranch maui.com; cnr Middle & Polipoli Rds; 2hr ride $100; ☺tour 10am) Join these folks for two-hour horseback rides across ranch land in the cool Upcountry bordering Polipoli Spring State Recreation Area. At elevations of 4000ft to 6000ft, it's a memorable ride for those who enjoy mountain scenery. Reserve ahead. Located 1 mile up Polipoli Rd on the left.

Keokea Park　　　Ultimate Frisbee
(Map p156) To get some exercise and meet some interesting people, join the ever-popular ultimate frisbee game held here Wednesday and Sunday from 4pm to sunset. The park is on the left just prior to entering town.

Scenic views, Maui Upcountry
FOTOSEARCH/GETTY IMAGES ©

Sleeping

Star Lookout — Cottage **$$**

(Map p156; ☎907-250-2364; www.starlook
out.com; 622 Thompson Rd; cottage $200) A
fabulous ocean view, outdoor hot tub and
grounds so quiet you can hear the flowers
bloom. Half a mile up a one-lane road
from Keokea center, this two-bedroom
cottage with a loft sleeps four comfort-
ably, six in a pinch. There's also a full
kitchen and wood-burning stove. Nice,
but what makes it spectacular is the set-
ting, which overlooks 1000 acres of green
pastureland with sweeping views of Lana'i
and West Maui.

Eating

Grandma's Coffee House — Cafe **$**

(Map p156; ☎878-2140; www.grandmascoffee.
com; 9232 Kula Hwy; pastries $3, breakfast $6-15,
sandwiches $8-10; ⏱7am-5pm, to 8pm Wed-Sat)
🌿 Worthy of a Norman Rockwell painting,
this charming island landmark with its
creaking screen door and carved wooden
tables grows its own coffee, dishes up deli
lunches and serves a varied dinner menu
Wednesday to Saturday. Take your good-
ies out on the lanai and eat right under
the coffee trees.

'Ulupalakua

This sprawling area is dominated by the
20,000-acre ranch of the same name.
Some 6000 head of cattle, as well as a
small herd of Rocky Mountain elk, dot the
hillside pastures. The ranch is still worked
by *paniolo*, Hawaiian cowboys who have
been here for generations.

Hwy 37 winds south through
ranch country, offering good views
of Kaho'olawe and the little island of
Molokini. After the vineyard, it's another
25 dusty, bumpy miles to Kipahulu along
the remote Pi'ilani Hwy.

Activities

Maui's Winery — Winery

(Map p156; ☎878-6058; www.mauiwine.com;
Kula Hwy; ⏱10am-5pm, tours 10:30am &
1:30pm) 🌿 Formerly Tedeschi Vineyards,
Maui's sole winery offers free tastings in
its historic stone cottage and twice-daily
tours. It produces a noteworthy variety,
from grape wines to novelty wines, using
local fruit to great effect. Try the sweet

Horses grazing at 'Ulupalakua Ranch

Maui Splash, a light blend of pineapple and passion fruit, the robust 'Ulupalakua, or the sophisticated dessert wine. Opposite the winery lie the remains of the Makee Sugar Mill, built in 1878.

Triple L Ranch   Horseback Riding

(📞280-7070; www.triplelranchmaui.com; 15900 Pi'ilani Hwy; 1hr $125, 2hr $150, half day $285, full day $375; ⏰8am-6:30pm) Unique on Maui, these personalized trail rides offer the opportunity to explore the volcanic Ka'naio region, from a one-hour outing around the cattle ranch to half- and full-day excursions to the sea and back. You won't be running into anyone else. For ages 12 and over. Reserve 24 hours ahead.

Festivals & Events

'Ulupalakua
Sunday Drive Event   Festival

(www.mauiwine.com/events) Twice a year, 'Ulupalakua Ranch sponsors a fun bash on the lawn of Maui's Winery with live slack key guitar music, glassblowing demonstrations, cowboy-centric food and exhibits of ecological goings-on. The music's a highlight. The festival currently takes place on a Sunday in December and June, but check ahead.

Eating

Bully's Burgers   Burgers $

(📞878-3272; www.triplelranchmaui.com; 15900 Pi'ilani Hwy, Triple L Ranch; burgers $9-12; ⏰11am-7pm winter, to 8pm summer) You've reached the end of the road. Or the beginning, if you wish. And what do you find but a burger shack decorated with cow skulls. No, Bully's has no Michelin stars, just one

The Best...
Upcountry-Grown Treats

1 Lunch tour, O'o Farm (p175)

2 Mango chèvre, Surfing Goat Dairy (p172)

3 Elk burgers, 'Ulupalakua Ranch Store

4 Maui Splash wine, Maui's Winery

5 Lavender scones, Ali'i Kula Lavender (p173)

6 Maui-grown coffee, Grandma's Coffee House

heck of a burger, thanks to the beef from Triple L Ranch and a few surprising twists, like the spicy chipotle sauce. Located about 4 miles past Maui's Winery – or the end of the road from Hana.

'Ulupalakua Ranch Store   Deli $

(Map p156; www.ulupalakuaranch.com; burgers $9-12; ⏰store 9:30am-5pm, grill 11am-3pm) 🌿 Sidle up to the life-size wooden cowboys on the front porch and say howdy. Then pop inside and check out the cowboy hats and souvenir T-shirts. If it's lunchtime, mosey over to the grill and treat yourself to an organic ranch-raised elk burger. Well yee-ha!

Haleakalā National Park

You haven't seen Maui – or at least peered into its soul – until you've reached the summit of Haleakalā. Like a yawning mouth, the huge crater opens beneath you, in all its raw volcanic glory, caressed by mist and, in the experience of a lifetime, bathed in the early light of sunrise. Lookouts on the crater's rim provide breathtaking views of the moonscape below, and the many cinder cones marching across it.

The rest of this amazing park is all about interacting with this mountain of solid lava, and the rare lifeforms that live upon it, some of them found only here. You can hike down into the crater, saddle-up on horse-back, or put your mountain bike through its paces. For the ultimate adventure, get a permit, bring a tent and camp overnight beneath the stars. However you do it, you will leave having touched something much, much larger than yourself.

Haleakalā Crater
SAMI SARKIS/GETTY IMAGES ©

183

Haleakalā National Park Itineraries

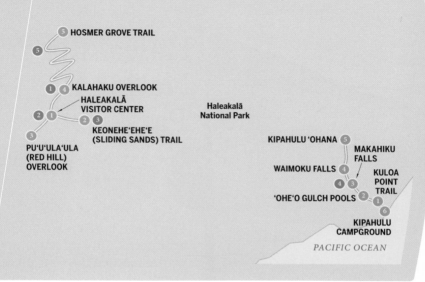

Day One

1 Haleakalā Visitor Center (p189) Haleakalā National Park has two distinct sections, and if you have just one day to visit, the summit is where you want to be. Whether you make a pre-dawn haul up the mountain to watch the sunrise, or mosey on up after breakfast, begin your explorations here. Not only is the visitor center the ideal perch for crater views, it's also a fine starting point for jaunts into the crater.

2 Keonehe'ehe'e (Sliding Sands) Trail (p191) Burn off the morning chill with an invigorating hike on the sun-warmed cinders of this unearthly trail.

3 Pu'u'ula'ula (Red Hill) Overlook (p189) Once you've completed your lunar-like crater hike, continue your road trip to Maui's highest point. Admire the *'ahinahina* (silversword) garden and take in a ranger talk.

4 Kalahaku Overlook (p187) It's time to head back down the mountain. Make your way to this lookout, a crater rim-hugger with an eye-popping, wide-angle view of the cinder cones dotting the crater floor.

5 Hosmer Grove Trail (p195) You've seen the starkly barren side of Haleakalā. Now make acquaintance with its lush green face by taking a half-mile walk in this forest brimming with birdsong. Like many animals in the park, some of these birds are found nowhere else.

➡ THIS LEG: 17 MILES

Day Two

① **Kuloa Point Trail** (p202) If you have two days for Haleakalā National Park, give the second day over to the wet and wild Kipahulu section. There's no food here, so bring a picnic basket and break it out at the trail's grassy knoll, savoring the ocean view.

② **'Ohe'o Gulch pools** (p202) These enticing pools cascade one into the next as they step down the hillside. The park service forbids swimming here, but you can hike Kuloa Point Trail to view the pools from a safe vantage point.

③ **Makahiku Falls** (p202) Now go back up Kuloa Point Trail and continue up the Pipiwai Trail. It's only 10 minutes to an overlook of the 200ft Makahiku Falls.

④ **Waimoku Falls** (p202) Enjoy the majestic view at Makahiku but don't stop there: keep going, keep going. There's a magical bamboo forest to walk through and the prize at the end of the trail is the towering 400ft cascade of Waimoku Falls.

⑤ **Kipahulu 'Ohana** (p203) Dig deeper by joining Native Hawaiian taro farmers for an ethnobotanical tour to learn firsthand the deeply rooted traditions of this sacred Hawaiian place.

⑥ **Kipahulu Campground** (p203) Now that you're in tune with the mana (spirit) of Kipahulu, pitch a tent at the site of an ancient Hawaiian settlement. Perched on the edge of a wild ocean, the surf will lull you to sleep. It's the perfect starlit finale to your Haleakalā experience.

⮕ THIS LEG: 8 MILES

Haleakalā National Park Highlights

① **Best Time to Visit: Sunrise** (p198) Because there's nothing more magical than our local star illuminating the ancient summit.

② **Best View: Haleakalā Visitor Center** (p189) Watch the clouds drifting through ancient cinder cones – and find out what those are!

③ **Best Hike: Keonehe'ehe'e (Sliding Sands) Trail** (p191) To really embrace a volcano, you have to trek into the crater.

④ **Best Waterfall: Makahiku Falls** (p202) A knockout view at the end of a short trail.

⑤ **Best Wildlife: Nene at Park Headquarters Visitor Center** (p187) The state bird loves to visit the lawn here, making it a prime viewing spot.

Hawaii's state bird, the nene, at Haleakalā National Park
ERIK AEDER/GETTY IMAGES ©

Discover Haleakalā National Park

Summit Area

Often referred to as the world's largest dormant volcano, the floor of Haleakalā is a colossal 7.5 miles wide, 2.5 miles long and 3000ft deep – nearly as large as Manhattan. In its prime, Haleakalā reached a height of 12,000ft before water erosion carved out two large river valleys that eventually merged to form Haleakalā crater. Technically, as geologists like to point out, it's not a true 'crater,' but to sightseers that's all nitpicking. Valley or crater, it's a phenomenal sight like no other in the US national park system.

HISTORY

The summit of Haleakalā was not inhabited by the ancient Hawaiians, but they came up the mountain and built heiau (temples) at some of the cinder cones. The primary goddess of Haleakalā, Lilinoe (also known as the mist goddess), was worshipped here. Today, Native Hawaiians still connect spiritually on the summit, and also come to study star navigation.

In 1916 Haleakalā became part of Hawai'i National Park, along with its Big Island siblings, Mauna Loa and Kilauea. In 1961 Haleakalā National Park became an independent entity; in 1969 its boundaries were expanded down into the Kipahulu Valley. And in 1980 the park was designated an International Biosphere Reserve by Unesco.

There are currently 55 endangered species in the park, the largest number in any US national park. This includes 26 plants, six birds, one bat, one seal, sea turtles and various invertebrates.

◉ Sights

Hosmer Grove   Forest

Hosmer Grove, off a side road just after the park's entrance booth, is primarily visited by campers and picnickers, but it's well worth a stop for its forested half-mile loop trail that begins at the edge of the campground. The whole area is sweetened with the scent of eucalyptus and alive with the red flashes and calls of native birds.

Leleiwi Overlook

VISUALS UNLIMITED, INC./GIPHOTOSTOCK/GETTY IMAGES ©

Drive slowly on the road in, as this is one of the top places to spot nene, a rare goose that is also the state bird.

Waikamoi Preserve   Nature Reserve
(📞572-4400; www.nature.org) This wind-swept native cloud forest supports one of the rarest ecosystems on earth. Managed by the Nature Conservancy, the 5230-acre preserve provides the last stronghold for 76 species of native plants and forest birds. You're apt to spot the 'i'iwi and the 'apapane (both honeycreepers with bright red feathers) and the yellow-green 'amakihi flying among the preserve's koa and ohia trees.

You might also catch a glimpse of the yellow-green 'alauahio (Maui creeper) or the 'akohekohe (crested honeycreeper), both endangered species found nowhere else on earth. The only way to see the area is to join one of the National Park Service's Waikamoi Preserve Hikes (p197).

Park Headquarters Visitor Center   Visitor Center
(📞572-4400; www.nps.gov/hale; 3-day pass car/individual on foot, bicycle or motorcycle $10/5; ⏱7am-3:45pm) Less than a mile beyond the entrance, this visitor center is the place to pick up brochures, buy nature books and get camping permits. It also has information on ranger talks and other activities being offered during your visit. If you're going hiking, you'll want to make sure your water bottles are filled before leaving here. Keep an eye out for nene wandering around the grounds; most nene deaths are the result of being hit by cars.

Leleiwi Overlook   Viewpoint
A stop at Leleiwi Overlook (8840ft), midway between the Park Headquarters Visitor Center and the summit, offers your first look into the crater, and gives you a unique angle on the ever-changing clouds floating in and out. You can literally watch the weather form at your feet. From the parking lot, it's a five-minute walk across a gravel trail to the overlook.

En route you'll get a fine view of the West Maui Mountains and the flat

Island Insights

Note well: Haleakalā National Park has two very different sections, the ethereal Summit Area and the coastal Kipahulu Area. *There is no direct road connection between them.* Thus travelers typically visit the summit on one day, and the Kipahulu Area on another (usually heading to or from Hana). One entrance ticket is good for both areas.

isthmus connecting the two sides of Maui. The trail has plaques identifying native plants, including the silver-leafed *hinahina* (a geranium found only at Haleakalā) and the *kukae-nene* (a member of the coffee family).

In the afternoon, if weather conditions are right, you might see the Brocken specter, an optical phenomenon that occurs at high elevations. Essentially, by standing between the sun and the clouds, your image is magnified and projected onto the clouds. The light reflects off tiny droplets of water in the clouds, creating a circular rainbow around your shadow.

Kalahaku Overlook   Viewpoint
Whatever you do, don't miss this one. Kalahaku Overlook (9324ft), 0.8 miles beyond Leleiwi Overlook, offers a bird's-eye view of the crater floor and the ant-size hikers on the trails snaking around the cinder cones below. At the observation deck, plaques provide information on each of the volcanic formations that punctuate the crater floor. From the deck you'll also get a perfect angle for viewing both the Ko'olau Gap and the Kaupo Gap on the rim of Haleakalā.

On a clear day you'll also be able to see the Big Island's Mauna Loa and Mauna Kea, Hawaii's highest mountaintops. It all adds up to one heck of a view.

Haleakalā Summit Area

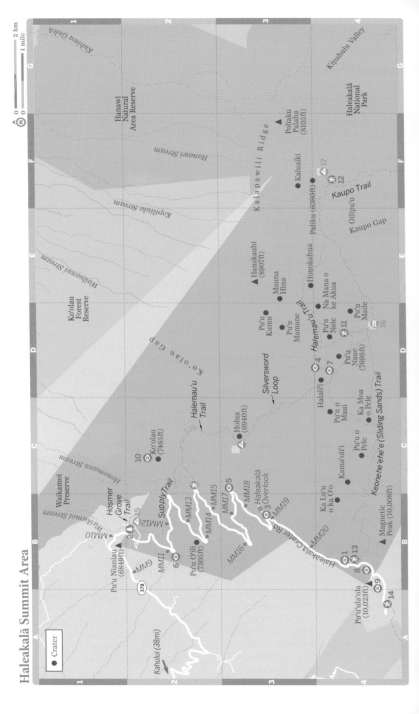

HALEAKALĀ NATIONAL PARK SUMMIT AREA

Haleakalā Summit Area

Between May and October the 'ua'u (Hawaiian dark-rumped petrel) nests in burrows in the cliff face at the left side of the observation deck. Even if you don't spot the birds, you can often hear the parents and chicks making their unique clucking sounds. Of about 2500 'ua'u pairs remaining today, most nest right here at Haleakalā, where they lay just one egg a year. These seabirds were thought to be extinct until sighted in the crater during the 1970s.

A short trail below the parking lot leads to a field of native 'ahinahina (silversword), ranging from seedlings to mature plants.

Haleakalā Visitor Center   Visitor Center
(www.nps.gov/hale; ☉sunrise-3pm) Perched on the rim of the crater at 9745ft, this visitor center is the park's main viewing spot. And what a magical sight awaits. The ever-changing interplay of sun, shadow and clouds reflecting on the crater floor creates a mesmerizing dance of light and color. The center has displays on Haleakalā's volcanic origins and details on what you're seeing on the crater floor 3000ft below.

Nature talks are given, books on Hawaiian culture and the environment are for sale, and there are drinking fountains and restrooms here.

By dawn the parking lot fills with people coming to see the sunrise show, and it pretty much stays packed all day. Leave the crowds behind by taking the 10-minute hike up **Pa Ka'oao** (White Hill), which begins at the eastern side of the visitor center and provides stunning crater views.

Pu'u'ula'ula (Red Hill) Overlook   Viewpoint
Sitting atop Pu'u'ula'ula (10,023ft), Maui's highest point, the summit building provides a top-of-the-world panorama from its wraparound windows. On a clear day you can see the Big Island, Lana'i, Moloka'i and even O'ahu. When the light's right, the colors of the crater are nothing short of spectacular, with an array of grays, greens, reds and browns. Brief natural and cultural history talks are given several times a day.

An 'ahinahina garden has been planted at the overlook, making this the best place to see these luminous silver-leafed plants in various stages of growth.

Magnetic Peak   Mountain
The iron-rich cinders in this flat-top hill, which lies immediately southeast of the summit building (the direction of the Big Island) pack enough magnetism to play havoc with your compass. Modest as it looks, it's also – at 10,008ft – the second-highest point on Maui.

Science City   Landmark
(www.ifa.hawaii.edu) Science City is the nickname for the collection of domes just behind the summit. Managed by the University of Hawai'i, this area is off-limits to visitors, unfortunately, as it houses some very interesting equipment.

Pan-STARRS surveys the heavens for earth-approaching objects, both asteroids and comets, that might pose a danger to our planet. It is the most powerful survey system in the world in terms of combined field of view, resolution and sensitivity. The Air Force's Ground-Based Electro-Optical Deep Space Surveillance system performs a similar function. It is capable of identifying a basketball-size object 22,000 miles away. The Faulkes Telescope is part of a global network of robotic telescopes dedicated to science education. After years of delay, the Daniel K Inouye Solar Telescope is now under construction. When complete it will be the world's largest solar telescope. Operations are expected to begin in 2019.

If all that sparks your interest, the Institute for Astronomy at the University of Hawai'i holds monthly public talks at its office in Pukalani. For more information see www.ifa.hawaii.edu/haleakalanew. The website contains fascinating videos of past lectures.

 Activities

Be sure to stop at the Park Headquarters Visitor Center to see what's happening. Free **ranger talks** on Haleakalā's unique natural history and Hawaiian culture are given at the Haleakalā Visitor Center and the Pu'u'ula'ula (Red Hill) Overlook; the schedule varies, but there's usually half a dozen to choose from each day.

STARGAZING

On clear nights, stargazing is phenomenal on the mountain. You can see celestial objects up to the seventh magnitude, free of light interference, making Haleakalā one of the best places on the planet for a sky view.

Stargazing Programs Stargazing
(☎ for schedule 572-4400; Hosmer Grove; program free; ⏰ 7pm Fri & Sat May-Sep) Hour-long evening programs are offered between May and September at Hosmer Grove. These talks, which are free and ranger-led, are occasionally held in the winter as

---

'Ahinahina Comeback?

Goats ate them by the thousands. Souvenir collectors pulled them up by their roots. They were even used to decorate parade floats. It's a miracle any of Haleakalā's famed *'ahinahina* (silverswords) are left at all.

It took a concerted effort to bring them back from the brink of extinction, but Haleakalā visitors can once again see this luminous relative of the sunflower in numerous places around the park, including Kalahaku and Pu'u'ula'ula (Red Hill) Overlooks and Silversword Loop.

The *'ahinahina* takes its name from its elegant silver spiked leaves, which glow with dew collected from the clouds. The plant lives for up to 50 years before blooming for its first and last time. In its final year it shoots up a flowering stalk that can reach as high as 9ft. During summer the stalk flowers gloriously with hundreds of maroon and yellow blossoms. When the flowers go to seed in late fall, the plant makes its last gasp and dies.

Today the *'ahinahina* faces new threats, including climate change and loss of pollinators from ants. But at least its fragile natural environment has been protected. After years of effort, the National Park Service has finished fencing the entire park with a 32-mile-long fence to keep out feral goats and pigs. You can do your part by not walking on cinders close to the plant; this damages the shallow roots that radiate out several feet just inches below the surface.

well; call for the schedule. If you have a pair of binoculars, bring them along.

If your visit doesn't coincide with a program, pick up a free star map of the night sky for the current month at the Park Headquarters Visitor Center and have your own cosmic experience.

HIKING

Strap on a pair of hiking boots and you can climb into the very heart of this otherworldly place. There's something for everyone, from short nature walks ideal for families to hardy treks that take a couple of days. Those who hike the crater will discover a completely different angle on Haleakalā's lunar landscape. Instead of peering down from the rim, you'll be craning your neck skyward at the walls and towering cinder cones. It's a world away from any place else. The crater is remarkably still. Cinders crunching underfoot are often the only sound, except for the occasional bark of a pueo (Hawaiian owl) or honking of a friendly nene. No matter what trail you take, give yourself plenty of time just to absorb the wonder of it all.

Keonehe'ehe'e (Sliding Sands) Trail Hiking

This trail starts at the southern side of the Haleakalā Visitor Center at 9740ft and winds down to the crater floor. If you take this hike after catching the sunrise, you'll walk directly into a gentle warmish wind and rays of sunshine. The path descends gently into an unearthly world of stark lava sights and ever-changing clouds.

The first thing you'll notice is how quiet everything is. The only sound is the crunching of volcanic cinders beneath your feet. If you're pressed for time, just walking down 20 minutes will reward you with an into-the-crater experience and fabulous photo opportunities. Keep in mind that the climb out takes nearly twice as long.

The full trail leads 9.2 miles to the Paliku cabin and campground, passing the Kapalaoa cabin at 5.6 miles after roughly four hours. The first 6 miles follow the southern wall. There are great views,

The Best...
Haleakalā Hikes

1 Keonehe'ehe'e (Sliding Sands) Trail

2 Pipiwai Trail (p202)

3 Kuloa Point Trail (p202)

4 Halemau'u Trail

5 Hosmer Grove Trail (p195)

but virtually no vegetation. Four miles down, after an elevation drop of 2500ft, Keonehe'ehe'e Trail intersects with a spur that leads north into the cinder desert, where it connects with the Halemau'u Trail after 1.5 miles.

Continuing on Keonehe'ehe'e, you head across the crater floor for 2 miles to Kapalaoa. Verdant ridges rise on your right, giving way to ropy *pahoehoe* (smooth-flowing lava). From Kapalaoa cabin to Paliku, the descent is gentle and the vegetation gradually increases. Paliku (6380ft) is beneath a sheer cliff at the eastern end of the crater. In contrast to the crater's barren western end, this area receives heavy rainfall, with ohia forests climbing the slopes.

Halemau'u Trail Hiking

Hiking the Halemau'u Trail down to the Holua campground and back – 7.4 miles return – can be a memorable day hike. Just be sure to start early before the afternoon clouds roll in and visibility vanishes. The first mile is fairly level and offers a fine view of the crater with Ko'olau Gap to the east.

The trail then descends 1400ft along 2 miles of switchbacks to the crater floor and on to the Holua campground (6940ft). You'll see impressive views of the crater walls rising a few thousand feet to the west. Several lava tubes are visible

191

from the trail, but since endangered species use them for shelter, the Park Service has made them off-limits.

If you have the energy, push on just another mile to reach some colorful cinder cones, being sure to make a short detour onto the **Silversword Loop**, where you'll see these unique plants in various stages of growth. If you're here during the summer, their tall stalks should be ablaze with hundreds of maroon and yellow blossoms. But be careful – half of all ʻahinahina today are trampled to death as seedlings, mostly by careless hikers who wander off trails and inadvertently crush the plants' shallow, laterally growing roots. The trail continues another 6.3 miles to the Paliku cabin.

The trailhead to Halemauʻu is 3.5 miles above the Park Headquarters Visitor Center and about 6 miles below the Haleakalā Visitor Center. There's a fair chance you'll see nene in the parking lot.

If you're camping at Hosmer Grove, you can take a shortcut over to the crater rim via the little-known, and less exciting,

Supply Trail that follows the old mule path used to get supplies down to the cabins on the crater floor. The trail starts on the campground turnoff road and after 1.5 miles opens up to broad vistas of the volcano's rainforest slopes and out to sea. After one more mile, the Supply Trail intersects with the Halemauʻu Trail and heads down into the crater.

Cinder Desert Trails   Hiking

Two spur trails connect Keonehe'ehe'e (Sliding Sands) Trail, near Kapalaoa cabin, with the Halemau'u Trail between Paliku and Holua cabins. If you're camping you may have time to do them both, as the trails are not very long. The spur trail furthest west takes in many of the crater's most kaleidoscopic cones, and the viewing angle changes with every step.

If you prefer stark, black and barren, the other spur trail takes you through ʻaʻa (rough, jagged lava) and pahoehoe (smooth-flowing lava) fields.

Both trails end up on the northern side of the cinder desert near **Kawilinau**, also known as the Bottomless Pit. Legend says the pit leads down to the sea, though the National Park Service says it's just 65ft deep. Truth be told, there's not much to see, as you can't really get a good look down the narrow shaft. The real prize is the nearby short loop trail, where you can sit for a while in the saddle of Pele's **Paint Pot Lookout**, the crater's most brilliant vantage point.

Kaupo Trail   Hiking

The most extreme of Haleakalā's hikes is the Kaupo Trail, which starts at the Paliku campground and leads down to Kaupo on the southern coast. Be prepared for ankle-twisting conditions, blistered feet, intense tropical sun and torrential showers. Your knees will take a pounding as you descend more than 6100ft over 8.6 miles.

The first 3.7 miles of the trail drop 2500ft in elevation before reaching the park boundary. It's a steep rocky path through rough lava and brushland, with short switchbacks alternating with level stretches. From here you'll be rewarded with spectacular ocean views.

The last 4.9 miles pass through Kaupo Ranch property on a rough jeep trail as it descends to the bottom of Kaupo Gap, exiting into a forest where feral pigs snuffle about. Here trail markings become vague, but once you reach the dirt road, it's another 1.5 miles to the end at the eastern side of the Kaupo Store.

The 'village' of Kaupo is a long way from anywhere, with light traffic. Still, you'll probably manage a lift. If you have to walk the final stretch, it's 8 miles to the 'Ohe'o Gulch campground.

Because this is such a strenuous and remote trail, it's not advisable to hike it alone. No camping is allowed on Kaupo Ranch property, so most hikers spend the

Responsible Hiking in Haleakalā

To protect Haleakalā's fragile environment, keep to established trails and don't be tempted off them, even for well-trodden shortcuts through switchbacks. And for your own sake, come prepared. Remember the climate changes radically as you cross the crater floor. In the 4 miles between Kapalaoa and Paliku cabins, rainfall varies from an annual average of 12in to 300in! Take warm clothing in layers, sunscreen, rain gear, a first-aid kit and lots of water. Hikers without proper clothing risk hypothermia.

Here are recommended day hikes, depending on how much time you have available:

Ten hours If you're planning a full-day outing, and you're in good physical shape, the 11.2-mile hike that starts down Keonehe'ehe'e (Sliding Sands) Trail and returns via Halemau'u Trail is the prize. It crosses the crater floor, taking in both a cinder desert and a cloud forest, showcasing the park's amazing diversity. Get an early start. As for getting back to your starting point, hitchhiking is allowed in the park and there's a designated place to hitch on Haleakalā Crater Rd opposite the Halemau'u trailhead.

Three hours For a half-day experience that offers a hearty serving of crater sights, follow Keonehe'ehe'e (Sliding Sands) Trail down to where it goes between two towering rock formations, before dropping steeply again. It takes one hour to get down. However, the way back is a 1500ft elevation rise, making the return a strenuous two-hour climb.

One hour Take to the forest on the Hosmer Grove Trail and see the green side of Haleakalā National Park.

night at the Paliku campground and then get an early start.

Skyline Trail   Hiking

This otherworldly trail, which rides the precipitous spine of Haleakalā, begins just beyond the summit at a lofty elevation (9750ft) and leads down to the campground at Polipoli Spring State Recreation Area (6200ft). It covers a distance of 8.5 miles and takes about four hours to walk. Get an early start to enjoy the views before clouds take over.

To get to the trailhead, go past Pu'u'ula'ula (Red Hill) Overlook and take the road to the left just before Science City. The road, which passes over a cattle grate, is signposted not for public use, but continue and you'll soon find a Na Ala Hele sign marking the trailhead.

The Skyline Trail starts in barren open terrain of volcanic cinder, a moon walk that passes more than a dozen cinder cones and craters. The first mile is rough lava rock. After three crunchy miles, it reaches the tree line (8500ft) and enters native mamane forest. In winter mamane is heavy with flowers that look like yellow sweet-pea blossoms. There's solitude on this walk. If the clouds treat you kindly, you'll have broad views all the way between the barren summit and the dense cloud forest.

Eventually the trail meets the Polipoli access road, where you can either walk to the paved road in about 4 miles, or continue via the Haleakalā Ridge Trail and Polipoli Trail to the campground.

If you prefer treads to hiking boots, the Skyline Trail is also an exhilarating adventure on a mountain bike. Just look out for hikers!

Hosmer Grove Trail Hiking

Anyone who is looking for a little greenery after hiking the crater will love this shaded woodland walk, as will birders. The half-mile loop trail starts at Hosmer Grove campground, three-quarters of a mile south of the Park Headquarters Visitor Center, in a forest of lofty trees.

The exotics here were introduced in 1910 in an effort to develop a lumber industry in Hawaii. Species include fragrant incense cedar, Norway spruce, Douglas fir, eucalyptus and various pines. Although the trees adapted well enough to grow, they didn't grow fast enough at these elevations to make tree harvesting practical.

After the forest, the trail moves into native shrubland, with 'akala (Hawaiian raspberry), mamane, pilo, kilau ferns and sandalwood. The 'ohelo, a berry sacred to the volcano goddess Pele, and the pukiawe, which has red and white berries and evergreen leaves, are favored by nene.

Listen for the calls of the native 'i'iwi and 'apapane; both are fairly common here. The 'i'iwi has a very loud squeaking call, orange legs and a curved salmon-colored bill. The 'apapane, a fast-moving bird with a black bill, black legs and a white undertail, feeds on the nectar of bright red ohia flowers, and its wings make a distinctive whirring sound.

HORSEBACK RIDING

Pony Express (p174) can get you in the stirrups for the ride of your life on a half-day horseback journey deep into Haleakalā crater. It starts near the summit and follows Keonehe'ehe'e (Sliding Sands) Trail, offering jaw-dropping scenery the entire way. If you're not hiking down to the crater this is the only other way to get eye to eye

with this geological marvel. Book early as there's a maximum of nine riders taken. The Pony Express office is on Hwy 378, 2.5 miles up from Haleakalā Hwy (Hwy 377).

CYCLING

Cycling downhill from the summit to the sea, via Makawao and Pa'ia, is an extraordinarily popular pursuit. There are companies that will lead a group tour, and others that will take you to the summit and let you ride down on your own. Many people combine this with sunrise, requiring a very early start. For more information see the Maui Downhill box, p155.

Alternatively, you can arrange bike and transportation on your own. This is not only cheaper, but less restrictive. Due to past problems, one-way downhill group cycle tours are not allowed to cycle within the park, but begin pedaling just below park boundaries. Individual cyclists are allowed to pedal without restriction. For rental equipment see Crater Cycles (p97) or Island Biker (p100) in Kahului, or Maui

Riders on Keonehe'ehe'e Trail (p191)
GREG ELMS/GETTY IMAGES ©

Volunteer Opportunities

Haleakalā National Park currently offers two different volunteer opportunities. One is a multiday trip sponsored by **Friends of Haleakalā National Park** (☏876-1673; www.fhnp.org). This totally volunteer-led operation involves up to a dozen visitors, who hike into the wild and stay for two nights in cabins owned by the National Park Service. Volunteers perform one of a number of tasks ranging from cabin maintenance to native planting to invasive species removal.

The second opportunity is a day trip run by Pacific Whale Foundation (p116) as part of its **Volunteers on Vacation** (☏ext 1 249-8811; www.volunteersonvacation.org) program, and occurs on the first and third Saturday of every month. Led by a certified naturalist and trained guide, volunteers work on projects that help protect Haleakalā National Park's ecosystem, such as removing invasive plants. There's also a short hike. Transportation is provided from Ma'alaea or Pukalani.

Both programs provide free admission into the park.

Sunriders (p155) in Pa'ia. Bike racks are available with the rental.

MOUNTAIN BIKING

For experienced mountain bikers, Skyline Trail (p194) is the island's ultimate wild ride, plunging some 3000ft in the first 6 miles with a breathtaking 10% grade. The trail starts out looking like the moon and ends up in a cloud forest of redwood and cypress trees that resembles California's northern coast. The route follows a rough 4WD road that's used to maintain Polipoli Spring State Recreation Area. Equip yourself with full pads and use a proper downhill bike. For rental equipment see Crater

Hosmer Grove Campground

Cycles (p97) or Island Biker (p100), both in Kahului.

Tours

Waikamoi Preserve　　Hiking Tour
(www.nps.gov/hale) The only way to see the unique Waikamoi Preserve is on this 3½-hour hiking tour run by the National Park Service. The tour departs Hosmer Grove campground at 8:45am. Dates vary, so check the schedule of events on the park website or stop by the Park Headquarters Visitor Center. It's best to make reservations, which you can do up to one week in advance. The hike is moderately strenuous. Bring rain gear.

Sleeping

Maui's best campgrounds are right in Haleakalā National Park. To spend the night at Haleakalā is to commune with nature. All of the camping options are primitive; none have electricity or showers. Backcountry campgrounds have pit toilets and limited nonpotable water supplies that are shared with the crater cabins. Water needs to be filtered or chemically treated before drinking; conserve it, as water tanks occasionally run dry. Fires are allowed only in grills and in times of drought are prohibited entirely. You must pack in all your food and supplies, and pack out all your trash. Also be aware that during periods of drought you'll be required to carry in your own water.

Keep in mind that sleeping at an elevation of 7000ft is not like camping on the beach. You need to be well equipped – without a waterproof tent and a winter-rated sleeping bag, forget it.

**Hosmer Grove
Campground**　　Campground
(campsite free) Wake up to the sound of birdsong at Hosmer Grove, the only drive-up campground in the mountainous section of Haleakalā National Park. Surrounded by lofty trees and adjacent to one of Maui's best birding trails, this campground at an elevation of 6800ft tends to be a bit cloudy, but a covered

The Sunrise Experience

Since ancient times people have been making the pilgrimage up to Haleakalā to watch the sunrise. It's an experience that borders on the mystical.

Plan to arrive at the summit an hour before the sunrise. Around that point the night sky begins to lighten and turn purple-blue, and the stars fade away. Ethereal silhouettes of the mountain ridges appear. The undersides of the clouds lighten first, accenting the night sky with pale silvery slivers and streaks of pink.

About 20 minutes before sunrise, the light intensifies on the horizon in bright oranges and reds. Turn around for a look at Science City, whose domes turn a blazing pink. For the grand finale, when the sun appears, all of Haleakalā takes on a fiery glow. It feels like you're watching the earth awaken.

Come prepared – it's going to be c-o-l-d! However many layers of clothes you can muster, it won't be too many.

The best photo opportunities occur before the sun rises. Every morning is different, but once the sun is up, the silvery lines and the subtleties disappear.

One caveat: a rained-out sunrise is an anticlimactic event after tearing yourself out of bed in the middle of the night to drive up a pitch-dark mountain. So check the weather report (☎866-944-5025) the night before to calculate your odds of having clear skies.

If you just can't get up that early, sunsets at Haleakalā have inspired poets as well.

---

picnic pavilion offers shelter should it start to rain.

Camping is free on a first-come, first-served basis, with a limit of 50 people. No permit is required, though there's a three-day camping limit per month. It's busier in summer than in winter and is often full on holiday weekends. The campground is just after the park entrance booth, and has grills, toilets and running water. Since you're close to the summit, it's a cinch getting up for sunrise.

Backcountry Campgrounds
Campground

(campsite free) For hikers, two backcountry campgrounds lie in the belly of Haleakalā Crater. The easiest to reach is at **Holua**, 3.7 miles down the Halemau'u Trail. The other is at **Paliku**, below a rainforest ridge at the end of Halemau'u Trail. Weather can be unpredictable at both.

Holua at 6940ft is typically dry after sunrise, until clouds roll back in the late afternoon. Paliku at 6380ft is in a grassy

meadow, with skies overhead alternating between stormy and sunny. Wasps are present at both campsites, so take precautions if you're allergic to stings.

Unlike at Hosmer Grove, permits are required for backcountry camping in the crater. They are free and issued at the Park Headquarters Visitor Center on a first-come, first-served basis between 8am and 3pm on the day of the hike. Camping is limited to three nights in the crater each month, with no more than two consecutive nights at either campground. Because only 25 campers are allowed at each site, permits can go quickly when larger parties show up, a situation more likely to occur in summer.

Haleakala Wilderness Cabins
Cabin $

(☎572-4400; www.recreation.gov; per cabin with 1-12 people $75) Three rustic cabins dating from the 1930s lie along trails on the crater floor at Holua, **Kapalaoa** and Paliku. Each has a wood-burning stove, a propane burner, 12 bunks with sleeping pads (but no bedding), pit toilets and a limited supply of water and firewood. There is no electricity.

Hiking distances to the cabins from the crater rim range from 4 to 9 miles. The driest conditions are at Kapalaoa, in the middle of the cinder desert off Keoneheʻeheʻe (Sliding Sands) Trail. Those craving lush rainforest will find Paliku serene. Holua has unparalleled sunrise views. There's a three-day limit per month, with no more than two consecutive nights in any cabin. Each cabin is rented to only one group at a time.

The cabins can be reserved online up to six months in advance. A photo ID is required for the permittee, and all of those staying in the cabin must watch an eight-minute wilderness orientation video.

ℹ Information

○ Pack plenty of snacks, especially if you're going up for the sunrise. No food or bottled water is sold anywhere in the park. You don't want a growling stomach to send you back down the mountain before you've had a chance to see the sights.

Backcountry camping at Paliku

○ Check out the current weather conditions at the summit by logging on to the crater webcam at Haleakalā Crater Live Camera (www.ifa.hawaii.edu/haleakalanew/webcams.shtml).

○ Bring extra layers of clothing. The temperature can drop dramatically at any point in the day.

Entrance Fees & Passes

Haleakalā National Park (☏572-4400; www.nps.gov/hale; 3-day pass car/individual on foot, bicycle or motorcycle $10/5) never closes, and the pay booth at the park entrance opens before dawn to welcome the sunrise crowd.

If you're planning several trips, or are going on to the Big Island, consider buying an annual pass ($25), which covers all of Hawaii's national parks.

Maps

A current hiking trail map can be downloaded from www.recreation.gov or the park's official website (www.nps.gov/hale). Other planning materials/books can be purchased online from the park's partner: www.hawaiipacificparks.org.

Dangers & Annoyances

This park can be seriously dangerous to drive in, due to a combination of sheer drops with no guardrails, daily doses of thick mist, and strong

wind. Exercise extra caution in winter afternoons, when a sudden rainstorm can add ice to the list.

Obey warning signs. They often mark a spot where a visitor has been hurt or killed by a fall, a flash flood or falling rocks.

The weather can change suddenly from dry, hot conditions to cold, windswept rain. Although the general rule is sunny in the morning and cloudy in the afternoon, fog and clouds can blow in at any time, and the windchill can quickly drop below freezing. Dress in layers and bring extra clothing.

At 10,000ft the air is relatively thin, so expect to tire more quickly, particularly if you're hiking. The higher elevation also means that sunburn is more likely.

Visitors rarely experience altitude sickness at the summit. An exception is those who have been scuba diving in the past 24 hours, so plan your trip accordingly. Children, pregnant women and those in generally poor health are also susceptible. If you experience difficulty breathing, sudden headaches and dizziness, or more serious symptoms such as confusion and lack of motor coordination, descend immediately. Sometimes driving down the crater road just a few hundred feet will alleviate the problem.

Panicking or hyperventilating only makes things worse.

ℹ️ Getting There & Around

Getting to Haleakalā is half the fun. Snaking up the mountain it's sometimes hard to tell if you're in an airplane or a car – all of Maui opens up below you, with sugarcane and pineapple fields creating a patchwork of green on the valley floor. The highway ribbons back and forth, and in some places as many as four or five switchbacks are in view all at once.

Haleakalā Crater Rd (Hwy 378) twists and turns for 11 miles from Hwy 377 near Kula up to the park entrance, then another 10 miles to Haleakalā summit. It's a good paved road all the way, but it's steep and winding. You don't want to rush it, especially when it's dark or foggy. Watch out for cattle wandering freely across the road.

The drive to the summit takes about 1½ hours from Pa'ia or Kahului, two hours from Kihei and a bit longer from Lahaina. If you need gas, fill up the night before, as there are no services on Haleakalā Crater Rd.

On your way back downhill, be sure to put your car in low gear to avoid burning out your brakes.

Kipahulu Area ('Ohe'o Gulch)

There's more to Haleakalā National Park than the cindery summit. The park extends down the southeast face of the volcano all the way to the sea. The crowning glory of the Kipahulu section of the park is 'Ohe'o Gulch, with its magnificent waterfalls and wide pools, each one tumbling into the next one below.

Back in the 1970s 'Ohe'o Gulch was dubbed the 'Seven Sacred Pools' as part of a tourism promotion, but at the request of community elders, park staff use the traditional names for the stream and gulch. 'Seven pools' is a complete misnomer anyway since there are 24 pools in all, extending from the ocean to Waimoku Falls, and they were never sacred – but they certainly are divine.

The waters once supported a sizable Hawaiian settlement of farmers who cultivated sweet potatoes and taro in terraced gardens beside the stream. Archaeologists have identified the stone remains of more than 700 ancient structures at 'Ohe'o.

One of the expressed intentions of Haleakalā National Park is to manage its Kipahulu area 'to perpetuate traditional Hawaiian farming and ho'onanea' – a Hawaiian word meaning to pass the time in ease, peace and pleasure. So kick back and have some fun!

👁 Sights & Activities

Kipahulu Visitor Center Visitor Center
(Map p230; ☎ 248-7375; www.nps.gov/hale; 3-day pass per car $10, per person on foot, bicycle or motorcyle $5; ☺ park 24hr, visitor center 9am-5pm) Rangers here offer cultural history talks and demonstrations on the lives and activities of the early Hawaiians who lived in the area now within park boundaries.

Nene Watch

The native nene, Hawaii's state bird, is a long-lost cousin of the Canada goose. By the 1950s, hunting, habitat loss and predators had reduced its population to just 30. Thanks to captive breeding and release programs, it has been brought back from the verge of extinction and the Haleakalā National Park's nene population is now holding steady at about 250.

Nene nest in shrubs and grassy areas from 6000ft to 8000ft, surrounded by rugged lava flows with sparse vegetation. Their feet have gradually adapted by losing most of their webbing. The birds are extremely friendly and love to hang out where people do, anywhere from cabins on the crater floor to the Park Headquarters Visitor Center.

Their curiosity and fearlessness have contributed to their undoing. Nene don't fare well in an asphalt habitat and many have been run over by cars. Others have been tamed by too much human contact, so no matter how much they beg for your peanut butter sandwich, don't feed the nene. It only interferes with their successful return to the wild.

The nonprofit Friends of Haleakalā National Park (p196) runs an Adopt-a-Nene program. For $30 you get adoption papers, information about your nene, a certificate and postcard. The money funds the protection of nene habitat.

Guided hikes are also routinely given. Check the schedule of events on the park's website.

Kuloa Point Trail Hiking, Swimming

(Map p230) Even if you're tight on time, you've got to take this 20-minute stroll! The Kuloa Point Trail, a half-mile loop, runs from the visitor center down to the lower pools and back. At the junction with Pipiwai Trail go right. A few minutes down, you'll come to a broad grassy knoll with a gorgeous view of the Hana coast. On a clear day you can see the Big Island, 30 miles away across 'Alenuihaha Channel. This is a fine place to stop and unpack your lunch.

The large **freshwater pools** along the trail are terraced one atop the other and connected by gentle cascades. They may look calm, but flash floods have taken several lives here, so the Park Service has closed the pools to swimming.

Waterfall Trails Hiking

The **Pipiwai Trail** (Map p230) runs up the 'Ohe'o streambed, rewarding hikers with picture-perfect views of waterfalls. The trail starts on the *mauka* (inland) side of the visitor center and leads up to Makahiku Falls (0.5 miles) and Waimoku Falls (2 miles). To see both falls, allow about two hours return. The upper section is muddy, but boardwalks cover some of the worst bits.

Along the path, you'll pass large mango trees and patches of guava before coming to an overlook after about 10 minutes. **Makahiku Falls**, a long bridal-veil waterfall that drops into a deep gorge, is just off to the right. Thick green ferns cover the sides of 200ft basalt cliffs where the water cascades – a very rewarding scene for such a short walk.

Continuing along the main trail, you'll walk beneath old banyan trees, cross Palikea Stream (killer mosquitoes thrive here) and enter the wonderland of the **Bamboo Forest**, where thick groves of bamboo bang together musically in the wind.

Beyond them is **Waimoku Falls**, a thin, lacy 400ft waterfall dropping down a sheer rock face. When you come out of the first grove, you'll see the waterfall in the distance. Forget swimming under

Waimoku Falls – its pool is shallow and there's a danger of falling rocks.

Tours

Kipahulu 'Ohana
Cultural Tour

(Map p230; 248-8558; www.kipahulu.org) Kipahulu was once a breadbasket, or more accurately a poi bowl, for the entire region. For fascinating insights into the area's past, join one of the ethnobotanical tours led by Kipahulu 'Ohana, a collective of Native Hawaiian farmers who have restored ancient taro patches within the national park. Some of these are in the most incredible places, including high bluffs overlooking waterfalls.

The tours include a sampling of Hawaiian foods and intriguing details on the native plants and ancient ruins along the way.

The two-hour outing ($49) includes about 2 miles of hiking, leaves at 10am and concentrates on the farm activities. The 3½-hour tour ($79) covers 4.5 miles and adds on a hike to Waimoku Falls. Both tours leave from the Kipahulu Visitor Center; advance reservations required.

Sleeping

Kipahulu Campground
Campground

(Map p230; campsite free) If you've got a tent, you're going to love this campground, which has an incredible setting on oceanside cliffs amid the stone ruins of an ancient Hawaiian village. Good mana here! This is a primitive campground. Facilities include pit toilets, picnic tables and grills. Drinking water is only available from the nearby visitor center restrooms. Camping is free but limited to three nights within a 30-day period. In winter you'll usually have the place to yourself, and even in summer there's typically enough space to handle everyone who shows up.

Bring mosquito repellent and gear suitable for rainy conditions. The campground is a quarter of a mile southeast of the Kipahulu Visitor Center.

Getting There & Around

The Kipahulu Area is on Hwy 31, 10 scenic miles south of Hana. There's no direct road access from here to the rest of Haleakalā National Park; the summit must be visited separately.

Makahiku Falls

The Road to Hana

You're about to experience the most ravishingly beautiful drive in Hawaii. Spanning the northeast shore of Maui, the legendary Hana Hwy delivers one jaw-dropping view after the other as it twists between jungle valleys and towering cliffs. Along the way, 54 one-lane bridges mark nearly as many waterfalls, some tranquil and inviting, others so sheer they kiss you with spray as you drive past.

But there's a lot more to this beauty than the drive. When you're ready to get out and stretch your legs the real adventure begins: hiking trails climb into cool forests, short paths lead to Eden-like swimming holes, side roads wind down to sleepy seaside villages. If you've never tried smoked breadfruit, taken a dip in a spring-fed cave or gazed upon an ancient Hawaiian temple, set the alarm early – you've got a big day ahead.

Road to Hana Itineraries

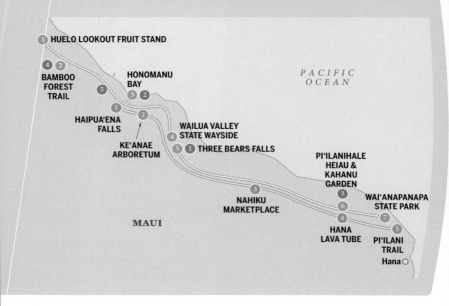

HUELO LOOKOUT FRUIT STAND

BAMBOO FOREST TRAIL

HONOMANU BAY

HAIPUA'ENA FALLS

KE'ANAE ARBORETUM

WAILUA VALLEY STATE WAYSIDE

THREE BEARS FALLS

PI'ILANIHALE HEIAU & KAHANU GARDEN

NAHIKU MARKETPLACE

WAI'ANAPANAPA STATE PARK

HANA LAVA TUBE

PI'ILANI TRAIL

Hana

MAUI

PACIFIC OCEAN

Day One

① **Huelo Lookout Fruit Stand** (p209) Start with a stop at this organic fruit stand for a mango crepe and a jolting java to kick off your road trip.

② **Bamboo Forest Trail** (p209) Now in your bathing suit, head deep into a bamboo forest and up a stream to find several waterfalls and pools. A few climbs and a swim make it a fun challenge.

③ **Honomanu Bay** (p212) You'll start getting glimpses as the Hana Hwy begins to wind down to the coast, but don't settle for just a glimpse – find the unmarked road into the bay and see a slice of untamed Hawaiian coast up close.

④ **Wailua Valley State Wayside** (p216) Next, climb the steps here and, bam, a 360-degree view unfolds from the mountains clear down to the sea.

⑤ **Three Bears Falls** (p216) Continue on to find the best in a magnificent run of roadside cascades that pop up between the 19- and 25-mile markers. Have a camera ready!

⑥ **Pi'ilanihale Heiau & Kahanu Garden** (p219) This preserved corner of ancient Hawaii is home to the largest heiau (temple) in Polynesia. You'll walk away with an entirely new appreciation for ancient Hawaiian life.

⑦ **Wai'anapanapa State Park** (p221) Your final stop harbors a beautiful black-sand beach, cool caves, a sea arch and a blowhole all within strolling distance of each other.

⟳ THIS LEG: 33 MILES

Day Two

1 **Haipua'ena Falls** (p212) If you've got two days for the Road to Hana, plan to take in the sights above and add the following to your itinerary. To begin, break out a beach towel and make your way to this Eden-like pool just begging for a dip.

2 **Ke'anae Arboretum** (p213) Take a streamside walk through this peaceful forest for a microcosm of the heady sights and scents you see along the Hana Hwy – painted eucalyptus trees, brilliant tropical flowers and patches of Hawaiian taro, to name just a few.

3 **Nahiku Marketplace** (p217) Hungry? This temporary structure is your best place to find lunch on the Road to Hana, with various options to choose from including Thai, seafood and Hawaiian.

4 **Hana Lava Tube** (p221) Easily the quirkiest site along the route, this place flips all the splendor above ground on its head, taking you into the bowels of the earth – a world of dripping stalactites and stalagmites. It's large enough to drive a train through, but it'll be just you and a flashlight on this one.

5 **Pi'ilani Trail** (p222) Follow with a walk in the footsteps of the early Hawaiians on this ancient coastal path that leads across a high shelf of lava with wild coastal vistas. Do the whole hike round-trip for a 6-mile outing, or take advantage of the way it packs the top sights into the first leg and make it an easy 2-mile jaunt.

➡ **THIS LEG: 27 MILES**

Road to Hana Highlights

1 **Best Waterfall: Three Bears Falls** (p216)
This triple-whammy rises above the rest.

2 **Best Beach: Honomanu Bay** (p212)
Where a tropical river spills out of a valley into the sea.

3 **Best Sight: Pi'ilanihale Heiau** (p219)
Polynesia's greatest temple is out of this world.

4 **Best Hike: Bamboo Forest Trail** (p209)
A magical forest, triple waterfalls, hidden pools and a bit of climbing.

5 **Best Adventure: Rappel Maui** (p212)
Ever rappelled down the face of a waterfall?

Three Bears Falls (p216)
DANITA DELIMONT/GETTY IMAGES ©

Discover the Road to Hana

Twin Falls

Once you've left Pa'ia and Ha'iku behind, houses give way to thick jungle, and the scenery gets more dramatic with every mile. Then the road does a sleight-of-hand. After the 16-mile marker on Hwy 36, the Hana Hwy changes numbers to Hwy 360 and the mile markers begin again at zero. Just after the 2-mile marker a wide parking area with a fruit stand marks the start of the trail to Twin Falls. Local kids and tourists flock to the pool beneath the lower falls, about a 10-minute walk in. Twin Falls gets a lot of attention as being the 'first waterfall on the road to Hana.' Truth be told, unless you're interested in taking a dip in muddy waters, this overcrowded stop is not worth the time. You'll find more idyllic options en route to Hana.

Huelo

With its abundant rain and fertile soil Huelo once supported more than 50,000 Hawaiians, but today it's a sleepy, scattered community of farms and enviable cliffside homes.

The double row of mailboxes and green bus shelter that come up after a blind curve 0.5 miles past the 3-mile marker mark the start of the narrow road that leads into the village. The only sight, Kaulanapueo Church, is a half-mile down.

It's tempting to continue driving past the church, but not rewarding, as the road shortly turns to dirt and dead-ends at gated homes. There's no public beach access.

Sights & Activities

Kaulanapueo Church — Church

Constructed in 1853 of coral blocks and surrounded by a manicured green lawn, this tidy church remains the heart of the village. It has been built in early Hawaiian missionary style, with a spare interior and a tin roof topped with a green steeple. Swaying palm trees add a tropical backdrop. There are no formal opening hours, but the church is typically unlocked during the day.

Kaulanapueo Church
JOHN ELK/GETTY IMAGES ©

Bamboo Forest Trail — Hiking

Beginning at the 6.5-mile marker, across the highway from a distinct line of conifers, this adventurous and uncrowded trail is one of the best on the Road to Hana. There are various roadside entrances through a thick stand of bamboo, the best being the last one, opposite the last conifer and next to an empty signpost.

After a half-mile, including crossing a stream with slippery rocks, you'll reach a small but scenic falls. The trail crosses a river, after which you'll climb a difficult rope ladder. Skirt to the left of the large pool above, where a wooden ladder takes you up a rock face. Now scamper up river rocks until you see another waterfall. Here you must swim across and climb the rocks near the falls to reach the last pool and falls above: the main attraction.

So yes, wear a bathing suit and don't bring anything you don't want to get wet (or do bring a waterproof bag).

 ## Sleeping & Eating

Tea House — Cottage $$

(☏ 572-8596; www.mauiteahouse.com; 370 Ho'olawa Rd; s/d $135/150; 🛜) 🍃 Built with walls recycled from a Zen temple, this one-of-a-kind cottage is so secluded it's off the grid and uses its own solar power. Yet it has everything you'll need, including a kitchen with gas burners and an open-air shower in a redwood gazebo.

The grounds also contain a Tibetan-style stupa with a spectacular cliff-top ocean view and a second cottage that rents by the week ($500). To get there follow Ulalama Loop, on the left after the 2-mile marker, to Ho'olawa Rd.

Huelo Point Lookout — B&B $$$

(☏ 871-8645; www.maui-vacationrentals.com; 222 Door of Faith Rd; cottages $255-355; @) Hidden well off the Hana Hwy, these four cottages, all linked together by covered walkways, form an extremely private and verdant 2-acre complex, with a parklike setting. A perennial honeymoon favorite, the cottages are well-stocked, including hot tubs, and share a lovely pool; the Lookout House in particular has gorgeous coastal and mountain views. The thick mattresses are heavenly.

The layout can be unconventional, but you won't mind. A three-night minimum and cancellation fee applies.

Huelo Lookout — Fruit Stand $

(☏ 280-4791; www.huelolookout.coconut protectors.com; 7600 Hana Hwy; snacks $5-8; ⏰ 7:30am-noon) 🍃 The fruit stand itself is tempting enough: drinking coconuts, smoothies and French crepes. But it doesn't stop there: take your goodies down the steps, where there's a shack selling waffles and sugarcane juice, and a table with a coastal panorama.

Ko'olau Forest Reserve

This is where it starts to get wild! As the highway snakes along the edge of the Ko'olau Forest Reserve, the jungle takes over and one-lane bridges appear around every other bend. Ko'olau means 'windward,' and the upper slopes of these mountains squeeze a mighty 200in to 300in of rain from passing clouds annually, making for some awesome waterfalls.

Hana Trip Tips

o With the highway now in excellent repair, hundreds of cars are making the journey each day. To beat the crowd, get a sunrise start.

o Fill up the tank in Pa'ia or Ha'iku; the next gas station isn't until Hana, and the station there sometimes runs dry.

o Bring snacks and plenty to drink.

o Wear a bathing suit under your clothes so you're ready for impromptu swims.

o Pull over to let local drivers pass – they're moving at a different pace.

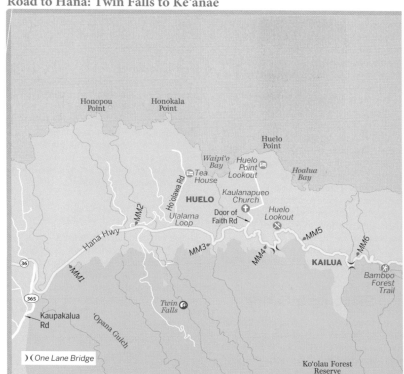

KAILUA

After the 5-mile marker you'll pass through the village of Kailua. This little community of tin-roofed houses is largely home to employees of the East Maui Irrigation (EMI) Company. EMI operates the irrigation system carrying water from the rainforest to the sugarcane fields in central Maui.

After leaving the village, just past the 6-mile marker, you'll be treated to a splash of color as you pass planted groves of **painted eucalyptus** with brilliant rainbow-colored bark. Roll down the windows and inhale the sweet scent given off by these majestic introduced trees.

KOʻOLAU DITCH

For more than a century the **Koʻolau Ditch** has been carrying up to 450 million gallons of water a day through 75 miles of flumes and tunnels from Maui's rainy interior to the dry central plains. Get a close-up look by stopping at the small pull-off just before the bridge that comes up immediately after the 8-mile marker. Just 30ft above the road you'll see water flowing through a hand-hewn, stone-block section of the ditch before tunneling into the mountain.

Waikamoi Nature Trail & Waterfalls

◉ Sights & Activities

Waikamoi Nature Trail   Hiking
Put on your walking shoes and relish the majestic sights and spicy scents along this half-mile loop trail. At the start you're welcomed by a sign that reads 'Quiet. Trees at work' and a stand of grand red-

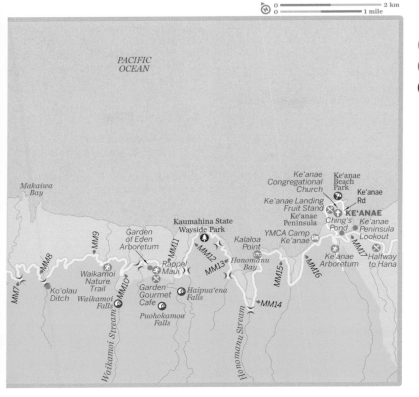

dish *Eucalyptus robusta,* one of several types of towering eucalyptus trees that grow along the path.

Once you reach the ridge at the top of the loop, you'll be treated to fine views of the winding Hana Hwy. At the turnoff to a spur, you'll enjoy great views of a huge green pincushion: a bamboo forest, facing you across the ravine. The spur leads up to a picnic area. Look for the signposted trailhead 0.5 miles past the 9-mile marker, where there's a dirt pull-off wide enough for several cars.

Waikamoi Falls   Waterfall
There's only space for a few cars before the bridge at the 10-mile marker, but unless it's been raining recently don't worry about missing this one. The East Maui Irrigation Company diverts water from the stream, so the falls are usually a

trickle. After the bridge, a green canopy of bamboo hangs over the road.

Garden of Eden Arboretum   Gardens
(www.mauigardenofeden.com; 10600 Hana Hwy; admission $15; ☼8am-4pm) So why pay a steep $15 per person – not per carload, mind you – to visit an arboretum when the entire road to Hana is a garden? Well, it does offer a tamer version of paradise. The winding paths are neatly maintained, the flowers are identified, and the hilltop picnic tables sport gorgeous views, including of Puohokamoa Falls and Keopuka Rock, which was featured in the opening shot of *Jurassic Park.*

There's also a nifty art gallery, the Fractal Gallery, located within, its entrance guarded by peacocks. The arboretum is 0.5 miles past the 10-mile marker.

211

The Best... Views

Puohokamoa Falls   Waterfall

Immediately after the 11-mile marker you'll pass Puohokamoa Falls. This waterfall no longer has public access, but you can get a glimpse of it from the bridge, or a bird's-eye view of the falls from the Garden of Eden Arboretum.

Haipuaʻena Falls   Waterfall

If you're ready for a dip, Haipuaʻena Falls, 0.5 miles past the 11-mile marker, provides a serene pool deep enough for the job. Since you can't see the pool from the road, few people know it's there. So it's not a bad choice if you *forgot* your bathing suit.

There's space for just a couple of cars on the Hana side of the bridge. To reach the falls, walk 50yd up the left side of the stream. Wild ginger grows along the path, and ferns hang from the rock wall beside the waterfall, creating an idyllic setting. Be aware of slippery rocks and flash floods.

Rappel Maui   Adventure Sports

(☎270-1500; www.rappelmaui.com; 10600 Hana Hwy, Garden of Eden Arboretum; per person $200; ⏰8am-2pm) 'Are you insane?' That's the general reaction to telling people you are rappelling (abseiling) down the face of a waterfall. The magic of this new outfit is that they make this way-out sport seem easy by the end, even if you have no previous experience.

After a 60ft instructional rappel down a dry cliff, you'll go straight down a 50ft waterfall, then a more difficult 30-footer, after which you'll swim to the finish line. This is real adventure, yet in the hands of the highly experienced and low-key Dave Black, it's also safe – and a compelling alternative to all those zip lines.

Eating

Garden Gourmet Cafe   Cafe $

(10600 Hana Hwy, Garden of Eden ticket booth; lunch mains $5-9; ⏰9:30am-4pm) Starving on the Hana Hwy? Pop into this local secret just outside the ticket booth at the Garden of Eden, where you'll find pizza, wraps, tacos and daily smoothies.

Kaumahina State Wayside Park

Clean restrooms and a grassy lawn with picnic tables make this roadside park a family-friendly stop. The park comes up 0.2 miles after the 12-mile marker and is open from 7am to 7pm. Be sure to take the short walk up the hill past the restrooms for an eye-popping view of coastal scenery.

For the next several miles, the scenery is absolutely stunning, opening up to a new vista as you turn round each bend. If it's been raining recently, you can expect to see waterfalls galore crashing down the mountains.

Honomanu Bay

Your first view of this striking stream-fed bay appears at the 13-mile marker, where there's a roadside pull-off that invites you to pause and take in the scene. This is the best stop on the first half of the Road to Hana. But you need to head down to the bay itself, via the inconspicuous road just after the 14-mile marker, to get the full effect.

Honomanu Bay's rocky black-sand beach (7am to 7pm) is used mostly by local surfers and fishers. Surfable waves form during big swells, but the rocky bottom and strong rips make it dangerous if you're not familiar with the spot; there's no lifeguard here.

Honomanu Stream, which empties into the bay, forms a little pool just inland from the beach that's good for splashing around, and on weekends local families take the young 'uns here to wade in its shallow water. Walk to the end of the beach, look back up the stream, and take in the valley – ooh!

Kalaloa Point   Lookout

For a fascinating view of the coast, stop at the pull-off on the ocean side of the highway 0.6 miles past the 14-mile marker. From the point you can look clear across Honomanu Bay and watch ant-size cars snaking down the mountain cliffs on the other side.

Ke'anae

Congratulations – you've made it to Ke'anae, halfway to Hana. Here's your reward: dramatic landscapes and the friendliest seaside village on the route.

Starting way up at the Ko'olau Gap in the rim of Haleakalā Crater and stretching clear down to the coast, Ke'anae Valley radiates green, thanks to the 150in of rainfall that drenches it each year. At the foot of the valley lies Ke'anae Peninsula, created by a late eruption of Haleakalā that sent lava gushing all the way down Ke'anae Valley and into the ocean. Unlike its rugged surroundings, the volcanic peninsula is perfectly flat, like a leaf floating on the water.

You'll want to see the peninsula up close. But keep an eye peeled, as sights come up in quick succession. After passing the YMCA Camp 0.5 miles past the 16-mile marker, the arboretum pops up on the right and the road to Ke'anae Peninsula heads off to the left around the next bend.

◉ Sights & Activities

Ke'anae Arboretum   Hiking

🚶 Up for an easy walk? Ke'anae Arbore-tum, 0.6 miles past the 16-mile marker,

follows the Pi'ina'au Stream past an array of magnificent shade trees, making for a lovely side trip that takes about 30 minutes total.

Park opposite the entrance gate and follow the paved trail. It turns to dirt and finally grows in after you hit a fence.

Ke'anae Peninsula   Village

This rare slice of 'Old Hawaii' is reached by taking Ke'anae Rd on the *makai* (seaward) side of the highway just beyond Ke'anae Arboretum. Families have tended stream-fed taro patches here for generations.

Marking the heart of the village is **Ke'anae Congregational Church** (**Lanakila 'Ihi'ihi o Iehova Ona Kaua**), built in 1860, and entered over the steps of the adjacent cottage. The church is made of lava rocks and coral mortar. It's a welcoming place with open doors and a guest book, although the roof has suffered storm damage (the community is taking up a collection to fix it). Note the cameo portraits in the adjacent cemetery.

Just past the church is **Ke'anae Beach Park** (🕙8am-7pm), with its scenic coastline of jagged black lava and hypnotic white-capped waves. Forget swimming, as the water is rough and there's no beach. The rock islets you see off the coast – Mokuhala and Mokumana – are seabird

sanctuaries. Turn around here, as there's a private residential area beyond with nothing else to see.

Ching's Pond   Outdoors

The stream that feeds Ke'anae Peninsula pauses to create a couple of swimming holes just below the bridge, 0.9 miles after the 16-mile marker. You won't see anything driving by, but if you pull off immediately before the bridge you'll find a deep crystal-clear pool beneath. Locals often swim here, but note the 'No trespassing' signs. Best to take your dip elsewhere.

Ke'anae Peninsula Lookout   Viewpoint

You'll get a superb bird's-eye view of the lowland peninsula and village, including the patchwork taro fed by Ke'anae Stream, by stopping at the paved pull-off just past the 17-mile marker on the *makai* side of the road. There's no sign, but it's easy to find if you look for the yellow tsunami speaker. If it's been raining

Left: Ke'anae Peninsula;
Below: Signpost for Ke'anae Landing Fruit Stand
(LEFT) RON DAHLQUIST/GETTY IMAGES ©; (BELOW) QUINCY DEIN/GETTY IMAGES ©

lately, look to the far left to spot a series of cascading waterfalls.

Sleeping & Eating

YMCA Camp Ke'anae　　Cabin **$**
(📞248-8355; www.ymcacampkeanae.org; 13375 Hana Hwy; campsite or van site s/f $20/35, cabin per person $20, apt $150) When they're not rented by groups, the YMCA's beat-up cabins, on a knoll overlooking the coast, are available to individuals as hostel-style dorms. You'll need your own sleeping bag, and cooking facilities are limited to simple outdoor grills. Another option is to pitch your tent on the grounds.

While facilities are weak, the location is superb, with great views across the bay to green sea cliffs cut by the highway. The great surprise is the duplex cottage down below, which is in much better shape and has spectacular ocean views. Each apartment has two bedrooms and a lanai (veranda). The camp is between the 16- and 17-mile markers.

Ke'anae Landing Fruit Stand　　Fruit Stand **$**
(📞248-7448; 210 Ke'anae Rd, Ke'anae Peninsula; banana bread $6, snacks $4-6; ⏱8:30am-2:30pm) 'Da best' banana bread on the entire road to Hana is baked fresh every morning by Aunty Sandy and her crew, and is so good you'll find as many locals as tourists pulling up here. You can also get fresh fruit and drinks at this stand, located in the village center just before Ke'anae Beach Park.

Halfway to Hana　　Fast Food **$**
(www.halfwaytohanamaui.com; 13710 Hana Hwy; lunch mains $5-9; ⏱8:30am-4pm) This aptly named old-timer has been slinging burgers, dogs and ice cream to midway travelers for 30 years. The only ATM on the highway is here, as well as portable restrooms. Homemade beef jerky will see you through to the other side.

215

The Best...
Roadside Eats

Waysides & Waterfalls

Sights

**Wailua Valley
State Wayside**   Viewpoint

Just before the 19-mile marker, Wailua Valley State Wayside lookout comes up on the right, providing a broad view into verdant Ke'anae Valley, which appears to be 100 shades of green. You can see a couple of waterfalls (when they're running), and Ko'olau Gap, the break in the rim of Haleakalā crater, on a clear day. If you climb up the steps to the right, you'll find an outstanding view of Wailua Peninsula as well – don't miss this.

A word of caution: the sign for the wayside appears at the last moment, so be on the lookout.

**Wailua
Peninsula Lookout**   Viewpoint

For the most spectacular view of Wailua Peninsula, stop at the large paved pull-off on the ocean side of the road 0.25 miles past the 19-mile marker. There's no sign but it's not hard to find as two concrete picnic tables mark the spot. Grab a seat, break out your snack pack and ogle the taro fields and jungle vistas unfolding below.

Three Bears Falls   Waterfall

A real beauty, Three Bears takes its name from the triple cascade that flows down a steep rockface on the inland side of the road, 0.5 miles past the 19-mile marker. Catch it after a rainstorm and the cascades come together and roar as one mighty waterfall. There's limited parking up the hill to the left after the falls.

You can scramble down to the falls via a steep ill-defined path that begins on the Hana side of the bridge. The stones are moss-covered and slippery, so either proceed with caution or simply enjoy the view from the road.

**Pua'a Ka'a
State Wayside Park**   Park

🖊 A delightful park with an odd name, Pua'a Ka'a (Rolling Pig) rolls along both sides of the highway 0.5 miles after the 22-mile marker. Some unlucky passersby see just the restrooms on the ocean side of the road and miss the rest. But you brought your beach towel, didn't you?

Island Insights

Every once in a while visitor stats make no sense at all, and here's a fine example: Pi'ilanihale Heiau & Kahanu Garden (p219) is easily the most important site on the Road to Hana, yet hundreds of visitors pass by every day without stopping. The reason is threefold. By the time they reach the outskirts of Hana, many visitors have run out of time, or hear 'garden' and think 'I've seen enough!' Since the heiau is part of the garden, it is often lost in the mix, rather than being seen as a destination unto itself. And finally, the resulting low visitation has meant a limited tour schedule and little marketing. In the end, though, all of this is good news for you, because you could well have this extraordinary place to yourself!

Cross the highway from the parking area and head inland to find a pair of delicious waterfalls cascading into pools.

The best for swimming is the upper pool, which is visible just beyond the picnic tables. To reach it, you'll need to cross the stream, skipping across a few rocks. Be aware of the possibility of falling rocks beneath the waterfall and flash floods.

To get to the lower falls, which drop into a shallow pool, walk back over the bridge and follow the trail upstream. And while you're at it, be sure to catch the view from the bridge.

Hanawi Falls   Waterfall
A waterfall with a split personality, Hanawi Falls sometimes flows gently into a quiet pool and sometimes gushes wildly across a broad rockface. No matter the mood, it always invites popping out the camera and snapping a pic. The falls are 0.1 miles after the 24-mile marker. There are small pull-offs before and after the bridge.

Makapipi Falls   Waterfall
Most waterfall views look up at the cascades, but this one offers a rare chance to experience an explosive waterfall from the top.

Makapipi Falls makes its sheer plunge right beneath your feet as you stand on the ocean side of the Makapipi Bridge. You don't see anything from your car so if you didn't know about it, you'd never even imagine this waterfall was here. And sometimes it isn't, as it flows intermittently.

Makapipi Falls is 0.1 miles after the 25-mile marker; you'll find pull-offs before and after the bridge.

Nahiku
The rural village of Nahiku is down near the coast, and cut by Nahiku Rd. Apart from an attractive lookout point, there's not much to tempt the visitor here. However, just before the 29-mile marker you'll come upon the Nahiku Marketplace, the jungle's best attempt at a strip mall, ranging from a tent to a tin roof. Inside you'll find a little coffee shop, a fruit stand, and several small eateries with very flexible opening hours.

If you're hungry, you'll want to stop. The food's tempting and this is the last place for a meal until you reach Hana.

◉ Sights

Nahiku Lookout   Lookout
(Nahiku Rd) If you're looking for a visual feast, turn left just past the 25-mile marker. After winding down to the sea over 2.5 miles, you'll find a great coastline view with waves crashing against the shore.

Waterfall along the Road to Hana
LOBSANG STUDIO/GETTY IMAGES ©

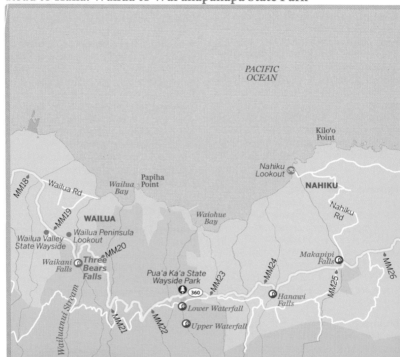

This is a fine picnic spot and a good place to stretch your legs.

Eating

Coconut Glen's
Ice Cream **$**

(📞979-1168; www.coconutglens.com; Hana Hwy, MM 27.5; scoop of ice cream $5; 🕐11am-5pm; 🍴) 🌿 Is it a commune, or an ice cream stand? Well, both. Out front Coconut Glen (aka Glen Simkins, who could double for Willy Wonka) is trying to 'change the world one scoop at a time' with his 100% vegan ice cream, served in a coconut shell with a coconut-shard for a spoon.

The ice cream comes in five flavors – try the chili chocolate – and is so tasty you won't even notice it's made from coconut milk, not cream. The adjacent eight-person commune is high on it as well.

Up In Smoke
Hawaii Regional **$**

(Hana Hwy, Nahiku Marketplace; mains under $9; 🕐10am-5pm Sun-Wed) Hawaiian food never tasted so good. This bustling barbecue stand at the Nahiku Marketplace is *the* place to try kiawe-smoked breadfruit and *kalua* pig tacos.

My Thai Food
Thai **$**

(Hana Hwy, Nahiku Marketplace; mains $8-10; 🕐11am-4pm) 🌿 Proof positive that you can now get Thai food absolutely anywhere. Owner Jen uses only fresh-caught Hana fish in her savory curries. The green papaya salad and pad Thai get rave reviews.

Island Chef
Seafood **$$**

(Hana Hwy, Nahiku Marketplace; mains $12-14; 🕐11am-6pm) The coconut shrimp here is so good that it brings people out from Hana.

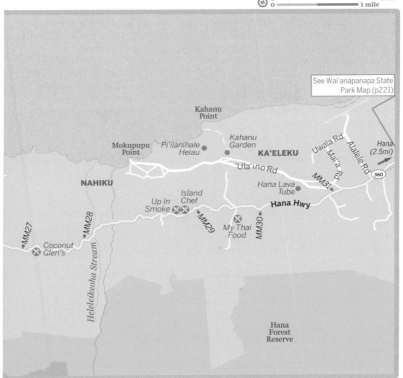

'Ula'ino Road

'Ula'ino Rd begins at the Hana Hwy, just south of the 31-mile marker.

◉ Sights & Activities

Pi'ilanihale Heiau
& Kahanu Garden   Historic Site
(☏248-8912; www.ntbg.org; 650 'Ula'ino Rd;
guided tour adult/child $25/free, self-guided tour
adult/child $10/free; ⏱9am-2pm Mon-Sat) The
most significant stop on the entire Road
to Hana, this site combines a 294-acre
ethnobotanical garden with the magnificent Pi'ilanihale Heiau, the largest
temple in all of Polynesia. A must-do
tour provides fascinating details into the
extraordinary relationship between the
ancient Hawaiians and their environment.

This is perhaps the best opportunity in
all of Hawaii to really feel what traditional
Hawaiian culture was like prior to contact
with the West. Amazingly, very few people
visit (see boxed text, p216).

Pi'ilanihale Heiau is an immense lava
stone platform with a length of 450ft.
The history of this astounding temple
is shrouded in mystery, but there's no
doubt that it was an important religious
site. Archaeologists believe construction
began as early as AD 1200 and continued
in phases. The grand finale was the work
of Pi'ilani (the heiau's name means House
of Pi'ilani), the 14th-century Maui chief
who is also credited with the construction
of many of the coastal fishponds in the
Hana area.

The temple occupies one corner
of **Kahanu Garden**, near the sea. An

219

outpost of the National Tropical Botanical Garden (which also runs the Allerton and McBryde gardens on Kaua'i), Kahanu Garden contains the largest collection of breadfruit species in the world, with over 127 varieties. Breadfruit is significant because, as its name suggests, its nutritional value makes it a dietary pillar, and hence a weapon to combat global hunger. The garden also contains a living catalog of so-called canoe plants, those essentials of traditional life brought to Hawaii in the canoes of Polynesian voyagers, along with a hand-crafted canoe house that is another step back in time.

The very best way to unlock the relationship between the heiau, the plants, and their beautiful, parklike surroundings, where palms sway in the breeze, is to take a guided tour, something the entire family will enjoy.

The King's Trail

Attention adventurers: this one is hard to beat.

Over 300 years ago, King Pi'ilani (of heiau fame) led the construction of a path around the entire island of Maui in an effort to improve commerce between its far-flung regions. Today the King's Trail, or what's left of it, offers the opportunity to see the island in a unique and unforgettable way: by walking around it.

The 200-mile trail skirts the coastline the entire way, providing access to remote areas where traditional Hawaiian life is still practiced. It can be covered in eight to nine days, if you push it. But be careful – this is not for the faint of heart. The trail has not been maintained in its entirety. There are places where it disappears, or where the highway has been built upon it. There are cars, steep cliffs and crazy dogs to contend with. And you'll need to bring lots of water.

If you only have time for a taste, try a section like the Lahaina Pali Trail (p116) from Ma'alaea to Papalaua Beach, the Hoapili Trail (p149) from La Pe'rouse Bay to Kanaio, or the Pi'ilani Trail (p222) between Wai'anapanapa State Park and Hana Beach Park, where the ancient trail once began. A complete itinerary looks like this:

- **Day 1** Ha'iku–Waihe'e

- **Day 2** Waihe'e–Kahakuloa

- **Day 3** Kahakuloa–Napili

- **Day 4** Napili–Oluwalu

- **Day 5** Oluwalu–Kihei

- **Day 6** Kihei–Kanaio

- **Day 7** Kanaio–Kaupo

- **Day 8** Kaupo–Hana

- **Day 9** Hana–Ha'iku

For more information, contact Daniel Sullivan at Indigo (p162) in Pa'ia. He's not only walked the entire trail, but created an extraordinary photographic record (www.danielsullivan.photoshelter.com).

These are only given Saturdays, at 10am and 1pm, and last two hours. Advance online reservations required.

The only other option is a self-guided tour by brochure. The site is located 1.5 miles down 'Ula'ino Rd from the Hana Hwy.

Hana Lava Tube   Cave

(Ka'eleku Caverns; ☏ 248-7308; www.maui cave.com; 305 'Ula'ino Rd; admission $12.50; ⏰ 10:30am-4pm; 🚻) One of the odder sights on this otherwise lushly green drive is this mammoth cave formed by ancient lava flows. The lava tube is so large that it once served as a slaughterhouse – 17,000lb of cow bones had to be removed before it was opened to visitors!

Winding your way through the extensive cave, which reaches heights of up to 40ft, you'll find a unique ecosystem of dripping stalactites and stalagmites. The journey is well-signed, takes about 45 minutes and is a perfect rainy-day activity.

Admission includes flashlights and hard hats. If you want to lose the kids, an adjoining **botanical maze** made from red ti plants is free. Hana Lava Tube is half a mile from the Hana Hwy.

Wai'anapanapa State Park

Swim in a cave, sun on a black-sand beach, explore ancient Hawaiian sites – this is one cool **park** (www.hawaiistateparks. org; off Hana Hwy (Hwy 360); ⏰ 7am-7pm Mon-Fri, 8am-6pm Sat & Sun). A sunny coastal trail and a seaside campground make it a tempting place to dig in for awhile.

Honokalani Rd, which leads into Wai'anapanapa State Park, is just after the 32-mile marker. The road ends overlooking the park's centerpiece, the jet-black sands at Pa'iloa Bay. Go early and you'll have it all to yourself.

🏖 Beaches

Pa'iloa Beach   Beach

The small beach here is a stunner – hands down the prettiest black-sand beach on Maui. Walk on down, sunbathe, enjoy. But if you're thinking of jumping in, be cautious. It's open ocean with a bottom that drops quickly and water conditions that are challenging, even for strong swimmers. Powerful rips are the

Wai'anapanapa State Park

| 0 | 1 km |
| 0 | 0.5 miles |

See Road to Hana: Wailua to Wai'anapanapa State Park Map (p218)

Pukaulua Point

Keawaiki Bay

Wai'anapanapa Campground

Pa'iloa Bay

Pa'iloa Beach

Lava Caves

Kuaiwa Point

PACIFIC OCEAN

Honokalani Rd

Wai'anapanapa State Park

Pa'ina

Kahului (50mi)

Water Tank

Hana Hwy

Hala Grove

Pi'ilani Trail

Pi'ilani Trail (King's Trail)

Kainalimu Bay

Luahaloa

Hana (1mi)

Right: Hiker ascending stairs towards a lava cave;
Below: Pa'iloa Bay (p221), Wai'anapanapa State Park
(RIGHT) DAVE FLEETHAM/GETTY IMAGES ©; (BELOW) ANN CECIL/GETTY IMAGES ©

norm (Pa'iloa means 'always splashing')
and there have been several drownings.

Sights & Activities

Lava Caves   Cave

A 10-minute loop path north from the
beach parking lot leads to a pair of lava-
tube caves. Their garden-like exteriors are
draped with ferns and colorful impa-
tiens, while their interiors harbor deep
spring-fed pools with some resident fish.
Wai'anapanapa means 'glistening waters'
and the pools' crystal-clear mineral waters reputedly rejuvenate the skin. They
certainly will invigorate – these sunless
pools are refreshingly brisk!

Pi'ilani Trail   Hiking

This gem of a coastal trail leads 3 miles
south from Wai'anapanapa State Park to
Kainalimu Bay, just north of Hana Bay.
It offers a private, reflective walk on top
of a raw lava field several meters above

the sea, with refreshing
views. It further packs a lot up
front, so even if you just have time
to do the first mile, you won't regret it.
There are a few spots where the loose
gravel path skirts sheer drops into the
sea below, from which there could be no
recovery – exercise caution and leave the
kids behind.

If you plan to hike the whole trail be
sure to bring water, as it's unshaded the
entire way, and good hiking shoes, as it
gets rougher as you go along. The trail
is indistinct sometimes, but as you are
paralleling the coast the entire way it is
impossible to get lost.

The route follows an ancient footpath
known as the King's Trail that once circled
the entire island (see boxed text, p220).
Some of the worn stepping stones along
the path date from the time of Pi'ilani, a
king who ruled Maui in the 14th century.
The trail begins along the coast just below
the camping area and parallels the ocean
along lava sea cliffs. Just a few minutes
along you'll pass a burial ground, a

natural sea arch and a blowhole that roars to life whenever there's pounding surf. This is also the area where you're most likely to see endangered Hawaiian monk seals basking onshore.

After three-quarters of a mile you'll view basalt cliffs lined up all the way to Hana, and ironwood encroaching the shoreline. Round stones continue to mark the way across lava and a grassy clearing, fading briefly on the way over a rugged sea cliff. A dirt road comes in from the right as the trail arrives at Luahaloa, a ledge with a small fishing shack. Inland stands of ironwood heighten the beauty of the scenic last mile of cliff-top walking to Kainalimu Bay. Stepping stones hasten the approach to the bay ahead, as the trail dips down a shrubby ravine to a quiet, black-cobble beach. Dirt roads lead another mile from here south to Hana. Alternatively, you can walk inland to the asphalt road, and either walk or hitch back to Wai'anapanapa State Park.

Sleeping

Wai'anapanapa Campground
Campground $

(📞984-8109; www.hawaiistateparks.org; Wai'anapanapa State Park; campsite $18; ⏰reservations 8:30am-3:30pm Mon-Fri) Fall asleep to the lullaby of the surf at this campground, located on a shady lawn near the beach in Wai'anapanapa State Park. It's a great spot, but since this is the rainy side of the island, it can get wet at any time. State camping permit required (see p326).

Wai'anapanapa Housekeeping Cabins
Cabin $

(📞984-8109; www.hawaiistateparks.org; Wai'anapanapa State Park; per cabin $90; ⏰reservations 8:30am-3:30pm Mon-Fri) Wai'anapanapa State Park has a dozen beat-up housekeeping cabins that are nonetheless extremely popular and may book up two to three months in advance. Each cabin sleeps six. They're located within walking distance of the parking area, facing the sea.

223

Hana &
East Maui

Where do Mauians go when they want to get away? To rugged East Maui, the most isolated part of the island. Instead of golf courses and beach resorts, you'll see a face that's hardly changed in ages. The awesome road to Hana is so special we've dedicated an entire chapter to it.

This one starts with time-honored Hana, where you'll relearn the meaning of s-l-o-w and talk story – l-o-n-g story – with people who take a personal approach to everything. Keep going and you'll reach sleepy Kipahulu, which makes Hana look urban. Then it's on to Kaupo, where the main street has one building. Finally, you'll disappear into miles of open country on the back side of Haleakalā: one spectacular drive.

From beginning to end you'll find off-the-grid farms, under-the-radar restaurants, secluded beaches and voices from the past. 'A journey like no other.' Well it's true.

Volcanic rock formations along the Hana coast
ROB HAMMER/GETTY IMAGES ©

Hana & East Maui Itineraries

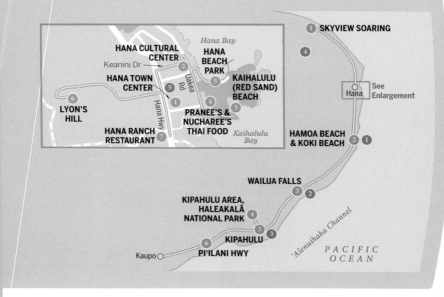

Day One

1 Hana Town Center (p228) If you've got one day it's all about slowing down to experience Hana's aloha. Wander around town, first taking in the 19th-century Wananalua Congregational Church, then stopping by the Hana Coast Gallery to peruse the museum-quality artwork.

2 Hana Cultural Center (p230) Head across town to this community museum, which harbors worthy sights within its walls and the historic grounds.

3 Kaihalulu (Red Sand) Beach (p229) It's time for a dip, so grab a towel (bathing suit optional) and sneak off to Hana's hidden red-sand strand.

4 Pranee's & Nucharee's Thai Food (p236) Hungry after that swim? Join the locals over an aromatic home-cooked lunch at this tasty Thai eatery.

5 Hana Beach Park (p230) Go see what's happening at the town's favorite hangout. When ex-Beatle George Harrison lived in Hana, he'd occasionally be seen at the beach park in the evening strumming a tune with Hana folk. Come see who's here today.

6 Lyon's Hill (p231) Top off the day with a hike through green pastures and past grazing cattle to the top of Hana's highest hill to watch the sun set over this timeless town.

7 Hana Ranch Restaurant (p237) Because after all that exercise, you've earned a thick Hana Ranch steak.

➡ **THIS LEG: 3 MILES**

Day Two

1 **Skyview Soaring** (p231) On day two, start off with a peaceful early morning flight over the crater of Haleakalā, then glide back to Hana Airport. Be sure to take a turn at the wheel.

2 **Hamoa Beach** (p229) **& Koki Beach** (p229) You have two fantastic beaches to choose from here, so take your choice – or see them both. Either way it's time to get wet.

3 **Wailua Falls** (p240) As you continue south the scenery gets lusher and greener, with the lofty cascades of Wailua Falls plunging by the roadside just begging for a picture.

4 **Kipahulu Area, Haleakalā National Park** (p201) Continue on to more watery delights at 'Ohe'o Gulch, where you can dip into heavenly pools, hike to towering waterfalls and take a look at ancient Hawaiian sites.

5 **Kipahulu** (p239) Quiet Kipahulu holds hidden treasures, including Charles Lindbergh's grave, where you can soak up the solitude that brought the great aviator to this remote village, and Ono Organic Farms. Here you'll take a superb ag tour through an exotic fruit farm, tasting along the way.

6 **Pi'ilani Hwy** (p241) Now it's time to continue your journey on the most remote road in all of Hawaii: the Pi'ilani Hwy around the southern flank of Haleakalā. In cowboy-centric Kaupo, step up to the counter at the Kaupo Store and take in the vintage scene. As you continue your adventure on the lonesome highway, enjoy the dramatic untouched coastal scenery, sea arches and lava flows along the way.

⊃ THIS LEG: 46 MILES

Hana & East Maui Highlights

1 **Best Beach: Hamoa Beach** (p229) The region's favorite sun and surf haunt.

2 **Best View: Wailua Falls** (p240) The most dramatic cascade on a drive full of drama.

3 **Best Activity: Ono Organic Farms tour** (p240) Because you've never tasted fruit like these.

4 **Best Restaurant: Hana Farms Clay Oven Pizza** (p237) Where else do they wrap it in a palm leaf?

5 **Best Night Out: Paniolo Bar** (p238) A festive bar at the end of the road.

Wailua Falls (p240)
JERRY ALEXANDER/GETTY IMAGES ©

Discover Hana & East Maui

Hana

Due to its history and its remote location at the end of Hawaii's most famous drive, Hana has a legendary aura about it. So many people are disappointed when they arrive to find a sleepy hamlet, population 1235. But that is only because Hana takes more than an hour or two to understand.

Contrary to what you might expect, Hana does not try to maximize its benefit from the many day-trippers who arrive each afternoon. This is one of the most Hawaiian communities in the state, with a timeless rural character, and also home to many transplants willing to accept certain privations for a slow, thoughtful and personal way of life in a beautiful natural setting. Though 'Old Hawaii' is an oft-used cliché, it's hard not to think of Hana in such terms. It takes time, however, to understand what this means, and to let it seep in. Hana is a story told through many personal interactions at a relaxed pace. Unfolding this story will engage the thoughtful traveler, someone open to discovering a different way of life. Those who invest the time are immensely rewarded by it.

HISTORY

It's hard to imagine little Hana as the epicenter of Maui, but this village produced many of ancient Hawaii's most influential *ali'i* (chiefs). Hana's great 14th-century chief Pi'ilani marched from here to conquer rivals in Wailuku and Lahaina, and become the first leader of unified Maui.

The landscape changed dramatically in 1849 when ex-whaler George Wilfong bought 60 acres of land to plant sugarcane. Hana went on to become a booming plantation town, complete with a narrow-gauge railroad connecting the fields to the Hana Mill. In the 1940s Hana could no longer compete with larger sugar operations in Central Maui and the mill went bust.

Enter San Francisco businessman Paul Fagan, who purchased 14,000 acres in Hana in 1943. Starting with 300 Herefords, Fagan converted the cane fields to ranch land. A few years later he opened a six-room hotel as a getaway resort for well-to-do friends and brought his minor-league baseball

Kaihalulu (Red Sand) Beach
MM SWEET/GETTY IMAGES ©

Island Insights

One of the keys to understanding Hana is contained in the local zoning regulations. In order to preserve Hana from development, the vast majority of properties are zoned agricultural. As a result, hardly anyone has the right to erect a commercial building. Consequently, almost all restaurants, and some other businesses, inhabit temporary structures, and sometimes hysterically so. You'll find them under thatched huts, tents and great blue tarps. Ice-cream trucks serve as semi-mobile kitchens. Technically, many of these businesses are still illegal, but as long as they benefit the community, no one cares. If they don't – well, the deserted mini-mall down the road from Hasegawa Store bears witness to how effective this informal system can be.

For visitors, the upshot is this: don't be afraid to eat under a blue tarp. Hana's many temporary structures are actually part of its charm.

team, the San Francisco Seals, to Hana for spring training. That's when visiting sports journalists gave the town its moniker, 'Heavenly Hana.'

Hana Ranch and the legendary Hana-Maui hotel (which changed hands many times) were the backbone of the local economy here for decades thereafter. In recent years, however, the hotel has been sold and transformed into Travaasa Hana. In 2012, 4500 acres of Hana Ranch was sold to a group of investors for $35 million, but the transaction has since been challenged in court.

 Beaches

Kaihalulu (Red Sand) Beach   Beach
(Map p232) This clothing-optional beach is dramatically sited in a hidden cove beneath a sheer red cliff. The turquoise cove is mostly protected by a volcanic dyke, the remains of an ancient fissure in the earth, but currents can still be powerful when the surf's up (Kaihalulu means 'roaring sea'). Water drains through a break on the left side, which should be avoided. The sea is calmest in the morning.

The adventurous coastal path here starts across the lawn at the lower side of Hana Community Center, where there's a barely discernible break in the foliage, and continues for 10 minutes along a steep hillside trail to the cove. The route

is narrow with a mix of loose volcanic cinders and slippery clay that can be treacherous, particularly when wet; wear appropriate shoes, as several unprepared beach-goers have fallen badly here. En route you'll pass an overgrown **Japanese cemetery** (Map p232), a remnant of the sugarcane days.

Hamoa Beach   Beach
(Haneo'o Rd) With its clear water, white sand and scenic cove, this famous beach is a little gem; author James Michener once called it the only beach in the North Pacific that actually looked as if it belonged in the South Pacific. When the surf's up, surfers and bodyboarders flock here, though beware of rip currents. When it's calm, swimming is good in the cove. The beach is used by Travaasa Hana hotel, but open to all. Public access is down the steps just north of the hotel's bus-stop sign; there's parking for seven or eight cars opposite. Facilities include restrooms.

Koki Beach   Beach
(Haneo'o Rd) This picturesque tan beach sits at the base of red cliffs with views toward tiny 'Alau Island. Bodysurfing is excellent, as it's shallow for quite a distance, but a rip current has been known to sweep people out to sea if they go too far. Shell-picking is good along tide pools by the edge.

229

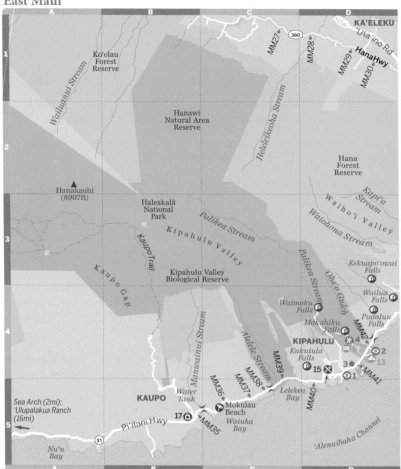

Hana Beach Park
Beach

(Map p232) Some towns have a central plaza. Hana's pulse beats from this bayside park. Families come here to take the kids for a splash, to picnic on the rocky black-sand beach and to strum their ukuleles with friends. When water conditions are very calm, snorkeling and diving are good out past the pier. Currents can be strong, and snorkelers shouldn't venture beyond the headland. Surfers head to **Waikoloa Beach** at the northern end of the bay.

◉ Sights

Hana Cultural Center
Museum

(Map p232; 248-8622; www.hanaculturalcenter.org; 4974 Uakea Rd; 10am-4pm Mon-Fri) FREE
This down-home museum displays some interesting local artifacts. The best is an entire three-bench courthouse (c 1871). Although it looks like a museum piece, this tiny court is still used on the first Tuesday of each month when a judge shows up to hear minor cases, sparing Hana residents the need to drive all the way to Wailuku to

See Wai'anapanapa State Park Map (p221)

See Hana Map (p232)

East Maui

◎ Sights

⊕ Activities, Courses & Tours

⊜ Sleeping

⊗ Eating

⊕ Shopping

🏃 Activities

Skyview Soaring
Glider

(Map p230; 📞 344-9663; www.skyviewsoaring.com; Hana Airport; 30min/1hr $165/300; ⊙by reservation) Haleakalā has excellent soaring conditions, and a sailplane is a unique, rewarding, and safe way to see the mountain. After he cuts the engine, experienced pilot Hans Pieters will fly over the crater (weather permitting) and let you fly too, before gliding silently back to Hana Airport. Call in advance for a reservation, or try your luck and visit the airport. Hans has clearly had his own share of luck, as he is one of the few people to have survived being struck by a propeller.

Lyon's Hill
Hiking

(Ka'uiki Hill; Map p232) This paved walkway up Ka'uiki Hill, behind the Travaasa Hana parking lot (take the small gate in the left corner), makes for a fine 15-minute walk. It leads to Hana's most dominant landmark, a tasteful memorial to former Hana Ranch owner Paul Fagan: like a mountaintop

contest a traffic ticket. Original paintings of Teddy Roosevelt and Admiral Dewey are a blast from the past.

Wananalua Congregational Church
Church

(Map p232; cnr Hana Hwy & Hauoli St) On the National Register of Historic Places, this church (c 1838) has such hefty walls it resembles an ancient Norman cathedral. The crumbling mausoleums in the cemetery, watched over by the draping arms of a banyan tree, are a poignant sight.

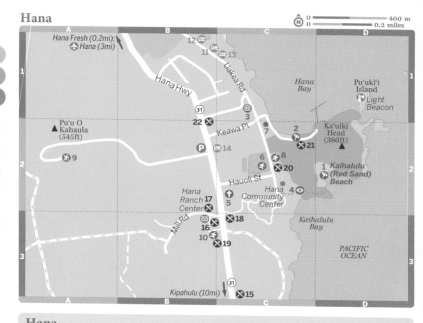

heiau with a huge cross. All of Hana is laid out below. Midway up the walkway you'll see a signed trail going off to your left. This leads to Koki Beach (2 miles).

Spa at Travaasa Hana
Spa

(Map p232; ☎270-5290; www.travaasa.com; 5031 Hana Hwy, Travaasa Hana; 1hr couples lomilomi $170) If the long drive to Hana has

tightened you up, this posh spa can work out the kinks with *lomilomi* (traditional Hawaiian massage). While nicely laid out, and big enough for an army, the rooms are a bit clinical.

Luana Spa
Day Spa

(Map p232; ☎248-8855; www.luanaspa.com; 5050 Uakea Rd; 1hr treatment $45-175) Offers massages and body treatments in a secluded yurt on Ka'uiki Hill, opposite Hana Ballpark. Lower office hidden next to Pranee's & Nucharee's Thai Food.

Travaasa
Hana Stables · Horseback Riding
(Map p232; ☎270-5276, reservations 359-2401; www.travaasa.com; 1hr ride $60) For a gentle trail ride along Hana's black-lava coastline. Riders must be at least nine years old and weigh less than 240lb.

Hana Ballpark · Tennis
(Map p232; cnr Uakea Rd & Hauoli St; ☉sunrise-sunset) Offers very nice public tennis courts and a playground for kids.

 ## Tours

Hana-Maui
Kayak & Snorkel · Snorkeling
(Map p232; ☎264-9566; www.hanabaykayaks.com; Hana Beach Park; snorkel trip $89) If you're an inexperienced snorkeler, or want to snorkel out beyond Hana Bay, then Kevin Coates is your man. You'll paddle out beyond the pier in Hana Bay and sample the reef before rounding the corner into open sea. Kevin's been doing this for 18 years, so has an endless number of stories to keep you entertained.

Also available are electric sea scooters for propelling you about. Snorkel trips generally depart 11am (9am for scooters) and return by 2pm, with a maximum of eight people. If you get seasick easily, study the conditions.

Festivals & Events

East Maui Taro Festival · Culture
(www.tarofestival.org) Maui's most Hawaiian town throws its most Hawaiian party. If it's native, it's here – outrigger canoe races, a taro pancake breakfast, poi making, hula dancing and a big jamfest of top ukulele and slack key guitarists. Held on the last weekend in April, it's Hana at its finest. Book accommodations well in advance.

First Friday Art Walk · Art
(☎248-7569; www.hanaarts.org) Hana Arts holds this art fest on the first Friday of

every month from 4pm to 8pm at Hana Farms Clay Oven Pizza. Includes an array of local visual and performing artists. Proceeds benefit local youth.

Hana Surfing Classic · Surf Meet
(www.mauisurfohana.org) Annual contest held at Koki Beach at the end of September.

Sleeping

In addition to the following, there are cabins and tent camping at Wai'anapanapa State Park (p221), just north of Hana, and camping at 'Ohe'o Gulch (p201), about 10

miles south. Maui County has tightened its regulation of rental accommodations, so you may see roadside signs indicating that a new permit has been applied for.

Bamboo Inn
Hotel $$

(Map p232; 248-7718; www.bambooinn.com; 4869 Uakea Rd; studio $195-210, ste $265;) Oh so Hana, the quiet Bamboo Inn looks down black-pebble Waikoloa Beach like a solitary traveler reflecting on their journey. There are three quality suites to choose from, all with nice seaward lanai offering great sunrises and interesting views of the Waikoloa Peninsula.

Two-person tubs are the place to end the day. One two-story suite can further be divided into two studios with reduced rates. A central location, and a long-time owner steeped in Hawaiian history, makes for a very convenient stay.

Hana's
Tradewind Cottages
Cottage $$

(Map p230; 248-8980; www.hanamauirentals. com; 135 Alalele Pl; 2 people $195, per extra person $25, Tradewind Cottage only) These two cottages on the same charming flower farm are extremely private and offer great value. The spotless Hana Cabana is a one-bedroom studio with full kitchen, lanai and a new hot tub, nestled in greenery. Wi-fi is unreliable, but you should be watching the stars anyway.

On the other side of the farm, the cozy two-bedroom Tradewind Cottage has enough space to accommodate a small family. The cottages are off the airport road just outside of town; look for the 'Tradewind Tropicals' sign. One-night stays accepted inside seven days.

Hale Ka'uiki
Yurt $$

(Map p232; 248-8855; www.luanaspa.com; 5050 Uakea Rd; d $170;) On a secluded hill overlooking Hana Bay, this back-to-nature yurt at Luana Spa Retreat fuses outdoor living with indoor comforts, including a well-equipped kitchenette. Shower outdoors in a bamboo enclosure, enjoy spectacular stargazing over the bay – this is pure Hana.

Left: Hamoa Beach (p229); **Below:** A yurt at Luana Spa Retreat (p232)

(LEFT) ANN CECIL/GETTY IMAGES ©; (BELOW) LONELY PLANET/GETTY IMAGES ©

Garden Room   B&B $$

(Map p230; ☏ 780-1312; www.
anyashouse.com/gardenroom.html; Kalo Rd;
r $147) This quiet and comfortable room,
in a private wing of a house 10 minutes
from Hana, overlooks a garden on 4 acres.
Amiable owner caters to one-night stays.
Continental breakfast.

Hana Sunrise House   Bungalow $$$

(Map p230; ☏ 248-7556; www.hanasunrise.com;
Kapia Rd; per day $250; 🛜) This split-level
Balinese bungalow is absolute perfection.
From the bamboo mats to the vaulted
ceiling, the owner has lavished attention to
ensure a profound simplicity prevails. One
entire wall can be removed to bring in the
outdoors. Irresistible day beds will keep
you contemplating the view for hours.
Delicate *shōji* screens rule out children.

Hamoa Bay
House & Bungalow   Cottage $$$

(Map p230; ☏ 248-7884; www.vrbo.com/28451;
Pi'ilani Hwy; d $265-295, q $395; 🛜) 'Tropical
Asian Fusion' describes these two beautifully designed and very private cottages
(one bedroom and two bedrooms) nestled
in greenery near Hamoa Beach. Slate
floors, soaking tubs, Balinese touches, and
fine woodwork create warm and comfortable spaces spiced with exotic romance
and set in peaceful gardens. Ideal for those
seeking a spiritual retreat; you may never
leave the lanai. Or the bamboo bed, which
is fit for a sultan.

Ekena   Vacation Rental $$$

(Map p230; ☏ 248-7047; www.ekenamaui.com;
Kalo Rd; 1br $245, 2br $320, upper fl $400, house
$645; 🛜) An impressive winding road leads
uphill to this two-story pole house with
vaulted ceilings, wraparound decks and
360-degree views of sea, forest and mountain. It's a bit rainier than the coast, but the
location is spectacular. The house can be
configured in multiple formats and prices
(only one party rents at a time). There's a
three-night minimum; resident manager.
Located at the very end of Kalo Rd.

Hale Kukuna II   Apartment $$$
(Map p232; ☏248-8980; www.halekukuna.com; 4821 Uakea Rd; apt $225, extra person $25; 🛜) This sparkling, centrally located apartment offers loads of space and a nice long deck overlooking a fishpond. Can be rented as one or two bedrooms.

Travaasa Hana   Boutique Hotel $$$
(Map p232; ☏359-2401, 855-868-7282; www.travaasa.com; 5031 Hana Hwy; d from $400; 🛜🏊) This historic resort has new owners, but mixed results. Known for decades as Hotel Hana-Maui, and locally as 'the hotel', it has left its roots behind in an effort to create a contemporary high-end resort experience. At this price, however, there is a surprising lack of attention to detail, from bent gutters to chipping paint and mold.

Some design elements, like chicken wire and chain link fencing, are definitely out of place. For some reason you can't order a drink by the pool. And the country-club atmosphere is really not what Hana is about.

The hotel is divided between the upper garden cottages and the coastal Sea Ranch, which only accepts children during school breaks. All guests share an elegant heiau-like pool, the hotel's best feature. If you just want a cottage, there are better rentals elsewhere at half the price.

Hana Kai-Maui   Condo $$$
(Map p232; ☏248-8426; www.hanakaimaui.com; 4865 Uakea Rd; studio/1br from $205/215; 🛜) Hana's only condo complex, a stone's throw from black-pebble Waikoloa Beach, comprises one ocean*front* building and an ocean*view* building behind it. Standard rooms have different owners and vary in decor; unit 1 has corner glass aimed straight down the beach. No minimum stay.

Guest Houses at Malanai   B&B $$$
(Map p230; www.hanaguesthouses.com; 6780 Hana Hwy; cottage 1br $250-295, 2br $250-345; 🛜) Two charming country cottages on 2 acres right off the highway.

Eating

To the chagrin of many visitors, only two restaurants are open for dinner Sunday through Thursday (Travaasa Hana and Hana Ranch, which have the same owner) and both are pricey; the weekend adds the Hana Farms Clay Pizza Oven (now you know why it's so popular). Grocery stores are also limited and expensive, even by Hawaii standards. So if you're bothered by a $9 gallon of milk, do what the locals do: load up on food in Kahului before coming.

Pranee's & Nucharee's Thai Food   Thai $
(Map p232; ☏248-8855; 5050 Uakea Rd; meals $10-12; ⏲10:30am-4pm) Hana's ever-popular Thai lunch stop is under one canvas roof, but changes identity depending on who's cooking: Nucharee (Tuesday to Friday) or Pranee (Saturday to Monday). Either way, you'll get one large and tasty meal, including fiery curries and fresh stir-fried dishes. The opaka (red snapper) and mango salad is a house special. Located opposite Hana Ballpark.

Bruddah Hutt's BBQ   Barbecue $
(Map p232; Hana Hwy; meals $8-13; ⏲11am-3:30pm) This entrepreneurial restaurant is like a neighborhood barbecue, with diners sitting on folding chairs under a canvas awning and an extended family cooking away over gas grills. Favorites are the barbecued chicken and the fish tacos. Expect a crowd at noon, and don't take the closing time too seriously: it shuts down when the food runs out.

Island Insights

There are so many organic farms wanting volunteer labor in Hawaii that Worldwide Opportunities on Organic Farms (WWOOF), which puts volunteers and organic farms together globally, runs a special Hawaii operation. In East Maui Hana Farms (p238) and Ono Organic Farms (p240) are both sponsors, among others. For a list of opportunities, see www.wwoofhawaii.org.

Uncle Bill's
American $

(Map p232; cnr Hana Hwy & Keanini Dr; sandwiches $8-10; ☺6am-1pm) We're not sure what's going on here. Is it really open? Why is there a sink in the yard? Am I sitting in someone's driveway? And where's Bill? Who knows, just grab a coffee mug, order at the lunch truck counter and enjoy the star attraction, Phyllis, the only cook in town prone to reciting erotic poetry to her guests. Now, where else can you get that with waffles?

Hana Fresh Market
Farm Stand $

(Map p230; ☎248-7515; www.hanahealth.org; 4590 Hana Hwy; lunch $5-9; ☺8am-4pm Mon-Fri, to 2pm Sat & Sun) This roadside stand in front of Hana Health sells organic produce grown on-site and healthy takeout plates featuring locally caught fish.

Tutu's
Snack Bar $

(Map p232; ☎248-8224; Hana Beach Park; snacks $4-10; ☺9am-4pm) Hana Beach Park's fast-food grill serves the usual shave ice, burgers and plate lunches. Nearby tables make for great beach-watching.

Ono Farmers Market
Farm Stand $

(Map p232; www.onofarms.com; Hana Hwy; $5-12; ☺10am-6pm) ✿ This is the place to pick up Kipahulu-grown coffee, jams and the most incredible array of fruit, from papaya to rambutan.

Hana Farms Clay Oven Pizza
Pizzeria $$

(Map p230; ☎248-7371; www.hanafarmsonline.com; 2910 Hana Hwy; pizza $12-17; ☺4-8pm Fri & Sat) ✿ Located behind the Hana Farms stand, this little gem is *the* local choice on Friday and Saturday nights. Gourmet pizzas with toppings sourced from the farm come out of clay ovens piping hot.

Banana bread at a roadside market
LONELY PLANET/GETTY IMAGES ©

The Best...
Locavore

1 Laulima Farms (p240)

2 Ono Organic Farms (p240)

3 Hana Fresh Market

4 Bruddah Hutt's BBQ

Gas lamps light picnic tables beneath thatched roofs. And the takeaway pizza box is a folded palm leaf – a Hana classic. Pre-order by phone to avoid waiting.

Hana Ranch Restaurant
American $$

(Map p232; ☎248-8255; Mill Rd, Hana Ranch Center; takeout meals $9-12, mains $22-30; ☺11am-8:30pm, takeout to 4pm) You've got

two choices here, at different ends of the spectrum. One is a steakhouse with extended menu (one pasta entrée, one chicken etc), including some great ribs and indoor/outdoor seating. The other is a lunchtime takeout window known far and wide for its Hana Ranch burgers. The adjacent picnic tables offer ocean views.

Hasegawa General Store — Supermarket

(Map p232; 5165 Hana Hwy; ⏰7am-7pm Mon-Sat, 8am-6pm Sun) This iconic mom-and-pop shop has been a local fixture for a century. It now sells mainly groceries, but you can pick up your 'I Survived the Hana Highway' T-shirt here.

Hana Ranch Store — Supermarket

(Map p232; ⏰7am-7:30pm) Groceries and liquor.

🍷 Drinking & Nightlife

Paniolo Bar — Bar

(Map p232; 5031 Hana Hwy, Travaasa Hana; ⏰11am-9pm) When it comes to Hana nightlife, this is the only game in town. But a great choice it is, particularly on Thursday and Friday nights, when live Hawaiian music attracts both locals and visitors, creating a festive ambience that is uniquely Hana – with a touch of Rick's Cafe.

🛍 Shopping

Hana Coast Gallery — Gallery

(Map p232; www.hanacoast.com; 5031 Hana Hwy; ⏰9am-5pm) Even if you're not shopping, visit this gallery at the northern side of Travaasa to browse the museum-quality wooden bowls, paintings and Hawaiian featherwork from over 100 different Hawaii artists. The Tahitian maoa shells carved with the Hawaiian Islands are uniquely beautiful.

Hana Farms — Food

(Map p230; www.hanafarmsonline.com; 2910 Hana Hwy; ⏰8:30am-8pm) This small 7-acre farm grows a large variety of tropical fruits, flowers and spices, and transforms them into interesting products. Its well-done roadside stand offers banana breads, exotic fruit preserves, tropical hot sauces, island candies, coffee and spices. This is a great place to find a unique and tasty gift.

Charles Lindbergh's grave (p240)

Charles Lindbergh: The Lone Eagle

In 1927, at the age of 25, Charles Lindbergh became the first man to fly across the Atlantic Ocean, navigating *Spirit of St Louis* from Long Island to Paris in 33½ hours. Six others had previously died in the attempt. His success brought him instant global fame.

In 1932, tragedy struck, when Lindbergh's young son was kidnapped and murdered. In the wake of unrelenting press coverage, Lindbergh and his American wife secretly fled to Europe, where they lived until returning to America in 1939. In the meantime Lindbergh helped the US military by providing reports on the growing capabilities of German aircraft.

Later in life Lindbergh traveled frequently to Europe, where he built a secret double life, fathering seven children with three different women in Germany and Switzerland, two of whom were sisters. In total, he had four different families at once. None of the children knew their cousins existed until well after Lindbergh's death.

Lindbergh's last years were spent in Kipahulu, where he retreated from the world almost entirely. *Spirit of St Louis* now hangs in the National Air & Space Museum in Washington DC, a fitting monument to a very transatlantic life.

ⓘ Information

Hana Ranch Center (Mill Rd) is the commercial center of town.

Bank of Hawaii (☎248-8015; www.boh.com; Mill Rd; ☉3-4:30pm Mon-Thu, 3-6pm Fri) No ATM.

Hana Health (☎248-8294; www.hanahealth.org; 4590 Hana Hwy; ☉8am-8pm Mon, to 5pm Tue-Fri, to noon Sat) At the northern side of town.

Hasegawa General Store (☎248-8231; 5165 Hana Hwy; ☉7am-7pm Mon-Sat, 8am-6pm Sun) Has an ATM.

Post Office (Map p232; 1 Mill Rd, Hana Ranch Center; ☉11am-4pm Mon-Fri)

ⓘ Getting There & Around

There are two ways to get to Hana: rent a car and drive down the winding Hana Hwy (two hours from Pa'ia), or take a 15-minute prop-plane flight from Kahului with Mokulele Airlines ($63). Flights depart at 2pm and 5:30pm, returning at 2:30pm and 6pm. Passengers must be under 350lb. The Maui Bus doesn't serve East Maui.

Travaasa Hana (p236) hotel operates a shuttle bus from Hana Airport (free for guests, $10 otherwise). The hotel concierge also offers two airport rental cars, a Chevy Malibu ($90) and a Jeep ($150). If you want to drive the Hana Hwy back to Kahului, the drop-off fee is $125.

Hana closes up early. The sole gas station in all of East Maui is **Hana Gas** (☎248-7671; cnr Mill Rd & Hana Hwy; ☉7am-8:30pm Mon-Sat, to 6pm Sun), so plan accordingly.

Kipahulu

South from Hana, the road winds down to Kipahulu. This lush stretch brims with raw natural beauty. Between its twists and turns, one-lane bridges and drivers trying to take in all the sights, it's a slow-moving 10 miles, so allow yourself a half-hour just to reach Kipahulu.

Along the way you'll pass 'Ohe'o Gulch, your entry point to the Kipahulu section of Haleakalā National Park. This is the undisputed highlight of the drive, offering fantastic falls, cool pools and paths galore. See the Haleakalā National Park chapter for more information (p201). Note: the rest of the park cannot be accessed from here by car.

The little village of Kipahulu lies less than a mile south of 'Ohe'o Gulch. It's hard to imagine, but this sedate community was once a bustling sugar-plantation town. After the mill shut down in 1922, most people left for jobs elsewhere. Today, mixed among modest homes, organic farms and back-to-the-landers living off the grid are a scattering of exclusive estates, including the former home of famed aviator Charles Lindbergh.

Sights

Wailua Falls
Waterfall

Before you reach Kipahulu, 0.3 miles after the 45-mile marker, you'll come upon these spectacular falls, which plunge a mighty 100ft just beyond the road. There's usually plenty of people lined up snapping photos. You'll see orchids growing out of the rocks, and jungles of breadfruit and coconut trees, all feeding on the mist.

Charles Lindbergh's Grave
Gravesite

(Map p230) Charles Lindbergh, the first man to fly across the Atlantic Ocean, moved to remote Kipahulu in 1968 (see boxed text, p239). After being diagnosed with terminal cancer, he decided to forgo treatment on the mainland and lived out his final days here. Following his death in 1974, Lindbergh was buried in the grave-yard of **Palapala Ho'omau Congregational Church**. The church is also noted for its window painting of a Polynesian Christ draped in the red-and-yellow feather capes of Hawaii's highest chiefs.

Lindbergh's grave is a simple granite slab laid upon lava stones in the yard behind the church. The epitaph is a quote from the Bible: 'If I take the wings of the morning, and dwell in the uttermost parts of the sea...CAL.' Walk seaward and you'll find a viewpoint aimed at those uttermost parts.

To find the church, turn left 0.2 miles south of the 41-mile marker and follow the road to the end.

Tours

Ono Organic Farms
Farm Tour

(Map p230; ☏248-7779; www.onofarms.com; Hana Hwy; 90min tours adult/child $35/free;

⏱1:30pm Mon-Fri) This fascinating two-hour tour of a wildly exotic business begins with a delicious tasting of tropical fruit. The variety is amazing: ever tried Surinam cherries, rambutan, red bananas, santol or jaboticaba? The tour then heads into the fields of the 300-acre farm, of which 70 acres are planted.

Here you'll pull your samples right off the trees as lively guides tell you the ins and outs of growing, harvesting and selling various species from around the globe – such as the cacao tree, whose avocado-sized fruit are like lanterns directly attached to all its limbs. Advance reservations required. The farm is well-hidden on the inland side of the road just south of the national park; look for 'Ono' on the mailbox. If you can't make it here, sample the goods at Ono Farmers Market (p237) in Hana.

Sleeping & Eating

Anya's House
Cabin $$

(Map p230; ☏248-8071; www.anyashouse.com; Kipahulu; 2 people $185, extra person $25, cleaning fee $75, 2-night minimum) You're really off the grid now. And in an Ohia-post cabin with spring-fed water, solar panels and great views across verdant hills to the sea. The serpentine drive through glorious uplands makes this destination special before you even arrive. The one-bedroom cabin has a large living area, a fully stocked kitchen and sleeps four (with couch).

Located on its own 16 acres, it offers extreme privacy, which is why the bath tub is alfresco. A great deal.

Laulima Farms
Farm Stand $

(Map p230; coffee $40/lb; ⏱9am-5pm) For hand-roasted coffee, veggies and fruit, fresh off the adjoining 13-acre farm. Located on Hana Hwy, between the 40- and 41-mile markers.

Kaupo

Leaving Kipahulu the road drops to parallel the edge of a rocky beach with breaking waves. At the 34-mile marker the open side of Haleakalā crater becomes visible.

The Other Spectacular Drive

The untamed Pi'ilani Hwy (Hwy 31) travels 25 ruggedly scenic miles between Kipahulu and 'Ulupalakua, skirting the southern flank of Haleakalā. Like the Road to Hana, this spectacular coastal drive starts out in lush jungle, with snaking bends through numerous gulches, but there the comparison ends. Once it enters the dry side of the island, the road breaks out into magnificent, wide-open scenery, from the crashing sea to the volcano above. And hardly anyone is on it.

The road is subject to tall tales about its condition, particularly from rental car companies. In reality it is rough and narrow in a few spots early on, but easily driveable, and the latter half has brand-new blacktop. There are no gas stations or other services along the way. Washouts sometimes close the road temporarily, so inquire about conditions at the Kipahulu Visitor Center (p201).

A mile later you'll reach Kaupo, a scattered community of *paniolo* (Hawaiian cowboys), many of them fourth-generation ranch hands working at Kaupo Ranch.

As the only lowlands on this section of coast, Kaupo was once heavily settled and is home to several ancient heiau (temples) and two 19th-century churches. However, those days are gone: the sole commercial venture on the entire road is **Kaupo Store** (Map p230; ☏ 248-8054; ☉ 10am-5pm Mon-Sat), which sells snacks and drinks. It's worth popping inside just to see the vintage displays lining the shelves.

A mile later **St Joseph Church** (1862) appears on the left. With its mountain backdrop, this is Kaupo's prettiest sight, and prime for photography. From here you can see enormous waterfalls through **Kaupo Gap**, the great gash in the side of majestic Haleakalā. If you're passing through on Sunday you may also hear singing in Hawaiian.

Kaupo to 'Ulupalakua Ranch

Past Kaupo village, you enter the dry side of the island. Near the 31-mile marker, a short 4WD road runs down to **Nu'u Bay**, favored by locals for fishing and swimming. If you're tempted to hit the water, stay close to shore to avoid riptides.

Just east of the 30-mile marker you'll see two gateposts that mark the path to dramatic **Huakini Bay**. Park at the side of the highway and walk down the rutted dirt drive. It takes just a couple of minutes to reach this rock-strewn beach whipped by violent surf. After the 29-mile marker, keep an eye out for a natural lava **sea arch** that's visible from the road.

At the 19-mile marker the road crosses a vast **lava flow** dating from between AD 1480 and 1600, Haleakalā's last-gasp eruption. This flow, part of the Kanaio Natural Area Reserve, is the same one that covers the La Pe'rouse Bay area. It's still black and barren all the way down to the sea.

Just offshore is Kaho'olawe and on a clear day you can even see the Big Island popping its head up above the clouds. It's such a wide-angle view that the ocean horizon is noticeably curved. You'll wonder how anyone could ever have thought the world was flat!

As you approach 'Ulupalakua, you find yourself back in civilization – sort of – at Bully's Burgers (p181). Don't mind the cow skulls! From there it's 4 miles to Maui's Winery (p180), where you can toast the end of one spectacular drive.

Side Trips: Lana'i & Moloka'i

Itching to get off the beaten track? Just a skip across the channel, Maui's sister islands of Lana'i and Moloka'i beg exploration.

Both have deep roots in farming, but each has taken a different route toward tourism. Lana'i has plowed under its pineapple fields and planted two Four Seasons resorts. Moloka'i, on the other hand, is damn proud of its success at keeping would-be developers at bay. It's barely changed a wink in decades – and may well have gone backwards.

But on both of these slow-paced islands you'll find people with time to talk story, wild untouched landscapes and miles of deserted beaches. Arriving in the towns of Lana'i City and Kaunakakai is like being transported to another era, free of traffic lights and chain restaurants. Just across the channel from Maui, yes – but a world apart.

Aerial view of the reefs off Kaunakakai (p260), Moloka'i
RON DAHLQUIST/GETTY IMAGES ©

Lana'i & Moloka'i Itineraries

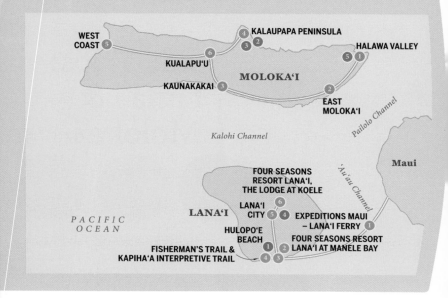

Day One

1 **Expeditions Maui–Lana'i Ferry** (p246) Ready for Lana'i in a day? Start by taking the early ferry (6:45am) from Lahaina – if you're lucky you'll see dolphins or even whales.

2 **Four Seasons Resort Lana'i at Manele Bay** (p254) It's only 8am, and you're already in the shuttle to your first luxe resort. Take in the panoramic views from One Forty while enjoying the breakfast buffet, or just a coffee.

3 **Hulopo'e Beach** (p252) Walk one of Hawaii's great beaches, plant yourself in the sand awhile, and snorkel the pristine waters (you did bring one?). Dry off by strolling out to striking Pu'u Pehe, a collapsed volcanic cone.

4 **Fisherman's Trail & Kapiha'a Interpretive Trail** (p253) Explore the other side of the bay, including the remains of an ancient village, while taking in fantastic views. End with a drink on the veranda at the

Challenge at Manele Clubhouse; staff will take you back to the shuttle stop.

5 **Lana'i City** (p247) In Lana'i's charming plantation town you'll circumnavigate Dole Park, taking in the Lana'i Culture & Heritage Center first. Choose from several tasty lunch spots, like Blue Ginger Cafe, Cafe 565 or Pele's Other Garden. Not hungry? Try a smoothie from Anuenue Juice Bar.

6 **Four Seasons Resort Lana'i, The Lodge at Koele** (p250) Having shuttled to the island's other resort, walk the Koloiki Ridge Trail as far as time allows before returning for tea in the Great Room. Catch the shuttle back in time for the last ferry (6:45pm), and you'll be in Lahaina for dinner.

➡ **THIS LEG: 33 MILES**

Days Two & Three

1 **Halawa Valley** (p266) After flying to Moloka'i, start off with the beautiful drive from Kaunakakai to Halawa Valley. Hike out to Moa'ula and Hipuapua Falls, and enjoy a spell on Halawa Beach upon your return. Hawaii as you dreamed it would be!

2 **East Moloka'i** (p264) On the way back to Kaunakakai, stop off to explore fishponds, historical spots and the stunning 'Ili'ili'opae Heiau, a lost temple in the jungle. Hungry? Mana'e Goods & Grindz will take care of you.

3 **Kaunakakai** (p260) Time to wander the island's retro capital. Make sure you stop by Kalele Bookstore to talk story. Head to Hula Shores, the oceanfront bar at Hotel Moloka'i, for a sunset drink and the best of local color. Lucky you if it's a Friday, when the ukuleles come out and hula dancers take to the stage. End the day with dinner on the patio at Paddler's Inn.

4 **Kalaupapa Peninsula** (p271) On day three hike or take a mule down the famous Kalaupapa Trail to one of the most unusual places in the national park system. Take the Damien Tour around the historic leprosy colony and enjoy the amazing view of the world's largest sea cliffs from Kalawao.

5 **West Coast** (p272) Time for a reality check. Catch the surfing action at beautiful Kepuhi Beach, in front of the defunct Kaluakoi Hotel. For a long, solitary walk on glorious windswept sands make your way to Papohaku Beach Park. Contemplate the ghost town of Maunaloa on the way back east.

6 **Kualapu'u** (p269) Celebrate your end-to-end experience of Moloka'i at Kualapu'u Cookhouse, an old roadhouse serving the island's best food.

THIS LEG: 99 MILES

Lana'i & Moloka'i Highlights

1 **Best Beach: Hulopo'e Beach** (p252) One of the finest beaches in Hawaii – and that's saying something.

2 **Best View: Pali Coast from Kalawao** (p272) The world's largest sea cliffs are an awesome sight.

3 **Best Hike: Kalaupapa Trail** (p271) Whether you do it by mule or on foot, this cliffside path will never be forgotten.

4 **Best Throwback: Lana'i City** (p247) Get lost in time in this welcoming 1930s plantation town.

5 **Best Valley: Halawa Valley** (p266) Mysterious, alluring, dramatic and gorgeous.

Halawa Valley (p266), Moloka'i
ROBERT JAMES DECAMP/GETTY IMAGES ©

Discover
Lana'i & Moloka'i

LANA'I

Lana'i's endearing oddity begins with its landscape, which often resembles East Africa. Miles of rough and deserted red-dirt roads penetrate thousands of acres of dry scrub and bluff, all that's left of the world's largest pineapple plantation. Almost all of its 3100 inhabitants reside in Lana'i City, the former company town, a grid of plantation cottages with charming Dole Park at its center. A remarkable 70% are Filipino, mostly Ilocano people from Luzon. Otherwise there are two somewhat discordant Four Seasons resorts: the coastal Manele Bay, which resembles an Asian palace, and the highland Lodge at Koele, which imitates an English country estate. The island is almost completely owned by billionaire Larry Ellison, who aims to transform it into a showcase of sustainable living. Major infrastructure upgrades are underway. So far most residents see this as an improvement, and are generally happy with life on Hawaii's quirkiest island.

ℹ️ Getting There & Around

Air

Flights to Lana'i are in small interisland planes with a 40lb limit per bag.

Island Air (📞800-652-6541; www.islandair.com) Flies several times daily to/from Honolulu; partners with Hawaiian Airlines and United.

Mokulele Airlines (📞426-7070; www.mokuleleairlines.com) Flies several times daily to/from Honolulu and Kahului (Maui); codeshares with intra-island carrier go!.

Boat

Expeditions Maui–Lana'i Ferry (📞800-695-2624, 661-3756; www.go-lanai.com; adult/child one-way $30/20) This small ferry is an unbeatable way to island hop between Maui and Lana'i. The one-hour journey departs Lahaina at 6:45am, 9:15am, 12:45pm, 3:15pm and 5:45pm. It departs Lana'i at 8am, 10:30am, 2pm, 4:40pm and 6:45pm. Sailing time is about an hour. You may see dolphins en route.

Car

Exploring Lana'i by vehicle generally means renting a 4WD, as there are only three paved roads outside

Garden of the Gods (p257), Lana'i
BRUCE YUANYUE BI/GETTY IMAGES ©

Day-Trip Logistics

Lana'i makes an interesting day trip from Maui. Visitors typically take the pleasant ferry from Lahaina to Manele Harbor first thing in the morning and return in the late afternoon. In the meantime they either take the Four Seasons shuttle around the island, thereby seeing Lana'i City and the two resort areas, or they rent a 4WD and explore further afield.

For most people, first-timers in particular, the shuttle will suffice. While a 4WD will get you to some remote beaches, the island is fairly flat and monotonous – no lush jungle, waterfalls or dramatic craters here – and sudden rains can make dirt roads treacherous, even for jeeps. Five-hundred dollar tows are not uncommon. Rental companies also limit where you can go in their pricey vehicles. In contrast, the shuttle hits the key sights for $10, with more than enough to fill a day's schedule (see p244). Just be sure to get back to the ferry in time!

of Lana'i City. Rental agencies are mom-and-pop operations with a few cars each.

ABB Executive Rentals (☑649-0644; per day $125-170) Three 4WD Jeeps, a pick-up and a 2WD car.

Dollar Rent-a-Car (☑800-533-7808, 565-7227; 1036 Lana'i Ave, Lana'i City; 4WD per day $125-150; ☺7am-7pm) Located inside Lana'i City Service gas station.

Lana'i Cheap Jeeps (☑311-6860; www.lanaicheapjeeps.com; per day $119-129) Best 4WD prices around.

Lana'i Hummer Rentals (☑286-9308; www.808hummers.com; per day $187) Rents Hummer H2s with no restrictions.

Shuttle

The Four Seasons shuttle runs between its two resorts and Lana'i City, as well as the airport and ferry dock. Shuttles run about every 30 minutes throughout the day in peak season, hourly in the slower months, from around 7am to 11pm. Fares may be included in the tariff for guests ($45 per week); others pay from $10 for a round-trip from the airport or ferry dock (credit cards only).

Lana'i City

Lana'i's one-and-only town glows with a unique charm. Built in the 1920s for Dole's Hawaiian Pineapple Company, the planned community consists of a grid of tin-roofed plantation cottages centered on rectangular Dole Park. The park is surrounded by a surprisingly rich collection of shops and tasty restaurants, but has not lost any of its authentic feel. Everything you need to see in town is within one block. Outgoing roads are lined with tall pines, a nice touch.

Sights

Lana'i Culture & Heritage Center   Museum

(Map p251; www.lanaichc.org; 111 Lana'i Ave; ☺8:30am-3:30pm Mon-Fri, 9am-1pm Sat) **FREE** Lana'i has done an admirable job of preserving its history in this engaging little museum. A visit should start here in order to understand the rest. Of particular note is the pre-contact collection (ie prior to the arrival of Captain Cook). History buffs may wish to pick up a walking tour guide of Dole Park ($3), which covers its individual buildings.

Luahiwa Petroglyphs   Petroglyphs

Lana'i's highest concentration of ancient petroglyphs are carved into three dozen boulders spread over a hillside. Many are quite weathered (so don't touch them), but you can still make out human figures, dogs and a canoe. Other than gusts of wind, the place is eerily quiet; you can almost feel the presence of the ancients.

Cat Sanctuary

If you like cats, particularly hundreds at once, then the **Lana'i Cat Sanctuary** (Map p249; ☎215-9066; www.lanaianimalrescue.org; ⏰11am-3pm) FREE is for you.

The absence of any natural predators, year-round breeding and no spaying program had bred a mighty army of strays, until Kathy Carroll built this huge open-air pen in 2009. Today 375 adorable critters wander about mewling and rubbing your legs: a strangely affecting experience. Feel a tug on your ticker? You can take one home or support it in situ for $20 per month. Otherwise, rest assured these little lions have a great sunset view.

You'll see two left-hand turns 0.6 miles past the airport; the leftmost leads to the sanctuary.

Wear long pants and shoes to defeat the underbrush.

To get to this seldom-visited site, head south from Lana'i City along tree-lined Manele Rd for about 2 miles. Take a left on the dirt track just prior to the obvious pump house. The petroglyphs are on the group of boulders on the distant hillside dead ahead. The road will turn away from them at first. Switch back sharply prior to a gate, and proceed to a turnout with a small stone marker on the left.

🏃 Activities

Koloiki Ridge Trail　　Hiking
This 2½-hour, 5-mile return hike leads up to one of the most scenic parts of the Munro Trail, offering sweeping views of remote valleys, Maui and Moloka'i. The trail begins at the rear of the Lodge at Koele, and is signed with numbered markers; printed guides are available in the lobby.

Experience at Koele　　Golf
(☎565-4653; www.golfonlanai.com; guests/nonguests $125/185; ⏰8am-6:30pm) Curving around the Lodge at Koele, this Greg Norman–branded course offers world-class golfing with knockout vistas. Check online for specials.

Lana'i Surf Safari　　Surfing
(☎649-0739; www.lanaisurfsafari.com; surf lessons per person $200, 2-person minimum) Veteran instructor Nick Palumbo offers two-hour surfing lessons at secluded spots, including 4WD transportation (travel time 1½ hours). Also has surfboard rentals from $60 per day.

Lana'i Grand Adventures　　Adventure Sports
(Map p249; ☎563-9385; www.lanaigrandadventures.com; horseback rides from $125, UTV rides 90min $188, 3hr $260; ⏰8am-5pm) Offers a sporting clays shooting course; utility training vehicle (UTV) rides along Monroe Trail; and one- to three-hour horseback rides. Staff are cowboys, born and bred. Located just past the Lodge at Koele entrance.

Cavendish Municipal Golf Course　　Golf
(Map p249; ☎565-7300; Keomuku Rd; greens fee free) If you think that's an open pasture below the Lodge at Koele, guess again. You've discovered a free golf course! This nine-hole par 36 was built for plantation workers in 1947. Today it serves free spirits who don't need a clubhouse, staff or tee times. Fairways may be wild, but the greens are well-maintained. Maps available in the Lodge lobby.

🎫 Tours

Hike Lana'i　　Hiking
(☎258-2471; www.hikelanai.com; per person $110-125) This well-managed enterprise offers two guided hikes, one to the ancient ruins of Kaunolou ($125) on Tuesday, Thursday and Saturday from 8am to 1pm, and a more strenuous ridgeline hike ($110) on Wednesday and Friday offering great views.

Lana'i

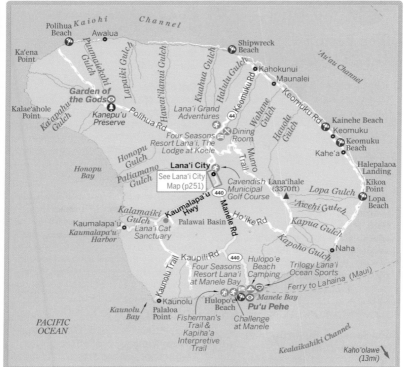

Rabaca's Limousine & Off-Road Tours
Driving Tour

(☏ 559-0230; 3hr tour per person for 2-6 people $75) 4WD tours of the island's key sights by an experienced guide, Bruce Harvey.

Festivals & Events

Pineapple Festival
Culture

(www.visitlanai.net) Lana'i's main bash is held on the first weekend in July to celebrate the island's plantation past with local *grinds* (food), games and live music at Dole Park.

Sleeping

Hotel Lana'i
Hotel $$

(Map p251; ☏ 565-7211; www.hotellanai.com; 828 Lana'i Ave; r $149-199, cottage $229; ☏) From 1923 to 1990, the Hotel Lana'i was the only hotel on the island. And it's still as charming as ever. The 10 renovated rooms have hardwood floors, antiques, pedestal sinks, patchwork quilts and very thin walls. Go for a room with – appropriately – a lanai (veranda) for viewing town. There's also a secluded two-bedroom cottage. Continental breakfast provided.

Plantation Home
Vacation Rental $$

(Map p251; ☏ 276-1528; craige@maui.net; cnr Gay & 13th Sts; per night $200) This small, renovated two-bedroom plantation-style house comes with a unique bonus: a free Jeep. Rooms are basic, but come with a long list of sports equipment, a full kitchen and laundry.

The Best...
Lana'i Hikes

Dreams Come True
Vacation Rental **$$**

(Map p251; ☎800-566-6961, 565-6961; www.dreamscometruelanai.com; 1168 Lana'i Ave; r daily/weekly $130/905; @🛜) This rustic plantation house is a bit lived in, and won't win any design awards, but it does have one good family room, a well-equipped kitchen and lots of fruit trees.

Four Seasons Resort Lana'i, The Lodge at Koele
Resort **$$$**

(Map p249; ☎800-321-4666, 565-4000; www.fourseasons.com/koele; 1 Keomuku Hwy; r from $349; ❄@🛜♨) Set on a rise above town, this pampering lodge affects the aristocratic demeanor of an English country estate, complete with afternoon tea, lawn bowling and a wood-panelled library. And that's the problem. While a stable full of horses certainly fits upcountry Hawaii, Downton Abbey is a square peg. The quality is what you would expect of the Four Seasons, with manicured grounds and an impressive Great Hall. But it is oddly quiet much of the year, attracting an unlikely mix of honeymooners and elderly visitors – or as the locals bluntly put it, 'the newly wed and the nearly dead.'

 Eating

For groceries, there are two supermarkets facing Dole Sq.

Anuenue Juice Bar & Cafe
Juice **$**

(Map p251; www.anuenuejuicebar.com; 338 8th St; smoothie $6; ⊙8am-3pm Mon, Tue, Thu & Fri, 10am-3pm Sat & Sun) A healthy and colorful juice bar with an explosion of tastes, served up with hip music. One of the best vibes in town.

Cafe 565
American **$**

(Map p251; 408 8th St; mains $6-12; ⊙10am-8pm Mon-Fri, to 3pm Sat; 🛜) This classic yellow plantation house on Dole Park serves amazing burgers, along with chicken, pizza and local *grinds*. The patio seating is a local favorite.

Blue Ginger Café
Cafe **$**

(Map p251; www.bluegingercafelanai.com; 409 7th St; breakfast & lunch $5-8, dinner $8-15; ⊙6am-8pm Thu-Mon, to 2pm Tue & Wed) This simple and friendly diner, with its large portions and checkered tablecloths, has been run by the same friendly family for decades. The long menu ranges from omelets and salads to burgers, delicious chicken katsu and more.

Canoes Lana'i
Cafe **$**

(Map p251; 419 7th St; meals $5-12; ⊙6:30am-1pm Sun-Thu, to 8pm Fri & Sat) Design your own omelet anytime at this old-time cafe, which has changed little since pineapple pickers filled the tables. That immigrant past is reflected in a tasty mix of Japanese, Chinese, Mexican, American and purely local flavors.

Pele's Other Garden
Italian **$$**

(Map p251; cnr 8th & Houston Sts; lunch $5-9, dinner $10-22; ⊙11am-3pm & 4:30-8pm Mon-Sat) Once the town brothel, this lively bistro now welcomes customers with the shades up. The kitchen leans Italian and serves up classic spaghetti and meatballs, gourmet pizza and first-rate pesto. There's an unusually fine beer list with 12 brews on tap, and happy hour from 4:30pm to 6:30pm.

Lana'i City Grille
Fusion **$$$**

(Map p251; ☎565-7211; www.hotellanai.com; 828 Lana'i Ave, Hotel Lana'i; mains $28-42; ⊙5-9pm Wed-Sun) The city's one fine dining experience is found at the historic Hotel Lana'i.

Sturdy 1930s schoolhouse furnishings give its dining room a vintage air, while the menu features fresh local seafood and organic meats in ways both familiar (a perfect rib-eye) and surprising (ahi *poke* tacos). The atmospheric bar comes alive on Friday night, when live music draws a crowd.

Dining Room
Hawaii Regional **$$$**

(Map p249; ☏565-7300; www.fourseasons.com/ koele; 1 Keomuku Hwy, Lodge at Koele; prix fixe $95, with wine $140; ☺6-9:30pm Fri-Tue) Leave your sandals in the room but bring your wallet to this very high-end restaurant at the Lodge at Koele. Locally sourced Hawaiian foods populate a prix fixe menu of expertly prepared creations. But really, you're missing the true Lana'i City experience here.

 Shopping

Mike Carroll Gallery
Art, Books

(Map p251; www.mikecarrollgallery.com; cnr 7th & Ko'ele Sts; ☺10am-5:30pm Mon-Sat, 9am-2pm Sun) Art lovers love this gallery, where you can find the eponymous owner either creating a new masterpiece or displaying the work of other local artists, such as the talented Billy O'Donnell.

Dis 'n Dat
Gifts

(Map p251; ☏565-9170; www.disndatshop.com; 418 8th St; ☺10am-5:30pm Mon-Sat) Noted for the Nash Metropolitan parked at the entrance, Lana'i's funkiest shop is an immediate head rush as 1001 wind chimes come to life upon entering. Add Asian jewelry, spiritual bric-a-brac and a headless zebra table, and there's more than enough 'cool stuff for you and your place.'

Lana'i Arts & Cultural Center
Art

(Map p251; www.lanaiart.org; cnr 7th & Houston Sts; ☺10am-4pm Mon-Sat) Staffed by volunteers, this local artists' cooperative offers works in many mediums. It's also a great place for local advice.

Local Gentry
Clothing

(Map p251; 363 7th St; ☺10am-6pm Mon-Sat, to 2pm Sun) Lovers of artful (mostly women's)

Lana'i City

threads flock to Local Gentry, a clothing store with color, flair and no polyester.

Information

Bank of Hawaii (www.boh.com; 460 8th St; ⊙8:30am-1pm & 2-4pm Mon-Thu, to 6pm Fri) Has a 24-hour ATM.

Lana'i City Service (☎565-7227; 1036 Lana'i Ave; ⊙6:30am-10pm)

Lana'i Community Hospital (☎565-6411; 628 7th St; ⊙24hr) Offers 24-hour emergency medical services.

Post Office (Map p251; 620 Jacaranda St; ⊙9am-3pm Mon-Fri, 9:30-11:30am Sat)

Hulopoʻe & Manele Bays

This area contains the ferry terminal, the coastal Four Seasons resort at Manele and Hulopo'e Beach, one of Hawaii's finest, all within walking distance. Below the water it's a marine conservation district,

making for great snorkeling and diving. Just be careful swimming in the rough winter months.

Beaches

Hulopoʻe Beach   Beach

Lana'i may only have one easy-access beach, but what a beauty it is. This gentle curve of white sand is long and broad, protected by a rocky point to the south, and well-kept by staff from the adjacent Four Seasons resort. Everybody loves it, yet it remains remarkably uncrowded. For the best snorkeling, head to the left side of the bay. Just beyond the sandy beach, you'll find steps down to a low lava shelf with tide pools and a splash pool, ideal for children. The beachside snack bar is for resort guests only.

Manele Harbor   Harbor

The island's main port contains some picnic tables for watching the action inside the breakwater, but the real action lies beyond. To the east is a small but empty

Left: Palms and picnic tables at Hulopo'e Beach, Lana'i;
Below: The Challenge at Manele golf course, Lana'i
(LEFT) QUINCY DEIN/GETTY IMAGES ©; (BELOW) RON DAHLQUIST/GETTY IMAGES ©

beach you can access via a short shoreline trail. Beyond the bay's western edge is **Cathedrals**, the island's most spectacular dive site, with grottoes galore and a 100ft lava tube. Coral is abundant near the cliffs, where the bottom quickly slopes off to about 40ft.

◎ Sights & Activities

Pu'u Pehe   Landmark
(Map p249) From Hulopo'e Beach, a short path leads south to the end of the point that separates Hulopo'e and Manele Bays (don't miss the steps down to the tide pools midway). The point is actually a volcanic cinder cone that has collapsed into the sea, leaving a rocky islet just offshore, known as **Sweetheart Rock**. For a fascinating view, continue to the top of the headland, where the trail ends, and look down into the semi-circular remains of the cone, washed by the sea.

Fisherman's Trail & Kapiha'a Interpretive Trail   Hiking
(Map p249; www.lanaichc.org/kapihaa/ kapihaa_lanai.html) The ancient Fisherman's Trail makes for a fine and refreshing walk with superb coastal views. It begins just beneath the Four Seasons at Manele Bay; you'll see a sign as you walk up from the beach. The trail is mostly flat, but dips down into gulches with wisps of beach, and gets very hot midday. It eventually merges with the Kapiha'a Interpretive Trail, a half-mile loop through the scant remains of a pre-contact village. The loop contains eight historical placards, and ends (or begins) at the Challenge at Manele clubhouse: a spectacular luncheon view.

Challenge at Manele   Golf
(Map p249; ☏565-2000; www.golfonlanai. com; Four Seasons Resort Lana'i at Manele Bay; guests/nonguests $210/225; ⏱7am-6:30pm)

253

The Future of Lana'i

Lana'i is in the midst of an historic transformation whose final scope remains to be seen. In 2012 Larry Ellison, the billionaire owner of Oracle Software, bought 98% of the island for $600 million, including its two resorts. The remaining 2% is government land and private homes (which Ellison is slowly buying up). So what does this mean for the future of the island?

Ellison has established a caretaker company, Pulama Lana'i (www. pulamalanai.com), whose stated goal is 'to achieve a new vision for Lana'i as a sustainable enterprise that meets the needs of residents for locally grown agriculture, affordable energy, housing, education, healthcare and hospice care, cultural preservation, conservation, water resources and economic growth.' In short, a model eco-society. In practical terms, this means transforming Lana'i into an island powered by solar energy, where electric cars replace gasoline-powered ones, and where seawater is transformed into fresh water, then used to sustain a new organic farming industry that feeds the island and supplies produce for export.

So far Pulama has won over the hearts and minds of the local community by improving public facilities in Lana'i City. A massive new desalinization plant is coming, as is an enlarged airport, a new low-rise luxury resort on lovely Halepalaoa Beach, and improvements to medical and educational infrastructure. One thing is for sure: Hawaii's quirkiest island is getting more interesting every day.

With an ocean view from every hole, this Jack Nicklaus–branded course offers spectacular play along seaside cliffs. The 12th hole challenges golfers to hit across the ocean.

Tours

Trilogy Lana'i
Ocean Sports   Diving, Snorkeling
(Map p249; ☏888-874-5649; www.scubalanai. com; boat dives from $190) Runs diving and snorkeling trips around Manele Bay, including the excellent Cathedrals dive site. Also offers varied catamaran trips to Lana'i from Maui.

Sleeping

Hulopo'e
Beach Camping   Campground $
(Map p249; permit $30, plus per person per night $15) The island's only campground is an excellent one. Located on the lawn above beautiful Hulopo'e Beach (only residents can camp on the beach itself), it has new restrooms, showers, drinking water, picnic tables, barbecue and great fishing. You have to take the shuttle to Lana'i City to get groceries. Call to reserve one of the eight spots and arrange a permit, which covers five or fewer people for three nights. Online reservations forthcoming.

Four Seasons Resort
Lana'i at Manele Bay   Resort $$$
(Map p249; ☏800-321-4666, 565-2000; www. fourseasons.com/manelebay; 1 Manele Bay Rd; r from $459; ❄@🛜🏊👪) This is the better choice of the two Four Seasons resorts on the island. It occupies a commanding location above Hulopo'e Bay (the resort's name is a misnomer), with beautiful views, especially from the sparkling pool. But like its sister ship, there's no snug fit with the dock.

The original Asian Palace design was inspirational, but never beachy, while recent attempts to mute it with Hawaiiana haven't fully succeeded. And the flat hues of the renovated rooms are frankly dull. It's not that you won't have a fine time, particularly in the $9229 Ali'i Suite, but at this price you deserve perfection. New blood points the way forward.

 Eating

Challenge at Manele Clubhouse
Hawaii Regional **$$**

(☏565-2000; www.fourseasons.com/manele bay; Four Seasons Resort Lana'i at Manele Bay; mains $12-34; ⏱11am-3pm) The fantastic coastal panorama from the private cliffside tables here is the best view of any island restaurant, and surprisingly unknown. The light menu, slanted toward seafood, may reveal a frozen heritage, but has moments of inspiration. The cutesy golf metaphors, from the 'approach shot' for appetizers and 'the green' for salads, are more difficult to swallow.

One Forty
Steakhouse **$$$**

(www.fourseasons.com/manelebay; 1 Manele Bay Rd, Four Seasons Resort Lana'i at Manele Bay; steak $45-67; ⏱6:30-11am & 6-9:30pm) Overlooking the ocean, this resort steakhouse may cook a fine rib-eye, but there's no connection to Hawaii, even though Hawaii has a long, long history of ranching, not to mention Maui beef. It's a great place for breakfast, though, whether it's the $32 buffet or just a coffee.

Munro Trail

This 12-mile adventure through verdant forest can be hiked, mountain biked or driven in a 4WD or UTV (p250). For the best views, get an early start.

Those hiking or cycling should be prepared for steep grades and allow a whole day. If you're driving give yourself two to three hours. However, be aware that rains create a swamp that has claimed many a 4WD. And watch out for sheer drop-offs, especially in the mist!

To start, head north from Lana'i City on Hwy 44. About a mile past the Lodge at Koele, turn right onto the paved road that ends in half a mile at the island's **cemetery**. The trailhead is to the left.

The trail passes through eucalyptus groves and climbs the ridge, where the path is studded with tall pines. Along the ridgeline, it looks down on deep ravines cutting across the eastern flank of the mountain, and passes **Lana'ihale** (3370ft), Lana'i's highest point.

On a clear day, you can see O'ahu, the Big Island, Maui, Kaho'olawe and Moloka'i. Stay on the main trail, descending 6 miles to the central plateau. Keep the hills to your left and turn right at the big fork in the road. The trail ends back on Manele Rd (Hwy 440) between Lana'i City and Manele Bay.

Driving the Munro Trail, Lana'i
RON DAHLQUIST/GETTY IMAGES ©

Keomuku Road

The best drive on Lana'i, Keomuku Rd (Hwy 44), heads north from Lana'i City into cool upland hills, where fog drifts above grassy pastures. Along the way, impromptu overlooks offer straight-on views of the undeveloped southeast shore of Moloka'i and its tiny islet Mokuho'oniki – a marked contrast to Maui's sawtooth highrises in Ka'anapali, seen to the right.

The surprisingly short 8-mile road gently slopes down to the coast in a series of switchbacks through a mostly barren landscape punctuated by oddly shaped rocks. The paved road ends near the coast, and in 4WD country. To the left, a dirt road leads to Shipwreck Beach, while turning right onto Keomuku Rd takes the adventurous to Keomuku Beach or all the way to Naha.

SHIPWRECK BEACH

This windswept stretch of sand extends 9 miles along Lana'i's northeast shore. The beach takes its name from the many ships that have run aground or been dumped here.

Start by taking the dirt road that runs 1.4 miles north from the end of Hwy 44, past some beach shacks. Park in the large clearing overlooking a rocky cove, known as Po'aiwa. This has good snorkeling among the rocks and reef, as well as protected swimming over the sandy bottom. The wreck of a WWII liberty ship lies about 440yd to the north. The hulls of these mass-produced cargo ships were made out of concrete, so they don't rust.

Close to the parking area is the site of a former lighthouse on a lava-rock point, though only the cement foundation remains. From here a trail leads inland about 100yd to the **Kukui Petroglyphs**. The simple figures are etched into large boulders on the right side of the path. Wild mouflon sheep are often spotted here; the curved horns are a giveaway.

Most people turn around at the lighthouse site, but it's possible to walk another 6 miles all the way to **Awalua**, where there's another shipwreck, the WWII tender YO-21. You'll pass the scant remains of over a dozen others along the way. The hike is windy, hot and dry (bring water!), but the further you go, the prettier it gets.

Polihua Beach, Lana'i

RON DAHLQUIST/GETTY IMAGES ©

SOUTH TO NAHA

The stretch of Keomuku Rd from the end of Hwy 44 to Naha is 4WD only, and best suited for true die-hards seeking an adventure. It's a barren stretch with a few marginal historical sites, scattered groves of coconuts and lots of kiawe trees. Keomuku Rd is likely to be either dusty or muddy, but if you catch it after it's been graded, it's drivable. Going the full 12 miles to Naha, at the end of the road, can take as long as two hours one way when the road is rough.

About 5.5 miles down is **Keomuku**, the former site of a short-lived sugarcane plantation. There's little left to see other than rustic **Ka Lanakila o Ka Malamalama Church** (1903), whose recent restoration makes it an incongruous sight, and the rusty boiler of a century-old locomotive abandoned when the sugarcane company went broke in 1901.

Halepalaoa Landing, 2 miles south of Keomuku, was the site of a wharf used to ship the sugarcane to Maui, and later became a recreation spot, Club Lana'i, which folded. There are plans to build the island's third major resort here, so you may see some new improvements to the area – as well as sea turtles, which commonly swim off the beach.

Another 4 miles brings you to **Naha**, the end of the road. With the wind whistling in your ears, you'll feel worlds away from more developed Maui, visible across the channel.

Polihua Road

Polihua Road starts near the stables at the Lodge at Koele. It's a fairly good road to the Garden of the Gods and takes about 30 minutes; from there to Polihua Beach is 4WD only, and may take 20 minutes to an hour, depending on road conditions.

Beaches

Polihua Beach
Beach

This broad, 1.5-mile-long white-sand beach at the northwestern tip of the island takes its name from the green sea turtles that nest here (*polihua* means 'eggs in the bosom'). Although the beach itself is gorgeous, strong winds may kick up stinging sand and swimming is treacherous.

Sights

Garden of the Gods
Natural Feature

(Map p249) Think rocks, not plants. This barren landscape of strange wind-sculpted forms looks more like Mars than earth. The colors change with the light – pastel in the early morning, rich hues in the late afternoon. A strangely affecting sight.

Kanepu'u Preserve
Forest

(Map p249) The 590-acre Kanepu'u Preserve is the last native dryland forest of its kind in Hawaii. Just 5 miles northwest of Lana'i City, the forest is home to 49 species of rare native plants, including the endangered *'iliahi* (Hawaiian sandalwood) and *na'u* (fragrant Hawaiian gardenia).

Kaunolu

Perched on a majestic bluff at the southwestern tip of the island, the ancient fishing village of Kaunolu thrived until its abandonment in the mid-19th century. Now overgrown and all but forgotten, Kaunolu boasts the largest concentration of stone ruins on Lana'i, including **Halulu Heiau**. Northwest of the heiau, a natural stone wall runs along the sea cliff. Look for a break in the wall at the cliff's edge, where there's a sheer 80ft drop known as **Kahekili's Jump**. In days past, Kamehameha the Great would test the courage of upstart warriors by having them make a death-defying leap from this spot.

To get here, follow Kaumalapa'u Hwy (Hwy 440) 0.6 miles past the airport, turning left onto a partial gravel and dirt road that runs south through abandoned pineapple fields for 2.2 miles. A carved stone marks the turn onto a much rougher but still 4WD-capable road down to the sea. After 2.5 miles you'll see a sign for a short **interpretive trail**, which

Moloka'i

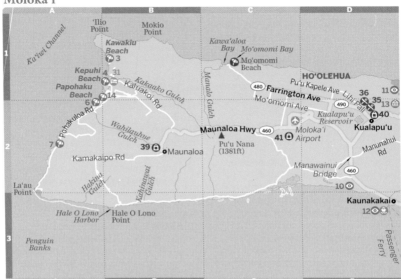

Moloka'i

◎ Don't Miss Sights

◎ Sights

◎ Activities, Courses & Tours

◎ Sleeping

◎ Eating

◎ Entertainment

◎ Shopping

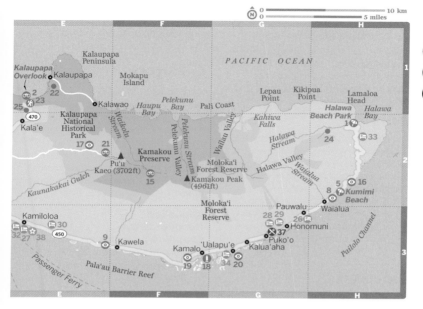

has well-weathered signs explaining the history of Kaunolu. Another 0.3 mile brings you to a parking area amid the ruins. Hike Lana'i (p248) specializes in guided hikes here.

MOLOKA'I

Moloka'i is the fickle goddess of Hawaii, both alluring and frustrating, profound and senseless, beautiful and angry.

The island is the product of vigorous opposition to virtually any form of development. If that sounds good in theory, the reality is mixed. The good has been shut down with the bad, cratering the economy.

The eastern half contains a spectacular tropical paradise, but you can't access most of it. The western half is accessible, but barren, except for its failed resort. There are no charming plantation towns here, for locals or tourists.

The people want to safeguard their heritage, but their greatest heiau lies lost in the jungle. Many think the island a timeless expression of old Hawaii; others

think it is going backwards. Visitors may come down on one side or the other. But the reality is, this island goddess has two faces, turning a challenging vacation into provocative travel.

ℹ️ Getting There & Around

Air

Island Air (📞 800-652-6541; www.islandair.com) Codeshares with Hawaiian Airlines.

Mokulele Airlines (📞 866-260-7070; www. mokuleleairlines.com) Partner with go! airlines.

Pacific Wings (📞 888-575-4546; www. pacificwings.com) These prop planes typically provide the cheapest flights from Maui and can cost less than the ferry.

Car

Renting a car is essential if you intend to fully explore Moloka'i, but keep to public roads; residents aren't too keen on trespassers. All main roads are paved, but some out-of-the-way sites, like Kamakou Preserve, require a 4WD. Rental cars can sell out, so book in advance; some prime condos include cars.

Moloka'i Outdoors (p261) rents several vehicles, including a Nissan 4WD for only $65 daily; **Mobettah Car Rentals** (📞970-227-8744; dustydancy@gmail.com) has a handful as well.

Alamo Rental Car (www.alamo.com)

Moloka'i Cars (📞336-0670; www.molokaicars. com; Moloka'i Airport; per day from $35) This newcomer is becoming ever-popular by providing clean cars at excellent prices, backed up by efficient service.

Boat

Moloka'i Ferry (📞667-9266, 877-500-6284; www.molokaiferry.com; adult/child round-trip $115/55) Runs a morning and late-afternoon ferry between Lahaina on Maui and Moloka'i's Kaunakakai Wharf. The 1½-hour crossing through the Pailolo Channel can get choppy, and is well-known for making people ill. Buy tickets online, by phone or on the *Moloka'i Princess* a half-hour before departure.

Kaunakakai

View a photo of Moloka'i's main town from 50 years ago and it won't look much different than today. Worn wooden buildings with tin roofs that roar in the rain seem like refugees from a western. But at least it's the real deal: no chain restaurants, no stoplights, and more pickup trucks than cars.

👁 Sights

Kaunakakai Wharf   Port
The days when pineapples were loaded here are gone, but the harbor still hums. A roped-off area with a floating dock provides the only swimming area. On the western side of the wharf, near the canoe shed, are the overgrown stone foundations of **King Kamehameha V's summer house**.

**Kapua'iwa
Coconut Grove**   Historic Site
(Maunaloa Hwy) Standing tall about a mile west of downtown is this 10-acre grove planted by King Kamehameha V. Careful of falling coconuts!

🏃 Activities

Moloka'i Ocean Tours   Rentals
(Map p263; 📞553-3290; www.molokaiocean tours.com; 40 Ala Malama Ave, Upstairs; ⏱10am-4pm Mon-Fri, 9am-noon Sat) All types of beach rentals: chairs, umbrellas, coolers, snorkel gear, boogie boards, surf boards...

**Moloka'i
Bicycle**   Bicycle Rental
(Map p263; 📞800-709-2453, 553-3931; www.mauimolokai-bicycle.com; 80 Mohala St; ⏱3-6pm Wed, 9am-2pm Sat & by appointment) Road and mountain bikes cost $15 to $24 per day and $70 to $100 per week. Hours are limited, so make an appointment.

👉 Tours

Moloka'i offers plenty of hiking, cycling, fishing, water sports and whale-

Kapua'iwa Coconut Grove, Moloka'i
RICH REID/GETTY IMAGES ©

watching (December to April). Its two tour operators can arrange anything on the island. For fishing, whale-watching and North Shore tours, you can also check out the charter boats at Kaunakakai Wharf yourself.

Moloka'i Fish & Dive Tour Operator
(Map p263; ☏553-5926; www.molokaifishand dive.com; 53 Ala Malama Ave; 3-tank boat dives $145-295; ⏲6am-7:30pm Mon-Sat, to 2pm Sun) Moloka'i's only licensed dive shop owns two boats. It also specializes in snorkeling ($79), whale watching ($79, December to April), kayaking ($69), Halawa Valley hikes ($75), sportfishing, Kalaupapa tours and gear rental. The office is located inside a gas station; look for the whale tail out front.

Moloka'i Outdoors Tour Operator
(☏877-553-4477, 553-4477; www.molokai-outdoors.com; Hio Pl; SUP/kayak tour adult/child $62/32; ⏲hours vary) Owned by a former pro-windsurfer, this outfit handles whatever you need for an adventure vacation, including rentals, transportation and accommodations. The focus is on surfing, kayaking and stand up paddle boarding (SUP), as well as driving tours. Its nifty SUP/kayak trip along the southern fringing reef is great for beginners. Co-located with Moloka'i Vacation Properties.

 Festivals & Events

For information on events held throughout the year see www.molokaievents.com.

Ka Moloka'i Makahiki Culture
Moloka'i's biggest annual event is an ancient winter harvest festival dedicated to the agricultural god Lono. Known as *makahiki,* it takes place in January and involves ancient Hawaiian sports, crafts and activities.

Moloka'i Ka Hula Piko Hula
(www.kahulapiko.com) Moloka'i's hula festival takes place in May.

The Best...
Moloka'i Views

1 Kalawao (p272)

2 Kalaupapa Overlook (p270)

3 Waikolu Lookout (p269)

4 Halawa Valley (p266)

5 Papohaku Beach (p273)

 Sleeping

For island-wide rentals, see **Friendly Isle Realty** (Map p263; ☏800-600-4158, 553-3666; www.molokairesorts.com; 75 Ala Malama Ave). **Moloka'i Vacation Properties** (☏800-367-2984, 553-8334; www.molokai-vacation-rental. com) and www.vrbo.com.

Ka Hale Mala B&B $
(☏553-9009; www.molokai-bnb.com; Kamehameha V Hwy; apt $90, incl breakfast $100; 🛜) Enjoy the spaciousness of a 900-sq-ft, one-bedroom apartment amid lush plantings, including trees laden with low-hanging fruit. The owners add to the bounty with organic vegetables and healthy breakfasts. It's about 5 miles east of Kaunakakai.

Moloka'i Shores Condo $$
(☏553-5954, reservations 800-367-5004; www.castleresorts.com; Kamehameha V Hwy; condos from $155; 🏊) This 1970s waterfront condo development is a good choice for location, price and friendliness. The units vary in quality based on their individual owners, so choose carefully; No 308 is a good option.

Hotel Moloka'i Hotel $$
(☏800-535-0085, 553-5347; www.hotelmolokai. com; Kamehameha V Hwy; r $169-259; 🛜🏊) Moloka'i's only hotel is slowly improving under new management. The barnlike

bungalows have never worked, but the quirky rooms have been upgraded. Upstairs rooms ($199) are best, with kitchenettes and airflow. A new restaurant opens in 2014.

Fishpond Cottage Cottage $$
(☎553-8334; www.staymolokai.com; 1120 Kamehameha V Hwy #1; cottage $150-175; ☜) This baby-blue, one-bedroom cottage sits right on a fishpond 1.5 miles from town. It's not alone, but has a freshly renovated interior and uninterrupted views. Sleeps four.

Eating

Moloka'i Burger Burgers $
(Map p263; www.molokaiburger.com; 20 Kamehameha V Hwy; burger $4-7; ☺7am-9pm; ☜) The island's top burger joint has made its name on its fast service and wild menu, from the holi moli pastrami burger to the no bun burger. Also serves chicken and a high-value breakfast.

Moloka'i Pizza Cafe Pizzeria $
(Map p263; Kaunakakai Pl; meals $9-15; ☺10am-10pm Mon-Thu, 10am-11pm Fri & Sat, 11am-10pm Sun) This unadorned pizza stop offers the usual salads, subs, burgers and pasta. It's all good, cheap and fast.

Kanemitsu Bakery Bakery $
(Map p263; 79 Ala Malama Ave; loaf of bread $5; ☺5:30am-5pm Wed-Mon) While no pretty face, this bakery is famous throughout the islands for its sweet bread and macnut lavosh crackers. The pastries are decent too. A local secret: every night except Monday you can slip down the alley to the bakery's back door at 8pm and buy loaves of hot bread fresh from the oven.

Maka's Korner Cafe $
(Map p263; cnr Mohala & Alohi Sts; meals $5-8; ☺7am-9pm Mon & Wed-Fri, to 4pm Tue, to 1pm Sat) Simple tasty fare, including a huge breakfast sandwich, excellent burgers and fries, and teri-beef. Pancakes served throughout the day. Outdoor/indoor seating.

Tiki's Coffee Shack Cafe $
(Map p263; 6 Mohala St; sandwiches $7-11; ☺6:30am-4pm Mon-Fri, 8am-2pm Sat, 9am-noon Sun) For your morning Joe. Also does paninis and sandwiches.

Moloka'i Drive-Inn Fast Food $
(Map p263; Kamehameha V Hwy; plate lunch $9-12; ☺6:30am-10pm; ☜) This timeless fast-food counter is popular for classic plate lunches and simple local pleasures such as teri-beef sandwiches, omelets with Spam and fried saimin noodles.

Friendly Market Supermarket
(Map p263; 90 Ala Malama Ave; ☺8:30am-8:30pm Mon-Fri, to 6:30pm Sat) Moloka'i's best supermarket.

 Drinking & Entertainment

Paddler's Inn Pub
(Map p263; 10 Mohala St; mains $8-20; ☺11:30am-2am Mon-Fri, 8am-2am Sat & Sun) Live music on the large outdoor patio makes this pub the town's main nightspot. The food is another reason. From deep-fried pub grub to burgers, steaks and simple pastas, the long menu holds few surprises, but the daily specials are excellent.

Hula Shores Live Music
(Kamehameha V Hwy, Hotel Moloka'i; ☺4-6pm Fri) Hands down the best place to have a sunset drink is this oceanfront bar at the Hotel Moloka'i. 'Aloha Fridays' from 4pm to 6pm is the most popular event on the island, with traditional Hawaiian musicians, spontaneous hula and a communal song at the end. Don't miss it!

Shopping

Kalele Bookstore Books
(Map p263; ☎567-9094; 64 Ala Malama Ave; ☺10am-5pm Mon-Fri, 9am-2pm Sat; ☜) New and used books, artwork, free maps, and loads of local culture and travel information. See Auntie Snooky for spiritual advice.

Kaunakakai

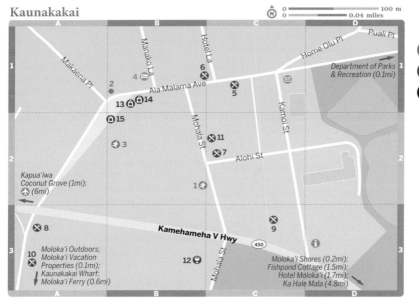

Kaunakakai

Saturday Morning Market Market
(Map p263; Ala Malama Ave; ⊙8am-2pm Sat)
This weekly market at the western end
of Ala Malama Ave is the place to browse
local crafts, try new fruits, stock up on organic produce and pick up some flowers.

Moloka'i Art from the Heart Art
(Map p263; 64 Ala Malama Ave; ⊙9:30am-5pm
Mon-Fri, 9am-2:30pm Sat) Local artists cooperative offering a variety of works from
150 members, at all levels of quality.

ⓘ Information

The **Moloka'i Visitor Center** (www.visitmolokai.
com) website has excellent links.

Bank of Hawaii (www.boh.com; Ala Malama Ave;
⊙8:30am-1pm & 2-4pm Mon-Thu, to 6pm Fri)
One of many locations with ATMs.

Moloka'i General Hospital (280 Homeolu Pl;
⊙24hr) Emergency services.

Post Office (Map p263; Ala Malama Ave; ⊙9am-
4:30pm Mon-Fri, to 11am Sat)

 Getting There & Around

Kaunakakai is a walking town, but you can gas up at **Rawlin's Chevron** (cnr Maunaloa Hwy/Hwy 460 & Ala Malama Ave; ⏰6:30am-8:30pm Mon-Sat, 7am-6pm Sun).

East Moloka'i

The 27-mile road from Kaunakakai to Halawa Valley skirts the ocean for much of the drive, with the mountains of east Moloka'i rising up to the north. It's all achingly pastoral, with small homes tucked into the valleys, horses grazing at the side of the road and silver waterfalls dropping down the mountainsides. There's no gas after Kaunakakai.

KAWELA TO KALUA'AHA

Sights

Kakahaia Beach Park   Outdoors

In Kawela you'll pass this beach park, a grassy strip wedged between the road and sea, shortly before the 6-mile marker. The park is the only part of the **Kakahaia National Wildlife Refuge** open to the public. Most of the refuge is marshland inland from the road. No camping.

St Joseph's Church   Church

Built by Father Damien in 1876, this simple, one-room wooden church 10 miles east of Kaunakakai has some of its original wavy glass panes. A lei-draped **statue of Father Damien** and a little cemetery are adjacent. The latter contains a statue of Joseph Dutton, who served the patients at Kalaupapa for 44 years.

Smith-Bronte Landing   Monument

Three-quarters of a mile past the 11-mile marker, at the base of four palm trees on the *makai* (seaward) side of the road, a little memorial plaque commemorates the first civilian flight from the US mainland to Hawaii. Ernest Smith and Emory Bronte were aiming for O'ahu, but safely crash-landed on Moloka'i in 1927.

'Ualapu'e Fishpond   Historic Site

A half-mile past the 13-mile marker, this impressive fishpond lies on the *makai* side of the road. Some walls are still under repair following the Japanese tsunami in 2012.

Kahinapohaku Fishpond, Moloka'i

Sleeping

Wavecrest Resort
Condo $$

(www.wavecrestaoao.com; per day/week 1br from $100/600, 2br from $150/800; 🏊) They look like bland cubes, but these well-kept condos at the 13-mile marker have a nice location between the mountains and the sea, with tennis and community pool, though no beach. The oceanfront units enjoy great views of Maui and Lanaʻi. Rent through www.vrbo.com, Molokaʻi Vacation Properties (p261) or Friendly Isle Realty (p261).

ʻILIʻILIʻOPAE HEIAU

Where's Unesco when you need it? ʻIliʻiliʻopae is Molokaʻi's biggest heiau and the second largest in Hawaii (after Piʻilanihale in Hana, Maui). Yet this remarkable artifact is barely known today, even by many locals.

Once a *luakini* (temple of human sacrifice), the heiau consists of an enormous platform of lava stones over 300ft long, 100ft wide, and between 11ft and 22ft tall, upon which other structures would have once stood. Archaeologists believe the original temple may have been three times this size! For the best view, follow the trail up the hill behind, from where you'll see the entire platform nestled in the jungle below. It's considered disrespectful to walk across the top.

Access is on the *mauka* (inland) side of the highway, just over half a mile past the 15-mile marker, immediately after the bridge. A small sign points down a gated dirt track into the trees, near a fire hydrant. Walk up this track, around a patch of trees and up the rocky road. Soon after, another sign indicates a trail on the left-hand side, opposite a house, that leads across a streambed. Follow to the temple in the jungle for an authentic Indiana Jones moment.

PUKOʻO TO ROCK POINT

Now just a few structures by the side of the road, sleepy Pukoʻo was once the seat

Fishponds

Starting just east of Kaunakakai and continuing past the 20-mile marker are dozens of *loko iʻa* (fishponds), huge circular walls of rocks that are part of one of the world's most advanced forms of aquaculture. Monumental in size, backbreaking in creation, the fishponds operate on a simple principle: little fish swim in through small holes, grow big and can't swim out. Some of the ponds are obscured and overgrown by mangroves, but others have been restored, such as Kahinapohaku and ʻUalapuʻe.

of island government until the plantation folks shifted everything to Kaunakakai.

Sights & Activities

Kahinapohaku Fishpond
Historic Site

This well-tended fishpond, a half-mile past the 19-mile marker, is in excellent shape.

Kumimi Beach
Beach

(Kamehameha V Hwy) Also known as Murphy's Beach (or Twenty Mile Beach because of the nearest mile marker), Kumimi Beach is protected by a reef, and has a large lagoon that is calm and shallow enough for kids, making this a top choice for families. Past the shallows, snorkelers will be rewarded with schools of fish, sponges, octopi and much more.

Rock Point
Landmark

The pointy clutch of rocks sticking out as the road swings left before the 21-mile marker is called Rock Point. This popular **surf spot** is the site of local competitions and the place to go for eastern-end swells.

LANAʻI & MOLOKAʻI EAST MOLOKAʻI

🛏 Sleeping

Dunbar Beachfront Cottages   Cottage $$

(📞800-673-0520, 558-8153; www.molokai-beachfront-cottages.com; Kamehameha V Hwy; 2br cottages from $190; 🛜) These two good-value cottages near the 18-mile marker are very nicely located on a bluff with great views toward Maui and Lana'i and a sliver of private beach apiece. Each is fitted with a full kitchen, ceiling fans, laundry and a lanai, and sleeps up to four people.

Hilltop Cottage   Cottage $$

(📞357-0139; www.molokaihilltopcottage.com; Kamehameha V Hwy; cottage per night $139-159; @) The huge wraparound lanai here allows you to savor views of neighbor islands by day and millions of stars by night. There's one nicely furnished bedroom, a full kitchen, laundry facilities and a two-night minimum stay. Excellent value.

Hale Lei Lani   Vacation Rental $$$

(📞415-457-3037, 415-218-3037; www.tranquil molokai.com; off Kamehameha V Hwy; per night $285; 🛜🏊) Perched on a hill near the 16-mile marker, this sparkling contemporary home offers two large bedrooms off a soaring great room, a great kitchen and sweeping ocean views. A small pool set into the wooden deck looks straight down the channel between Maui and Lana'i. A slightly smaller two-bedroom guesthouse ($240) is also available.

🍴 Eating

Mana'e Goods & Grindz   Hawaiian $

(Kamehameha V Hwy/Hwy 450, MM 16; meals $5-12; 🕐kitchen 6:30am-4pm Mon-Fri, 7:30am-4:30pm Sat & Sun, store 7am-6pm Mon-Fri, to 4pm Sat & Sun; 🛜) Even if it wasn't your only option east of Kaunakakai, you'd still want to stop here. The plate lunches are something of a local legend: tender yet crispy chicken katsu, specials such as pork and squash, and standards such as excellent teriyaki burgers. The attached market is small but well stocked.

HALAWA VALLEY

After Rock Point the road starts to wind upwards, narrowing to one lane in spots. It levels out just before the 24-mile marker, where there's a fine view of the islet of **Mokuho'oniki**, a seabird sanctuary. Afterwards the jungle closes in, with lots of beep-as-you-go hairpin bends. A quarter mile past the 26-mile marker there's a turnoff with a **panoramic view** of Halawa Valley.

Now this is the gorgeous valley you came to Hawaii to see: steep verdant walls, waterfalls and a central stream flowing to the beach. While occupied since 650 AD, it has only a few families now due to past tsunamis. The road descends into the valley at a steep but

Halawa Beach, Moloka'i
RITA ARIYOSHI/GETTY IMAGES ©

Pu'u O Hoku Ranch

The **Pu'u O Hoku Ranch** (☎558-8109; www.puuohoku.com; 2br cottage $225, 4br house $300; ⊠) contains 14,000 extraordinary acres on the eastern tip of Moloka'i, including beautiful Halawa Valley. New management is slowly trying to reinvent it in various ways, including through organic farming, renewable energy and eco-tourism. Some outbuildings have been turned into rustic accommodations – your entrée to a low-key, private and entirely real experience, in which you can hike, swim, learn about the ranch and wonder at the stars.

The charming one-bedroom Sunrise Cottage ($225) has a full kitchen, enclosed lanai (veranda), wide hardwood floors and bamboo furniture. Perfect for a family getaway, the larger Grove House ($300) has a stone fireplace and Balinese furnishings. Both are surrounded by towering trees and rolling grassland, while enjoying the ranch's incredible views. Also available is an entire lodge, with a fireplace, a swimming pool and sleeping accommodations for 21 people ($165 each per night, all-inclusive). Reserve online.

If you're driving to Halawa Valley, you'll come upon the small **Pu'u O Hoku Ranch Store** at the 25-mile marker. This has snacks, drinks, some of the ranch's fine produce and a few locally made gifts.

manageable rate, ending at Halawa Beach Park.

Beaches

Halawa Beach Park
Beach

You'll feel like one happy castaway on this beautiful tropical beach, with jaw-dropping Halawa Valley as background. The beach has double coves separated by a rocky outcrop, with the northern side a bit more protected than the south. When the water is calm, there's good swimming, but both coves are subject to dangerous rip currents otherwise. The park has picnic pavilions, restrooms and nondrinkable running water.

Activities

Moa'ula & Hipuapua Falls
Hiking

The hike to these twin 250ft falls, which cascade down the back of the lush Halawa Valley, is a highlight of many people's Moloka'i visit. The straightforward 1.7-mile trail passes some archaeological sites, including an ancient burial ground and a seven-tiered stone temple. A bracing plunge into the pools at the bottom of the falls is a fine end.

Access is somewhat complicated. Pu'u o Hoku Ranch, which owns the valley, authorizes a single local guide, longtime-resident **Pilipo Solatario** (☎551-1055; www.halawavalleymolokai.com; adult/child $60/35). His 9am tour includes a wealth of cultural knowledge and lasts three to four hours. Pilipo must be called in advance, as he lives out of cell-phone range and only responds to messages.

Unofficial 'guides' at Halawa Beach Park offer to fill in for $20, but know far less. You can also organize a guide with tour operators in Kaunakakai ($80). Local transplants report having done the walk themselves many times without any problem, or fee.

In any case, prepare for mosquitoes and muddy conditions. Wear stout shoes for river crossings. Bring water, lunch and plenty of sunscreen.

Right: Kalaupapa Peninsula (p271), Moloka'i; **Below:** Mosses and ferns along the Pepe'opae Trail, Kamakou Preserve, Moloka'i
(RIGHT) LIYSA LIYSA/GETTY IMAGES ©; (BELOW) JONATHAN KINGSTON/GETTY IMAGES ©

Central Moloka'i

Central Moloka'i takes in Mo'omomi Beach, the former plantation town of Kualapu'u and the forested interiors of Kamakou Preserve. On the remote northern end of it all is Kalaupapa Peninsula, Hawaii's infamous leprosy colony.

The most trodden route in central Moloka'i is the drive up Hwy 470, past the coffee plantation, restored sugar-mill museum, mule stables and the trailhead down to Kalaupapa Peninsula. The road ends at Pala'au State Park.

KAMAKOU AREA

The mountains that form the spine of Moloka'i's eastern side reach up to Kamakou, the island's highest peak (4970ft). Few visitors make it up this way. If you're lucky enough to be one of them, you'll be rewarded with spectacular views of the island's impenetrable northern coast and an opportunity to explore a near-pristine rainforest. Kamakou is a treasure but not an easily reached one. It's accessed via a narrow rutted dirt road (Maunahui Rd) requiring a 4WD. The turnoff for Kamakou begins between the 3- and 4-mile markers on Hwy 460, immediately east of the Manawainui Bridge. The road is marked with a sign for Homelani Cemetery.

◉ Sights

Moloka'i Forest Reserve · Park
The 10-mile drive up to Waikolu Lookout takes about 45 minutes, depending on road conditions. A mile before the lookout you'll find the 19th-century **Sandalwood Pit**, a grassy depression on the left. The pit was dug to the exact measurements of a ship's hold. After being filled with fragrant sandalwood logs, the wood was strapped to the backs of laborers, who hauled it down to the harbor for shipment to China.

Waikolu Lookout, just before the Kamakou Preserve entrance, offers a breathtaking view of remote Waikolu Valley. If it's been raining recently, waterfalls stream down the sheer cliff sides. Morning is the best time for views, as afternoon trade winds commonly bring clouds.

Kamakou Preserve Park

Hiking back through three million years of evolution on the **Pepe'opae Trail** is Kamakou's star attraction. Crossed by a boardwalk, this undisturbed Hawaiian montane bog is a miniature primeval forest of stunted trees, dwarfed plants and lichens that make it feel like the dawn of time.

From the trail's end at **Pelekunu Valley Overlook**, you'll be rewarded with a fantastic view of majestic cliffs and (if it's not too cloudy) the ocean beyond. The marked trailhead is located 2.2 miles beyond Waikolu Lookout.

KUALAPU'U

Moloka'i's second town, Kualapu'u is a small, spread-out farming community with a pint-size town center.

Kualapu'u was a pineapple-plantation town until Del Monte pulled out in 1982. In 1991 coffee saplings were planted on the fallow pineapple fields, and now cover some 600 acres beneath the town center.

Eating

Coffees of Hawaii Cafe $

(www.coffeesofhawaii.com; cnr Hwys 470 & 490; sandwiches $5-8; ⊙7am-4pm Mon-Sat) Coffees of Hawaii grows and roasts its own coffee. You can survey the scene from the veranda and enjoy a cup with a sandwich or salad. Try the signature Mocha Mama.

Kualapu'u Cookhouse Hawaiian $$

(Hwy 490; lunch $13-15, dinner $19-33; ⊙8am-8pm Tue-Sat, 9am-2pm Sun, 7am-2pm Mon) This low-key roadhouse has some of the island's best food – and largest portions. Breakfast includes perfect omelets,

Monte Cristo sandwiches join the plate-lunch brigade, and dinner stars inventive fare such as ahi in lime cilantro sauce. Live music Thursday night. Beer and wine available across the street. Cash only.

Shopping

Blue Monkey   Gifts
(☏567-6776; www.bigwindkites.com/blue monkey; cnr Hwys 470 & 490; ◷10am-5pm Mon-Sat) This large and colorful gift shop next to Coffees of Hawaii offers an excellent selection of local goods.

HO'OLEHUA

Ho'olehua, the dry central plains that separate eastern and western Moloka'i, is home to a community of Native Hawaiian homesteaders operating small farms.

Kumu Farms (www.kumufarms.com; ◷9am-4pm Tue-Fri) grows bananas, papayas, herbs, tomatoes, lettuce and much more. Its attractive farm store offers fresh treats at picnic tables and diverse natural products – honey, soap, jelly, salt, pesto – for export. Look for the signs off Hwy 460 just south of the airport.

MO'OMOMI BEACH

Mo'omomi Beach, on the western edge of the Ho'olehua Plains, is a spectacular stretch of wild dunes – long, lonely and windswept. It's also a nesting ground for green sea turtles, and home to several endangered native plant species. A red-dirt road at the end of Farrington Hwy leads 2.2 miles to the beach. An ideal place for a reflective walk in the elements.

Mo'omomi Bay, a small sandy beach that is part of Hawaiian Home Lands, is marked by a picnic pavilion. A broad, white-sand beach (often mistakenly called Mo'omomi) is at **Kawa'aloa Bay**, a windy 20-minute walk to the west. Because of the fragile ecology of the dunes, visitors should stay along the beach and on trails.

KALA'E

Kala'e is known mainly for the **Moloka'i Museum & Cultural Center** (☏567-6436; adult/child $5/1; ◷10am-2pm Mon-Sat), which contains a nicely restored 19th-century sugar mill. A self-guided tour by brochure provides a simple yet engaging look at a long-gone industry; you can almost feel the place in operation. The adjacent cultural center contains intriguing displays on Moloka'i's history. It's located 3.8 miles up Hwy 470, toward Kalaupapa Overlook.

PALA'AU STATE PARK

Sights

Kalaupapa Overlook   Lookout
Perched on the edge of a 1500ft cliff, this overlook is the highlight of this woodsy park at the end of Hwy 470. The stunning view of the peninsula far below reveals why Kalaupapa means 'flat leaf'.

Kauleonanahoa   Cultural Site
Hawaii's premier phallic stone pokes up in a little clearing inside an ironwood grove near Kalaupapa Overlook. Nature has endowed it well, but it's obviously been touched up by human hands. Women who wish to become pregnant leave offerings underneath; some are left limp by the sight.

 Sleeping

Camping is allowed in a grassy field near the park entrance, but keep in mind this is one of the wetter parts of the island.

Kalaupapa National Historical Park

Wildly beautiful and strikingly isolated, Kalaupapa Peninsula is fronted by tumultuous waters and backed by the world's highest sea cliffs. Because of its remoteness, around 8000 people suffering from leprosy (Hansen's disease) were forced into isolation here. Although the isolation policies were abandoned in 1969, a few elderly patients still remain, along with around 90 staff, in what otherwise feels like a well-restored ghost town.

The remote settlement is now a national historical park uniquely managed by both the State of Hawaii Department of Health and the **National Park Service (www.nps.gov/kala)**.

The 3-mile trail down the *pali* (cliffs) is the only land route to the peninsula. You can either take a mule down, or hike it yourself. Otherwise you have to fly in. In any case, you have to book with Damien Tours to see the peninsula, which is otherwise off-limits.

HISTORY

In 1835 doctors diagnosed Hawaii's first case of leprosy, one of many diseases introduced by foreigners. Alarmed by the spread of the disease, King Kamehameha V signed a law banishing people with leprosy to Kalaupapa Peninsula.

Hawaiians call leprosy *mai ho'oka'awale,* which means 'separating sickness,' a reference to the fact that it tore families apart. Once the afflicted arrived on Kalaupapa Peninsula, there was no way out, not even in a casket. Early conditions were unspeakably horrible and lifespans short.

Father Damien (Joseph de Veuster), a Belgian priest, arrived at Kalaupapa in 1873. A talented carpenter, he built 300 simple houses, nursed the sick and buried the dead. Damien's work inspired others, including Mother Marianne Cope, who stayed 30 years and came to be known as the mother of the hospice movement. Damien died of leprosy in 1889 at the age of 49. In 2009 he became Hawaii's (and America's) first Catholic saint.

Activities

Kalaupapa Trail   Hiking

One of Hawaii's great experiences, the Kalaupapa Trail has 26 switchbacks along its 3-mile descent, making for a dramatic cliffside hike. While steep, the trail is paved with stones and manageable by anyone in fit condition. Begin by 8am to avoid walking in fresh mule dung, and

Hikers on the Kalaupapa Trail
DAVID CORNWELL/GETTY IMAGES ©

allow an hour to descend comfortably. At the bottom, you'll break out of the jungle onto a long and empty beach, welcomed by the sound of waves. Magical.

The trailhead is on the eastern side of Hwy 470, just north of the mule stables, where there's roadside parking. Note that it's possible to hike down and then fly out, although the 1½ hour walk up is not as difficult as it seems.

Tours

Damien Tours   Bus Tour
(☏567-6171; tour $50, with lunch $70; ⏰Mon-Sat) This 3½ hour bus tour is the only way to see Kalaupapa's ghostly settlement, which feels deserted. You'll be taken to various well-restored sites, including churches, a store, a cemetery, a bar and a visitors center with period photos. The tour is a bit long, but includes magical Kalawao, on the eastern side of the peninsula, where you'll enjoy a gorgeous view along the world's highest sea cliffs (*pali*), a ripple of green valleys towering 3300ft in the air. Reserve in advance.

Molokai Mule Ride   Tour
(☏800-567-7550, 567-6088; www.muleride.com; rides $200; ⏰Mon-Sat) This 2½ hour round-trip by mule will leave you thrilled but sore. While the mules move none too quickly, there's a certain thrill in trusting your life to these sure-footed beasts as they descend the 3 miles of Kalaupapa Trail. Make reservations well in advance. Lunch and the land tour with Damien Tours are included in the rate.

❶ Getting There & Around

Makani Kai Air Charters (☏834-1111; www.makanikaiair.com) Runs regular flights from Ho'olehua on Moloka'i ($197 return) and O'ahu ($315 return) that include the Damien Tour. Some combine a hike down with a one-way flight out.

West End

Moloka'i's arid western side has been shaped by local resistance to, and the ultimate collapse of, the island's largest employer, Moloka'i Ranch – and the local economy with it. The result is an eerie emptiness, beginning with the ghost town

A mule ride through Kalaupapa, Moloka'i

of Maunaloa, and ending with the ghost resort of Kaluakoi, where all the fairways have gone to seed. It's worth a day trip for the beaches, but you only stay here to put the world in the rear-view mirror.

MAUNALOA

In the 1990s, Moloka'i Ranch largely bulldozed the town of Maunaloa and rebuilt it in the same plantation style. When the ranch subsequently closed, the new development withered. Much of it is now shuttered, creating a modern ghost town.

Stop in at **Big Wind Kite Factory & Plantation Gallery** (www.bigwindkites.com; 120 Maunaloa Hwy; ⊗8:30am-5pm Mon-Sat, 10am-2pm Sun) for custom-made kites of all shapes and sizes – how it got blown here is anyone's guess.

Maunaloa General Store (⊗8am-6pm Mon-Sat) is the only grocery store in the West End.

KALUAKOI RESORT & AROUND

The Kaluakoi Resort once included a fine hotel beautifully located above a fantastic beach, and a large development of upscale condos interspersed with golf links. Today it looks like a neutron bomb has gone off. The hotel is closed, the wild fairways can hardly be recognized and the condo owners struggle with depressed valuations. Ironically, this stretch of coast has Moloka'i's best beaches, located one after another. They can easily occupy a full day of exploration.

 Beaches

Kepuhi Beach   Beach
This amazing white-sand beach below the defunct Kaluakoi Resort is even more striking for its ominous backdrop. Popular with surfers, it's OK for sunbathing, but swimming conditions are usually dangerous due to a tough shorebreak and strong currents.

Kawakiu Beach   Beach
The northernmost of the West End beaches is reached by walking north along the coastal golf 'greens' and up over a rocky point. It's a white-sand crescent with bright turquoise waters and good swimming when seas are calm, most often in summer.

Papohaku Beach Park   Beach
The 2.5-mile-long Papohaku Beach is often windy, with gusts of sand, and usually too treacherous for swimming. It's fantastic for walks, however, and has a choice **campground** – beautiful and quiet, with the surf lulling you to sleep beneath a field of stars. Full facilities as well. Permits available through the **Department of Parks & Recreation** (☎553-3204; www.co.maui.hi.us; 90 Ainoa St, Mitchell Pauole Center, Kaunakakai; ⊗8am-1pm & 2:30-4pm Mon-Fri).

Dixie Maru Beach   Beach
This beach at the southern end of Pohakuloa Rd is the most protected cove on the western shore, and popular with local swimmers, especially on weekends. The waters are generally calm, except when the surf is high enough to break over the mouth of the bay.

 Sleeping

Ke Nani Kai   Condo $$
(www.kenanikai.com; Kaluakoi Rd; 1br/2br from $140/150; ⊠) An oasis in the desert, these 100-plus units are large and well-maintained, and the pool attractive. Kepuhi and Papohaku Beaches are a short walk.

Hale Puhi   Vacation Rental $$$
(☎553.8334; molokai-vacation-rental.com; Dixie Maru Beach; $250-325) Set on 30 acres fronting Dixie Maru Beach, this converted garage offers total seclusion in an amazing location. The layout is odd – the downstairs bedroom is more like a safari tent – but you can pack eight people in, and there's laundry, a barbecue and a hot tub. Perfect for a surfing party.

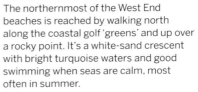

Maui

In Focus

Wailea Beach (p138)
ROB DECAMP/GETTY IMAGES ©

Maui Today

Snorkelers viewing coral formations off Olowalu (p61)

66

Few topics raise more debate on Maui than development issues

99

ethnicity
(% of population)

29 **19** **40** **10** **2**

Asian
American | Mixed
Race | White | Native
Hawaiian | Other

if Maui were 100 people

29 would be
0-24 years old

28 would be
25-44 years old

28 would be
45-64 years old

14 would be
65+ years old

population per sq mile

♛ ≈ 45 people

Maui | Big Island | O'ahu

Staying Hawaiian

Hawaiian culture today is about much more than melodic place names and luau shows. Traditional arts and healing arts are experiencing a revival, ancient heiau temples and fishponds are being restored, native forests replaced and endangered birds bred and released.

Although few island residents can agree on what shape the fragmented Native Hawaiian sovereignty movement should take, or even if it should exist at all, its grassroots political activism has achieved tangible results. Decades of protest and a federal lawsuit filed by sovereignty activists finally pressured the US military into returning the island of Kaho'olawe, which it had used for bombing practice since WWII, to the state in 1994. In 2011 Governor Neil Abercrombie signed into law a bill recognizing Native Hawaiians as the state's only indigenous people.

Eco-Awareness

Mauians know intimately the consequences of global warming. Extended periods of drought have become commonplace. Some years these end with record-setting bursts of torrential rains that wash down the slopes, flooding low-lying communities and muddying the coral reefs. Most Mauians take the issue seriously. Even big-wave surfer Laird Hamilton attributes climate change as a source of the 100ft surf he rides off Maui's North Shore.

Maui has a long history of protecting the environment. It was the first island in Hawaii to ban single-use plastic bags, and in a move to decrease their own carbon emissions, Mauians supported the erection of windmills. Many residents have called for the end of sugarcane burning by Hawaiian Commercial & Sugar Co, the last sugarcane company on the island. There are concerns that the resulting smoke is linked to lung disease.

RON DAHLQUIST/GETTY IMAGES ©

Headline Grabbers

Two mainland celebrities have been garnering local headlines in recent years. Larry Ellison, co-founder of Oracle Corporation, bought 98% of Lana'i in 2012. And in 2013 TV personality Oprah Winfrey, who owns an estate on the slopes of Haleakalā in Keokea, shared her plan to sell organic produce grown on her property.

The biggest newsmaker, though? The tiger shark. There were eight shark attacks off Maui in 2013, two of them fatal. In a normal year there are typically only four attacks statewide. According to island lore, run-ins increase when the wili wili tree blooms, which is typically in the fall. But recent incidents spanned the calendar. The Department of Land & Natural Resources has commissioned a two-year study to analyze the recent spike.

Paving Paradise

Few topics raise more debate on Maui than development issues. The latest target of corporate bulldozers is Olowalu, a lush coastal village in West Maui known for its thriving coral reef. If plans are finalized, developers will construct 1500 housing units just south of the town village. Although 50% of the units will be set aside as affordable housing, environmentalists are concerned that the project could harm the coral reef.

Two high-profile projects took advantage of pre-existing commercial sites in 2013. The Hyatt's new Andaz Maui resort hotel took over the former Renaissance Hotel in Wailea. The Outlets of Maui, a collection of high-end outlet stores, rejuvenated a decaying strip mall in Lahaina.

History

Outrigger canoe

RON DAHLQUIST/GETTY IMAGES

Hawaii has lured adventurous travelers to its shores for more than 1500 years. The first Polynesian voyagers to arrive were so enamored by the sight that they paddled back across 2400 miles of ocean to spread the word. So began the perilous Pacific voyages, Western colonization, island kingdom intrigue and plantation-era immigration – all making the island chain's history compelling.

The Great Canoe Voyages

The earliest Polynesian settlers of Hawaii came ashore around AD 500. Archaeologists disagree on exactly where these explorers came from, but artifacts indicate the first to arrive were from the Marquesas Islands. The next wave of settlers were from Tahiti and arrived around AD 1000. Unlike the Marquesans, who sparsely settled the tiny islands at the northwest end of the Hawaiian Islands, the Tahitians arrived in great numbers and settled each of the

900,000 years ago
The volcanoes that formed Maui rise from the sea; the buildup continues until 400,000 BC.

major islands in the Hawaiian chain. Though no one knows what set them on course for Hawaii, when they arrived in their great double-hulled canoes they were prepared to colonize a new land, bringing with them pigs, dogs, taro roots and other crop plants.

Their discovery of Hawaii may have been an accident, but subsequent journeys were not. The Tahitians were highly skilled seafarers, using the wind, stars and wave patterns to guide them. Yet, incredibly, they memorized their route over 2400 miles of open Pacific and repeated the journeys between Hawaii and Tahiti for centuries.

And what a story they must have brought back with them, because vast waves of Tahitians followed to pursue a new life in Hawaii. So great were the number of Tahitian migrations that Hawaii's population reached a peak of approximately 250,000 by the year 1450. The voyages back and forth continued until around 1500, when all contact between Tahiti and Hawaii appears to have stopped.

European Explorers

On January 18, 1778, an event occurred on the islands that would change the life of Hawaiians in ways inconceivable at the time. On that day British explorer Captain James Cook sighted Hawaii while en route to the Pacific Northwest in search of a possible 'northwest passage' between the Pacific and Atlantic Oceans.

Cook's appearance was not only the first Western contact, it also marked the end of Hawaii's 300 years of complete isolation that followed the end of the Tahiti voyages. Cook anchored on the Big Island, across the channel from Maui, and stayed long enough to refresh his food supplies before continuing his journey north.

Cook sighted Maui but never set foot on the island. The first Westerner to land on Maui was French explorer Jean François de Galaup La Pérouse, who sailed into Keone'o'io Bay (now called La Pe'rouse Bay) on Maui's southern shore in 1786, traded with the Hawaiians and left after two days of peaceful contact.

Royal Power Struggles

From the early days of Polynesian settlement, Maui was divided into separate kingdoms, with rival chiefs occasionally rising up to battle for control of the island.

In the 16th century Pi'ilani, the king of the Hana region, marched north to conquer Lele (now Lahaina) and Wailuku, uniting Maui for the first time under a single royal rule.

During the 1780s Maui's king Kahekili became the most powerful chief in all Hawaii, bringing both O'ahu and Moloka'i under Maui's rule.

In 1790, while Kahekili was in O'ahu, Kamehameha the Great launched a bold naval attack on Maui. Using foreign-acquired cannons and two foreign seamen, Isaac Davis

---

AD 500

Polynesian colonists traveling thousands of miles across open seas in double-hulled canoes arrive in Hawaii.

1500

The migration voyages between the South Pacific and Hawaii end.

1778

British Captain James Cook becomes the first-known Westerner to sight Maui.

A Bloody Confrontation

In January 1790, the American ship *Eleanora* arrived on Maui, eager to trade Western goods for food and sandalwood. Late one night a party of Hawaiian men stole the ship's skiff. In retaliation, Captain Simon Metcalf lured a large group of Hawaiians to his ship under the pretense of trading with them. Instead he ordered his men to fire every cannon and gun aboard the ship at the Hawaiians, murdering over 100 men, women and children. This tragic event, one of the first contacts between Westerners and Maui islanders, is remembered as the Olowalu Massacre.

and John Young, Kamehameha defeated Maui's warriors in a fierce battle at 'Iao Valley that was so bloody the waters of 'Iao Stream ran red for days.

An attack on his own homeland by a Big Island rival forced Kamehameha to withdraw from Maui, but the battle continued over the years. When the aging Kahekili died in 1794, his kingdom was divided among two quarreling heirs, which left a rift that Kamehameha quickly exploited.

In 1795 Kamehameha invaded Maui again, with a force of 6000 canoes. This time he conquered the entire island and brought it under his permanent rule. Later that year Kamehameha went on to conquer O'ahu and unite the Hawaiian Islands under his reign.

In 1810 Kamehameha became the first *mo'i* (king) of the Kingdom of Hawaii. He established Lahaina as his royal court, where he built a royal residence made of brick, the first Western-style building in Hawaii. Lahaina remained the capital of the kingdom until 1845, when King Kamehameha III moved the capital to Honolulu on O'ahu.

Here Come the Westerners

After Captain Cook's ships returned to England, news of his discovery quickly spread throughout Europe and America, opening the floodgates to a foreign invasion of explorers, traders, missionaries and fortune hunters. By the 1820s Hawaii had become a critical link in the growing trade route between China and the US, with British, American, French and Russian traders all using Hawaii as a mid-Pacific stop for provisioning their ships.

Soul Savers

Shortly after the first missionaries arrived on Maui they made inroads with Hawaiian leaders. By a twist of fate, they arrived at a fortuitous time, when Hawaiian society was in great upheaval after the death of Kamehameha the Great in 1819. It made the missionar-

1786
French explorer La Pérouse becomes the first Westerner to land on Maui.

1790
Kamehameha the Great invades Maui, decimating island warriors in a bloody battle at 'Iao Valley.

MICHAEL DEFREITAS/GETTY IMAGES ©

ies' efforts to save the souls of the 'heathen' Hawaiians much easier. The *ali'i* (royalty), in particular, were keen on the reading lessons offered by the missionaries in the Hawaiian language, which had never before been put into written form. Indeed, by the middle of the 1850s, Hawaii had a higher literacy rate than the USA.

Lahaina became a center of activity. In 1831 Lahainaluna Seminary (now Lahainaluna High School), in the hills above Lahaina, became the first secondary school to be established west of the Rocky Mountains. Lahaina was also home to the first newspaper, *Ka Lama Hawaii,* printed west of the Rocky Mountains.

But the New England missionaries also helped to destroy traditional Hawaiian culture. They prohibited the dancing of the hula because of its lewd and suggestive movements and they denounced the traditional Hawaiian chants and songs that paid homage to the Hawaiian gods. In the late 19th century they even managed to prohibit the speaking of the Hawaiian language in schools as another means of turning Hawaiians away from their 'hedonistic' cultural roots – a major turnaround from the early missionary days when all students were taught in Hawaiian.

The Best...
Native Hawaiian Sites

1 Pi'ilanihale Heiau (p219)

2 Haleki'i-Pihana Heiau State Monument (p105)

3 Brick Palace & Hauola Stone (p38)

4 Hoapili Trail (p149) (King's Hwy Trail)

5 Hana Cultural Center (p230)

Whalers

The first whaling ship to stop in Maui was the *Balena,* which anchored at Lahaina in 1819. The crew was mostly New England Yankees with a sprinkling of Gay Head Indians and former slaves. As more ships arrived, men of all nationalities roamed Lahaina's streets. Most were in their teens or twenties, and ripe for adventure. Lahaina became a bustling port of call with shopkeepers catering to the whalers. Saloons, brothels and hotels boomed.

A convenient way station for whalers of both the arctic and Japanese whaling grounds, by the 1840s Hawaii was the whaling center of the Pacific. In Lahaina the whalers could transfer their catch to trade ships bound for America. This allowed whalers to stay in the Pacific for longer periods of time without having to return home with their payload, resulting in higher profits. At the peak of the whaling era, more than 500 whaling ships were pulling into Lahaina each year.

Whaling brought big money to Maui and the dollars spread beyond Lahaina. Many Maui farmers got their start supplying the whaling ships with potatoes. Hawaiians themselves made good whalers, and sea captains gladly paid a $200 bond to the Hawaiian government for each Hawaiian sailor allowed to join their crew. Kamehameha

1810

Kamehameha the Great moves to Maui, declaring Lahaina the royal seat of the Hawaiian kingdom.

Left: Kamehameha the Great statue

1819

Kamehameha the Great dies and the Hawaiian religious system is cast aside.

1819

The first whaling ship anchors in Lahaina, Maui.

IV even set up his own fleet of whaling ships that sailed under the Hawaiian flag.

Whaling in the Pacific peaked in the mid-19th century and quickly began to burn itself out. In a few years all but the most distant whaling grounds were being depleted and whalers were forced further afield to make their kills.

The last straw for the Pacific whaling industry came in 1871, when an early storm in the arctic caught more than 30 ships by surprise, trapping them in ice floes above the Bering Strait. Although more than 1000 seamen were rescued, half of them Hawaiian, the fleet itself was lost.

Sugar & Immigration

In the 1840s, sugar growing began to emerge as an economic force. Maui's role in sugar production began in 1839, when King Kamehameha III issued small parcels of land to individual growers who were required to have their crop processed at a mill built by the king in Wailuku. Half of the crop went to the king. Of the remaining half, one-fifth was taken as a tax to support the government and the remainder went to the grower.

In the heyday of sugar, there were as many as 10 plantations on Maui, cultivating thousands of acres of land throughout the island. One of the most prominent mills, the Pioneer Mill in Lahaina, was founded in 1863 by American entrepreneurs. In 1876 the Hamakua Ditch began transporting water from the rainy mountains to the dry plains, allowing sugar plantations to spread. In 1890 the first train to run in West Maui was opened to bring freshly cut sugarcane to the mill.

As sugar production grew, sugar barons were worried about the shortage of field laborers, who were mostly Hawaiian. There had been a severe decline in the Native Hawaiian population due to introduced diseases, such as typhoid, influenza and smallpox, for which the Hawaiians had no immunities. To expand their operations, plantation owners began to look overseas for a cheap labor supply. First they recruited laborers from China. In 1868 recruiters went to Japan, and in the 1870s they brought in Portuguese workers from Madeira and the Azores Islands.

The labor contracts typically lasted for two to three years, with wages as low as $1 per week. Workers lived in ethnically divided 'camps' set up by the plantations that included modest housing, a company store, a social hall and other recreational amenities. At the end of their contracts, some returned to their homelands, but most remained on the islands, integrating into the multicultural mainstream.

The Best... Missionary- Era Sites

1 Baldwin House (p35)

2 Hale Pa'i (p42)

3 Bailey House Museum (p106)

4 David Malo's Church (p126)

1820
Christian missionaries arrive, filling the gap left by the abandonment of Hawaii's traditional religion.

1831
Lahainaluna Seminary, the first secondary school west of the Rocky Mountains, is built in Lahaina.

1848
Under the influence of Westerners, the first system of private land ownership is introduced.

After Hawaii's 1898 annexation, US laws, including racially biased prohibitions against Chinese immigration, were enforced in Hawaii. Because of these new restrictions, plantation owners turned their recruiting efforts to Puerto Rico and Korea. Filipinos were the last group of immigrants brought to Hawaii to work in the fields and mills between 1906 and 1946.

The Great Land Grab

Throughout the monarchy period, the ruling sovereigns of Hawaii fought off continual efforts on the part of European and American settlers to gain control of the kingdom.

In 1848, under pressure from foreigners who wanted to own land, a sweeping land reform act known as the Great Mahele was instituted. This act allowed, for the first time, the ownership of land, which had previously been held exclusively by monarchs and chiefs. The chiefs had not owned the land in the Western sense but were caretakers of the land, and the commoners who lived on the land worked it, giving a portion of their harvest in return for the right to stay.

Baldwin House (p35), Lahaina

1868
Thousands of Japanese laborers arrive on Maui to work newly planted sugarcane fields.

1893
While attempting to restore Native Hawaiian rights, Queen Lili'uokalani is overthrown by American businessmen.

1898
Hawaii is annexed by the USA and becomes a US territory.

The reforms of the Great Mahele had far-reaching implications. For foreigners, who had money to buy land, it meant greater economic and political power. For Hawaiians, who had little or no money, it meant a loss of land-based self-sufficiency and forced entry into the low-wage labor market, primarily run by Westerners.

When King David Kalakaua came to power in 1874, American businessmen had wrested substantial control over the economy and were bent on gaining control over the political scene as well. Kalakaua was an impassioned Hawaiian revivalist, known as the 'Merrie Monarch.' He brought back the hula, reversing decades of missionary repression against the 'heathen dance,' and he composed the national anthem *Hawaii Ponoi,* which is now the state song. Kalakaua also tried to ensure a degree of self-rule for Native Hawaiians, who had become a minority in their own land.

Overthrow of the Monarchy

When King Kalakaua died in 1891, his sister ascended the throne. Queen Lili'uokalani was a staunch supporter of her brother's efforts to maintain Hawaiian independence.

In January 1893, Queen Lili'uokalani was preparing to proclaim a new Constitution to restore royal powers when a group of armed US businessmen occupied the Supreme Court and declared the monarchy overthrown. They announced a provisional government, led by Sanford Dole, son of a pioneer missionary family.

After the overthrow of the monarchy, the new government leaders pushed hard for annexation, believing that it would bring greater stability to the islands, and more profits to Caucasian-run businesses. Although US law required that any entity petitioning for annexation must have the backing of the majority of its citizens through a public vote, no such vote was held in Hawaii.

Nonetheless on July 7, 1898, President William McKinley signed a joint congressional resolution approving annexation. Some historians feel that Hawaii would not have been annexed if it had not been for the outbreak of the Spanish–American War in April 1898, which sent thousands of US troops to the Philippines, making Hawaii a crucial Pacific staging point for the war.

WWII

On December 7, 1941, when Japanese warplanes appeared above the Pearl Harbor area, most residents thought they were mock aircraft being used in US Army and Navy practice maneuvers. Even the loud anti-aircraft gunfire didn't raise much concern. Of course it was the real thing, and by the day's end hundreds of ships and airplanes had been destroyed, more than 1000 Americans had been killed and the war in the Pacific had begun. The impact on Hawaii was dramatic. The army took control of the islands, martial law was declared and civil rights were suspended. Unlike on the mainland, Japanese-Americans in Hawaii were not sent to internment camps because they made

1901
The Pioneer Inn, Maui's first hotel, is built on the waterfront in Lahaina.

1927
Convict road gangs complete the construction of the Hana Hwy.

1941
Japanese warplanes attack Pearl Harbor, turning Hawaii into a war zone under martial law.

up most of the labor force in the cane fields in Hawaii's sugar-dependent economy.

The Japanese-Americans' loyalty to the USA was still questioned and they were not allowed to join the armed forces until 1943. When the US government reversed its decision and approved the formation of an all-Japanese combat unit, called the 100th Infantry Battalion, more than 10,000 men answered the recruitment call. The 442nd Regimental Combat Team of the battalion, made up largely of Hawaii's Japanese-American population, saw fierce action in Europe and fought so bravely that they became the most decorated fighting unit in US history.

Statehood

Throughout the 20th century numerous statehood bills were introduced in Congress, only to be shot down. One reason for this lack of support was racial prejudice against Hawaii's multi-ethnic population. US congressmen from a still-segregated South were vocal in their belief that making Hawaii a state would open the doors to Asian immigration and the so-called 'Yellow Peril' threat that was so rampant at the time. Others believed Hawaii's labor unions were hotbeds of communism.

However, the fame of the 442nd Regimental Combat Team in WWII went a long way toward reducing anti-Japanese sentiments on the mainland and increasing support for statehood. In March 1959 Congress voted again, this time admitting Hawaii into the Union. On August 21, President Eisenhower signed the admission bill that officially deemed Hawaii the 50th state.

Statehood had an immediate economic impact, most notably in boosting the tourism industry. Coupled with the advent of jet airplanes, which could transport thousands of people per week to the islands, tourism exploded, creating a hotel-building boom previously unmatched in the US. Tourism became the largest industry on Maui.

Hawaiian Renaissance & Sovereignity Movement

By the 1970s, Hawaii's rapid growth meant new residents (mostly mainland transplants) and tourists were crowding island beaches and roads. Runaway construction was rapidly transforming resorts almost beyond recognition, and the relentless peddling of 'aloha' got some islanders wondering what it meant to be

The Best...
History & Culture Museums

1 Whalers Village Museum (p67)

2 Alexander & Baldwin Sugar Museum (p119)

3 Lahaina Heritage Museum (p34)

4 Story of Hawaii Museum (p115)

5 Wo Hing Museum (p37)

IN FOCUS HISTORY

1959
On August 21, Hawaii becomes the 50th state of the USA.

1962
Hawaii's first resort destination outside of Waikiki is built at Ka'anapali Beach in Maui. Right: Ka'anapali Beach

AEDER ERIK/GETTY IMAGES ©

Hawaiian. Some Native Hawaiians turned to *kapuna* (elders) and the past to recover their heritage, and by doing so became more politically assertive.

In 1976, a group of activists illegally occupied Kaho'olawe, aka 'Target Island,' which the government had taken during WWII and used for bombing practice until 1990. During another protest occupation attempt in 1977, two members of the Protect Kaho'olawe 'Ohana (PKO) – George Helm and Kimo Mitchell – disappeared at sea, instantly becoming martyrs. Saving Kaho'olawe became a rallying cry and it radicalized a nascent Native Hawaiian rights movement.

When the state held its landmark Constitutional Convention in 1978, it passed a number of important amendments of special importance to Native Hawaiians. For example, it made Hawaiian the official state language (along with English) and mandated that Hawaiian culture be taught in public schools. At the grassroots level, the islands were experiencing a revival of Hawaiian culture, with a surge in residents – of all ethnicities – joining hula *halau* (schools), learning to play Hawaiian instruments and rediscovering traditional crafts like feather lei making.

In 2011 Governor Neil Abercrombie signed into law a bill recognizing Native Hawaiians as the state's only indigenous people and establishing a commission to create and maintain a list of qualifying Native Hawaiians.

Whaleboat at Whalers Village Museum (p67), Ka'anapali
JOHN ELK/GETTY IMAGES ©

1976
Native Hawaiian activists illegally occupy the island of Kaho'olawe.

1993
President Clinton signs 'Apology Bill,' acknowledging US government's role in the kingdom's illegal takeover 100 years earlier.

2012
Born and raised in O'ahu, Barack Obama is re-elected US president. He wins with more than 70% of the Hawaiian vote.

The People of Maui

Woman making lei, Ka'anapali (p65)

The bond that unites all Mauians is a sense of aloha 'aina – a love of the land. Add to this strong family ties and a culture that embraces generosity and hospitality, and you've got a style of community rarely seen anymore on the hard-charging, rootless US mainland. There's also an appreciation for chitchatting, known as 'talking story' – a refreshingly 'retro' mode of communication still in fashion.

Island Identity

Nobody sweats the small stuff on Maui. It's all good. No worries. No problem. And if somebody is noticeably wound-up? They're from the mainland, guaranteed. Folks on Maui tend to have sunny disposi-tions, and they're more laid-back than their mainland cousins, dressing more casually and spending more time outside. On weekends everybody can be found hanging on the beach in T-shirts and biki-nis, and wearing those ubiquitous flip-flops known in Hawaii as *slippahs*.

Located 2500 miles from the nearest continent, the Hawaiian Islands are practically another country. On Maui, most streets have Hawaiian names, mixed-race people are the norm, and school kids participate in hula contests. You'll find no daylight savings time and no significant

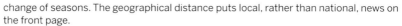

change of seasons. The geographical distance puts local, rather than national, news on the front page.

People on Maui never walk by anybody they know without partaking in a little talk story, stopping to ask how someone is doing (and mean it) and to share a little conversation. Islanders prefer to avoid heated arguments and generally don't jump into a controversial topic just to argue a point. Politically, most residents are middle-of-the-road Democrats and tend to vote along party, racial, ethnic, seniority, and local and nonlocal lines.

To locals, it is best to avoid embarrassing confrontations and to 'save face' by keeping quiet. At community meetings or activist rallies, the most vocal, liberal and passionate will probably be mainland transplants. Of course, as more and more mainlanders settle in Hawaii, the traditional stereotypes are fading.

Mauians tend to be self-assured without being cocky. Though Honolulu residents may think other Hawaiian Islands are 'da boonies,' they generally give a different nod to Maui. In the greater scheme of Hawaiian places, Maui is considered the more sophisticated sister, with a more polished scene than the Big Island or Kaua'i.

Lifestyle

Take a Sunday afternoon drive along the West Maui coast and you'll see the same scene repeated at the different beach parks: overflowing picnic tables, smoking grills and multigenerational groups enjoying the sun and surf. On Maui, the 'ohana (family) is central to island lifestyles. 'Ohana includes all relatives, as well as close family friends. Growing up, 'auntie' and 'uncle' are used to refer to those who are dear to you, whether by blood or friendship. Weekends are typically set aside for family outings, and it's not uncommon for as many as 50 people to gather for a family picnic.

People are early risers, often taking a run along the beach or hitting the waves before heading to the office. Most work a 40-hour week – overtime and the workaholic routine common elsewhere in the US are the exceptions here.

In many ways, contemporary culture in Maui resembles contemporary culture in the rest of the US. Mauians listen to the same pop music and watch the same TV shows. The island has rock bands and classical musicians, junk food and nouvelle cuisine. The wonderful thing about Maui, however, is that the mainland influences largely stand beside, rather than engulf, the culture of the island.

Not only is traditional Hawaiian culture an integral part of the social fabric, but so are the customs of the ethnically diverse immigrants who have settled here. Maui is more than a meeting place of East and West; it's a place where the cultures merge, typically in a manner that brings out the best of both worlds.

Recent decades have seen a refreshing cultural renaissance in all things Hawaiian. Hawaiian-language classes are thriving, local artists and craftspeople are returning to traditional mediums and themes, and hula classes are concentrating more on the nuances behind hand movements and facial expressions than on the stereotypical hip-shaking.

Visitors will still encounter packaged Hawaiiana that seems almost a parody of island culture, from plastic lei to theme-park luau. But the growing interest in traditional Hawaiian culture is having a positive impact on the tourist industry, and authentic performances by hula students and Hawaiian musicians are now the norm. Resorts are adding cultural talks and outrigger canoe tours.

Folks on Maui are quite accepting of other people, which helps explain the harmonious hodgepodge of races and cultures here. Sexual orientation is generally not an issue and gays and lesbians tend to be accepted without prejudice. In 2013, Hawaii became the 15th state to legalize marriage between same-sex couples.

Who's Who

Haole White person, Caucasian. Often further defined as 'mainland haole' or 'local haole.'

Hapa Person of mixed ancestry, most commonly referring to *hapa haole* who are part white and part Asian.

Hawaiian Person of Native Hawaiian ancestry. It's a faux pas to call a non-native Hawaii resident 'Hawaiian.'

Kama'aina Person who is a resident of Hawaii, literally defined as 'child of the land.'

Local Person who grew up in Hawaii. Locals who move away retain their local 'cred,' at least in part. But longtime transplants never become local. To call a transplant 'almost local' is a compliment.

Neighbor Islander Person who lives on any Hawaiian Island other than O'ahu.

Transplant Person who moves to the islands as an adult.

Most locals strive for the conventional 'American dream': kids, home ownership, stable work and ample free time. Generally, those with less-standard lifestyles (eg B&B owners, artists, singles and world travelers) are mainland transplants.

The median price of a home on Maui dropped during the recession, from $700,000 to about $450,000, but single-family home prices appeared to be rising in the fall of 2013. Nearly half a million is a steep purchase price when the median annual income for a household hovered around $64,000 between 2008 and 2012. For working-class people, it generally takes two incomes to make ends meet. Considering that the cost of living in Hawaii is 78% higher than on the mainland, it can be a tough go in paradise. And that's without mentioning Ka'anapali, where the cost of living is 172% higher than the national average! Yet most agree that nothing compares to living on Maui and would leave only if absolutely necessary.

Multiculturalism

Maui is one of the most ethnically diverse places in the US. Need proof? Just look at its signature dish: the plate lunch. This platter, with its meat, macaroni salad and two scoops of rice, merges the culinary habits of Native Hawaiians with those of a global array of immigrants – Portuguese, Japanese, Korean, Filipino – to create one heaping plate of deliciousness. A metaphor never tasted so good.

But the diversity is both eclectic and narrow at once. That's because Hawaii's unique blend of races, ethnicities and cultures is quite isolated from the rest of the world. On one hand, Hawaii is far removed from any middle-American, white-bread city. On the other, it lacks major exposure to certain races and ethnicities, particularly blacks and Mexican Hispanics, that are prevalent in the US mainland population.

Any discussion regarding multiculturalism must address whether we are talking about locals (insiders) or nonlocals (outsiders). Among locals, social interaction has hinged on old plantation stereotypes and hierarchies since statehood. During plantation days, whites were the wealthy plantation owners. For years afterward, minorities would joke about their being the 'bosses' or about their privileges due to

Shaka Sign

Islanders greet each other with the *shaka* sign, made by folding down the three middle fingers to the palm and extending the thumb and little finger. The hand is then shaken back and forth in greeting. On Maui, it's as common as waving.

race. As the Japanese rose to power economically and politically, they tended to capitalize on their 'minority' status, emphasizing their insider status as former plantation laborers. But the traditional distinctions and alliances are fading as the plantation generation dies away.

Of course, any tensions among local groups are quite benign compared with racial strife on the US mainland. Locals seem slightly perplexed at the emphasis on 'political correctness.' Just consider the nickname for overdeveloped Kihei in South Maui. It's been dubbed 'Haole-wood' by the locals. Haole? It's the Hawaiian term for Caucasian. Among themselves, locals good-naturedly joke about island stereotypes: talkative Portuguese, stingy Chinese, goody-goody Japanese and know-it-all haole.

When nonlocals enter the picture, the balance shifts. Generally, locals feel bonded with other locals. While tourists and transplants are welcomed, they must earn the trust and respect of the locals. It is unacceptable for an outsider to assume an air of superiority and to try to 'fix' local ways. Such people will inevitably fall into the category of 'loudmouth haole.'

That said, prejudice against haole is minimal. If you're called a haole, don't worry. It's generally not an insult or threat (if it is, you'll know). Essentially, locals are warm and gracious to those who appreciate island ways.

Island Etiquette

Dial it down a notch when you get to Maui. Big city aggression and type-A maneuvering won't get you far. As the bumper sticker here says, 'Practice Aloha.'

When driving on narrow roads like the Road to Hana and the Kahekili Highway, the driver who reaches a one-way bridge first has the right of way, if the bridge is otherwise empty. If facing a steady stream of cars, yield to the entire queue.

Remember the simple protocol when visiting sacred places: don't place rocks at the site as a gesture of thanks; better to use words instead. It is also considered disrespectful to stack rocks or build rock towers. Finally, don't remove rocks from national parks.

When surfing there's a pecking order, and tourists are at the bottom. The person furthest outside has the right of way. When somebody is up and riding, don't take off on the wave in front of them. Wait your turn, be generous and surf with a smile.

Hawaii's Cuisine

Hawaiian feast of meats and tropical fruit

ANN CECIL/GETTY IMAGES ©

Hawaii's cuisine has a sense of inclusive fun. Yes, there are the official culinary distinctions that fascinate gourmands: local food, Hawaii Regional cuisine and Native Hawaiian. But that's not why we love it. We love it for its tasty exuberance and its no-worries embrace of foreign flavors. The plate lunch. Loco moco. Even Spam musubi has a sassy – if salty – charm. So join the fun, sample the unknown...and savor the next bite.

Staples & Specialties

Sticky white rice is more than just a side dish in Hawaii; it's a culinary building block, an integral partner in everyday meals. Without rice, Spam *musubi* would be a slice of canned meat. *Loco moco* would be nothing more than an egg-covered hamburger. And without two-scoop rice, the plate lunch would be a ho-hum conversation between meat and macaroni rather than a multicultural party.

And by the way, sticky white rice means sticky white rice. While you might find couscous or mashed potatoes at fancy restaurants, day-to-day meals are served with sticky white rice. Not flaky rice. Not wild rice. Not flavored rice. And *definitely* not Uncle Ben's. Locals can devour mounds of the stuff and it typically comes as two scoops.

Spam a Lot

Spam arrived in Hawaii during WWII, when fresh meat imports were replaced by this GI ration. By the war's end, Hawaiians had developed a taste for the fatty canned stuff. Today, locals consume about 7 million pounds of Spam annually!

Spam looks and tastes different in Hawaii. It's eaten cooked (typically sautéed to a light crispiness in sweetened *shōyu*), not straight from the can, and served as a tasty meat dish. The popular Spam *musubi* is a rice ball with a slice of fried Spam on top, or in the middle, wrapped with a strip of sushi nori (dried seaweed). It's commonly seen at grocers and convenience stores.

The top condiment is soy sauce, known by its Japanese name *shōyu*, which combines well with sharp Asian flavors such as ginger, green onion and garlic.

Meat, chicken or fish are often key components of a meal, too. For quick, cheap eating, locals devour anything tasty, from Portuguese sausage to hamburger steak to corned beef. But the dinner-table highlight is always seafood, especially freshly caught fish.

One word of caution: Maui's attempts at nonlocal classics such as pizza, bagels, croissants and southern barbecue can be disappointing. Stick with *local* local food.

Local Food

Day-to-day eats reflect the state's multicultural heritage, with Asian, Portuguese and Native Hawaiian influences the most immediately evident. Cheap, fattening and tasty, local food is also the stuff of cravings and comfort.

The classic example of local food is the ubiquitous plate lunch. Picture this: chunky layers of tender *kalua* pork, a dollop of smooth, creamy macaroni and two hearty scoops of white rice. Yum, right? The pork can be swapped for other proteins like fried mahimahi or teriyaki chicken. Served almost like street food, the plate lunch is often served on disposable plates and eaten using chopsticks. A favorite breakfast combo includes fried egg and spicy Portuguese sausage (or bacon, ham, Spam etc) and, always, two scoops of rice.

Pupu is the local term used for all kinds of munchies or 'grazing' foods. Much more than just cheese and crackers, *pupu* represent the ethnic diversity of the islands and might include boiled peanuts in the shell, *edamame* (boiled fresh soybeans in the pod) and universal items such as fried shrimp.

Not to be missed is *poke* (raw fish marinated in *shōyu*, oil, chili peppers, green onions and seaweed). It comes in many varieties – sesame ahi (yellowfin tuna) is particularly delicious and goes well with beer.

Another local 'delicacy' is Spam *musubi* (a rice ball topped with sautéed Spam and wrapped with dried seaweed). Locals of all stripes enjoy this 'only in Hawaii' creation.

And, finally, there's shave ice. Ignore those joyless cynics who'll tell you that shave ice is nothing more than a snow cone. Shave ice is *not* just a snow cone. It's a tropical 21-gun salute – the most spectacular snow cone on earth. The specifics? The ice is shaved as fine as powdery snow, packed into a paper

Eating Price Ranges

The following ranges refer to a standard main, excluding tax.

$ less than $12

$$ $12–30

$$$ more than $30

cone and drenched with sweet fruit-flavored syrups in dazzling hues. For added decadence, add Kauai cream, azuki beans and ice cream.

Native Hawaiian

Kalua pig (which is traditionally baked in an underground oven) and poi are the 'meat and potatoes' of native Hawaiian food. Poi is served as the main side dish with every Hawaiian-style meal. The purple paste is pounded from cooked taro roots, with water added to make it pudding-like. It's nutritious and easily digested, but for many nonlocals it is also an acquired taste, largely because of its pasty consistency.

A common main dish is *laulau* (a bundle of pork or chicken and salted butterfish wrapped in a taro leaf that's steamed until it has a soft spinach-like texture). Other Hawaiian foods include baked *'ulu* (breadfruit), which has a texture similar to a potato, and *haupia* (a delicious pudding made of coconut cream thickened with cornstarch or arrowroot). *Haupia* ice cream made on Maui offers a nice cross between traditional and modern cuisine.

Hawaii Regional Cuisine

Twenty years ago Hawaii was a culinary backwater. Sure, you could slum it on local *grinds* (food) and get by on the slew of midrange Asian eateries, but fine dining was typically a European-style meal that ignored locally grown fare and the unique flavors of the islands.

In the 1990s a handful of island chefs smashed this tired mold and created a new cuisine, borrowing liberally from Hawaii's various ethnic influences. They partnered with local farmers, ranchers and fishers to highlight fresh local fare and transform their childhood favorites into grown-up, gourmet masterpieces. The movement was dubbed 'Hawaii Regional cuisine' and the pioneering chefs became celebrities. A trio with Maui connections are Roy Yamaguchi (Roy's Ka'anapali), Beverly Gannon (Hali'imaile General Store) and Mark Ellman (Mala Ocean Tavern & Honu in Lahaina).

The *real* catchwords for Hawaii Regional cuisine are fresh, organic and locally grown. Think Upcountry greens, Maui chèvre (goat cheese), Kula onions, free-range Hana beef and locally caught fish. The spread of the movement has been a boon to small-scale farmers. Some Maui chefs, like James McDonald (O'o Farm in Kula), have even started their own organic farms. And it's all contributing to a greening of Maui's gardens and menus.

Drinks

Hawaii is the only US state that grows coffee commercially. Both Maui and Moloka'i have coffee farms, and their final products are certainly worth a try. However, the only Hawaiian coffee with gourmet cachet is the world-renowned Kona coffee, grown on the Big Island. Aficionados rave about Kona coffee's mellow flavor that has no bitter aftertaste.

Fruit drinks are everywhere on Maui, but inexpensive canned drinks are usually not pure juice. One native Hawaiian juice tonic is *noni* (mulberry), which grows with wild

The Best...
Food Experiences

1 Hawaii Regional cuisine, Lahaina Grill (p50)

2 Island-caught seafood, Mama's Fish House (p162)

3 Plate lunch, Da Kitchen Express (p133)

4 Food truck, Geste Shrimp (p101)

5 Local scene, Hana Farms Clay Oven Pizza (p237)

abandon alongside roads. Proponents claim that *noni* reduces inflammation, boosts energy and helps cure everything from arthritis to cancer. *Noni* is pungent, if not repulsive, in smell and taste, so it's typically mixed with other juices.

Nineteenth-century whalers introduced Hawaiians to alcohol, even teaching them to make their own, *'okolehao* (alcohol distilled from the *ti* root). Instead of alcohol, Hawaiians used *'awa* (kava) as a mild intoxicant. Today, Wow-Wee Maui's Kava Bar & Grill in Kahului serves this bitter, mouth-numbing drink. The lactones in *'awa* are believed to relieve anxiety and fatigue, while fostering restful sleep and vivid dreams. The effect is mildly narcotic, but not mind-altering. *'Awa* is not recommended for pregnant women or for daily use.

Beer is cheap and widely available. Maui has its own microbrewery, Maui Brewing Company, which brews a range of beers that can be found in convenience stores and restaurants across the island.

At Maui's Winery at Tedeschi Vineyards you can sample Maui-made wines, including its popular pineapple wine.

And, of course, at every beachside bar you can order a colorful tropical drink topped with a fruit garnish and a tiny umbrella. Three favorites are piña colada, made with rum, pineapple juice and cream of coconut; mai tai, a mix of rum, grenadine, and lemon and pineapple juices; and Blue Hawaii, a vodka drink colored with blue curaçao.

Celebrations

The traditional Hawaiian feast marking special events is the luau. Local luau are still commonplace in modern Hawaii for christenings, anniversaries and other celebrations. These gatherings, typically big, include extended family, co-workers and friends.

The main dish at any luau is *kalua* pig, which is roasted in an earthen oven called an *imu*. The *imu* is readied for cooking by building a fire and heating rocks in the pit. When the rocks are glowing red, layers of moisture-laden banana trunks and green *ti* leaves are placed over the stones. A pig that has been slit open is filled with the hot rocks and laid on top of the bed. Other foods wrapped in *ti* and banana leaves are placed around it. It's all covered with more *ti* leaves and a layer of coconut-frond mats, then topped with dirt to seal in the heat. This bakes and steams the food. The process takes about four to eight hours depending on the size of the pig and the amount of other food added. Anything cooked in this style is called *kalua*.

It's Perfectly Clear

Hawaii's top-selling spirit? It's Ocean Vodka, an organic, distilled-on-Maui vodka made with desalinated water drawn from the depths of the ocean. Observe the production process on a tour (p172) of its new facility – with samples – on the slopes of Haleakalā in Kula.

Food takes center stage in many Hawaiian celebrations and festivities. On Sunday the beach parks are packed full of large family gatherings and picnic tables covered with massive spreads of potluck dishes. On standard American holidays, mainstream foods like Super Bowl beer and Thanksgiving turkey appear along with local fare such as rice, sweet-potato tempura and hibachi-grilled teriyaki beef.

Maui food festivals such as the East Maui Taro Festival and the Maui Onion Festival showcase home-style island crops. At the Kapalua Wine & Food Festival, top Maui chefs whip up island foods with gourmet flair.

Where to Eat & Drink

For quick takeout, plate-lunch eateries are great choices. They pack things tidily so you can carry your meal to a nearby beach for an impromptu picnic lunch. One tip: at lunchtime, decide what you want before reaching the register. Lines typically move quickly and the indecisive can muck up the system. Lunch vans and food trucks, known as *kaukau* (food) wagons, have become more common on Maui. They typically park near the beach. Bring cash.

Maui has a happening cafe scene, and these are the best places to relax over a good lunch in an engaging setting at a fair price. If the setting isn't important, there are plenty of diner-style Asian restaurants with Formica tables and vinyl chairs, no view and no decor. They generally offer quick service and often have surprisingly good food at decent prices. Maui's top-end restaurants are outright impressive and include some of the most highly rated chef-driven places in Hawaii. These establishments are typically found on prime oceanfront perches as well as in resorts and golf course clubhouses. Most forgo the pompous fastidiousness common to upscale urban restaurants on the US mainland. Meals start at $30 per person. To sample top cuisine at a good price, visit during happy hour when prices on appetizers are often reduced.

For groceries, head to farmers markets and locally owned supermarkets. Note that in Hawaii, about 90% of groceries are imported from the mainland, including milk and eggs (unless labeled 'Island fresh'), chicken, pork, produce and most beef. If absolute freshness matters to you, choose locally raised beef, island-caught fish and Maui-grown produce. For information on some of the best places to eat with children, see the Family Travel chapter on p302.

Mai tai cocktails

Habits & Customs

Locals eat meals early and on the dot: typically 6am for breakfast, noon for lunch and 6pm for dinner. Restaurants are packed around the habitual mealtimes, but they clear out an hour or two later, as locals are not lingerers. If you dine at 8:30pm you might not have to wait at all. But bear in mind that restaurants also close early and night owls must hunt for places to eat.

Locals tend to consider quantity as important as quality – and the portion sizes are telling, especially at plate-lunch places. If you're a light eater, feel free to split a meal or take home the leftovers.

Home entertainment for local folks always revolves around food, which is usually served 'potluck style' with all the guests adding to the anything-goes smorgasbord. Locals rarely serve dinner in one-at-a-time courses. Rather, meals are served 'family style,' where diners help themselves. Throwaway paper plates and wooden chopsticks make for an easy cleanup, and the rule is 'all you can eat' (and they definitely mean it!).

If you're invited to someone's home, show up on time and bring a dish – preferably homemade, but a bakery cake or *manju* (Japanese cakes filled with sweet bean paste) from Sam Sato's in Wailuku are always a certain hit. Remove your shoes at the door. And don't be surprised if you're forced to take home a plate of leftovers.

Vegetarians & Vegans

While most locals are omnivores, vegetarians and vegans can feast on Maui, too. That said, vegetarians aren't the target market: a plate lunch without meat or fish is not quite a plate lunch, and high-end restaurants tend to focus on seafood, though some feature at least one vegetarian main dish nightly. Greens and veggies grow so prolifically in the Upcountry that salads have a leading role on menus and the smarter cafes will invariably have meal-size vegetarian salads.

The Asian influence guarantees lots of vegetable and tofu options – walk into any Thai or Vietnamese restaurant and you'll find an extensive listing of vegetarian dishes. If you want to be in a totally meat-free space, there are vegetarian-only restaurants in Lahaina, Ha'iku and Pa'ia.

Food Glossary

Island food, with its blend of Pacific influences, is unique enough to require translation.

'awa Kava; a native plant used to make an intoxicating drink

bento Japanese-style box lunch

broke da mout Delicious; literally 'broke the mouth'

donburi Meal-sized bowl of rice and main dish

grind To eat

grinds Food; *'ono kine grinds* is good food

guava Fruit with green or yellow rind, moist pink flesh and lots of edible seeds

haupia Coconut pudding

hulihuli chicken Rotisserie-cooked chicken

imu Underground earthen oven used to cook *kalua* pig and other luau food

kalo Hawaiian word for taro

kalua Method of cooking pork and other luau food in an *imu*

kamaboko Steamed fish cakes; used to garnish Japanese dishes

katsu Deep-fried fillets, usually chicken

kaukau Food

laulau Bundle of pork or chicken and salted butterfish wrapped in taro and *ti* leaves and steamed

liliko'i Passion fruit

loco moco Dish of rice, fried egg and hamburger patty topped with gravy or other condiments

lomilomi salmon Minced and salted salmon, diced tomato and green onion

luau Hawaiian feast

mai tai 'Tiki bar' drink typically containing rum, grenadine, and lemon and pineapple juices

malasada Portuguese sugared fried doughnut

manju Japanese bun filled with sweet bean paste

mochi Japanese sticky-rice dumpling

noni Type of mulberry with smelly yellow fruit; used medicinally

nori Japanese seaweed, usually dried

'ono Delicious

pho Vietnamese soup of beef broth, noodles and fresh herbs

pipikaula Hawaiian beef jerky

poi Staple starch made of steamed, mashed taro

poke Cubed, marinated raw fish

pupu Snacks or appetizers

saimin Local-style noodle soup

shave ice Cup of shaved ice sweetened with colorful syrups

shōyu Soy sauce

star fruit Green-yellow fruit with five ribs like the points of a star and sweet, juicy pulp

taro Plant with edible corm used to make poi and with leaves eaten in *laulau; kalo* in Hawaiian

teppanyaki Japanese style of cooking with an iron grill

tonkatsu Japanese breaded and fried pork cutlets

The Best...
Hawaiian Cookbooks

IN FOCUS HAWAII'S CUISINE

1 **Roy's Feasts From Hawaii** Roy Yamaguchi

2 **Hali'imaile General Store Cookbook** Beverly Gannon

3 **Maui Tacos Cookbook** Mark Ellman

4 **What Hawaii Likes to Eat** Muriel Miura and Betty Shimabukuro

5 **Aloha Cuisine** Sam Choy

Name that Fish

In Hawaii, most fish go by Hawaiian names. Browse the Hawaii Seafood Buyers' Guide at www.hawaii-seafood.org to learn more about local fish. The fish in the following list are good sustainable choices – if they are caught in Hawaiian waters. Ask before ordering, as some fish are imported. For a handy list of sustainable choices, download the free pocket guide from the **Monterey Bay Aquarium** website (www.seafoodwatch.org).

ahi Yellowfin or bigeye tuna with red flesh; excellent raw or rare

aku Red-fleshed skipjack tuna; strong flavor; *katsuo* in Japanese

kajiki Pacific blue marlin; *a'u* in Hawaiian

mahimahi Dolphin fish or dorado; pink flesh, popular cooked

ono White-fleshed wahoo

opah Moonfish; firm and rich

'opakapaka Pink snapper; delicate flavor, premium quality

'opelu Pan-sized mackerel scad; delicious fried

shutome Swordfish; succulent and meaty

tako octopus

Hawaiian Arts & Crafts

Ukuleles in a store, Lahaina (p53)

SUPERSTOCKCOLLECTION/GETTY IMAGES ⊙

'Hula is the language of the heart, and therefore the heartbeat of the Hawaiian people,' said King Kalakaua, the 19th-century ruler who resurrected hula and other native art forms after years of suppression by zealous missionaries. Today that heartbeat is strong, especially in Maui where traditional hula shows, slack key guitar festivals and stone-carving workshops embrace the island's heritage.

Music

Spanish cowboys arrived in the Hawaiian Islands in the 1830s, and some brought their guitars with them. But Hawaiians made the instrument uniquely their own. In 1889, Joseph Kekuku, a Native Hawaiian, designed the steel guitar, one of only two major musical instruments invented in what is now the USA. (The other is the banjo.) The Hawaiian steel guitar is usually played with slack key tunings. For the slack key method the six strings are slacked from their standard tuning to facilitate a full sound on a single guitar. The thumb plays the bass and rhythm chords, while the fingers play the melody and improvisations, in a picked style.

The most influential slack key artist was Gabby Pahinui (1921–80), who launched the modern slack key era with his first recording in 1946. Other pioneering slack key masters were Sonny Chillingworth and Atta Isaacs. Today the tradition lives on in Dennis Kamakahi, Keola Beamer, Led Ka'apana and Cyril Pahinui. For live slack key performances, head to Napili on Wednesday night for the weekly Masters of Hawaiian Slack Key Concert Series at Napili Kai Beach Resort, hosted by slack key legend George Kahumoku Jr.

Universally beloved is the ukulele, derived from the *braguinha* (a Portuguese instrument introduced to Hawaii in the late 19th century). Ukulele means 'jumping flea' in Hawaiian, referring to the way players' deft fingers swiftly 'jump' around the strings. Hawaii's ukulele masters include Eddie Kamae, Herb Ohta and contemporary uke whirlwind Jake Shimabukuro.

The ukulele and the steel guitar were essential to the lighthearted, romantic music popularized in Hawaii between the 1930s and 1950s, during which time 'My Little Grass Shack' and 'Lovely Hula Hands' became classics.

In the 1970s Hawaiian music enjoyed a rebirth, and artists such as Cecilio & Kapono and the Beamer Brothers remain icons in Hawaii. The Hawaiian sound spurred offshoots like reggae-inspired 'Jawaiian,' but the traditional style lives on in gifted contemporary voices, such as Keali'i Reichel (also a hula master) and Raiatea Helm, who has been scooping up Hawaii's top music awards. Still, the most famous island musician is the late Israel Kamakawiwo'ole, whose album *Facing Future* went platinum in 2005. It contains his beloved track 'Somewhere Over the Rainbow/What a Wonderful World.' Also in 2005 a Grammy Award for Best Hawaiian Music Album was established. In that year the award went to a slack key collection featuring Maui's own Jeff Peterson and Keoki Kahumoku.

To learn more about slack key guitar, visit George Winston's Dancing Cat Records (www.dancingcat.com). For guitar and ukulele information, check out www.taropatch.net.

Hula

In ancient Hawai'i, hula was not entertainment but a type of religious expression. Dancers used hand gestures, facial expression and rhythmic movement to illustrate historical events, legendary tales and the accomplishments of the great *ali'i* (royalty). Rhythmic chants and drum beatings accompanied performances, serving to connect with the spirit world. Dancers wore *kapa* (bark cloth), never the stereotypical grass skirts.

There are many hula troupes active on Maui. Some practice in public places, such as in school grounds and at parks, where visitors are welcome to watch. Although many of the *halau* (schools) rely on tuition fees, others receive sponsorship from hotels or shopping centers and give weekly public performances in return. Two places presenting authentic hula are the Old Lahaina Luau and the Lahaina Cannery Mall, both in Lahaina. If you're in Maui in early November, don't miss the Hula O Na Keiki competition in Ka'anapali.

Local Arts & Craftwork

Woodworking is an ancient skill that remains popular and commercially viable. In old Hawai'i, the best artisans used giant logs to build canoes. Today, the most common creations are hand-turned wooden bowls and furniture – impossibly smooth and polished – made from a variety of hardwood. Traditionally koa was the wood of choice but, for variety, other gorgeous island woods are also used. Don't be fooled by cheap monkeypod bowls made in the Philippines.

Lei-making (p322) is a more transitory art form. Although the lei most visitors wear are made of fragrant flowers such as plumeria and tuberose, traditional lei of *mokihana* berries and maile leaves were more commonly worn in old Hawai'i. Both types are still made and sold today.

Lauhala weaving is another traditional craft. Weaving the *lau* (leaves) of the *hala* (pandanus) tree is the fun part, while preparing the leaves, which have razor-sharp spines, is difficult, messy work. Traditionally *lauhala* served as mats and floor coverings, but today smaller items such as hats, place mats and baskets are most commonly made.

Literature

'I went to Maui to stay a week and remained five,' wrote Mark Twain in *Letters from the Sandwich Islands*. 'I never spent so pleasant a month before or bade a place good-bye so regretfully.' Twain's 1860s observations, along with those of 19th-century British adventurer Isabella Bird, began a long tradition of Hawaii literature dominated by nonlocal Western writers observing the state's exoticism.

Novels of this type include *Hawaii*, James Michener's ambitious saga of Hawaii's history, and *Hotel Honolulu,* Paul Theroux's novel about a washed-up writer who becomes the manager of a run-down hotel.

Today, a growing body of local writers is redefining Hawaii literature. Stories don't consciously highlight Hawaii as an exotic setting but instead focus on the lives of universal characters. Bamboo Ridge Press (www.bambooridge.com) publishes contemporary local fiction and poetry in a biannual journal and has launched many local writers' careers. Some have hit the national scene, such as Nora Okja Keller, whose first novel, *Comfort Woman,* won the 1998 American Book Award, and Lois-Ann Yamanaka, who introduced pidgin to literary circles with *Saturday Night at the Pahala Theatre* – winner of the 1993 Pushcart Prize for poetry – and critically acclaimed novels such as *Behold the Many*.

Much locally written literature features pidgin English, especially in dialogue. The book *Growing Up Local: An Anthology of Poetry and Prose from Hawaii* (Bamboo Ridge Press) is a good introduction. Also highly amusing are the pidgin writings by Lee Tonouchi, author of *Living Pidgin: Contemplations on Pidgin Culture* (essays) and *Da Kine Dictionary* (pictorial dictionary).

Hawaiian Quilting

Christian missionaries introduced the concept of patchwork quilting, but the Hawaiians didn't have a surplus of cloth scraps. Cutting up new lengths of fabric simply to sew them back together in small squares seemed absurd.

Instead, Hawaiian women created designs using larger cloth pieces, typically with stylized tropical flora on a contrasting background. The story goes that when the first group of Hawaiian quilters spread their white cloth on the ground, a breadfruit leaf cast its shadow onto the cloth. The outline of the leaf was traced to produce the first native design.

Maui Quilt Shop in Kihei sells Hawaiian quilting materials.

Best Hawaiian Sounds

Familiarize yourself with the dynamic panoply of Hawaiian music:

Genoa Keawe No one epitomizes Hawaii like 'Aunty Genoa,' whose extraordinary signature falsetto sets the standard. (www.genoakeawe.com)

Israel Kamakawiwo'ole A discussion of Hawaiian music isn't complete without honoring the late 'Braddah Iz,' whose album *Facing Future* is Hawaii's all-time bestseller.

Jake Shimabukuro A ukulele virtuoso and exhilarating performer, Shimabukuro is known for lightning-fast fingers and a talent for playing any musical genre on the ukulele. (www.jakeshimabukuro.com)

Keali'i Reichel Charismatic vocalist Reichel is also a *kumu hula* (hula teacher) and the founder of a Hawaiian-language immersion school on Maui. (www.kealiireichel.com)

Cinema & TV

O'ahu's North Shore doubled as the deadly fighting arena in 2013's blockbuster *The Hunger Games: Catching Fire,* the second movie from author Suzanne Collins' popular *Hunger Games* book series. As for TV productions, a reboot of *Hawaii-5-0* hit the prime time lineup in 2010. For *Lost* fans mourning the loss of Hawaiian scenery from their TV screens, this slick reincarnation came none too soon.

Hollywood's love affair with Hawaii began in 1913 and bloomed in the 1930s, when the islands captured the public's imagination as a sultry, care-free paradise. In film classics such as *Waikiki Wedding* (featuring Bing Crosby's Oscar-winning song, 'Sweet Leilani'), *Blue Hawaii* (an Elvis favorite) and a spate of WWII dramas, including the 1953 classic *From Here to Eternity,* viewers saw Hawaii through foreigners' eyes.

Hundreds of feature films have been filmed in Hawaii, including the most recent *Godzilla, The Descendants, Pearl Harbor, Raiders of the Lost Ark,* and *Jurassic Park* and its two sequels. Unless homegrown films are produced, expect to see the same themes and stereotypes in Hollywood movies. Essentially, Hawaii is often just a colorful backdrop for mainland characters. Viewers might not even realize they're seeing Hawaii, as the islands often serve as stand-ins for Costa Rica, Africa, Vietnam and similar settings.

Maui is rarely the island seen in these productions. Kaua'i is the celluloid darling, while O'ahu (*Magnum PI, Lost* and the *Hawaii 5-0* series) draws directors with its more advanced facilities. Movies filmed in part on Maui include *Pirates of the Caribbean: At World's End* (2007), *The Hulk* (2003), *Jurassic Park III* (2000) and the James Bond film *Die Another Day* (2002).

For an insider's look at surf culture, don't miss Stacy Peralta's *Riding Giants,* which features three titans in big-wave surfing – Greg Noll, Jeff Clark and Laird Hamilton – hitting the waves on Maui.

For more information about movies or TV shows recently filmed in Hawaii, see the Hawaii Film Office website (www.filmoffice.hawaii.gov).

Family Travel

Children are welcome everywhere on Maui. Hawaiians love kids – large families are common and na keiki (children) are an integral part of the scenery. Maui has everything a child on vacation could dream of: sandy beaches, fun hotel pools, all sorts of yummy food and tons of outdoor activities. Maui also offers plenty of cool cross-cultural opportunities, from hula lessons to outrigger canoe rides.

Sights & Activities

Brimming with glorious beaches and abundant resort activities, South Maui and West Maui are the top destinations for families. Both have excellent opportunities for swimming, snorkeling, boogie boarding, catamaran sails and whale-watching – that alone could keep the whole family in splashy fun for a week! Older kids will gravitate toward the more challenging water activities such as kayaking and stand up paddle boarding.

In Lahaina, kids can climb America's largest banyan tree. The dangling aerial roots invite at least one Tarzan-style swing. Little tots will want to ride the Sugar Cane Train. And the rest of the clan can take the plunge with a surfing lesson on Lahaina's gentle waves.

Speaking of Tarzan, Maui is zip-line heaven. For thrills galore, opt for Pi'iholo Ranch Zipline or the Kapalua Adventures zip line; both have dual lines that allow family members to zip along side by side.

Be sure to take a day for Haleakalā National Park. Every kid loves playing astronaut on a crunchy walk into the wildly lunar-like crater.

Hotel luau offer up flashy dances, fire tricks and a large buffet where kids can pick and choose their own meal – what's not to love? Children get a discount, usually half-price, and are often invited to go on stage and enjoy the fun.

Keep an eye out for festivals, even small local events. They're invariably family oriented with plenty of *keiki*-geared activities tied in. The **Friday Town Parties** (www.mauifridays.com) are entertaining and filled with distractions.

Eating With Kids

Maui's family-oriented, casual atmosphere means children will feel at home almost everywhere. Sit-down restaurants are quick to accommodate kids with high chairs and booster seats.

You might assume that all fancy restaurants frown on parties that include children, but many cater to them with special kids' menus. The trend toward exhibition-kitchen restaurants – one large open area with a loud dining room – means that kid chatter will blend into the overall din. At hotel luau, kids receive a discount and most will enjoy the show. As for the food, the local palate tends toward the sweet and straightforward, which typically agrees with kids' tastes, without too much garlic or pungent flavors.

Kids love a picnic, and impromptu picnicking on Maui is a cinch – you can scarcely go a mile without finding a park with picnic tables. Many restaurants pack food for takeout, and grocery stores invariably have extensive deli sections with grab-and-go meals. Finding treats is also easy. Premium ice cream, shave ice, home-style cookies and chocolate-covered macadamias are omnipresent temptations.

When you're traveling around the island, stop at roadside fruit stands to let everyone pick their own healthful snack. It's fun watching a coconut being cracked open with a machete and then slurping up the coconut water through a straw.

Practicalities

○ Restaurants, hotels and sights that especially cater to families, and have good facilities for children, are marked with a family-friendly icon (⛹) throughout this guide.

○ Children are welcome at hotels throughout Maui and those under 17 typically stay free when sharing a room with their parents and using existing bedding.

○ Many sights and activities offer children's rates, sometimes as cheap as half price.

○ Car-hire companies on Maui lease child-safety seats, but they don't always have enough on hand so don't wait until the last minute to book your car.

The Best...
One-of-a-Kind Kids' Activities

1 Haleakalā crater walk (p199)

2 Exploring the Hana Lava Tube (Ka'eleku Caverns; p221)

3 Snorkeling Molokini Crater (p128)

4 Ogling Pi'ilanihale Heiau (p219)

5 Watching windsurfers at Ho'okipa Beach Park (p154)

o If you're traveling with infants and forget to pack some of your gear, go online to www. akamaimothers.com to rent cribs, strollers and other baby items.

o For an evening out alone, the easiest and most reliable way to find a babysitter is through the hotel concierge.

o Maui is an open-minded place, and although public breast feeding is not commonplace, it's unlikely to elicit unwanted attention.

Children's Highlights

Each regional chapter also includes advice about family-friendly sights and activities.

Water Adventures

Surf lessons in Lahaina (p40) Gentle waves. Surf schools line the streets.

Snorkeling at Honolua Bay (p79) Fantastic underwater sights are a few kicks from shore. Careful on the slippery entry!

Whale-watching (p42) From mid-December to April, hop on a boat in Lahaina or Maʻalaea to glimpse these mighty beasts.

Plants & Animals

Maui Ocean Center (p114) A 54ft clear tunnel funnels families through a fish-filled 750,000-gallon tank.

Surfing Goat Dairy (p172) Kids can hang with the kids – of the goat variety.

Ono Organic Farm (p240) Sample exotic fruit as you explore a 300-acre farm.

Maui Tropical Plantation (p113) Enjoy two zip lines, a touch of history and exotic fruit at the Coconut Station.

Am I Old Enough?

Some popular activities require that children be of a certain age, height or weight to participate. Always ask about restrictions when making reservations to avoid disappointment.

To learn how to surf Kids who can swim comfortably in the ocean are candidates for lessons. Teens can usually join group lessons, although younger kids may be required to take private lessons.

To take a snorkel cruise Depending on the outfitter and type of boat (catamaran, raft), tours sometimes set minimum ages, usually from five to eight years. Larger boats may allow tots as young as two to ride along.

To go zip-lining Minimum age requirements range from eight to 10 years, depending on the company. Participants must also meet weight minimums (usually 60lb to 80lb).

To ride a horse For trail rides the minimum age ranges from eight to 10 years, depending on the company. It helps if your kid already has some riding experience. Short pony rides may be offered to younger kids.

Let 'em Explore

Banyan Tree Square (p35) With its sprawling canopy and thick trunks, this tree would make the Swiss Family Robinson feel at home.

Fourth Marine Division Memorial Park (p163) In Haiku, this jungle gym looks like a sprawling castle.

Kealia Coastal Boardwalk (p118) Burn off energy at this elevated boardwalk through coastal wetlands.

For Older Kids & Teens

Skyview Soaring (p231) From Hana, glide along Haleakalā's crater in a sailplane.

Hana-Maui Kayak & Snorkel (p233) Paddle beyond Hana Bay.

Makena Stables (p149) Ride through coastal lava fields on horseback.

Need to Know

● **Car-safety seats** Reserve in advance with your car rental.

● **Changing facilities** Found in shopping malls and resorts.

● **Cots** Request in advance when booking a room.

● **Highchairs** Available at most restaurants.

● **Kids' menus** Family-oriented restaurants have them.

● **Nappies (diapers)** Grocery and convenience stores sell them.

● **Strollers** Bring your own or rent in Maui.

Children's Programs

● Many of Maui's beach resorts have *keiki* day programs where kids can do fun things while you head for the spa.

● Visitors to Haleakalā National Park should take advantage of the free junior ranger program geared for ages seven to 12.

● The Pacific Whale Foundation (p42) provides a free Junior Marine Naturalist handbook that introduces kids to Hawaii marine life through quizzes, anagrams and the like. Pick up one on board a whale-watching cruise.

Natural Wonders

Volcanic rock formations, Wai'anapanapa State Park (p221)

LASZLO PODOR/GETTY IMAGES

You don't have to be a geologist, botanist or marine biologist to appreciate the valley isle's myriad natural charms, although you might find yourself picking up an interest in a new field of study after a morning snorkel or a hike atop Haleakalā. Trust us, it won't take long to feel the 'aloha 'aina (love for the land), too.

Environment

Breaching whales, flowery tropical blooms and fascinating underwater sights that exist nowhere else on the planet – Maui's environmental wonders are in a class by themselves.

The Land

Maui is the second-largest Hawaiian island, with a land area of 728 sq miles. Set atop a 'hot spot' on the Pacific Plate, Maui rose from the ocean floor as two separate volcanoes. Lava flows and soil erosion eventually built up a valley-like isthmus between the volcanic masses, linking them in their present form. This flat region provides a fertile setting for sugarcane fields and is home to Maui's largest urban center, the twin towns of Kahului and Wailuku.

The eastern side of Maui, the larger and younger of the two volcanic masses, is dominated by the lofty Haleakalā (10,023ft). This dormant volcano, whose craterlike floor is dotted with cinder cones, last erupted between AD 1480 and 1600. The second, more ancient volcano formed the craggy West Maui Mountains, which top out at the Pu'u Kukui (5778ft). Both mountains are high enough to trap the moisture-laden clouds carried by the northeast trade winds, bringing abundant rain to their windward eastern sides. Consequently, the lushest jungles and gushiest waterfalls are found along the Hana Hwy, which runs along Haleakalā's eastern slopes, while the driest, sunniest beaches are on the western coasts.

Wildlife

All living things that reached Maui were carried across the sea on wing, wind or wave – seeds clinging to a bird's feather, or insects in a piece of driftwood. Scientists estimate that successful species arrived once every 70,000 years – and they included no amphibians and only two mammals: a bat and a seal.

However, the flora and fauna that made it to Maui occupied an unusually rich and diverse land. In a prime example of 'adaptive radiation,' the 250 flowering plants that arrived evolved into 1800 native species. Lacking predators, new species dropped defensive protections – thorns, poisons and strong odors disappeared, which explains why they fare so poorly against modern invaders. So many plant and animal species have been lost that the state has been dubbed 'the extinction capital of the world.'

The Polynesians brought pigs, chickens, coconuts and about two dozen other species, not to mention people. The pace of change exploded after Western contact in the late 18th century. Cattle and goats were introduced and set wild, with devastating consequences. Even today, sitting on a Kihei beach looking out at Kaho'olawe in the late afternoon, you'll notice a red tinge from the dust whipping off the island, a consequence of defoliation by wild goats released there a century ago.

But there is progress. On Kaho'olawe the goats are gone and native reforestation has begun; Haleakalā National Park has made great strides in reintroducing and protecting native species; and the first public garden totally dedicated to endemic Hawaiian species, Maui Nui Botanical Gardens, sits on the site of a former exotic zoo.

If you see a wild animal in distress, report it to the state **Division of Conservation & Resource Enforcement** (DOCARE; ☎984-8110).

Animals

Most of Maui's wildlife attractions are found in the water or on the wing. Hawaii has no native land mammals.

Marine Life

Of the almost 700 fish species in Hawaiian waters, nearly one-third are found nowhere else in the world. Maui's nearshore waters are a true rainbow of color: turquoise parrot fish, bright yellow tangs and polka-dotted pufferfish, to name a few.

Honu (green sea turtles) abound in Maui's waters. To the thrill of snorkelers and divers, *honu* can often be seen feeding in shallow coves and bays. Adults can grow to

The Best...
Places to Honor the Sun

1 Haleakalā Crater (p199) for sunrise

2 Wai'anapanapa State Park (p221) for sunrise

3 Big Beach (Oneloa; p146) for sunset

4 Papawai Point (p61) for sunset

5 Downtown Lahaina (p34) for sunset

Maui's Top Protected Areas

'Ahihi-Kina'u Natural Area Reserve (p148) A pristine bay, lava flows and ancient sites; good for hiking and snorkeling.

Haleakalā National Park (Summit Area; p199) With towering waterfalls, cascading pools and ancient sites; good for hiking, swimming and camping.

Haleakalā National Park (Kipahulu Area; p199) Large, dormant volcano; good for hiking, camping and horseback riding.

'Iao Valley State Park (p111) Features streams, cliffs and swimming holes; good for hiking and photography.

Pi'ilanihale Heiau & Kahuna Garden (p219) A national botanic garden and ancient site; good for walking.

Kealia Pond National Wildlife Refuge (p118) Good for bird-watching.

Molokini Crater (p114) A submerged volcanic crater; ideal for snorkeling and diving.

Polipoli Spring State Recreation Area (p178) With cloud forest and uncrowded trails; good for hiking, camping and mountain biking.

Wai'anapanapa State Park (p221) Lava tubes and a trail over rugged sea cliffs to Hana; good for hiking and camping.

more than 3ft – an awesome sight when one swims past you in the water. Much less common is the hawksbill turtle, which occasionally nests on Maui's western shores.

The sheltered waters between Maui, Lana'i and Moloka'i are the wintering destination for thousands of North Pacific humpback whales. The majestic creatures are the fifth-largest of the great whales, reaching lengths of 45ft and weighing up to 45 tons. Humpback whales are coast-huggers and are visible from the beach in winter along Maui's west and southwest coasts.

Maui is also home to a number of dolphins. The spinner dolphin (named for its acrobatic leaps) comes into calm bays during the day to rest.

With luck you might see the Hawaiian monk seal, which lives primarily in the remote Northwestern Hawaiian Islands, but occasionally hauls out on Maui beaches. It was nearly wiped out by hunting in the 1800s, but conservation efforts have edged the species back from the brink of extinction – barely, with a population of about 1200 seals.

Don't touch, approach or disturb marine mammals; most are protected, making it illegal to do so. Watch dolphins, whales, seals and sea turtles from a respectful distance.

Birds

Many of Hawaii's birds have evolved from a single species in a spectacular display of adaptive radiation. For example, all 54 species of Hawaiian honeycreepers likely evolved from a single finch ancestor. Left vulnerable to introduced predatory species and infectious avian diseases after humans arrived, half of Hawaii's native bird species are already extinct, and more than 30 of those remaining are still under threat.

The endangered nene, Hawaii's state bird, is a long-lost cousin of the Canada goose. Nene nest in high cliffs on the slopes of Haleakalā and their feet have adapted to the rugged volcanic environment by losing most of their webbing. Nene have black heads, light-yellow cheeks, a white underbelly and dark gray feathers.

At least three birds native to Maui – the Maui parrotbill, 'akohekohe (crested honeycreeper) and 'alauahio (Maui creeper) – are found nowhere else in the world. The Maui Parrotbill and 'akohekohe are federally listed endangered species. The Maui Parrotbill exists solely in the Kipahulu section of Haleakalā National Park and in a small section of high elevation forest on the northeast slope of Haleakalā volcano. The cinnamon-colored po'ouli was last seen in 2004 and may already be extinct. Alas, it's unlikely you'll see any of those birds. But other native forest birds, including the 'apapane (a vivid red honeycreeper), can be sighted in Hosmer Grove in Haleakalā National Park.

Maui's two waterbird preserves, the Kanaha Pond Bird Sanctuary and Kealia Pond National Wildlife Refuge, are nesting sites for the ae'o (Hawaiian black-necked stilt), a wading bird with a white underbelly and long orange legs.

For information about honeycreepers and the Maui Parrotbill (there are only 500 left!), visit the Maui Forest Bird Recovery Project website (www.mauiforestbirds.org). The group specializes in recovering endangered honeycreepers. Through the group, you can sponsor a tree to be planted on Maui, which will aid in habitat recovery for the birds.

Plants

Maui seems suitable for just about anything with roots. On a mile-for-mile basis, Hawaii has the highest concentration of climatic and ecological zones anywhere on earth. They vary from lowland deserts along the coast to lush tropical rainforests in the mountains. And the diversity within a small region can be amazing. In the Upcountry there are so many microclimate zones that hillside farms, such as Enchanting Floral Gardens in Kula, can grow tropical fruit trees just a few sloping acres from where temperate roses thrive. Another mile up, don't even bother looking for tropical fruit trees as you're now in the zone for cool-weather crops.

Many native species have adapted to very narrow geographic ecosystems, such as Maui's endangered silversword (p190), which grows at the summit of Haleakalā.

Flowering Plants & Ferns

For travelers, the flower most closely identified with Hawaii is the hibiscus, whose generous blossoms are worn by women tucked behind their ears. Thousands of varieties of hibiscus bushes grow in Hawaii; on most, the flowers bloom early in the day and drop before sunset. The variety most frequently seen is the introduced red Hibiscus rosa-sinensis, which is used as a landscape hedge throughout Maui. Much rarer is the koki'o ke'oke'o, a native white hibiscus tree that grows up to 40ft high; it can be seen at Maui Nui Botanical Gardens in Kahului.

Two native plants at the beach are pohuehue, a beach morning glory with pink flowers that's found just above the wrack line; and beach naupaka, a shrub with oval leaves and a small white five-petal flower that looks as if it's been torn in half.

Throughout the Upcountry you'll find gardens filled with protea, a flashy flower originally from South Africa that takes many forms. Named after the Greek god Proteus (who could change shape at will), blossoms range from small pincushiony heads to tall stalklike flowers with petals that look like feathers. You'll also see plenty of other showy exotic flowers throughout Maui, including the brilliantly orange-and-blue bird-of-paradise and various heliconias with bright orange and red bracts.

There are about 200 varieties of Hawaiian ferns and fern allies (such as mosses) found in rainforests and colonizing lava flows.

Trees & Shrubs

The most revered of the native Hawaiian forest trees is koa, found at higher elevations on Maui. Growing up to 100ft high, this rich hardwood is traditionally used to make canoes, surfboards and even ukuleles.

Brought by early Polynesian settlers, the *kukui* tree has chestnutlike oily nuts that the Hawaiians used for candles, hence its common name, candlenut tree. It's recognizable in the forest by its light silver-tinged foliage.

Two coastal trees that were well utilized in old Hawaii are *hala,* also called pandanus or screw pine, whose spiny leaves were used for thatching and weaving; and the *niu* (coconut palm), which loves coral sands and yields about 75 coconuts a year.

Kiawe, a non-native tree, thrives in dry coastal areas. A member of the mesquite family, kiawe is useful for making charcoal but is a nuisance for beachgoers as its sharp thorns easily pierce soft sandals. Also plentiful along the beach are stands of ironwood, a conifer with drooping needles that act as windbreaks and prevent erosion.

Other trees that will catch your eye include the African tulip tree, a rainforest tree abloom with brilliant orange flowers that grows profusely along the road to Hana; plumeria, a favored landscaping tree whose fragrant pink-and-white blossoms are used in lei making; and majestic banyan trees, which have a canopy of hanging aerial roots with trunks large enough to swallow small children.

National, State & County Parks

Haleakalā National Park accounts for nearly 10% of Maui's land area. The park not only offers superb hiking and other recreational activities but also protects Hawaiian cultural sites and the habitat of several endangered species. Maui's numerous state and county parks also play an important role in preserving undeveloped forest areas and much of Maui's coastline. The parks are well used by Maui residents – from surfers to pig hunters – as well as by tourists.

The state's **Department of Land & Natural Resources** (DLNR; ☎ 984-8100; http://dlnr.hawaii.gov) has useful online information about hiking, aquatic safety, forestry and wildlife. The DLNR oversees the **Division of State Parks** (☎ 984-8109; www.hawaiistateparks.org), which issues camping permits on Maui, and **Na Ala Hele** (www.hawaiitrails.org), which coordinates public access to hiking trails.

Protea flower, Maui
DANITA DELIMONT/GETTY IMAGES ©

Outdoor Adventures

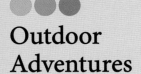

Surfer, Honolua Bay (p79)

QUINCY DEIN/GETTY IMAGES ©

After climbing Haleakalā in 1866, Mark Twain wrote that the sunrise there was 'the sublimest spectacle I ever witnessed'. Today, outdoor adventurers might pay the same compliment to the whole of Maui. Kiteboarders skip across swells. Surfers ride monster waves. Snorkelers float beside green sea turtles. And hikers climb misty mountains. It is a spectacle sublime.

At Sea

The Pacific Ocean is Maui's ultimate playground. And take note, when renting ocean gear, you'll pay premium prices at resort beach shacks. Stop by a surf or snorkel shop in town for the best rates.

Shark Attacks: Do You Need to Worry?

Bringing up shark attacks in a guidebook seems rather, well, rude. Our apologies. But shark attacks off the coast of Maui have garnered headlines in recent years. There were seven shark attacks in Maui waters in 2012 and 10 statewide. In 2013 there were eight off the Maui coast, two of them fatal, and 13 across the state. The norm for Hawaii is about four attacks per year.

The reason for the spike? No one is 100% sure. Some scientists think that there may be an increase in incidents in the fall, when

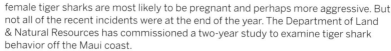

female tiger sharks are most likely to be pregnant and perhaps more aggressive. But not all of the recent incidents were at the end of the year. The Department of Land & Natural Resources has commissioned a two-year study to examine tiger shark behavior off the Maui coast.

Do you need to be concerned? Not particularly. Before 2013, the last shark attack fatality in Hawaii was 2004. And according to the International Shark Attack File your odds of being bitten are about 1 in 11.5 million. To be extra cautious, though, try not to swim or snorkel in murky water (which is more likely to appear later in the day) and try to swim where there are lots of people.

Bodysurfing & Boogie Boarding

If you want to catch your waves lying down, bodysurfing and boogie boarding are suitable water activities for anybody.

There are good beginner to intermediate shorebreaks at the Kamaʻole Beach Parks and Charley Young Beach in Kihei, and at Ulua Beach and Wailea Beach in Wailea. Experienced bodysurfers should head to DT Fleming Beach Park and Slaughterhouse Beach in Kapalua, Big Beach in Makena and HA Baldwin Beach Park near Paʻia.

Special bodysurfing flippers, which are smaller than snorkel fins, will help you paddle out. Boogie board rentals range from $5 to $20 per day.

Diving

Excellent visibility. Warm water temperatures. Hundreds of rare fish species. Maui is a diving mecca for a reason. Here you can often see spinner dolphins, green sea turtles, manta rays and moray eels. With luck you might even hear humpback whales singing underwater – you'll never forget it.

Most dive operations on Maui offer a full range of dives as well as refresher and advanced certification courses. Introductory dives for beginners get you beneath the surface in just a couple of hours. Experienced divers needn't bring anything other than a swimsuit and certification card. Don't monkey around with activity desks – book directly with the dive operators.

On Maui, the granddaddy of dives is crescent-shaped Molokini. The other prime destination is untouched Cathedrals on the south side of Lanaʻi, which takes its name from the amazing underwater caverns, arches and connecting passages.

For a basic but helpful map of dive and snorkel spots around Maui, pick up the free *Maui Dive and Surf Magazine* at a Maui Dive Shop (www.mauidiveshop.com), which are scattered across the island.

Molokini Crater

This fascinating volcanic crater lies midway between the islands of Maui and Kahoʻolawe. Extremely popular with travelers, this underwater site can see more than 1000 visitors in a day. Half of the crater rim has eroded away, leaving a crescent-moon shape that rises 160ft above the ocean surface, with a mere 18 acres of rocky land high and dry. But it's what's beneath the surface that draws the crowds. Snorkelers and divers will be thrilled by steep walls, ledges, white-tipped reef sharks, manta rays, turtles and abundant fish.

The legends about Molokini are myriad. One says Molokini was a beautiful woman who was turned to stone by jealous Pele,

Parks & Beaches

Details about county parks and beaches in Maui, including contact information and lifeguard availability, can be found on the Maui County government (www.mauicounty.gov) website.

goddess of fire and volcanoes. Another claims one of Pele's lovers angered her by secretly marrying a *mo'o* (shape-shifting water lizard). Pele chopped the sacred lizard in half, leaving Molokini as its tail and Pu'u Ola'i in Makena as its head. Yet another tale alleges that Molokini, which means 'many ties' in Hawaiian, is the umbilical cord left over from the birth of Kaho'olawe.

The coral reef that extends outward from Molokini is awesome, though it's lost some of its variety over the years. Most of the black coral that was once prolific in Molokini's deeper waters made its way into Lahaina jewelry stores before the island was declared a marine conservation district in 1977. During WWII the US Navy shelled Molokini for target practice, and live bombs are still occasionally spotted on the crater floor. In 2006 a tour boat with an inexperienced captain sank at Molokini. No one was injured, but after an inept salvage job, 1200 coral colonies had been destroyed. The company incurred a $396,000 state-imposed fine.

There are a few things to consider when planning a Molokini excursion. The water is calmest and clearest in the morning, so don't fall for discounted afternoon tours – go out early for the smoothest sailing and best conditions. For snorkelers, there's simply not much to see when the water's choppy. The main departure points for Molokini trips are Ma'alaea and Lahaina Harbors. You'll get out there quicker if you hop on a boat from Ma'alaea, which is closer to Molokini. Going from Lahaina adds on more sail time, but if it's winter it will also increase the possibilities for spotting whales along the way, so it's sometimes worth an extra hour out of your day.

Responsible Diving

The popularity of diving is placing immense pressure on many sites. Consider the following tips to help preserve the ecology and beauty of reefs:

○ Avoid touching living marine organisms with your body or dragging equipment across the reef. Polyps can be damaged by even the gentlest contact. Never stand on coral. If you must hold on to the reef, touch only exposed rock or dead coral.

○ Be conscious of your fins. Even without contact, the surge from heavy fin strokes near the reef can damage delicate organisms. When treading water in shallow reef areas, take care not to kick up clouds of sand. Settling sand can easily smother the delicate reef organisms.

○ Don't use reef anchors and take care not to ground boats on coral.

○ Minimize your disturbance of marine animals. It is illegal to approach endangered marine species too closely; these include whales, dolphins, sea turtles and the Hawaiian monk seal. In particular, don't ride on the backs of turtles!

○ Practice and maintain proper buoyancy control. Major damage can be done by divers descending too fast and colliding with the reef. Make sure you are correctly weighted and that your weight belt is positioned so that you stay horizontal.

The Best...
Beaches

1 Honolua Bay (p79) Surf in winter, snorkel in summer.

2 DT Fleming Beach Park (p79) A beauty that makes you wonder if you've reached the South Pacific.

3 Ka'anapali Beach (p66) A happening resort beach with all the expected facilities.

4 Keawakapu Beach (p125) Perfect for a sunset swim.

5 Malu'aka Beach (p144) The best place to snorkel with turtles.

6 Big Beach (p146) For long beach strolls, boogie boarding and bodysurfing.

○ Resist the temptation to feed marine animals. You may disturb their normal eating habits, encourage aggressive behavior or feed them food that is detrimental to their health.

○ Spend as little time in underwater caves as possible, as your air bubbles may be caught within the roof and leave previously submerged organisms high and dry.

○ Don't leave any rubbish, and remove any litter you find. Plastics in particular are a serious threat to marine life. Turtles can mistake plastic for jellyfish and eat it.

○ Don't collect (or buy) coral or shells. Aside from ecological damage, taking marine souvenirs depletes the beauty of a site and spoils the enjoyment of others.

○ **Divers Alert Network** (DAN; ☎800-446-2671, emergency 919-684-9111; www.diversalertnetwork.org) gives advice on diving emergencies, insurance, decompression services, illness and injury.

Diving & Snorkeling Outfitters

○ Lahaina Divers (p39) Boat dives and snorkeling; departs Lahaina.

○ Maui Dive Shop (p39) Boat dives and snorkeling; departs Lahaina.

○ Maui Dreams Dive Co (p127) Shore dives and boat dives; departs Kihei and Ma'alaea.

○ Pacific Whale Foundation (p116) Snorkeling; departs Ma'alaea.

Fishing

Deep-sea sportfishing charters set out from Maui for such legendary game as ahi (yellowfin tuna) and, most famous of all, Pacific blue marlin, which can reach 1000lb. Licenses aren't required, and charter boats are available on the pier in Lahaina Harbor and Ma'alaea. Sharing a boat costs around $195 to $250 per person for eight hours. Shorter trips are offered. Many boats let you keep only a small fillet from your catch; see Maui Fishing (www.mauifishing.com) for reasons why...and more.

Kayaking

There's a lot to see underwater just off the coast, so most outfitters offer snorkel-and-kayak combos. The top spot is Makena, an area rich with marine life, including sea turtles, dolphins and wintering humpback whales. In the calmer summer months, another excellent destination is Honolua–Mokule'ia Bay Marine Life Conservation District at Slaughterhouse Beach and Honolua Bay north of Kapalua, where there are turtles aplenty and dolphin sightings. Water conditions on Maui are usually clearest and calmest early in the morning, so that's an ideal time to go.

For tours in South Maui try Aloha Kayaks (p147) or South Pacific Kayaks (p127), which also provide kayaks for rent.

Kitesurfing

Kitesurfing is a bit like strapping on a snowboard, grabbing a huge kite and riding with the wind across the water. It looks damn hard and certainly takes stamina, but if

The Best...
Beaches for Children

1 Kalepolepo Beach Park (p124)

2 Spreckelsville Beach (p155)

3 Launiupoko Beach Park (p60)

4 Kapalua Beach (p79)

5 Wailea Beach (p138)

you already know how to ride a board, there's a good chance you'll master it quickly. According to surf legend Robby Naish, who pioneered kitesurfing, it's the most accessible of all extreme sports.

There's no better place to learn than on Maui's Kite Beach, at the western end of Kanaha Beach Park. Visiting kitesurfers need to check with locals to clarify the no-fly zones. Get the lowdown from the Maui Kiteboarding Association (www.mauikiteboardingassociation.com) and Maui Kitesurfing Community (www.mauikitesurf.org).

Outrigger Canoeing

Polynesians were Hawaii's first settlers, paddling outrigger canoes across 2000 miles of open ocean – so you could say canoeing was Hawaii's earliest sport. The first Europeans to arrive were awestruck at the skill Hawaiians displayed, timing launches and landings perfectly, and paddling among the waves like dolphins.

Today canoe clubs keep the outrigger tradition alive. Hawaiian Sailing Canoe Adventures in Wailea offers guided outrigger canoe tours, sharing cultural insights as you paddle along the coast. Many resorts, including the Four Seasons, Andaz Maui and Makena Beach & Golf Resort, have also begun offering tours.

Parasailing

Soaring 200ft above the ocean tethered to a speedboat towline is a quick seven-minute thrill, available from beach huts at Ka'anapali Beach. Because parasailing upsets humpback whales, the activity is banned in Maui during the winter season. But from mid-May to mid-December, the rush is on. Expect to pay around $70 to $75 per trip.

Sailing

Breezy Lahaina is the jump-off point for most sails. If you're in the mood to just unwind, hop on a sunset sail. For an exciting day-long journey consider a sail to Lana'i.

Stand up paddle surfing (SUP), Pa'ia (p154)
QUINCY DEIN/GETTY IMAGES ©

Snorkeling

The waters around Maui are a kaleidoscope of coral, colorful fish and super-big sea turtles. Best of all, you don't need special skills to view them. If you can float, you can snorkel – it's a cinch to learn. If you're a newbie, fess up at the dive shop or beach hut where you rent your snorkel gear – mask, snorkel and fins – and they'll show you everything you need to know. And it's cheap: most snorkel sets rent for $10 or less per day.

Snorkelers should get an early start. Not only does the first half of the morning offer the calmest water, but at some of the popular places crowds begin to show by 10am.

The hottest spots for snorkeling cruises are the largely submerged volcanic crater of Molokini, off Maui's southwest coast, and Lana'i's Hulopo'e Beach. Both brim with untouched coral and an amazing variety of sealife.

Stand Up Paddle Surfing

The stand up paddle surf invasion has begun. For proof, drive from Papawai Point northwest to Lahaina and look seaward. Platoons of paddle-wielding surfers, standing on 9ft to 11ft boards, are plying the waves just off the coast at seemingly every beachside park.

Abbreviated SUP, and known in Hawaii as Ku Hoe He'e Nalu, this quickly emerging sport is great for less limber adventurers since you don't need to pop up into a stance. It takes coordination to learn but isn't harder than regular surfing – although you should be a strong swimmer. Consider a class with paddle surf champ Maria Souza in Kihei, or with the instructors at Maui Wave Riders in Lahaina. Beachside rentals run $35 to $40 per hour.

Surfing

Maui lies smack in the path of all the major swells that race across the Pacific, creating legendary peaks for surfing. The island's north shore sees the biggest waves, which roll in from November to March, though some places, like famed Ho'okipa Beach, have good wave action year-round.

Newbies should head directly to Lahaina, which has beginner-friendly waves and instructors that can get you up on a board in just one lesson. You won't be tearing across mammoth curls, but riding a board is easier than it looks and there's no better place to get started. Two primo owner-operated surf schools that have the perfect blend of patience and persistence are Goofy Foot Surf School and Maui Surf Clinics.

The Original Boardriders

Hawaii is the birthplace of surfing. Researchers have traced chants mentioning *he'e nalu* (surfing) and petroglyphs depicting surfers back to at least 1500 AD.

When the first missionaries arrived in Hawaii in the 1820s they promptly started stamping out the 'hedonistic' act of surfing and, save a few holdouts, by 1890 surfing was all but extinct.

Then in the early 1900s modern surfing's first icon, Duke Kahanamoku, stepped off the beach and into history. Kahanamoku grew up on the sands of Waikiki, where he rode the reefs on traditional *olo*-style boards. After winning Olympic gold in swimming at Stockholm in 1912, Duke began to travel the world demonstrating the Hawaiian 'Sport of Kings.'

Get a surf and weather report online at OMaui (www. omaui.com).

Surf Beaches & Breaks

While there are hippie holdouts from the 1960s who believe the spirit of Jimi Hendrix roams the Valley Isle's mountains, today Maui's beaches are where most of the island's action is found. On the north shore, near the town of Ha'iku, is the infamous big-wave spot known as Pe'ahi, or Jaws. Determined pro surfers, such as Laird Hamilton, Dave Kalama and Derrick Doerner, have helped put the planet's largest, most perfect wave on the international map, appearing in everything from American Express commercials to mutual fund ads. Jaws' waves are so high that surfers must be towed into them by wave runners.

Not into risking your life on your vacation? No worries, there are plenty of other waves to ride. Maui's west side, especially around Lahaina, offers a wider variety of surf. The Lahaina Breakwall and Harbor's fun reef breaks cater to both beginner and intermediate surfers. To the south is Ma'alaea Pipeline, a fickle right-hand reef break that is often considered one of the fastest waves in the world. On the island's northwest corner is majestic Honolua Bay. This right point break works best on winter swells and is considered one of the premier points not just in Hawaii, but around the world.

Gentler shorebreaks good for bodysurfing can be found around Pa'ia, Kapalua and the beaches between Kihei and Makena.

The Best...
Snorkel Spots

1 Malu'aka Beach (p144)

2 Ulua Beach (p138)

3 Honolua Bay (p79)

4 'Ahihi-Kina'u Natural Area Reserve (p148)

5 Molokini Crater (p114)

6 Pu'u Keka'a (Black Rock; p66)

Swimming

Whoever coined the phrase 'Maui *no ka 'oi*' (Maui is the best) was surely thinking of Maui's beaches, which are arguably the best in the Hawaiian Islands.

Along the northwest coast from Ka'anapali to Kapalua and the southwest coast from Kihei to Makena Harbor are scores of sandy beaches with good year-round swimming conditions. The windward northern and eastern coasts are generally rough for swimming in winter but quieten down in summer, when they can become as calm as a swimming pool.

Whale-Watching

With their tail-slaps, head lunges and spy hops, humpback whales sure know how to impress a crowd. Each winter, about 12,000 of these graceful leviathans – two-thirds of the entire North Pacific humpback whale population – come to the shallow coastal waters off the Hawaiian Islands to breed and give birth. And like other discerning visitors to Hawaii, these intelligent creatures favor Maui. The western coastline of the island is their chief birthing and nursing ground. Luckily for whale-watchers, humpbacks are coast-huggers, preferring shallow waters to protect their newborn calves.

Much of Hawaii's ocean waters are protected as the Hawaiian Islands Humpback Whale National Marine Sanctuary, whose Kihei headquarters is abuzz with cool whale happenings. Along the coast there's great whale-watching at many places, including Papawai Point, and along beach walks in Kihei and Wailea.

If you want to get within splashing distance of 40-ton leviathans acrobatically jumping out of the water, take a whale-watching cruise. No one does them better than

317

Pacific Whale Foundation (p42), a conservation group that takes pride in its green, naturalist-led whale-watch trips. Maui's peak whale-watching season is from January through March, although whales are usually around for a month or so on either side of those dates.

Windsurfing

This sport reaches its peak on Maui. Ho'okipa Beach, near Pa'ia, hosts top international windsurfing competitions. The wind and waves combine at Ho'okipa in such a way that makes gravity seem arbitrary. Ho'okipa is for experts only, as hazards include razor-sharp coral and dangerous shorebreaks. For kick-ass wind without risking life and limb, the place to launch is Kanaha Beach in Kahului, but avoid the busy weekends when the water becomes a sea of sails.

Overall, Maui is known for its consistent winds. Windsurfers can find action in any month, but as a general rule the best wind is from June to September and the flattest spells are from December to February.

At Ma'alaea, where the winds are usually strong and blow offshore toward Kaho'olawe, conditions are ripe for advanced speed sailing. In winter, on those rare occasions when *kona* (leeward) winds blow, the Ma'alaea–Kihei area can be the only place windy enough to sail. Get the inside scoop on the windsurfing scene at Maui Windsurfing (www.mauiwindsurfing.net).

Most windsurfing shops are based in Kahului and handle rentals, give lessons and sell windsurfing gear.

Golf course, Makena (p144)

ARIYOSHI RITA/GETTY IMAGES

On Land

Adventures here aren't limited to the sea; there are a plethora of things to do on land. Maui's hiking and horse trails traverse some of the most unique ecosystems on earth. And if knocking around a little white ball is your thing, would-be Tigers can stalk the very greens where the real Tiger plays.

Cycling

Cyclists on Maui face a number of challenges: narrow roads, heavy traffic, an abundance of hills and mountains, and the same persistent winds that so delight windsurfers. Many roads, however, including the Pi'ilani Hwy in South Maui, do have bike lanes. Reliable shops include West Maui Cycles in Lahaina, South Maui Bicycles in Kihei and Island Biker in Kahului.

The *Maui County Bicycle Map* is no longer printed, but you can peruse it online at West Maui Cycles (www.westmauicycles.com) and South Maui Bicycles (www. southmauibicycles.com). It shows all the roads on Maui that are suitable for cycling and gives other nitty-gritty details. It's worth a look if you intend to explore by pedal power. West Maui Cycles also provides basic maps for several mountain-biking trails.

Golf

Flanked by scenic ocean vistas and emerald mountain slopes, golfing just doesn't get much better. The most prestigious of Maui's courses is the Plantation course in Kapalua, which kicks off the annual PGA tour. Only slightly less elite are the championship greens at Wailea and Ka'anapali.

At the other end of the spectrum, you can enjoy a fun round at the friendly Waiehu Municipal Golf Course and at lesser-known country clubs around the island.

A good resource, with course reviews, is Maui Golf (www.golf-maui.com).

Helicopter Tours

Helicopters go into amazing places that you otherwise might not experience. When you book, ask about seat guarantees, and let it be known you want a seat with a window, not a middle seat. On Maui, winds pick up by midday and carry clouds up the mountains with them. For the clearest skies and calmest ride, book a morning flight. There are four main tours:

West Maui tour (20 to 30 minutes) Takes in jungly rainforest, remote waterfalls and 'Iao Valley – this is Maui's prettiest face.

East Maui tour (45 minutes) Highlights Hana, Haleakalā Crater and 'Ohe'o Gulch. This is the rainiest side of Maui. The good news: waterfalls stream down the mountainsides if you hit clear weather after a rainstorm. The bad news: it can be socked in with clouds.

Circle Island tour (one hour) Combines the West and East Maui tours.

West Maui & Moloka'i tour (one hour) Includes the drama of West Maui as well as a zip along the spectacular coastal cliffs of Moloka'i. Definitely the Big Kahuna of knockout photo ops!

All operate out of the Kahului Heliport, at the southeast side of Kahului Airport. For recommended tour companies, see (p100). Discounts off the list prices are common; ask when you book or look for coupons online or in the free tourist magazines.

Hiking

The diversity is what makes hiking on Maui so cool. Trails here hug lofty ridges, twist through bamboo forests and green jungles, and meander across jagged lava fields. The most extraordinary trails are in Haleakalā National Park, where hikes range

319

Preserving Hiking Trails

Of special interest to hikers and naturalists is the work of **Na Ala Hele** (www.
hawaiitrails.org), a group affiliated with Hawaii's Division of Forestry & Wildlife.
Na Ala Hele was established in 1988 with the task of coordinating public access
to hiking trails and also maintaining and preserving historic trails. On Maui, the
group has negotiated with private landowners and the military to gain access
to previously restricted areas and re-establish abandoned trails. Visit its website
for trail descriptions. The Na Ala Hele logo signpost – a brown sign featuring a
yellow hiking petroglyph figure – marks an increasing number of trailheads.

from half-day walks to quad-busting multiday treks meandering across the moonscape of Haleakalā Crater. In the Kipahulu ('Ohe'o Gulch) section of the park, a trail
climbs past terraced pools and on to the towering waterfalls that feed them.

In Maui's Upcountry, Polipoli Spring State Recreation Area has an extensive trail
system in cloud forest, including the breathtaking Skyline Trail that connects with
Haleakalā summit.

North of Wailuku is the lofty Waihe'e Ridge Trail. This wonderful footpath penetrates
deep into the misty West Maui Mountains, offering sweeping views of green valleys
and the rugged northern coast. Near Ma'alaea Bay, the Lahaina Pali Trail follows an old
footpath on the drier western slope of the same mountain mass.

The Kapalua Resort has opened several trails offering a range of scenery. The
Coastal Trail links Kapalua Beach and DT Fleming Beach while the Village Walking Trails
wander through an overgrown golf course. A complimentary shuttle drops hikers at
the flora-filled Maunalei Arboretum Trail, which begins in the mountainous foothills
above the resort. Follow it to the jungle-like Honolua Ridge Trail. The diverse Mahana
Ridge Trail drops through lush slopes to the shimmering coast.

Several pull-offs along the road to Hana offer short nature walks that lead to hidden
waterfalls and unspoiled coastal views, including the Waikamoi Nature Trail. A longer
coastal trail between Wai'anapanapa State Park and Hana Bay follows an ancient
Hawaiian footpath past several historic sights, as does the Hoapili Trail (the King's
Hwy) from La Pe'rouse Bay on the other side of the island.

Short nature walks that combine bird- and whale-watching include the Kealia
Coastal Boardwalk in Ma'alaea and the Kihei Coastal Trail.

One of Maui's top environmental shakers, the Sierra Club (www.mauisierraclub.org/
hikes-service-programs), sponsors guided hikes, often educational, to various places
around the island. Everyone is welcome; nonmembers are asked to pay a $5 donation.
Not only will you be sharing the trails with other eco-minded hikers, but the Sierra Club
sometimes hikes into fascinating places that are otherwise closed to the public.

Hiking Considerations

○ Maui has no snakes, no poison ivy and few wild animals that will fuss with hikers. There's
only the slimmest chance of encountering a large boar in the backwoods, but they're
unlikely to be a problem unless cornered.

○ Be careful on cliffs since cliffside rock in Maui tends to be crumbly. Flash floods are a
threat in many of the steep, narrow valleys on Maui that require stream crossings. Warning
signs are a distant rumbling, the smell of fresh earth and a sudden increase in the stream's
current. If the water begins to rise, get to higher ground immediately.

○ A walking stick is good for bracing yourself on slippery approaches, gaining leverage and testing the depth of streams.

○ Darkness falls fast once the sun sets, and ridgetop trails are no place to be caught unprepared in the dark. Always carry a flashlight. Wear long pants for protection from overgrown parts of the trail, and sturdy footwear with good traction. Pack 2L of water per person for a day hike, carry a whistle to alert rescue workers if necessary, wear sunscreen and start early.

Horseback Riding

With its abundant ranch land and vibrant cowboy culture, Maui offers some of Hawaii's best riding experiences. Choose a ride based on the landscape you'd like to see, since all are friendly, reputable outfitters.

The most unusual ride, offered by Pony Express, meanders down into the barren hollows of Haleakalā Crater via Keonehe'ehe'e (Sliding Sands) Trail. Makena Stables takes riders along the volcanic slopes that overlook pristine La Pe'rouse Bay, while Mendes Ranch rides along the cliffs of the Kahekili Hwy. Families will like the easy rides at Thompson Ranch in Keokea.

Mountain Biking

To explore the wilderness on a mountain bike, head to the Upcountry (p155). Experienced downhill riders will find adrenaline-stoked thrills on the Skyline Trail (p194), which follows the mountain's spine from Haleakalā National Park into Polipoli Spring State Recreation Area. Closer in, you'll find single track trails at the Makawao Forest Reserve. See www.westmauicycles.com for a basic map of the reserve's trails.

Spas

Hawaiian spa treatments may sound a bit whimsical, but they're based on herbal traditions. Popular body wraps and 'cocoons' use seaweed to nourish; ginger, papaya and healing plants are applied as moisturizers. Other tropical treatments sound good enough to eat: coconut-milk baths and coffee-chocolate scrubs...mmm.

Most spas are in the large resort hotels, such as the Hotel Travaasa and Grand Wailea Resort Hotel & Spa, but if you prefer a more traditional setting consider the Luana Spa Retreat, which offers treatments under a thatched hut in Hana.

Tennis

Singles? Doubles? Or perhaps a lesson? Take your pick at the world-class facilities at Wailea Tennis Club, Royal Lahaina Tennis Ranch in Ka'anapali and Kapalua Tennis. If you just want to knock a ball around, many hotels have tennis courts for their guests and the county maintains free tennis courts at many public parks.

Zip-Lining

Click in. Grab tight. Thumbs up. And whooooosh...you're off. Quick as a flash, Maui's zip lines let you soar freestyle on a series of cables over gulches, woods and waterfalls while strapped into a harness. The hardest part is stepping off the platform for the first zip – the rest is pure exhilaration!

The Pi'iholo Ranch Zipline in Makawao is winning rave reviews with its 2800ft long final line – Hawaii's longest. It also offers side-by-side zip lines, allowing you to swoop the course alongside up to three of your friends. First on the Maui scene was Skyline Eco-Adventure's Haleakalā tour. It often books out months in advance. The company has opened a second zip line in the hills above the resort; this one is pricier but easier to book. The zip line course in Kapalua reopened in late 2013 as Kapalua Ziplines. The course still offers side-by-side zipping on dual lines as well as moonlight rides.

Lei

Lei woven with orchids

Fragrant and ephemeral, lei embody the beauty of nature and the embrace of the community, freely given and freely shared. Greeting. Honor. Respect. Peace. Love. Celebration. Spirituality. Good luck. Farewell. These beautiful garlands, handcrafted from fresh tropical flora, can signify all of these meanings, and more.

The Art of the Lei

Lei making is a sensuous and transitory art form. In choosing their materials, lei makers tell a story – since flowers and plants embody place and myth – and express emotions. They may use feathers, nuts, shells, seeds, seaweed, vines, leaves and fruit, in addition to more familiar fragrant tropical flowers. Handmade lei are typically created by knotting, braiding, winding, stringing or sewing the raw natural materials together.

Worn daily, lei were integral to ancient Hawaiian society. In the islands' Polynesian past, lei were made part of sacred hula dances and given as special gifts to loved ones, healing medicine to the sick and offerings to the gods, all practices that continue in Hawaii today. So powerful a symbol were they that on ancient Hawaii's battlefields, the right lei could bring peace to warring armies.

Today, locals continue to wear lei for special events, such as weddings, birthdays, anniversaries, graduations and public ceremonies. In general, it's no longer common to make one's own lei, unless you're a devoted member of a *hula halau* (hula school). For ceremonial hula (as opposed to popular competitions or shows for entertainment), performers are often required to make their own lei, even gathering the raw materials by hand.

Modern Celebrations

For visitors to Hawaii, the tradition of giving and receiving lei dates back to the 19th-century steamships that first brought tourists to the islands. In the heyday of cruise ship tourism, disembarking passengers were greeted by local vendors who would toss garlands around the necks of *malihini* (newcomers, or foreigners).

The tradition of giving a kiss with a lei began during WWII, allegedly when a hula dancer at a USO club was dared by her friends to give a military serviceman a peck on the cheek when she placed a flower lei over his head.

In 1927, the poet Don Blanding and Honolulu journalist Grace Tower Warren called for making May 1 a holiday to celebrate lei. The next year, Leonard and Ruth Hawk composed the popular tune 'May Day is Lei Day in Hawaii,' a song that later became a hula *mele* (song). Today, Lei Day is celebrated across the islands with Hawaiian music, hula dancing, parades, lei-making workshops and contests, and more fun.

Lei Etiquette

◦ Don't wear a lei hanging directly down around your neck. Instead, drape a closed (circular) lei over your shoulders, making sure that equal lengths are hanging over your front and back.

◦ When traditionally presenting a lei, bow your head slightly and raise the lei above your heart. Don't drape it with your own hands over the head of the recipient, as this isn't respectful. Let them do it themselves.

◦ Don't give a closed lei to a pregnant woman, as it may bring bad luck to the unborn child; choose an open (untied) lei or *haku* (head) lei instead.

◦ Resist the temptation to wear a lei intended for someone else. It's bad luck.

◦ Never refuse a lei, and don't take one off in the presence of the giver.

◦ When you stop wearing your lei, don't throw it in the trash. Untie the string and return the lei's natural elements to the earth (eg scatter flowers in the sea, bury seeds or nuts) instead.

Island Variations

Lei are a universal language in Hawaii, but some special lei evoke a particular island.

O'ahu The yellow-orange *'ilima* is the island's official flower, and a symbol of Laka, the Hawaiian goddess of hula dancing. Once favored

Lei Overboard

When you're leaving the islands, it's tradition to cast a lei into the ocean; if it returns to the beach, it's said you will one day return to Hawaii. But don't throw your lei into the water without first removing the string and the bow.

by royalty, an *'ilima* lei may be made of up to a thousand small blossoms strung together.

Hawai'i the Big Island Lei made from lehua, the pom-pom flowers of the ohia plant, are most often colored red or pink. According to Hawaiian legend, the very first lei was made of lehua and given by Hi'iaka, goddess of healing, to her sister Pele, goddess of fire and volcanoes.

Maui The *lokelani* (pink damask rose, or 'rose of heaven') is a soft, velvety and aromatic flower. It was first planted on the island by early-19th-century Christian missionaries in the gardens of Lahaina. Today it's Maui's official flower, the only exotic species of flora to be so recognized in Hawaii.

Lana'i A yellowish-orange vine, *kaunaoa* is traditionally gathered from the island's windward shores, then twisted into a lei. One traditional Hawaiian chant sings of this plant growing on Lana'i like a feathered cape lying on the shoulders of a celebrated chief.

Lei in Print

Ka Lei: The Leis of Hawaii (Ku Pa'a Publishing, 1995) Written by Marie McDonald, a recognized *kapuna* (elder), this is an in-depth look at the art of Hawaiian lei making before Western contact and during contemporary times.

Na Lei Makamae: The Treasured Lei (University of Hawai'i Press, 2003) This artful, beautiful blend of botany and culture by Marie McDonald and Paul Weissich surveys the Hawaiian flowers traditionally used in lei and their meaning and mythology.

Moloka'i *Kukui* lei are either made from the laboriously polished, dark-brown nuts of Hawaii's state tree (in which case, they're usually worn by men) or the tree's white blossoms, which are Moloka'i's official flower.

Kaua'i On the 'Garden Island,' leathery *mokihana* berries that faintly smell of licorice are often woven with strands of glossy, green maile vines. *Mokihana* trees grow in the rain-soaked forests on the western slopes of mighty Mt Wai'ale'ale.

Shopping for Lei

A typical Hawaiian lei costs anywhere from $10 for a single strand of orchids or plumeria to thousands of dollars for a 100% genuine Ni'ihau shell lei necklace. Beware that some *kukui* (candlenut) and *puka* shell lei are just cheap (even plastic) imports.

When shopping for a lei, ask the florist or shopkeeper for advice about the most appropriate lei for the occasion (eg for a bride, pick a string of pearl-like *pikake* jasmine flowers), and indicate if you're giving the lei to a man or a woman. Of course, it's OK to buy a lei for yourself any time!

On Maui you can buy fresh lei at Whole Foods Market in Kahului, just a mile from the airport. Its lei ($14 to $15) are made from Maui-grown flora. Check the case at the front of the store.

Survival
Guide

Sunset over Kama'ole Beach (p125)
GARRY BLACK/GETTY IMAGES ©

A-Z

Directory

Accommodations

Be it a luxury resort, a rural B&B, a beachside condominium or a national park campground, Maui has accommodations to suit every taste. In this guide we've listed reviews in order of author preference. See the inside front cover for an explanation of lodging symbols.

Costs Maui has the highest average room rates of any Hawaiian island. That said, costs vary widely depending on which type of accommodations you select and its proximity to the beach.

Price icons The following price ranges refer to a double room with bathroom in high season (mid-December to mid-April). Unless otherwise stated breakfast isn't included in the price. Tax is not included in the prices.

- ◦ **$** less than $100
- ◦ **$$** $100–275
- ◦ **$$$** more than $275

Season Rates are typically up to a third lower outside of peak season. Holiday periods, especially between Christmas and New Year, command premium prices and often book up far in advance.

Booking It's wise to reserve in advance almost any time of the year to lock in a good deal. Many hotels and condos offer year-round internet specials well below the advertised 'rack rates.'

Cancellation policies Although a reservation guarantees your room, most require a deposit, after which, if you change your mind, there are typically stiff cancellation fees on Maui. Note the cancellation policies and other restrictions before making a deposit.

B&Bs & Inns

If you're considering a B&B, plan ahead.

Most are small operations with just a couple of rooms and hence can book out weeks in advance. Some require a minimum stay of a few days. Same-day reservations are hard to get, though there are sometimes last-minute openings. If you're lucky, you may be able to snag a one-night rental. But always call ahead – B&B owners don't want unannounced visitors disturbing their guests.

Some B&Bs book only through agencies. The following agencies cover B&Bs on Maui:

Affordable Paradise (☏ 261-1693; www.affordable -paradise.com)

Bed & Breakfast Hawaii (☏ 822-7771; www.bandb-hawaii.com)

Hawaii's Best B&B (☏ 885-4550; www.bestbnb.com)

Camping

On Maui there's a very clear pecking order when it comes to camping. At the top, offering the best and safest options, are the campgrounds at Haleakalā National Park. After that, the state parks – most notably Wai'anapanapa State Park – are a better option than the county parks.

National parks Haleakalā National Park has excellent drive-up camping at the summit area at Hosmer Grove and in the seaside section at Kipahulu Campground. There are no fees, reservations or permits required for drive-up camping. Haleakalā also offers free backcountry camping on the crater floor with a permit, as well as $75 cabin rentals, though the cabins are in high demand and difficult to score.

Book Your Stay Online

For more accommodations reviews by Lonely Planet authors, check out http://hotels. lonelyplanet.com. You'll find independent reviews, as well as recommendations on the best places to stay. Best of all, you can book online.

Those overnighting in the backcountry must watch a short orientation video at the Headquarters Visitor Center.

State parks Maui has campgrounds and cabins at Wai'anapanapa State Park near Hana and at the remote Polipoli Spring State Recreation Area in the cool Upcountry, as well as tent camping at Pala'au State Park on Moloka'i. Book cabins well in advance to avoid disappointment. Each state park allows a maximum stay of five consecutive nights per month. Tent camping is $18 per night per site. Cabins cost $90. For reservations, contact the **Division of State Parks** (Map p108; ☑ 984-8109; www. hawaiistateparks.org; 54 S High St, Wailuku; ⊙ 8am-noon Mon-Fri).

County parks Maui County allows camping at Kanaha Beach Park in Kahului (except Monday and Tuesday) and at Papalaua Beach Park south of Lahaina (except Wednesday and Thursday). Camping is allowed for three consecutive nights and costs $5 to $8 per day ($2 to $3 for children under 18). For reservations at either site, contact the **Department of Parks & Recreations – Central District** (Map p102; ☑ 270-7389; www.co.maui. hi.us; 700 Halia Nakoa St, War Memorial Gymnasium, Wailuku; ⊙ 8am-1pm & 2:30-4pm Mon-Fri) or the **Department of Parks & Recreation – West District** (Map p64; ☑ 661-4685; www.co.maui.hi.us; 1840 Honoapi'ilani Hwy; ⊙ 8am-noon Mon-Sat, 1:30-4pm Mon-Fri).

Leeward & Windward

Maui's high central mountains trap the trade winds that blow from the northeast, capturing moisture-laden clouds and bringing abundant rainfall to the windward side of Maui. The jungly road to Hana lies smack in the midst of windward Maui and simply gushes with waterfalls.

The same mountains keep clouds and hence rain from reaching the southwest side of the island. So it's in places such as Kihei and Makena that you'll find the driest, sunniest conditions. It's no coincidence that the great majority of Maui's resorts are found on its dry leeward side.

Gear If you're going to be camping in the Upcountry or in Haleakalā National Park, bring a waterproof tent, a winter-rated sleeping bag, rain gear and layers of warm clothing. Camping on the beach is another matter entirely – a very lightweight cotton bag and a tent is all you'll need.

Condominiums

◦ Condos are incredibly popular on Maui. Indeed, some top destinations such as Kihei and Napili have far more condominiums than hotels.

◦ Condos are more spacious than hotel rooms, and often furnished with everything a visitor needs, from a kitchen to a washer and dryer. They typically work out cheaper than hotels, especially if you're traveling with a group.

◦ In most places condo units are individually owned and then placed in a rental pool, so the furnishings and decor can vary from one unit to the next. Whenever possible, ask to see a few units before settling in.

◦ Maui condos usually have built-in discounts for longer stays: as a general rule the weekly rate is six times the daily rate and the monthly rate three times the weekly.

◦ Don't forget to ask about cleaning fees, which might be tacked onto your bill. These fees are becoming more commonplace on Maui.

◦ Some condo complexes are booked only through rental agencies. Others operate more like a hotel with a front desk, though even in these places some units are usually handled by rental agencies. Some properties may charge a reservation fee.

◦ Most condos, especially those handled through rental agencies, have a three- to seven-day minimum stay.

◦ Search online for condos at **HomeAway** (www.homeaway. com) or **Vacation Rentals by Owner** (VRBO; www.vrbo.com).

◦ The following agents handle condos and vacation rentals:

Bello Realty (☑ 879-3328; www.bellomaui.com)

Kihei Maui Vacations (☑ 879-4000; www.kmvmaui. com)

Hostels

There are no Hostelling International (HI) hostels on Maui, but there are a few simple places in older buildings that provide a cheap place to crash.

These hostels aren't up to US mainland standards, but for travelers on a budget they do provide a dorm bed and kitchen facilities from around $30 to $45 per night.

Hotels

o It's very common for hotels to discount their published rack rates, especially when booked via the internet. Some hotels discount by the season or day depending on demand, and others throw in a free rental car, so look for specials.

o Within a particular hotel, the main thing that impacts room rates is the view and the floor you're on. An ocean view can cost 50% to 100% more than a parking-lot view, euphemistically called a 'garden view.'

o In addition to checking the hotel's website, try www. kayak.com, which compares rate deals from a variety of discount sites. If you have a smartphone, download the Hotel Tonight app for last-minute discounted rooms.

Resorts

Maui's top resorts are designed to be pleasure palaces that anticipate your every need and provide 'the best' of everything.

They provide myriad dining options, multiple swimming pools, children's programs, cultural activities, nightly entertainment and spas.

Climate

Haleakalā

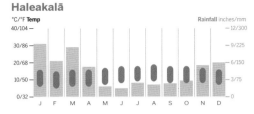

Hana

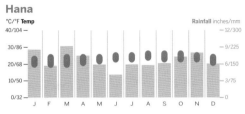

Lahaina

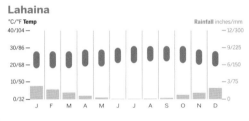

At the priciest ones, beach sands are without blemishes, coconut trees are trimmed of drooping fronds and every aspect of your experience is managed seamlessly.

They are intentionally contrived visions of paradise – and once you accept that, they're quite nice.

●●●
Customs Regulations

o Currently each international visitor is allowed to bring 1L of liquor (if 21 years of age or older) and 200 cigarettes into the USA. You may also bring in up to $100 worth of gift merchandise without incurring any duty. For more complete, up-to-date information, visit the US Customs & Border Protection website (www. cbp.gov).

o Hawaii is a rabies-free state and there are strict regulations regarding the importation of pets, so don't plan on bringing your furry friend on a short vacation.

o Many fresh fruits and plants cannot be brought into Hawaii. For complete details, visit the Hawaii Department of Agriculture website (http:// hawaii.gov/hdoa).

Electricity

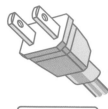

120V/60Hz

120V/60Hz

Gay & Lesbian Travelers

Maui is a popular destination for gay and lesbian travelers. The state has strong legislation to protect minorities and a constitutional guarantee of privacy that extends to sexual behavior between consenting adults. In 2013 Hawaii became the 15th state to legalize same-sex marriage. That said, people tend to be private so you won't see much public hand-holding or open displays of affection.

LGBT Maui is not terribly organized. There isn't a big, boisterous 'out' scene. Kihei is the most open town on Maui, low-key as it is, and has a hotel, the Maui Sunseeker, catering to gay and lesbian travelers.

Maui Pride (www.mauipride. org) Visit the Maui Pride website for a calendar of LGBTQ events, including hikes and weekly gatherings.

Hawaii Gay Travel (✆ 800-508-5996; www. hawaiigaytravel.com) Arranges travel geared for gay and lesbian travelers.

Pacific Ocean Holidays (✆ 800-735-6600; www. gayhawaiivacations.com) Vacation packages for gays and lesbians.

Purple Roofs (www.purple roofs.com) Directory of gay-owned and gay-friendly B&Bs, vacation rentals and hotels.

Health

Staphylococcus

○ In 2007 Hawaii led the nation in Staphylococcus aureus infection, having over twice the rate of infection as the US mainland. Some types of antibiotic-resistant staph infections can be fatal.

○ Staph infections are caused by bacteria that enter the body through an open wound.

○ To prevent infection, practice good hygiene. Apply antibiotic ointment to any open cuts or sores and keep them out of recreational water; if they're on your feet don't go barefoot, even on the sand.

○ If a wound becomes painful, looks red, inflamed or swollen, leaks pus or causes a rash or blisters, seek medical help immediately.

International Travelers

Entry Requirements

○ For current information about the USA's entry requirements for travelers, access the Visa section of the US State Department website (www.travel.state.gov) and also the Travel section of the US Customs & Border Protection website (www. cpb.gov).

○ The Department of Homeland Security's registration program (DHS; www.dhs.gov), called Office of Biometric Identity Management, includes every port of entry and covers nearly every foreign visitor to the USA. For most visitors (excluding, for now, most Canadian and some Mexican citizens), registration consists of having a digital photo and electronic (inkless) fingerprints taken; the process takes less than a minute.

Passports

❍ A machine readable passport (MRP) is required for all foreign citizens to enter the USA.

❍ Your passport must be valid for six months beyond your expected stay in the US.

❍ If your passport was issued or renewed after October 26, 2006, you need to have an 'e-passport' containing a digital photo and an integrated chip that stores biometric data.

Visas

❍ Depending on your home country, you may not need a visa. Under the Visa Waiver Program (VWP), visas are not required for citizens of 37 countries for stays of 90 days or less.

❍ With the exception of Canadians and visitors who qualify for the Visa Waiver Program, foreign visitors to the USA need a visa. Under the VWP you must have a return ticket (or an onward ticket to any foreign destination) that's nonrefundable in the US.

❍ All VWP travelers must register online at least 72 hours before arrival with the Electronic System for Travel Authorization (ESTA; https://esta.cbp.dhs.gov), which currently costs $14. Once approved, registration is valid for two years (or until your passport expires).

❍ Visa applicants may be required to 'demonstrate binding obligations' that will ensure their return home. Because of this requirement,

those planning to travel through other countries before arriving in the USA are better off applying for their US visa in their home country, not on the road.

❍ Foreign visitors who don't qualify for the VWP must apply for a tourist visa. The process is not free, involves a personal interview and can take several weeks.

Internet Access

❍ There are coffee shops with computers in Maui's main tourist destinations. Some hotels offer online computers in their lobbies for guests.

❍ Most Maui hotels and many condos and B&Bs have wi-fi. You can also find free wi-fi at Queen Ka'ahumanu Center (p104) in Kahului and at most McDonald's fast food restaurants. When wi-fi is available in an establishment, it's marked in this guide with a symbol (📶).

❍ If you bring a laptop from outside the USA, make sure you bring along a universal AC and plug adapter.

Legal Matters

Legal rights Anyone arrested in Hawaii has the right to have the representation of a lawyer from the time of their arrest to their trial, and if a person cannot afford a lawyer, the state must provide one for free. You're presumed

innocent unless or until you're found guilty in court.

Alcohol laws The legal drinking age is 21. It's illegal to have open containers of alcohol in motor vehicles, and drinking in public parks or on the beaches is also illegal. Drunk driving is a serious crime and can incur stiff fines, jail time and other penalties. In Hawaii, anyone caught driving with a blood alcohol level of 0.08% or greater is guilty of driving 'under the influence' and will have their driver's license taken away on the spot.

Money

The US dollar is the only currency used on Maui.

ATMs, Cash & Checks

Major banks such as the **Bank of Hawaii** (www.boh.com) and **First Hawaiian Bank** (www.fhb.com) have ATM networks throughout Maui that give cash advances on major credit cards and allow cash withdrawals with affiliated ATM cards. In addition to bank locations, you'll find ATMs at most grocery stores, mall-style shopping centers and convenience stores.

If you're carrying foreign currency, it can be exchanged for US dollars at larger banks around Maui. Out-of-state personal checks are not readily accepted on Maui.

Credit Cards

Major credit cards are widely accepted on Maui, including at car-rental agencies and at most hotels, restaurants, gas stations, grocery stores and tour operators. Some B&Bs and condos (including some handled through rental agencies) may refuse them.

Tipping

In restaurants, good waiters are tipped 15% to 20%, while very dissatisfied customers make their ire known by leaving 10%. There has to be real cause for not tipping at all.

Taxi drivers are typically tipped about 15% of the metered fare, rounded up to the next dollar, and hotel bellhops about $2 per bag. Pay parking valets at least $2 when your car is returned.

Traveler's Checks

Traveler's checks are becoming obsolete. Foreign visitors carrying traveler's checks will find things easier if the checks are in US dollars. Most midrange and top-end restaurants, hotels and shops accept US dollar traveler's checks and treat them just like cash.

●●●
Opening Hours

Opening hours may vary slightly throughout the year. We've provided high-season opening hours; hours will generally decrease in the shoulder and low seasons.

Banks 8:30am to 4pm Monday to Friday; some to 6pm Friday and 9am to noon or 1pm Saturday

Bars & clubs noon to midnight daily; some to 2am Thursday to Saturday

---

Practicalities

○ **Newspapers** Maui's main daily newspaper is the *Maui News* (www.mauinews.com). The *Maui Weekly* (www.mauiweekly.com) covers news and entertainment for all of Maui. *Lahaina News* (www.lahainanews.com) is a weekly newspaper focusing on West Maui.

○ **Radio** For Hawaiian music and personalities tune into **KPOA 93.5FM** (www.kpoa.com). Hawaii Public Radio **KKUA 90.7FM** (www.npr.com) features island programs and music.

○ **Smoking** Tobacco smoking is prohibited in enclosed public places, including restaurants and hotel lobbies.

○ **TV** All major US TV networks and cable channels are available.

○ **Weights & measures** As on the US mainland, distances are measured in feet, yards and miles; weights are in ounces, pounds and tons.

Businesses 8:30am to 4:30pm Monday to Friday

Post offices 8:30am to 4:30pm Monday to Friday; some 9am to noon Saturday

Shops 9am to 5pm Monday to Saturday, some also noon to 5pm Sunday; major shopping areas and malls keep extended hours

●●●
Public Holidays

When a public holiday falls on the weekend, it's often celebrated on the nearest Friday or Monday instead. These long weekends can be busy, as people from other Hawaiian Islands often take advantage of the break to visit Maui. If your visit coincides with a holiday be sure to book your hotel and car well in advance.

New Year's Day January 1

Martin Luther King Jr Day Third Monday of January

Presidents Day Third Monday of February

Good Friday March or April

Prince Kuhio Day March 26

Memorial Day Last Monday of May

King Kamehameha Day June 11

Independence Day July 4

Statehood Day Third Friday of August

Labor Day First Monday of September

Discoverer's Day Second Monday of October (celebrated as Columbus Day on the US mainland)

Election Day Second Tuesday of November in even-numbered years

Veterans Day November 11

Thanksgiving Fourth Thursday of November

Christmas Day December 25

Safe Travel

Hazards

Flash floods, rock falls, tsunami, earthquakes, volcanic eruptions, shark attacks, jellyfish stings and, yes, even possibly getting brained by a falling coconut – the potential dangers of traveling in Hawaii might seem alarming at first. But as the old saying goes, statistically you're more likely to get hurt crossing the street at home. The key pieces of advice? Pay attention to your surroundings and watch for changing conditions.

Theft

Maui is notorious for rip-offs from parked rental cars. It can happen within seconds, whether from a secluded parking area at a trailhead or from a crowded beach parking lot. Do not leave anything valuable in your car – ever.

If you must, pack things well out of sight *before* you arrive at your destination; thieves wait and watch to see what you put in the trunk.

Trespassing

When exploring, remember to mind your manners and watch your step. Hawaii has strict laws about trespassing on both private and government land not intended for public use. Trespassing is always illegal, no matter how many other people you see doing it. As a visitor to the islands, it's important to respect all 'Kapu' or 'No trespassing' signs.

Always seek explicit permission from the land owner or local officials before venturing onto private or public land that is closed to the public, regardless of whether it is fenced or signposted as such. Doing so not only respects the *kuleana* (rights) of local residents and the sacredness of the land, but also helps to ensure your own safety.

Tsunamis

Tidal waves, or tsunamis as they're called in the Pacific, are rare, but when they do hit they can be deadly.

Maui has a warning system, aired through yellow speakers mounted on telephone poles around the island. They're tested on the first working day of each month at 11:45am for about one minute.

If you should hear one at any other time and you're in a low-lying coastal area, immediately head for higher ground.

Telephone

Pay phones are a dying breed but you may find them at larger public parks and local community centers. To make long-distance calls consider buying a prepaid phone card at a convenience store or pharmacy.

Always dial '1' before toll-free numbers (800, 888 and 877). Some toll-free numbers may only work within the state or from the US mainland, while others work from Canada, too. But you'll only know by making the call.

Agricultural Checks

All luggage and carry-on bags leaving Hawaii for the US mainland are checked by an agricultural inspector using an X-ray machine.

You cannot take out fresh flowers of jade vine and Mauna Loa, citrus or citrus-related flowers, leaves or plant parts, even in lei, though most other fresh flowers and foliage are permitted. You can take home pineapples and coconuts, but most other fresh fruits and vegetables are banned. Other things not allowed to enter mainland states include plants in soil, berries including fresh coffee berries (roasted beans are OK), cactus and sugarcane.

However, seeds, fruits and plants that have been certified and labeled for export aren't a problem. For more information contact the **Plant Protection & Quarantine Office** (☎877-5261; www.aphis.usda.gov).

Important Numbers

Area code	☎808
Country code	☎1
Emergencies	☎911
International access code	☎011

Cell (Mobile) Phones

Coverage Cell-phone coverage is good on most of Maui, but spotty in remote areas such as the Road to Hana. Verizon has the most extensive cellular network on Maui, but AT&T and Sprint also have decent coverage.

Equipment International travelers, take note: most US mobile-phone systems are incompatible with the GSM 900/1800 standard used throughout Europe and Asia, and will need a multi-band phone. Check with your cellular service provider before departure about using your phone on Maui.

Long-Distance & International Calls

Calls to Hawaii If you're calling Maui from abroad, the international country code for the US is '1'. All calls to Hawaii are then followed by the area code 808 and the seven-digit local number.

International calls from Maui To make international calls direct from Maui to any country other than Canada, dial 011 + country code + area code + number. To make calls direct to Canada, dial 1 + area code + number.

Operator assistance For international operator assistance, dial 0. The operator can provide specific rate information and tell you which time periods are the cheapest for calling.

Calls within Hawaii If you're calling from one place on Maui to any other place on Maui you do not need to dial the 808 area code. However, you must dial 1 + 808 when making a call from one Hawaiian island to another.

Time

Hawaii does not observe daylight saving time. It has about 11 hours of daylight in midwinter and almost 13½ hours in midsummer. In midwinter the sun rises at about 7am and sets at about 6pm. In midsummer it rises before 6am and sets after 7pm.

Tourist Information

Maui County's tourist organizations have loads of visitor information on their websites and will mail out material to those not online. There's an information desk (p105) at the Kahului airport.

Maui Visitors Bureau (www.gohawaii.com/maui) Visit the website to download or order a Maui visitor's guide. Also represents Lana'i and Moloka'i.

Moloka'i Visitors Association (MVA; Map p263;

☎ 553-3876, 800-800-6367; www.gohawaii.com/molokai)

Destination Lana'i (☎ 800-947-4774, 565-7600; www.gohawaii.com/lanai)

Tours

A number of tour-bus companies operate half-day and full-day sightseeing tours on Maui, covering the most visited island destinations. Popular routes include day-long jaunts to Hana, and Haleakalā trips that take in the major Upcountry sights.

There are also specialized adventure tours such as whale-watching cruises, snorkeling trips to Lana'i and helicopter tours. Details are in the Activities sections under each town.

Polynesian Adventure Tours (☎ 833-3000; www.polyad.com; tours $102-154) Part of Gray Line Hawaii, it's a big player among Hawaiian tour companies; offers tours to Haleakalā National Park, Central Maui and 'Iao Valley State Park, and the Road to Hana. Also runs short trips from Maui to Pearl Harbor in O'ahu ($456 per person).

Roberts Hawaii (☎ 800-831-5541; www.robertshawaii.com; tours $74-106) In operation for more than 70 years, Roberts Hawaii runs three tours: Hana, 'Iao Valley and Lahaina, and Haleakalā National Park.

Valley Isle Excursions (☎ 661-8687; www.tourmaui.com; tours $142) Costs a bit

333

more but hands-down the best Road to Hana tour. Vans take just 12 passengers and guides offer more local flavor and less canned commentary. Includes continental breakfast and, in Hana, a barbecue lunch.

Travelers with Disabilities

○ Maui has decent infrastructure for travelers with disabilities, and most public places comply with *Americans with Disabilities Act* (ADA) regulations.

○ Many of the major resort hotels have elevators, TTD-capable phones and wheelchair-accessible rooms.

○ Major car-rental companies will install hand controls and provide accessible transportation to the vehicle pickup site with advance notification.

○ Most public buses are wheelchair accessible.

○ A disability parking placard issued by other states or countries for parking in designated accessible parking spaces is valid in Hawaii.

○ Travelers with visual impairments are allowed to bring guide dogs into Hawaii without quarantine, provided they meet the Department of Agriculture's requirements. Contact the **Animal Quarantine Station** (☏483-7151; http://hdoa. hawaii.gov).

○ For more tips for visitors with disabilities on Maui, check out www.gohawaii.com/maui/

about/travel-tips/special-needs.

Disability & Communication Access Board (www.hawaii.gov/health/dcab) This website has the scoop on services for visitors with disabilities in Hawaii.

Society for Accessible Travel & Hospitality (www.sath.org) A good resource with travel tips and access information for travelers with disabilities.

Volunteering

Opportunities for volunteering abound on Maui. Some require extended time commitments but many ask for just a few hours.

The Pacific Whale Foundation and the Hawaii Tourism Authority organize short-term projects on Maui through their joint Volunteers on Vacation program (see the boxed text, p196).

Kaho'olawe Island Reserve Commission (KIRC; ☏ 243-5020; www.kahoolawe.hawaii.gov/volunteer.shtml) Runs four-day volunteer trips to Kaho'olawe for restoration work. Volunteers pay a $125 fee. There's a two-year waiting list, but a volunteer program launched in 2014 by KIRC is now providing volunteer opportunities at the future site of the Kaho'olawe Cultural Center in Kihei.

National Park Service (www.nps.gov/hale)

Coordinates one-day projects (non-native plant and trash removal) at Haleakalā National Park with Pacific Whale Foundation and three-day backcountry projects with Friends of Haleakalā.

Transport

Getting There & Away

 Air

Airports

○ Most mainland flights to Maui involve at least one stopover, but direct flights to Maui are currently possible from some cities, including Los Angeles, San Diego, San Francisco, Seattle, Dallas, Phoenix and Vancouver, BC.

○ If you don't have a direct transpacific flight to Kahului then you'll be flying into O'ahu at **Honolulu International Airport** (www.honoluluairport.com) and taking an inter-island flight from there.

• To reach Lana'i or Moloka'i by air, you'll have to fly via Honolulu, Kahului or Kapalua.

Kahului International Airport (Map p98; ☎ 872-3830; www.hawaii.gov/ogg; 1 Kahului Airport Rd) All transpacific flights arrive here.

Kapalua Airport (www.hawaii.gov/jhm) Off Hwy 30, south of Kapalua, this regional airport has flights to other Hawaiian islands on small carriers and chartered planes, currently including **Mokulele Airlines** (www.mokulele airlines.com).

Hana Airport (☎ 248-4861; www.hawaii.gov/hnm) There are twice-daily flights from Kahului to this small airport with Mokulele Airlines, cutting a two-hour drive to a 20-minute flight.

Lana'i Airport (☎ 565-7942; www.hawaii.gov/lny; Lana'i Ave, Lana'i City) This small airport is a few miles outside Lana'i City.

Moloka'i Airport (Map p258; ☎ 567-9660; www.hawaii.gov/mkk; Ho'olehua) Moloka'i's main airport.

Tickets

• With so many airlines flying into Hawaii, good airfare deals often pop up. Check both the airline websites and the usual travel websites for the best price.

• If you're going to Maui on a short getaway, don't rule out package tours – they may cost little more than what an airfare alone would have cost.

Pleasant Holidays (☎ 800-742-9244; www.pleasantholidays.com) offers competitive vacation packages from the US mainland and **Air Tech** (☎ 212-219-7000; www.airtech.com) finds discounted airfare between the US mainland and Maui.

Sea

The following cruise lines offer tours to Hawaii with stops on Maui.

Holland America Cruise Line (www.hollandamerica.com) Typically departs from San Diego or Vancouver.

Norwegian Cruise Line (☎ 866-234-7350; www.ncl.com) Operates a cruise between the Hawaiian Islands that starts and ends in Honolulu.

Princess Cruises (www.princess.com) Offers cruises departing from Los Angeles, San Francisco and Vancouver.

Getting Around

To explore Maui thoroughly, and reach off-the-beaten-path sights, you'll need to rent a car.

Public transportation is limited to the main towns and tourist resorts.

 Air

Several inter-island airlines connect Maui with its neighboring Hawaiian islands.

Hawaiian Airlines (☎ 800-367-5320; www.hawaiianair.

Climate Change & Travel

Every form of transport that relies on carbon-based fuel generates CO_2, the main cause of human-induced climate change. Modern travel is dependent on airplanes, which might use less fuel per kilometer per person than most cars but travel much greater distances. The altitude at which aircraft emit gases (including CO_2) and particles also contributes to their climate change impact. Many websites offer 'carbon calculators' that allow people to estimate the carbon emissions generated by their journey and, for those who wish to do so, to offset the impact of the greenhouse gases emitted with contributions to portfolios of climate-friendly initiatives throughout the world. Lonely Planet offsets the carbon footprint of all staff and author travel.

com) The largest inter-island carrier flies from O'ahu to Maui and the other main Hawaiian Islands.

Island Air (☎ 800-652-6541; www.islandair.com) Currently flies 64-seat passenger planes between Honolulu and Moloka'i, Lana'i, Kaua'i and Maui.

Mokulele Airlines (☎ 866-260-7070; www.mokuleleairlines.com) On Maui, offers flights from Kahului to Hana. Also flies to the other major Hawaiian Islands except Kaua'i.

To/From the Airport

Shuttle

If you want a shuttle ride from Kahului airport but forgot to make reservations, try **Roberts Hawaii** (www.airportmauishuttle.com), which provides on-demand shuttle service. Rates are competitive; a one-way trip to Lahaina costs $48 per person.

You can also make reservations with the two companies below. Reserve in advance for your return to the airport.

Price depends on the destination and the size of the group.

Speedi Shuttle (☏ 877-242-5777; www.speedishuttle.com) Fares for one person from Kahului airport cost about $50 to Lahaina, $54 to Ka'anapali, $74 to Kapalua, $33 to Kihei and $39 to Wailea. Add $4 to $6 more per additional person.

Hawaii Executive Transportation (☏ 800-833-2303, 669-2300; www.hawaiiexecutivetransportation.com; ☺ reservations 7am-11pm) Runs shuttles between Kahului Airport and Lahaina, West Maui and South Maui. For one person, the fare is $31 to Kihei, $47 to Lahaina and $49 to Ka'anapali.

Taxi

From Kahului Airport Taxi dispatchers are near the exit of the baggage-claim area. Approximate fares from the airport: to Kihei $30 to $55; to Lahaina $70 to $75; to

Ka'anapali $80 to $85; and to Kapalua $100 to $105.

Bicycle

○ Cyclists on Maui face a number of challenges: narrow roads, an abundance of hills and mountains, and the same persistent winds that so delight windsurfers. Maui's stunning scenery certainly will entice hard-core cyclists, but casual riders hoping to use a bike as a primary source of transportation around the island may well find such conditions daunting.

○ Getting around by bicycle within a small area can be a reasonable option for the average rider, however. For example, the tourist enclave of Kihei is largely level and now has cycle lanes on its two main drags, S Kihei Rd and the Pi'ilani Hwy.

○ The full-color *Maui County Bicycle Map,* although out-of-print, can be found on the websites of two Maui bike rental shops, West Maui Cycles and South Maui Bicycles. The map shows all the roads on Maui that have cycle lanes and gives other nitty-gritty details.

○ For information about bicycle rentals, see specific destinations around the island. Rental rates range from $15 to $60 per day, depending on performance needs.

○ Bringing your own bike to Hawaii costs upwards of $100 on flights from the mainland. The bicycle can usually be checked at the airline counter, the same as any baggage, but you'll need to prepare the bike by wrapping the handlebars and pedals in foam or by fixing the handlebars to the

side, removing the pedals and putting it all in a box or hard case.

○ In general, bicycles are required to follow the same state laws and rules of the road as cars. State law requires all cyclists under the age of 16 to wear helmets.

Boat

Passenger ferry services connect Maui with Lana'i and Moloka'i. You can buy tickets online, by phone or on the boat. Advance reservations are always a good idea, though they are not required.

Bus

The buses on Maui can take you between the main towns, but they're not going to get you to many prime out-of-the-way places, such as Haleakalā National Park, Hana or Makena's Big Beach. And some of the buses, such as the ones between Ma'alaea and Lahaina, make a direct beeline, passing trailheads and beaches without stopping.

Maui Bus (☏ 871-4838; www.mauicounty.gov/bus; $2 per boarding) is the island's public bus system. The main routes run once hourly throughout the day and several have schedules that dovetail with one another for convenient connections.

Routes The handiest buses for visitors:

○ Lahaina Islander (Kahului–Lahaina)

○ Kihei Islander (Kahului–Wailea)

○ Wailuku Loop (Kahului–Wailuku)

- Haiku Islander
  (Kahului–Haiku)

- Kihei Villager
  (Ma'alaea–Kihei)

- Ka'anapali Islander
  (Lahaina–Ka'anapali)

- Napili Isander (Ka'anapali–
  Napili)

Costs Fares are $2 per ride, regardless of the distance. There are no transfers; if your journey requires two separate buses, you'll have to buy a new ticket when you board the second bus. Best deal is a daily pass for just $4.

Carry-on All buses allow you to carry on only what fits under your seat or on your lap, so forget the surfboard.

Resort shuttles The Ka'anapali Resort Shuttle runs complimentary service between Whalers Village and the major resorts in Ka'anapali from 10am to 8pm. Some resorts provide limited complimentary shuttle service.

Car & Motorcycle

The majority of visitors to Maui rent their own vehicles.

Automobile Associations

Members of the **American Automobile Association** (AAA; ☎808-593-2221, from Neighbor Islands 800-736-2886; www.hawaii.aaa.com; 1130 N Nimitz Hwy, Honolulu; ⊙9am-5pm Mon-Fri, 9am-2pm Sat) get discounts on car rentals and some air tickets, hotels and sightseeing attractions.

For emergency road service and towing, members should call ☎800-222-4357.

Hitting the Road

Most main roads on Maui are called highways whether they're busy four-lane thoroughfares or just quiet country roads. Indeed there are roads in remote corners of the island that narrow down to barely the width of a driveway but nonetheless are designated highways. So when you're scanning a map don't let the term 'highway' fool you into thinking you'll be whizzing along.

What's more, islanders refer to highways by name, and rarely by number. If you stop to ask someone how to find Hwy 36, chances are you'll get a blank stare – ask for the Hana Hwy instead.

AAA has reciprocal agreements with automobile associations in other countries, but be sure to bring your membership card, and check coverage, from your country of origin. The closest AAA office to Maui is in Honolulu in O'ahu.

Driver's License

International visitors can legally drive in Hawaii with a valid driver's license issued by their home country (minimum age 18). An International Driving Permit, obtained before you leave home, is only necessary if your country of origin is a non-English-speaking one.

Fuel & Towing

- When you take a country drive on Maui, you need to be conscious of your fuel gauge. There are no gas stations on several long stretches of road, including the Road to Hana; the Kahekili Hwy between Wailuku and Kapalua; and the Haleakalā Crater Rd to the national park.

- Expect to pay about 25% more per US gallon than on the mainland. At the time of research, the average gas price

on Maui was about $4.30 per gallon.

- Towing is expensive on Maui. Make sure your car is in good shape before taking off into any remote areas, and be aware that some of these places may be 'off limits' according to your car-rental agreement. Always ask when booking if the company has any road restrictions for its vehicles.

Insurance

Liability insurance covers people and property that you might hit. For damage to the actual rental vehicle, a collision damage waiver (CDW) is available for about $28 a day. If you have collision coverage on your vehicle at home, it might cover damages to car rentals; inquire before departing. Additionally, some credit cards offer reimbursement coverage for collision damages if you rent the car with that credit card; again, check before departing.

Rentals

- Note: reserve your car in advance, especially if you're traveling during high season or arriving on a weekend

Driving Distances & Drive Times from Kahului

Average driving times and distances from Kahului are as follows. Allow more time during weekday morning and afternoon rush hours, and any time the surf is up on the North Shore if you're heading that way.

DESTINATION	MILES	TIME
Haleakalā Summit	36	1½ hours
Hana	51	2 hours
Ka'anapali	26	50 minutes
Kapalua	32	1 hour
Kihei	12	25 minutes
La Pe'rouse Bay	21	50 minutes
Lahaina	23	40 minutes
Makawao	14	30 minutes
'Ohe'o Gulch	61	2¾ hours
Pa'ia	7	15 minutes
Wailuku	3	15 minutes

when some agencies book out altogether. That said, with advance notice, you shouldn't have a problem getting something, possibly on another part of the island, but avoid the stress.

◦ Similar to airfares, car-rental rates vary significantly with demand. Rental rates on Maui spike if you pick the car up on a holiday such as Christmas or Thanksgiving.

◦ With advance reservations, the daily rate for a small car from a national company starts at about $45 per day, while typical weekly rates run about $235 or more, excluding taxes and fees. Those who book at the last minute are most likely to get the worst rate.

◦ Try an aggregator site like www.kayak.com for the best rates and a quick comparison.

◦ Rental rates generally include unlimited mileage, but confirm that when you book.

◦ If you drop the car off at a different location from where you picked it up, there's usually an additional fee.

◦ One consideration regarding car sizes: if you are going to drive the Road to Hana or around the north side of Maui, these roads are very narrow and driving a wide, full-size car gives you less of a margin than a mid-size or compact vehicle would. You may want to opt for the smallest car you're comfortable in.

◦ For budget rental cars also try **Maui Craigslist** (http://honolulu.craigslist.org/mau/cta).

Rental agents Most major car-rental agencies have operations at Kahului Airport.

Several of them also have branches in Ka'anapali and will pick you up at the nearby Kapalua Airport.

The following are contacts for car rentals serving Maui.

Road Conditions & Hazards

◦ Maui has a lot of ranchland, much of it open pasture, so you'll need to keep an eye out for livestock on the road in rural areas.

◦ Narrow, winding or steep roads sometimes wash out after heavy rains. Sections of some roads, including the Road to Hana and the Kahekili Hwy, are particularly susceptible to wash-outs. If it's been raining heavily recently it's best to inquire before setting out.

◦ Stay alert for one-lane-bridge crossings: one direction of traffic usually has the right of way while the other must obey the posted yield sign. Downhill traffic must yield to uphill traffic where there is no sign.

Road Rules

◦ Maui enacted a cell-phone driving ban in 2010, meaning it is illegal to use your cell phone or electronic device while driving, unless you are using a headset or hands-free product. The hands-free device exemption does not apply to drivers under the age of 18.

◦ Drivers at a red light can turn right after coming to a stop and yielding to oncoming traffic, unless there's a sign at the intersection prohibiting the turn.

◦ Locals will tell you there are three golden rules for driving on the Hawaiian Islands: don't honk your horn, don't follow too closely and let people pass whenever it's safe to do so. Any cool moves like this are acknowledged by waving the *shaka* (Hawaiian hand greeting) sign.

○ Horn honking is considered rude unless required for safety, or for urging cattle off the road.

○ Hawaii requires the use of seat belts. Heed this, as the ticket is stiff.

Hitchhiking

Hitchhiking, though technically illegal statewide, is not unusual on Maui. However, hitchhiking anywhere is not without risks, and we don't recommend it. Hitchers should size up each situation carefully before entering cars, and women should be wary of hitching alone. People who do choose to hitchhike will be safer if they travel in pairs and let someone know where they are going.

Moped & Motorcycle

○ You can legally drive both mopeds and motorcycles in Hawaii as long as you have a valid driver's license issued by your home country.

○ The minimum age for renting a moped is 16 (with signed parental approval until 18 at most rental companies); for a motorcycle it's 21.

○ Keep in mind that the windward side of Maui generally requires hard-core foul-weather gear, since it rains early and often.

○ State law requires mopeds to be ridden by one person only and prohibits their use on sidewalks and freeways.

○ Mopeds must always be driven in single file and may not be driven at speeds in excess of 30mph.

○ Riders 17 and under must wear helmets; otherwise there are no helmet laws in the state of Hawaii. Most rental agencies provide free helmets, and cautious riders will use them.

Taxi

○ On Maui, you can't just flag a taxi down in the street. Call ahead for a scheduled pickup.

○ Pickups from remote locations (for instance, after a long through-hike) can sometimes be arranged in advance, though you may have to also pay in advance.

○ Fares are county-regulated. The drop charge is $3.50 and then it costs $3 per additional mile.

Maui Pleasant Taxi (☎ 344-4661; www.mauipleasanttaxi.com) Serves airports at Kahului and Kapalua.

Royal Taxi (☎ 874-6900; www.royaltaximaui.com)

A-Z

Glossary

For food terms, see p296.

'a'a – type of lava that is rough and jagged

ae'o – Hawaiian black-necked stilt

ahu – stone cairns used to mark a trail; an altar or shrine

ahupua'a – traditional land division, usually in a wedge shape that extends from the mountains to the sea (smaller than a *moku*)

'aina – land

ali'i – chief, royalty

ali'i nui – high chiefs

aloha – the traditional greeting meaning love, welcome, good-bye

aloha 'aina – love of the land

'aumakua – protective deity or guardian spirit, deified ancestor or trustworthy person

'awa – see *kava*

'awa 'awa – bitter

'awapuhi – wild ginger

azuki bean – often served as a sweetened paste, eg as a topping for shave ice

braguinha – a Portuguese stringed instrument introduced to Hawaii in the late 19th century from which the ukulele is derived

broke da mout – delicious; literally, 'broke the mouth'

crack seed – Chinese preserved fruit; a salty, sweet and/or sour snack

e koko mai – welcome

grinds – food; to *grind* means to eat

ha – breath

hale – house

haole – Caucasian; literally, 'without breath'

hapa – portion or fragment; person of mixed blood

hapa haole – Hawaiian music with predominantly English lyrics

hau – indigenous lowland hibiscus tree whose wood is often used for making canoe outriggers (stabilizing arms that jut out from the hull)

he'e nalu – wave sliding, or surfing

heiau – ancient stone temple; a place of worship in Hawaii

honu – turtle

ho'okipa – hospitality

ho'olaule'a – celebration, party

hula – Hawaiian dance form, either traditional or modern

hula 'auana – modern hula, developed after the introduction of Western music

hula halau – hula school or troupe

hula kahiko – traditional hula

ipo – sweetheart

issei – first-generation Japanese immigrants; born in Japan

kahili – a feathered standard, used as a symbol of royalty

kahuna – knowledgable person in any field; commonly a priest, healer or sorcerer

kahuna lapa'au – healer

kahuna nui – high priest(ess)

kalo – taro

kama'aina – person born and raised or a longtime resident in Hawaii; literally, 'child of the land'

kanaka – man, human being, person; also Native Hawaiian

kane/Kane – man; if capitalized, the name of one of four main Hawaiian gods

kanoa – hidden meaning

kapa – see *tapa*

kapu – taboo, part of strict ancient Hawaiian social and religious system

kapuna – elders

kava – a mildly narcotic drink (*'awa* in Hawaiian) made from the roots of *Piper methysticum*, a pepper shrub

keiki – child

ki ho'alu – slack key

kiawe – a relative of the mesquite tree introduced to Hawaii in the 1820s, now common; its branches are covered with sharp thorns

kika kila – Hawaiian steel guitar

ki'i – see *tiki*

ki'i akua – temple images

kipuka – an area of land spared when lava flows around it; an oasis

ko – sugarcane

ko'a – fishing shrine

koa – native hardwood tree used in making native crafts and canoes

koki'o ke'oke'o – native Hawaiian white hibiscus tree

kokua – help, cooperation

kona – leeward side; a leeward wind

konohiki – caretakers

ko'olau – windward side

Ku – Polynesian god of many manifestations, including god of war, farming and fishing (husband of Hina)

kukui – candlenut tree and the official state tree; its oily nuts were once burned in lamps

kuleana – rights

kumu hula – hula teacher

kupuna – grandparent, elder

ku'ula – a stone idol placed at fishing sites, believed to attract fish; also, the god of fishermen

Laka – goddess of the hula

lanai – veranda; balcony

lau – leaf

lauhala – leaves of the *hala* plant, used in weaving

lei – garland, usually of flowers, but also of leaves or shells

lokelani – pink damask rose, or 'rose of heaven,' Maui's official flower

loko i'a – fishpond

lolo – stupid, feeble-minded, crazy

lomi – to rub or soften

lomilomi – traditional Hawaiian massage; known as 'loving touch'

Lono – Polynesian god of harvest, agriculture, fertility and peace

loulu – native fan palms

luakini – a type of heiau dedicated to the war god Ku and used for human sacrifices

luau – traditional Hawaiian feast

mahalo – thank you

mahele – to divide; usually refers to the sugar industry–initiated land divisions of 1848

mai ho'oka'awale – leprosy; literally, 'the separating sickness'

maka'ainana – commoners; literally, 'people who tend the land'

makai – toward the sea; seaward

make – dead

malihini – newcomer, visitor

malo – loincloth

mana – spiritual power

mauka – toward the mountains; inland

mele – song, chant

menehune – 'little people' who, according to legend, built many of Hawaii's fishponds, heiau and other stonework

milo – a native shade tree with beautiful hardwood

moku – wedge-shaped areas of land running from the ridge of the mountains to the sea

mokupuni – island

mo'i – king

mo'o – water spirit, water lizard or dragon

muumuu – a long, loose-fitting dress introduced by the missionaries

na keiki – children

Neighbor Islands – the term used to refer to the main Hawaiian Islands outside of O'ahu

nene – a native goose; Hawaii's state bird

nisei – second-generation Japanese immigrants

'ohana – family, extended family; close-knit group

'olelo Hawai'i – the Hawaiian language

oli – chant

'ope'ape'a – Hawaiian hoary bat

pahoehoe – type of lava that is quick and smooth-flowing

palaka – Hawaiian-style plaid shirt made from sturdy cotton

pali – cliff

paniolo – cowboy

Papa – earth mother

pau – finished, no more

pau hana – happy hour

Pele – goddess of fire and volcanoes; her home is in Kilauea Caldera

pidgin – distinct local language and dialect, influenced by its multiethnic immigrants

pili – a bunchgrass, commonly used for thatching houses

pohaku – rock

pono – righteous, respectful and proper

poi – staple Hawaiian starch made of steamed, mashed taro

pueo – Hawaiian owl

puka – any kind of hole or opening; puka shells are small, white and strung into necklaces

pupu – snack or appetizer; also a type of cowry shell

pu'u – hill, cinder cone

pu'uhonua – place of refuge

raku – a style of Japanese pottery with a rough, handmade appearance

rubbah slippah – rubber flip-flops

seine – a large net used for fishing

shaka – hand gesture used in Hawaii as a greeting or sign of local pride

stink-eye – dirty look

taiko – Japanese drumming

talk story – to strike up a conversation, make small talk

tapa – cloth made by pounding the bark of paper mulberry, used for early Hawaiian clothing (*kapa* in Hawaiian)

ti – common native plant; its long shiny leaves are used for wrapping food and making hula skirts (*ki* in Hawaiian)

tiki – wood- or stone-carved statue, usually depicting a deity (*ki'i* in Hawaiian)

tutu – grandmother or grandfather; also term of respect for any member of that generation

'ua'u – dark-rumped petrel

ukulele – stringed musical instrument derived from the *braguinha,* which was introduced to Hawaii in the 1800s by Portuguese immigrants

'ulu – breadfruit

'ulu maika – ancient Hawaiian stone bowling game

wa'a kaulua – an ancient Hawaiian long-distance sailing vessel

wahi pana – sacred place

Wakea – sky father

wiliwili – the lightest of the native woods

Behind the Scenes

Author Thanks

Amy C Balfour

Maholo to my intrepid coauthor Paul Stiles who added new trails, intriguing history and one unexpected architectural find. Thanks also to Beckee Morrison, Libby Fulton, Craig Lowell, Laura Berthold with Maui Forest Bird Recovery Project, and local experts Theo Morrison, Kevin Cooney, Peter Hamilton and Griff Dempsey.

Paul Stiles

To Bonnie in Kula; Daniel in Pa'ia; Sandy in Ha'iku; Tad, Dean and John in Hana; Terry and Bart on Lana'i; and Margaret, Clare, Kip and Leslie on Moloka'i: thank you. Also Balbi for the intros, Craig for the plane, Brother Eric for Kalaupapa, and Amy for the teamwork. I couldn't have done it without you all.

Acknowledgments

Climate map data adapted from Peel MC, Finlayson BL & McMahon TA (2007) 'Updated World Map of the Köppen-Geiger Climate Classification', *Hydrology and Earth System Sciences*, 11, 1633–44.

Cover photographs
Front: green sea turtle swimming over a coral reef, MM Sweet/Getty Images ©
Back: black sand beach at Wai'anapanapa State Park, David Olsen/Alamy ©

This Book

This 2nd edition of Lonely Planet's *Discover Maui* guidebook was researched and written by Amy C Balfour and Paul Stiles. The previous edition was written by Ned Friary, Glenda Bendure and Amy C Balfour. This guidebook was commissioned in Lonely Planet's Oakland office, and produced by the following:

Commissioning Editors Catherine Craddock-Carrillo, Emily K Wolman
Coordinating Editor Gabrielle Innes
Product Editor Catherine Naghten
Senior Cartographer Mark Griffiths
Book Designer Mazzy Prinsep
Managing Editors Martine Power, Angela Tinson
Senior Editor Claire Naylor
Assisting Editor Anne Mulvaney
Assisting Cartographers Corey Hutchison, Rachel Imeson
Cover Researcher Naomi Parker
Thanks to Anita Banh, Kate Chapman, Penny Cordner, Brendan Dempsey, Lauren Egan, Ryan Evans, Larissa Frost, Anna Harris, Briohny Hooper, Genesys India, Jouve India, Virginia Moreno, Karyn Noble, Anthony Phelan, Rene Reixach, Dianne Schallmeiner, Juan Winata, Wendy Wright

Index

000 Map pages

000 Map pages

How to Use This Book

These symbols give you the vital information for each listing:

- ☑ Telephone Numbers
- ☺ Opening Hours
- ℗ Parking
- ☺ Nonsmoking
- ✳ Air-Conditioning
- @ Internet Access

- ☺ Wi-Fi Access
- ☒ Swimming Pool
- ☑ Vegetarian Selection
- ⓘ English-Language Menu
- ☒ Family-Friendly
- ☺ Pet-Friendly

- ☐ Bus
- ☺ Ferry
- Ⓜ Metro
- Ⓢ Subway
- ☺ Tram

Look out for these icons:

★ Must-visit recommendation

 No payment required

🍃 A green or sustainable option

Our authors have nominated these places as demonstrating a strong commitment to sustainability – for example by supporting local communities and producers, operating in an environmentally friendly way, or supporting conservation projects.

All reviews are ordered in our authors' preference, starting with their most preferred option. Additionally:

Sights are arranged in the geographic order that we suggest you visit them, and within this order, by author preference.

Eating and Sleeping reviews are ordered by price range (budget, mid-range, top end) and within these ranges, by author preference.

Map Legend

Sights
- 🏖 Beach
- 🛕 Buddhist
- 🏰 Castle
- ✝ Christian
- 🕉 Hindu
- ☪ Islamic
- ✡ Jewish
- 🗼 Monument
- 🏛 Museum/Gallery
- 🏚 Ruin
- 🍷 Winery/Vineyard
- 🦓 Zoo
- ◎ Other Sight

Activities, Courses & Tours
- 🤿 Diving/Snorkelling
- 🛶 Canoeing/Kayaking
- ⛷ Skiing
- 🏄 Surfing
- 🏊 Swimming/Pool
- 🚶 Walking
- 🏄 Windsurfing
- ➊ Other Activity/ Course/Tour

Sleeping
- 🛏 Sleeping
- ⛺ Camping

Eating
- 🍴 Eating

Drinking
- ☕ Drinking
- ☕ Cafe

Entertainment
- 🎭 Entertainment

Shopping
- 🛍 Shopping

Information
- 📮 Post Office
- ⓘ Tourist Information

Transport
- ✈ Airport
- 🚫 Border Crossing
- 🚌 Bus
- 🚡 Cable Car/ Funicular
- 🚲 Cycling
- ⛴ Ferry
- 🚝 Monorail
- Ⓟ Parking
- Ⓢ S-Bahn
- 🚕 Taxi
- 🚉 Train/Railway
- 🚊 Tram
- 🚇 Tube Station
- Ⓤ U-Bahn
- Ⓜ Underground Train Station
- • Other Transport

Routes
- Tollway
- Freeway
- Primary
- Secondary
- Tertiary
- Lane
- Unsealed Road
- Plaza/Mall
- Steps
-)= = Tunnel
- Pedestrian Overpass
- Walking Tour
- Walking Tour Detour
- Path

Boundaries
- – – – International
- – – – – State/Province
- – – – Disputed
- Regional/Suburb
- Marine Park
- Cliff
- Wall

Population
- ✪ Capital (National)
- ◉ Capital (State/Province)
- ● City/Large Town
- ○ Town/Village

Geographic
- 🏠 Hut/Shelter
- 🚩 Lighthouse
- 🔭 Lookout
- ▲ Mountain/Volcano
- 🌴 Oasis
- 🌳 Park
-)(Pass
- 🦋 Picnic Area
- 🌊 Waterfall

Hydrography
- River/Creek
- Intermittent River
- Swamp/Mangrove
- Reef
- Canal
- Water
- Dry/Salt/ Intermittent Lake
- Glacier

Areas
- Beach/Desert
- Cemetery (Christian)
- Cemetery (Other)
- Park/Forest
- Sportsground
- Sight (Building)
- Top Sight (Building)

Our Story

A beat-up old car, a few dollars in the pocket and a sense of adventure. In 1972 that's all Tony and Maureen Wheeler needed for the trip of a lifetime – across Europe and Asia overland to Australia. It took several months, and at the end – broke but inspired – they sat at their kitchen table writing and stapling together their first travel guide, *Across Asia on the Cheap*. Within a week they'd sold 1500 copies. Lonely Planet was born.

Today, Lonely Planet has offices in Franklin, London, Melbourne, Oakland, Beijing and Delhi, with more than 600 staff and writers. We share Tony's belief that 'a great guidebook should do three things: inform, educate and amuse'.

Our Writers

AMY C BALFOUR

Coordinating Author, Lahaina, West Maui, Kihei & South Maui Amy first visited Hawaii as a toddler. For this book she clutched the wheel on the Kahekili Highway, paddled past green turtles in Makena Bay, devoured triple berry pie at Lahaina Grill, snapped photos of a roaring blowhole and checked out the sunset drum circle at Little Beach. Amy has authored or coauthored 20 books for Lonely Planet, including the 1st edition of *Discover Maui*, *Hawaii*, *California*, *Southwest USA*, *Southwest USA's Best Trips*, *Florida & the South's Best Trips* and *USA*.

PAUL STILES

'Iao Valley & Central Maui, North Shore & Upcountry, Haleakalā National Park, The Road to Hana, Hana & East Maui, Side Trips: Lana'i & Moloka'i When he was 21, Paul bought an old motorcycle in London and drove it to Tunisia. That did it for him. Since then he has explored 60 countries. With a passion for exotic islands, he's covered Madagascar, Borneo, and five of the Hawaiian Islands for Lonely Planet, and lived for four years at the base of El Teide, the tallest volcano in the Atlantic. For this book he circumnavigated Maui in a convertible, thanking God for every moment.

Read more about Paul at:
lonelyplanet.com/members/paulwstiles

Published by Lonely Planet Publications Pty Ltd
ABN 36 005 607 983
2nd edition – Sep 2014
ISBN 978 1 74220 628 8
© Lonely Planet 2014   Photographs © as indicated 2014
10 9 8 7 6 5 4 3 2 1
Printed in China